Meeeow!

Ken-ichi Sakura

When I first started drawing *Dragon Drive*, I often felt lonely. I went back to my hometown every month after meeting my deadline. But lately I haven't been back at all. I'm a total Tokyo native now. I get lost on the subway, I can't take any route except the ones I already know, but I'm a real Tokyoite!

Ken-ichi Sakura's manga debut was *Fabre Tanteiki*, which was published in a special edition of *Monthly Shonen Jump* in 2000. Serialization of *Dragon Drive* began in the March 2001 issue of *Monthly Shonen Jump* and the hugely successful series has inspired video games and an animated TV show. Sakura's latest title, *Kotokuri*, began running in the March 2006 issue of *Monthly Shonen Jump*. *Dragon Drive* and *Kotokuri* have both become tremendously popular in Japan because of Sakura's unique sense of humor and dynamic portrayal of feisty teen characters.

DRAGON DRIVE

DRAGON DRIVE
VOLUME 13

The SHONEN JUMP Manga Edition

STORY AND ART BY
KEN-ICHI SAKURA

Translation/Martin Hunt, HC Language Solutions, Inc.
English Adaptation/Ian Reid, HC Language Solutions, Inc.
Touch-up Art & Lettering/Jim Keefe
Cover Design/Mark Griffin
Interior Design/Julie Behn
Editor/Shaenon K. Garrity

Editor in Chief, Books/Alvin Lu
Editor in Chief, Magazines/Marc Weidenbaum
VP, Publishing Licensing/Rika Inouye
VP, Sales & Product Marketing/Gonzalo Ferreyra
VP, Creative/Linda Espinosa
Publisher/Hyoe Narita

Printed in Canada

Published by VIZ Media, LLC
P.O. Box 77010
San Francisco, CA 94107

SHONEN JUMP Manga Edition
10 9 8 7 6 5 4 3 2 1
First printing, April 2009

THE WORLD'S
MOST POPULAR MANGA

www.shonenjump.com

www.viz.com

RATED
PARENTAL ADVISORY
DRAGON DRIVE is rated A
and is suitable for readers
of all ages.
ratings.viz.com

DRAGON DRIVE

SHONEN JUMP MANGA EDITION

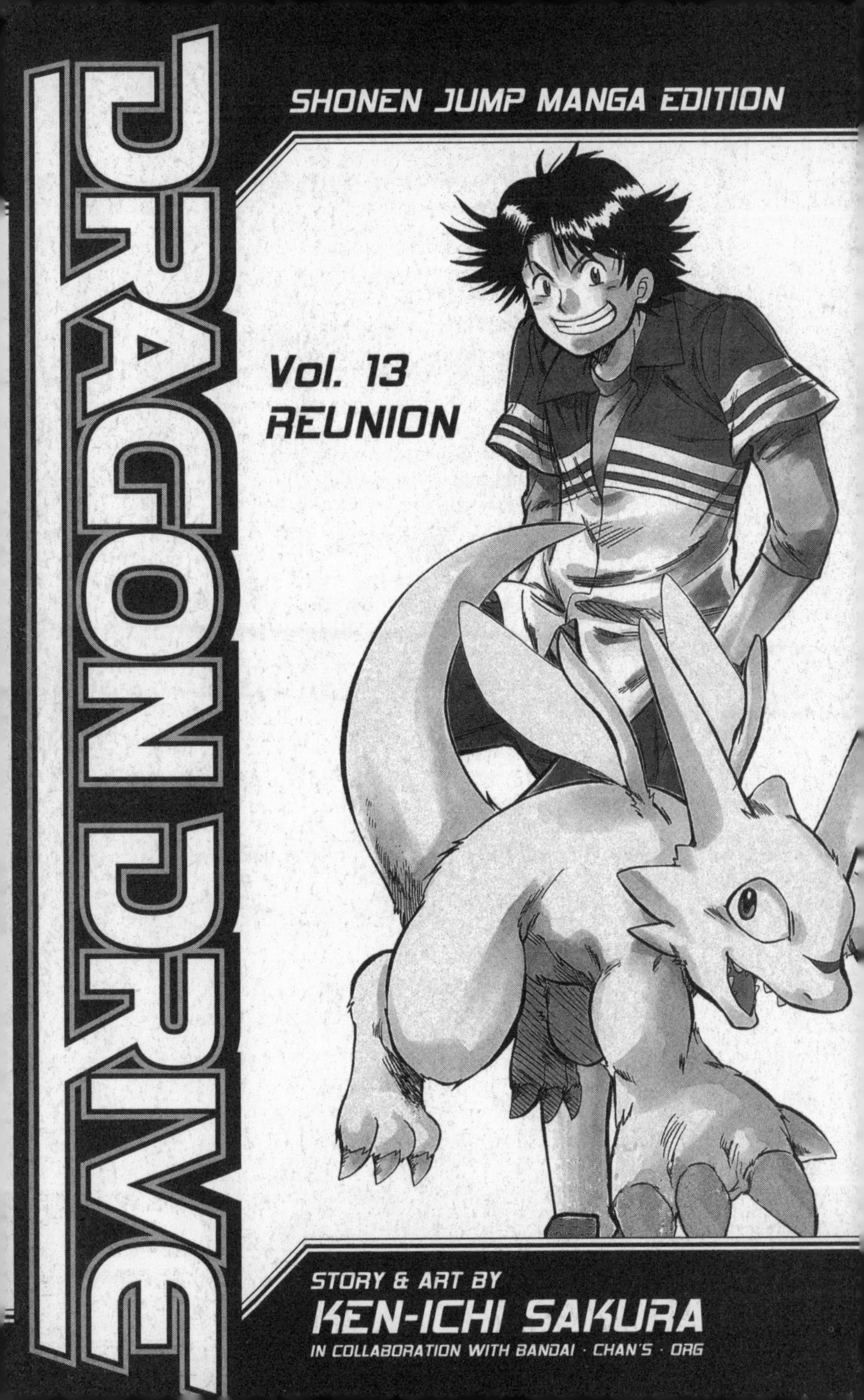

Vol. 13
REUNION

STORY & ART BY

KEN-ICHI SAKURA

IN COLLABORATION WITH BANDAI · CHAN'S · ORG

CHARACTERS

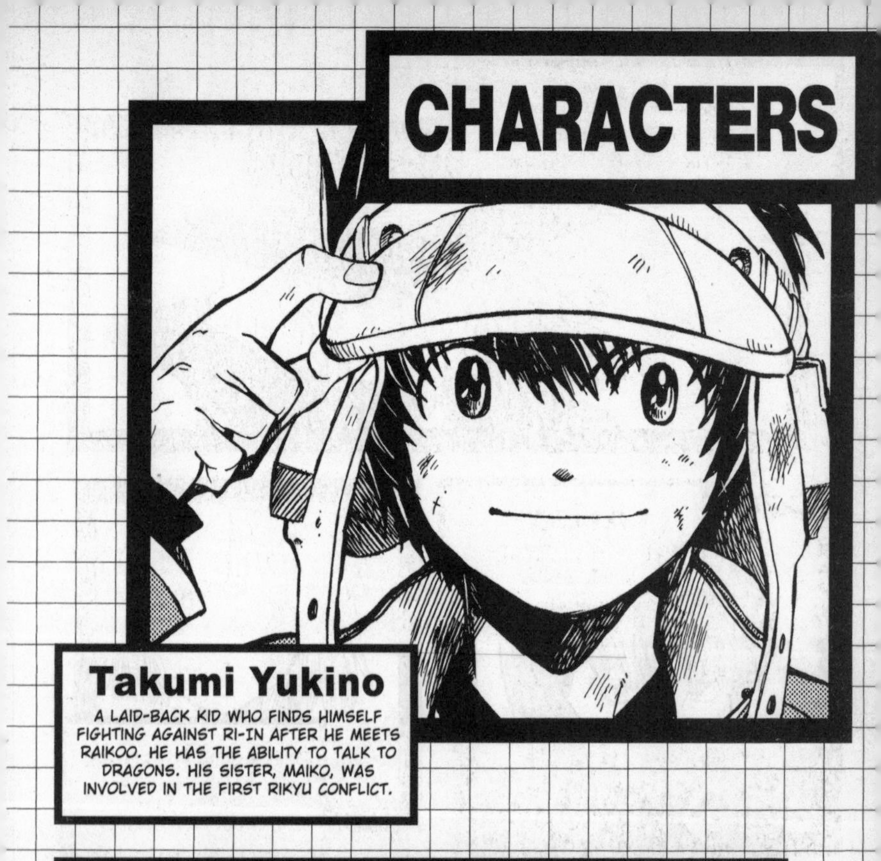

Takumi Yukino

A LAID-BACK KID WHO FINDS HIMSELF FIGHTING AGAINST RI-IN AFTER HE MEETS RAIKOO. HE HAS THE ABILITY TO TALK TO DRAGONS. HIS SISTER, MAIKO, WAS INVOLVED IN THE FIRST RIKYU CONFLICT.

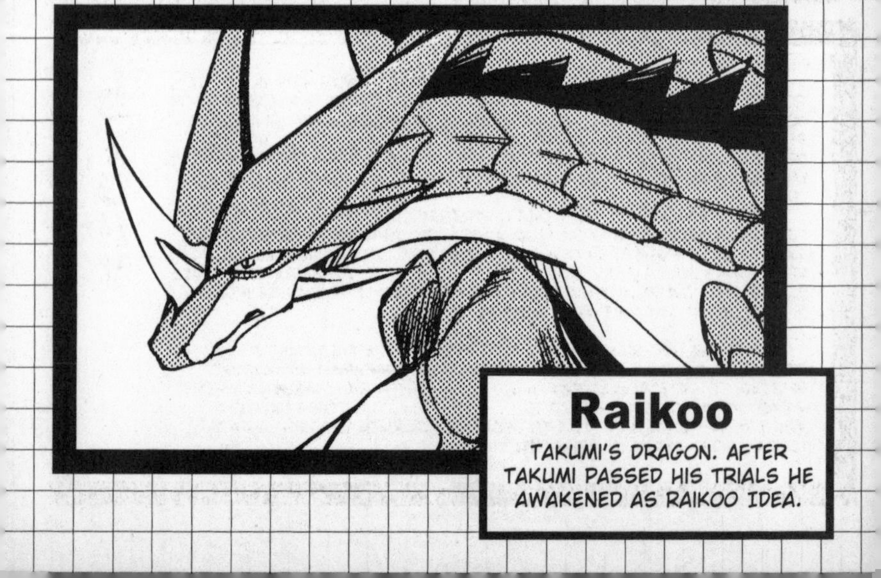

Raikoo

TAKUMI'S DRAGON. AFTER TAKUMI PASSED HIS TRIALS HE AWAKENED AS RAIKOO IDEA.

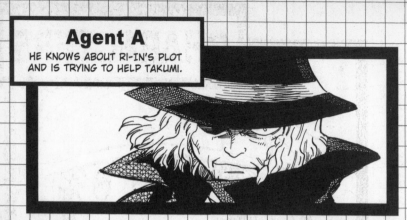

Agent A

HE KNOWS ABOUT RI-IN'S PLOT AND IS TRYING TO HELP TAKUMI.

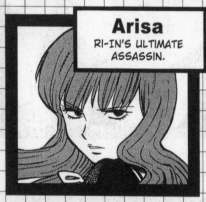

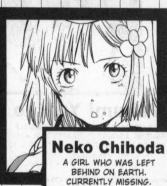

Neko Chihoda

A GIRL WHO WAS LEFT BEHIND ON EARTH. CURRENTLY MISSING.

Arisa

RI-IN'S ULTIMATE ASSASSIN.

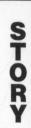

STORY

A GAME CALLED DRAGON DRIVE IS WILDLY POPULAR WITH KIDS ALL OVER THE WORLD. ONE DAY, TAKUMI YUKINO RECEIVES A DECK OF D.D. CARDS FROM AGENT A AND JOINS A TOURNAMENT. EVEN THOUGH HE'S NEVER PLAYED BEFORE, HE MANAGES TO MAKE IT TO THE NATIONAL FINALS WITH THE HELP OF HIS DRAGON, RAIKOO. TAKUMI TURNS OUT TO BE A TRANSLATOR, A PERSON WITH THE RARE ABILITY TO TALK TO DRAGONS.

BEFORE THE FINALS, TAKUMI HAS A STRANGE DREAM. HE'S TOLD THAT TO AWAKEN THE TRUE RAIKOO FROM AMONG THE 99 RAIKOO CARDS, ALL THE RAIKOOS MUST FIGHT EACH OTHER. A WEEK LATER, AN ORGANIZATION CALLED RI-IN HACKS INTO THE D.D. COMPUTER SYSTEM. THE D-ZONE DRAGONS TRADE PLACES WITH THE PEOPLE OF EARTH. ONLY THE PEOPLE WHO WERE INSIDE A D.D. CENTER AT THE TIME ARE LEFT BEHIND.

TAKUMI AND HIS FRIENDS SET OUT TO RESTORE THE EARTH AND ITS PEOPLE. IN A BATTLE WITH THE POWERFUL ASSASSIN ARISA, RAIKOO IS DELETED. TO SAVE RAIKOO, TAKUMI AND NEKO ENTER RAIKOO'S MIND, WHERE RAIKOO REAWAKENS AS RAIKOO IDEA. MEANWHILE, THE OTHER RAIKOO MASTERS OF THE WORLD PLAN TO ESCAPE FROM RI-IN THROUGH A GATE TO RIKYU, THE REALM OF DRAGONS...

Vol. 13 PROMISE
CONTENTS

DRAGON DRIVE

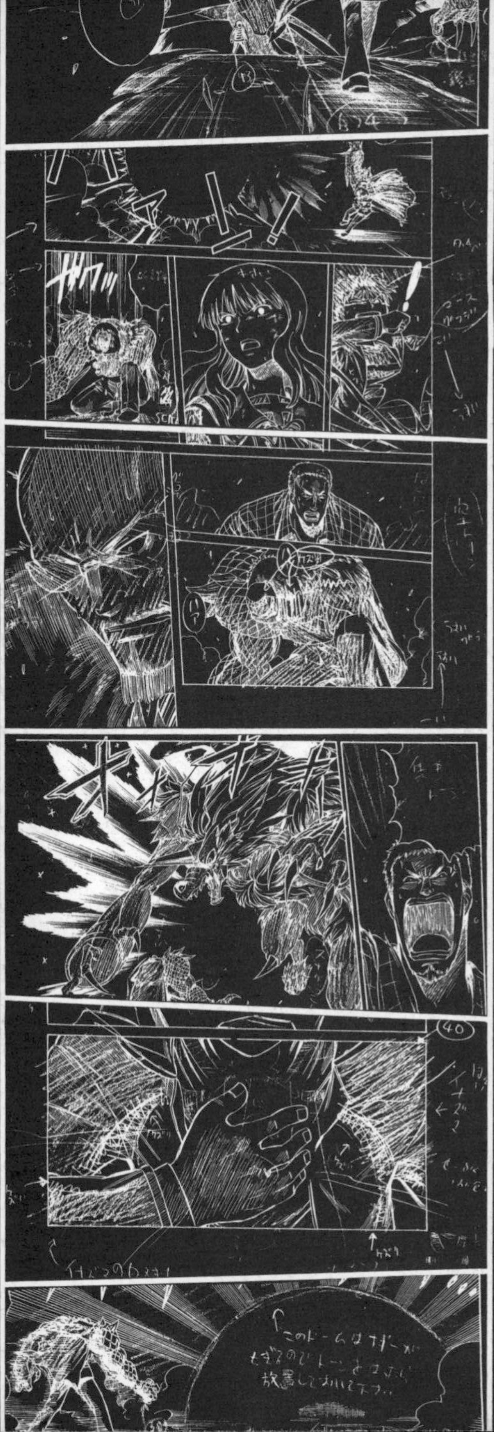

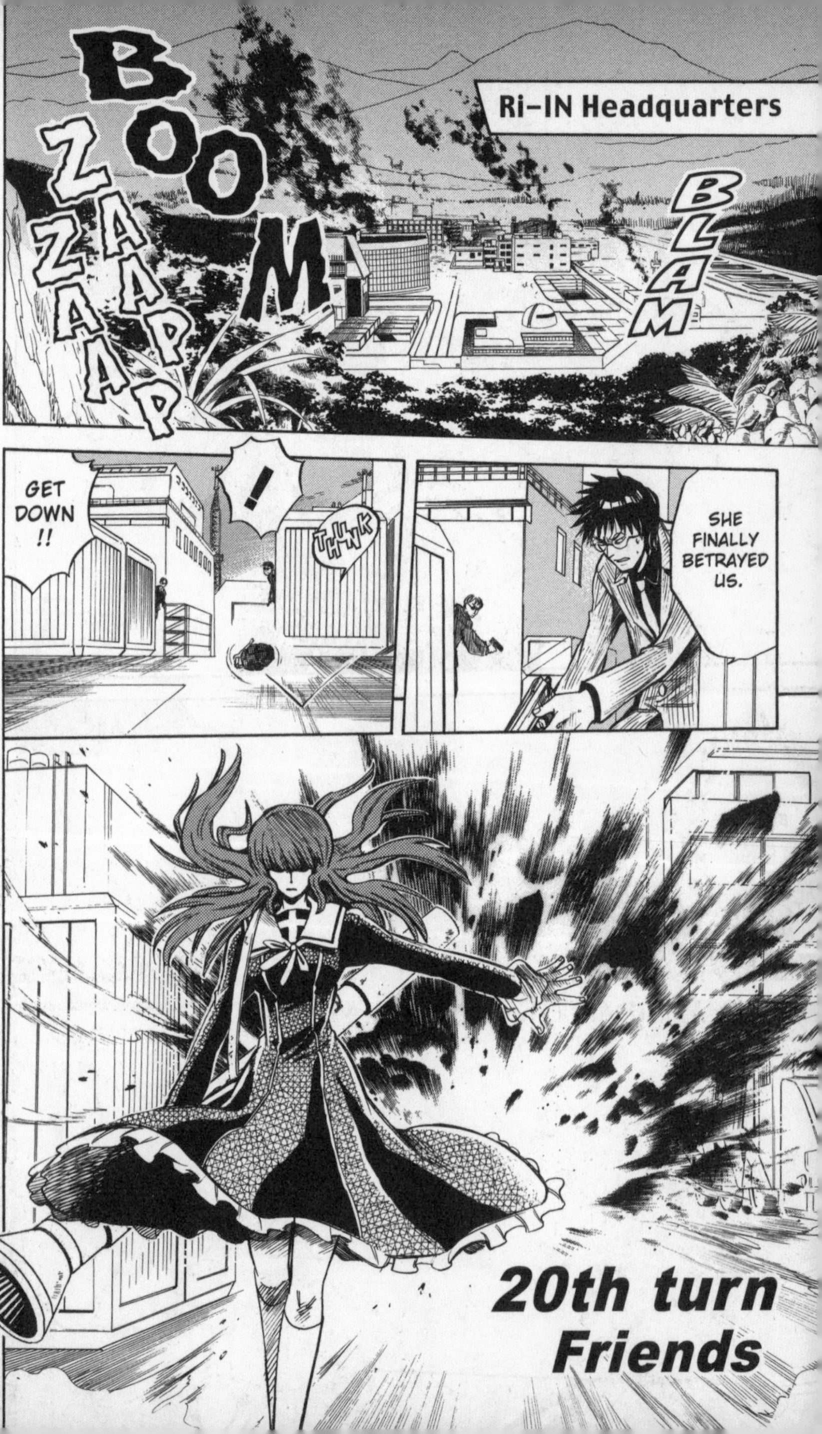
Ri-IN Headquarters
BLAM
BOOM
ZAAP
ZAAP
SHE FINALLY BETRAYED US.
!
THUNK
GET DOWN !!
20th turn
Friends

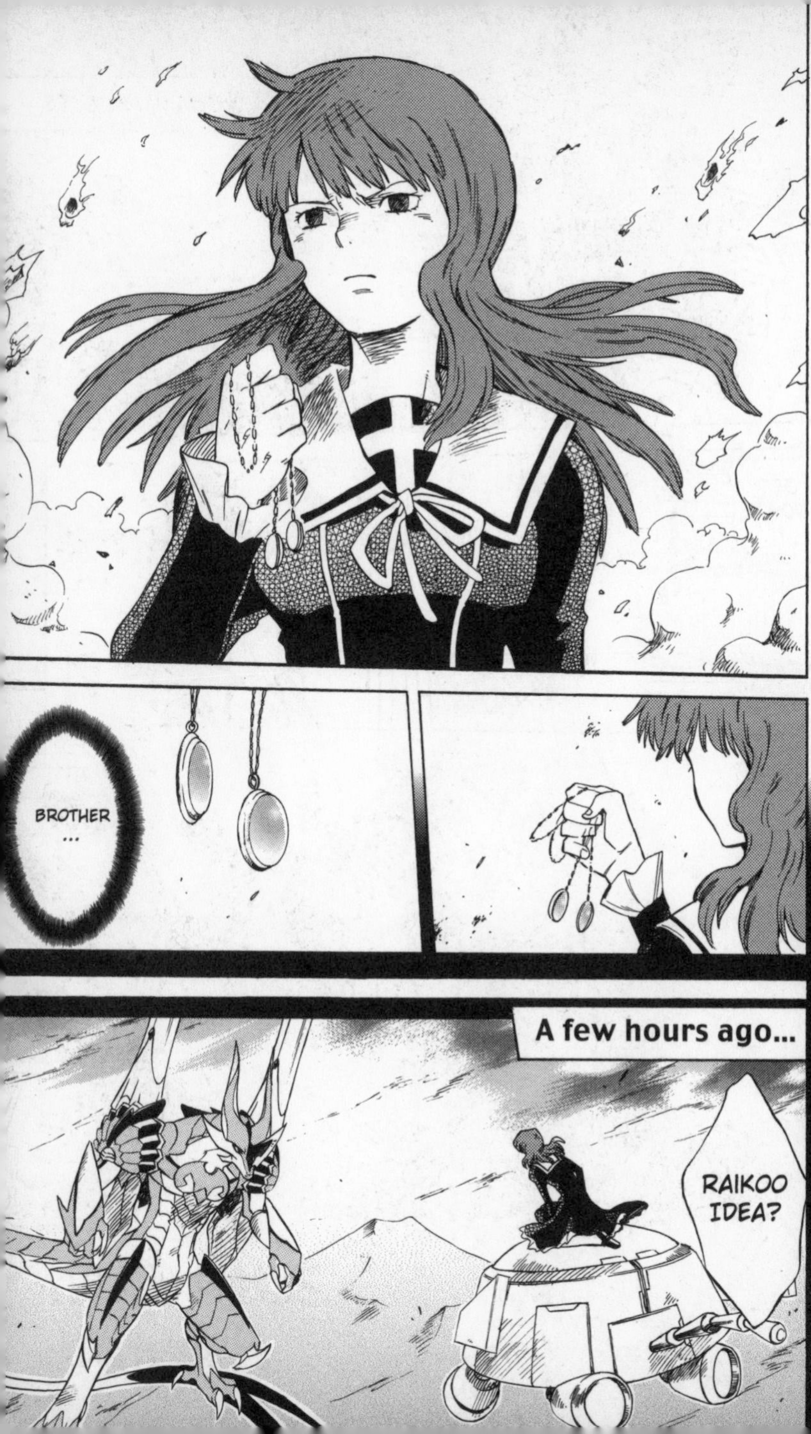
BROTHER
...
A few hours ago...
RAIKOO
IDEA?

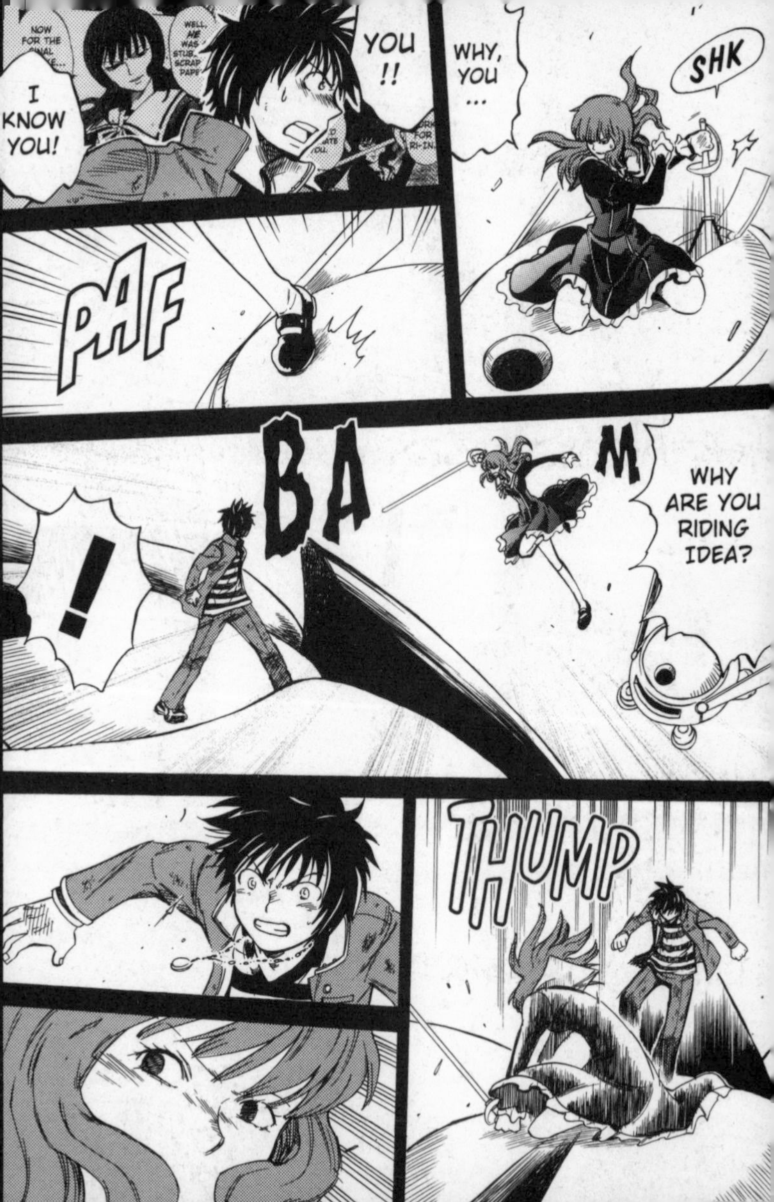
SHK
WHY, YOU ...
YOU !!
I KNOW YOU!
PAF
WHY ARE YOU RIDING IDEA?
BAM
!
THUMP

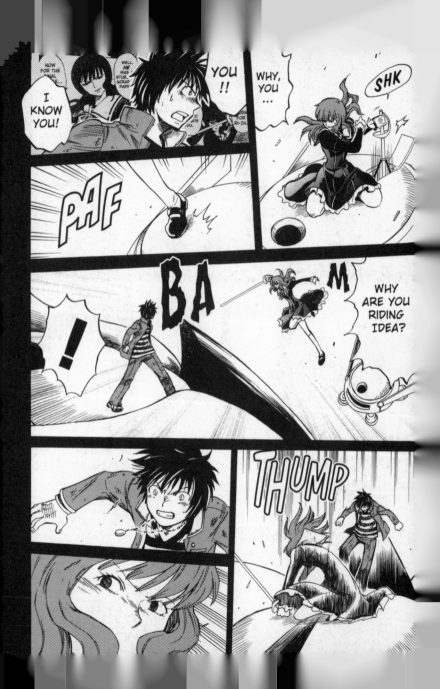

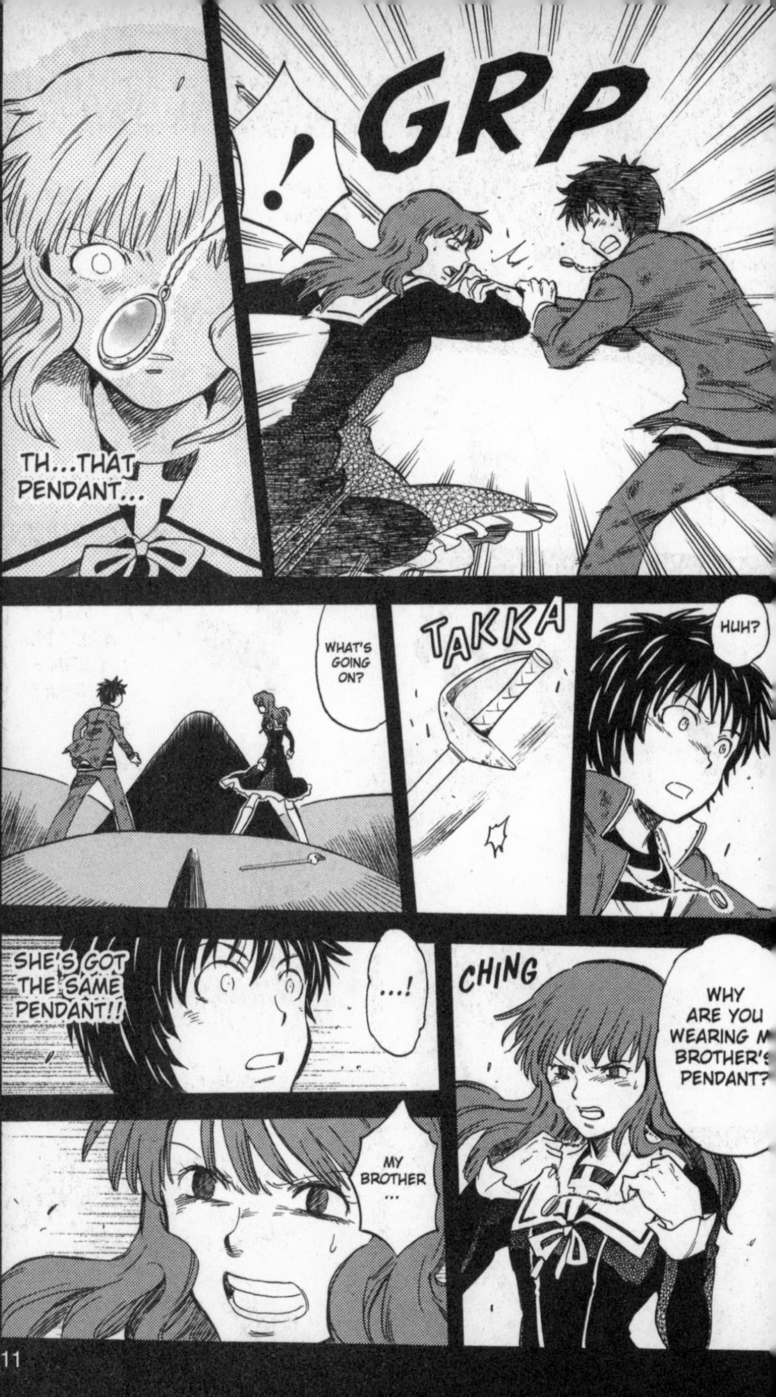
GRP
!
TH...THAT PENDANT...
HUH?
TAKKA
WHAT'S GOING ON?
CHING
WHY ARE YOU WEARING M BROTHER'S PENDANT?
SHE'S GOT THE SAME PENDANT!!
...!
MY BROTHER ...

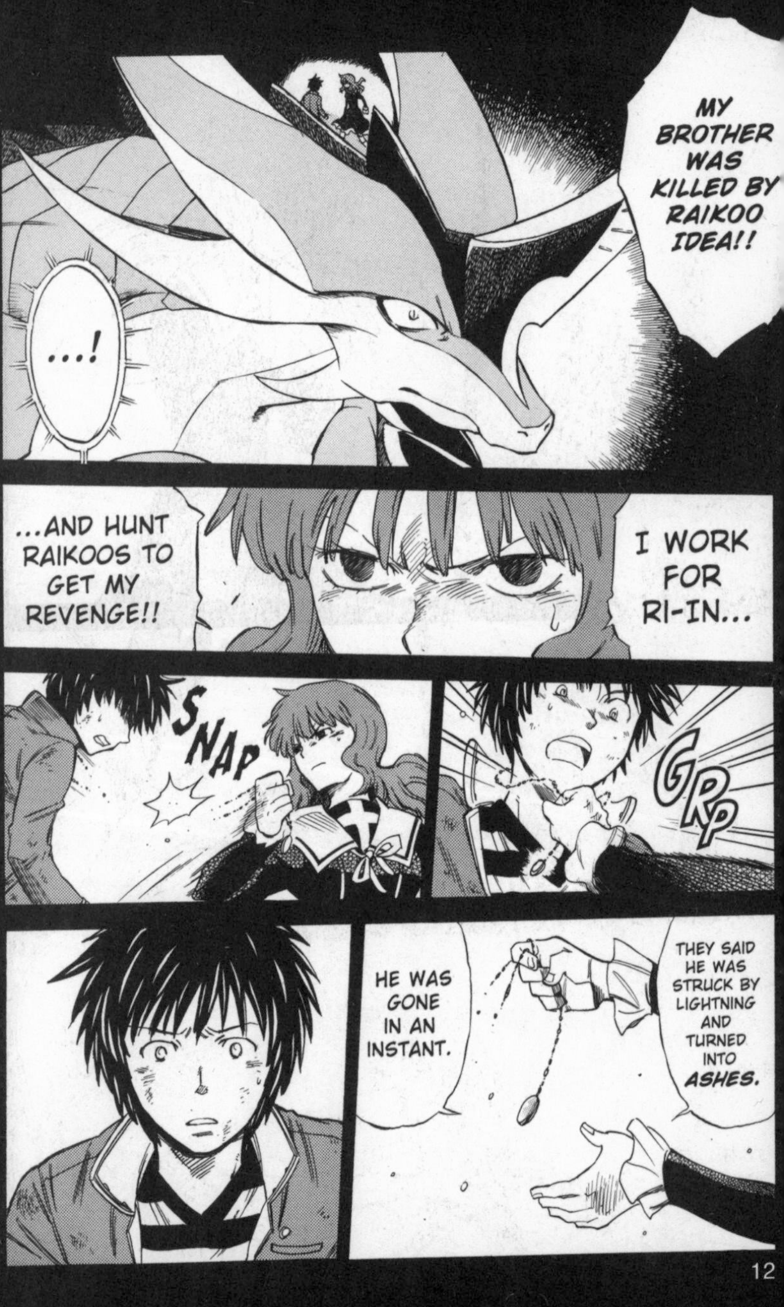
MY BROTHER WAS KILLED BY RAIKOO IDEA!!
...!
I WORK FOR RI-IN...
...AND HUNT RAIKOOS TO GET MY REVENGE!!
GRP
SNAP
THEY SAID HE WAS STRUCK BY LIGHTNING AND TURNED INTO **ASHES.**
HE WAS GONE IN AN INSTANT.

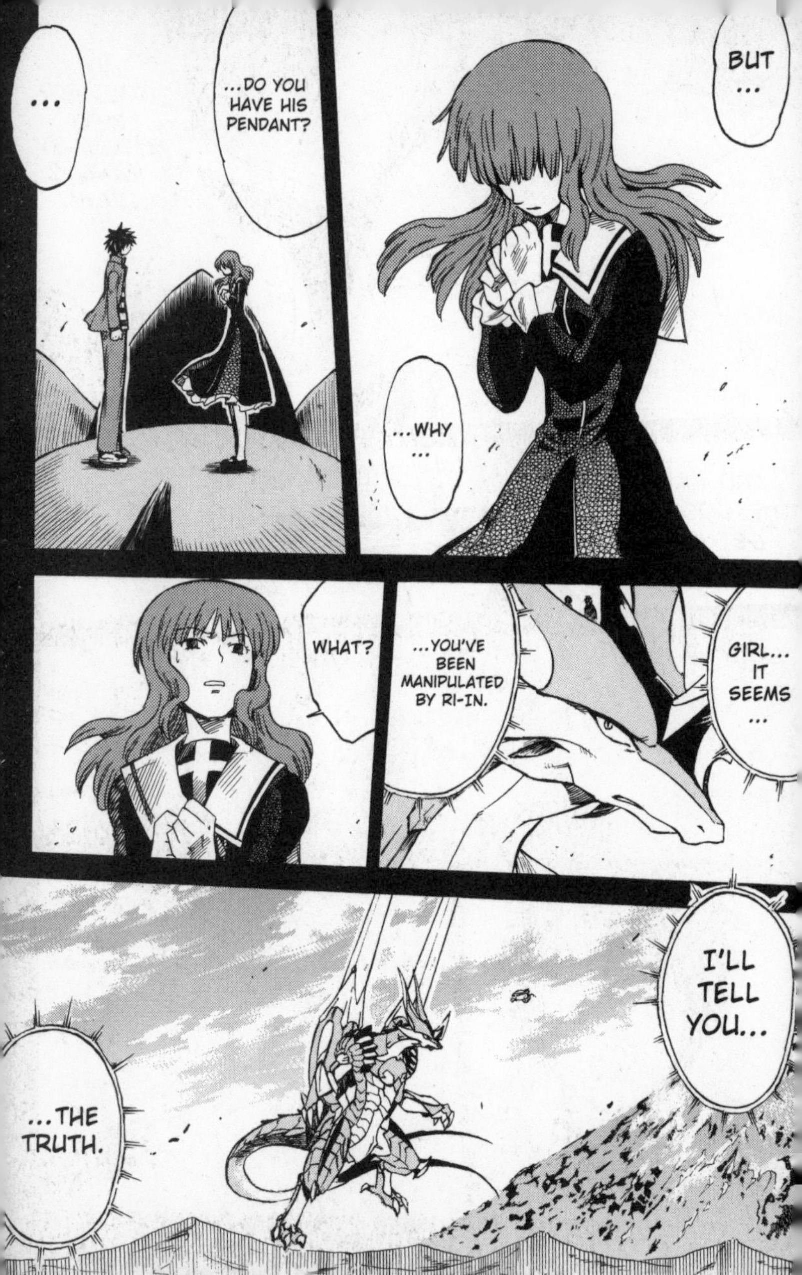
BUT ...
...WHY ...
...DO YOU HAVE HIS PENDANT?
...
GIRL... IT SEEMS ...
...YOU'VE BEEN MANIPULATED BY RI-IN.
WHAT?
I'LL TELL YOU...
...THE TRUTH.

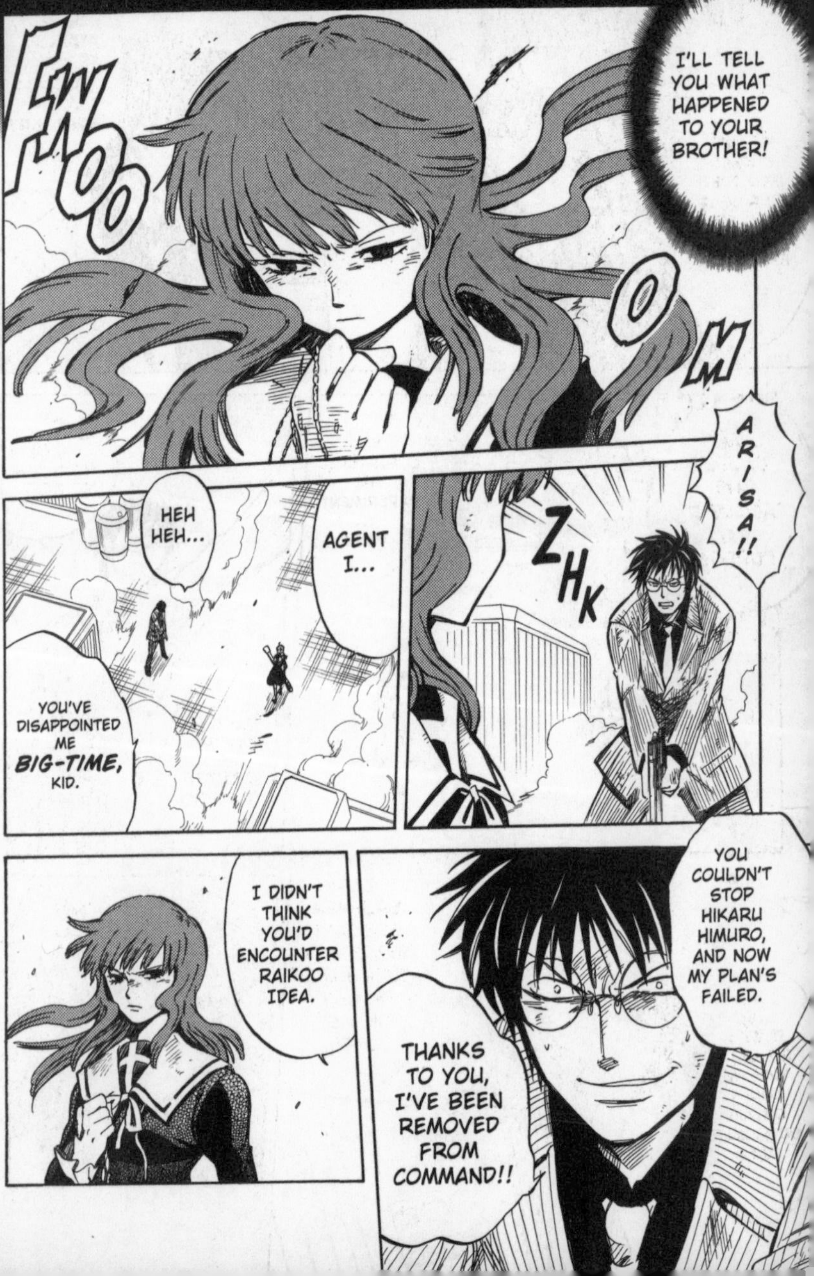
I'LL TELL YOU WHAT HAPPENED TO YOUR BROTHER!
FWOO
OM
ARISA!!
ZHK
HEH HEH...
AGENT I...
YOU'VE DISAPPOINTED ME BIG-TIME, KID.
YOU COULDN'T STOP HIKARU HIMURO, AND NOW MY PLAN'S FAILED.
THANKS TO YOU, I'VE BEEN REMOVED FROM COMMAND!!
I DIDN'T THINK YOU'D ENCOUNTER RAIKOO IDEA.

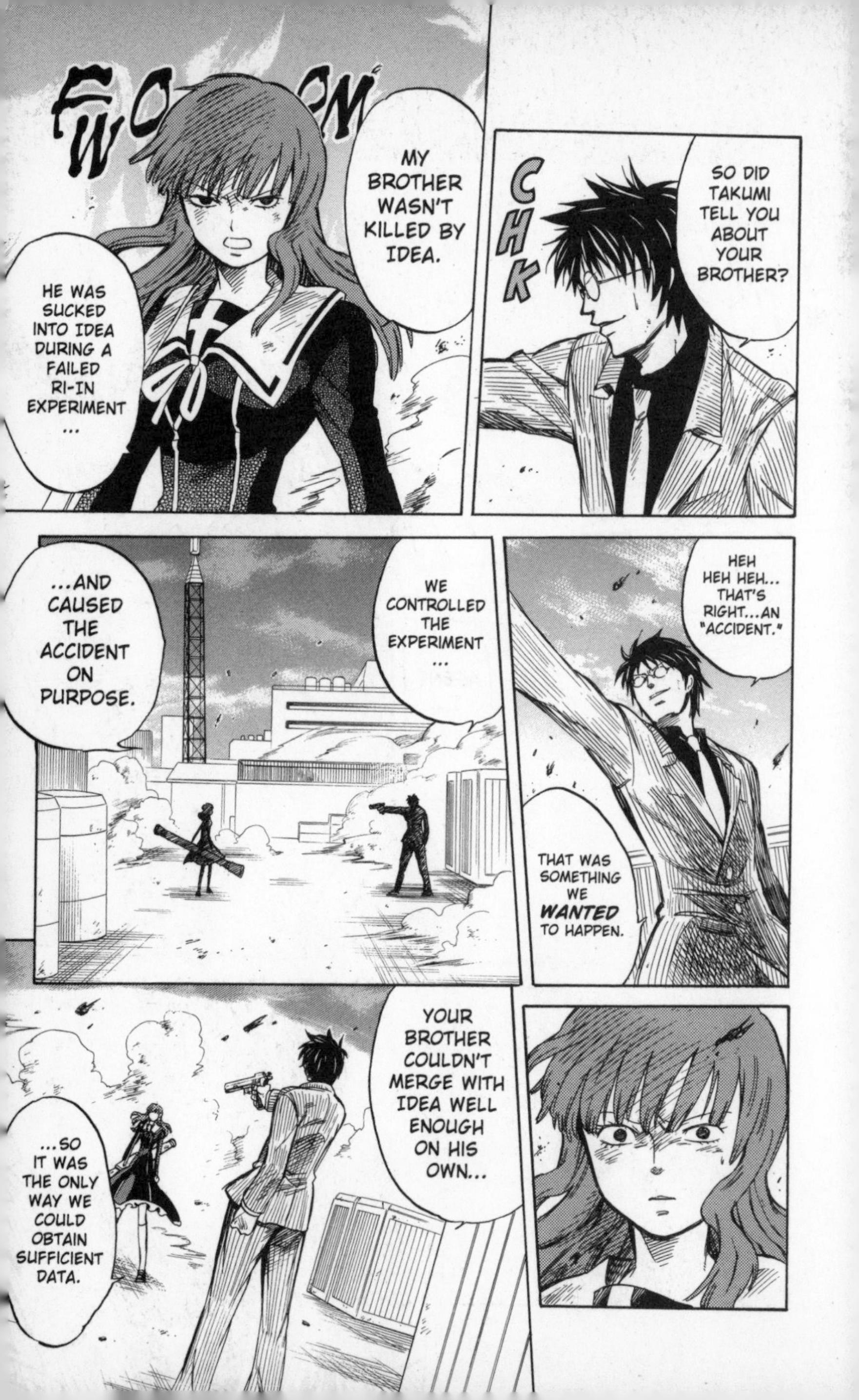

CHK
SO DID TAKUMI TELL YOU ABOUT YOUR BROTHER?
FWOOOM
MY BROTHER WASN'T KILLED BY IDEA.
HE WAS SUCKED INTO IDEA DURING A FAILED RI-IN EXPERIMENT...
HEH HEH HEH... THAT'S RIGHT...AN "ACCIDENT."
THAT WAS SOMETHING WE *WANTED* TO HAPPEN.
WE CONTROLLED THE EXPERIMENT...
...AND CAUSED THE ACCIDENT ON PURPOSE.
YOUR BROTHER COULDN'T MERGE WITH IDEA WELL ENOUGH ON HIS OWN...
...SO IT WAS THE ONLY WAY WE COULD OBTAIN SUFFICIENT DATA.

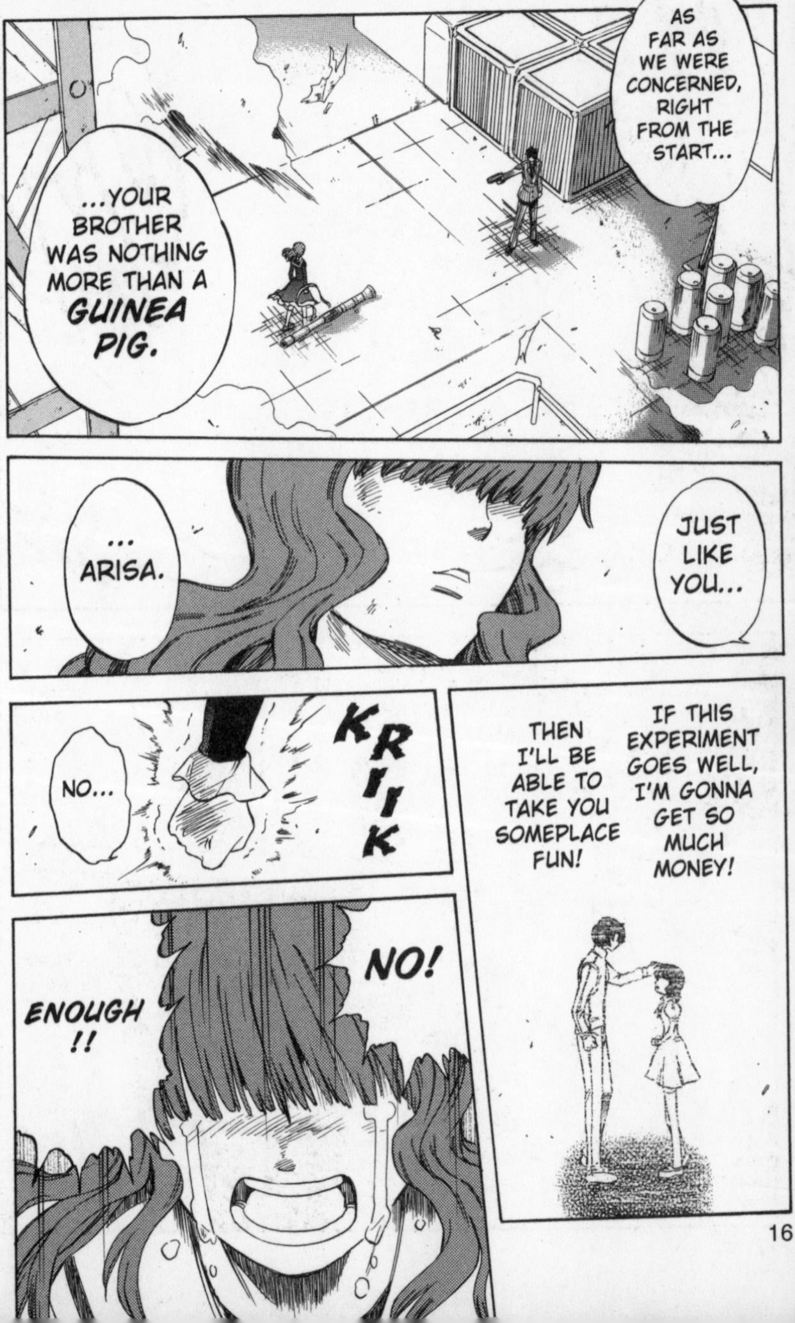
AS FAR AS WE WERE CONCERNED, RIGHT FROM THE START...
...YOUR BROTHER WAS NOTHING MORE THAN A GUINEA PIG.
JUST LIKE YOU...
... ARISA.
IF THIS EXPERIMENT GOES WELL, I'M GONNA GET SO MUCH MONEY!
THEN I'LL BE ABLE TO TAKE YOU SOMEPLACE FUN!
KRIIK
NO...
NO!
ENOUGH !!

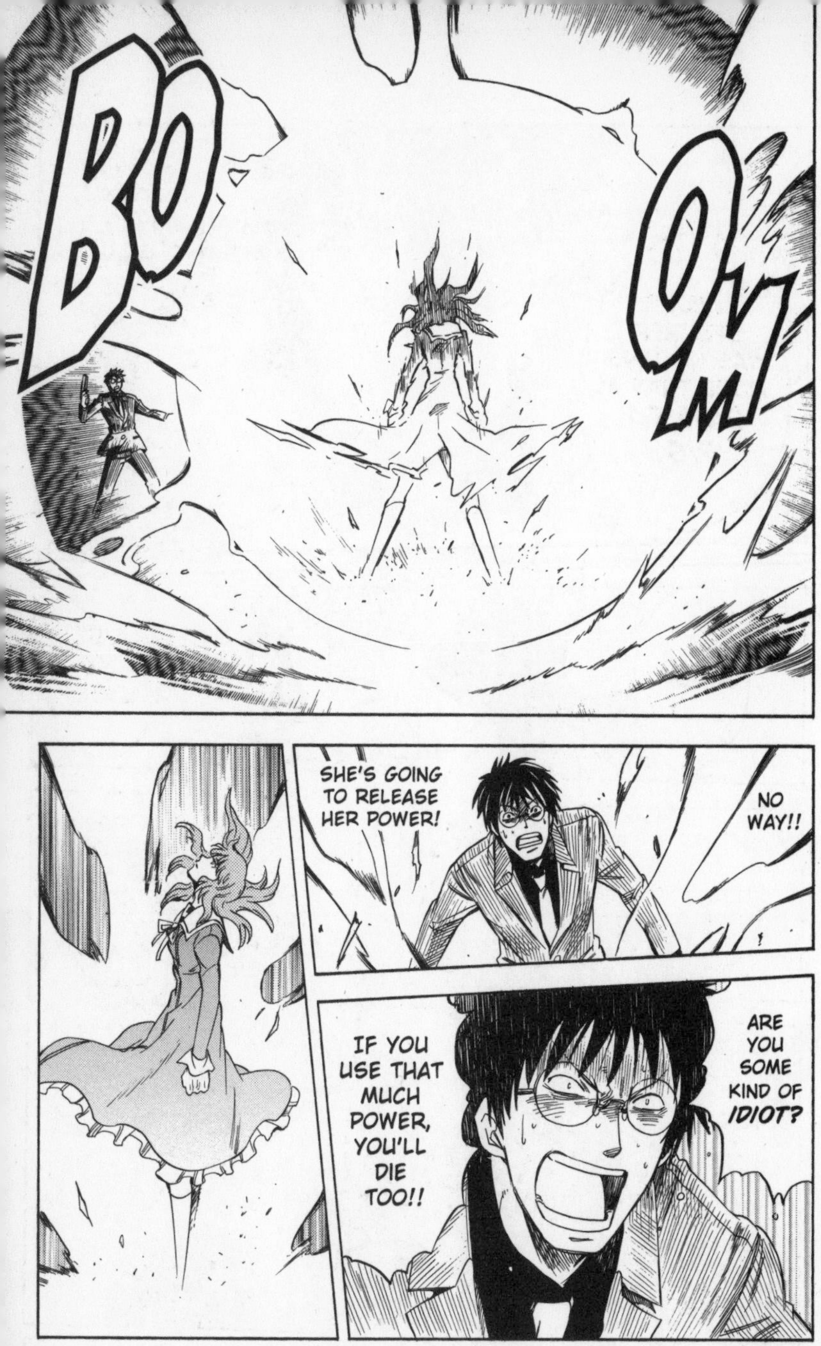
BOOM
NO WAY!!
SHE'S GOING TO RELEASE HER POWER!
ARE YOU SOME KIND OF *IDIOT*?
IF YOU USE THAT MUCH POWER, YOU'LL DIE TOO!!

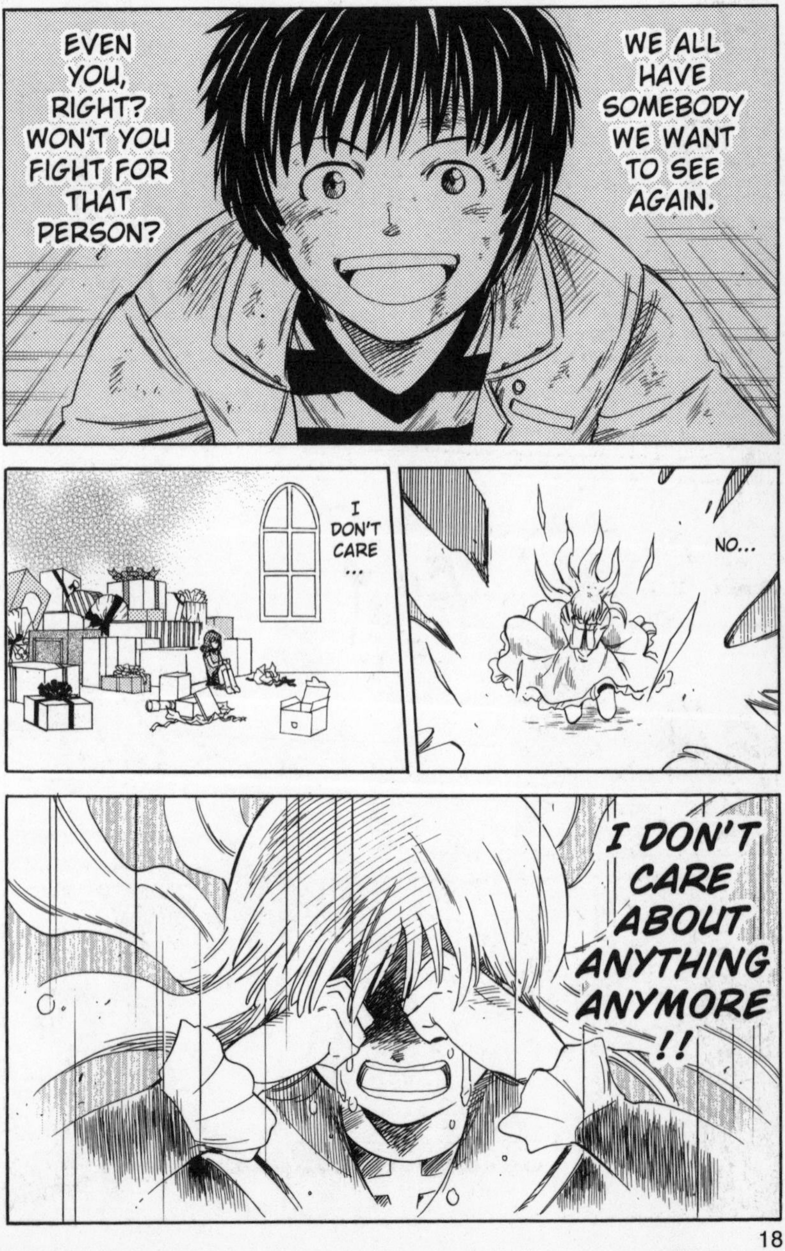
WE ALL HAVE SOMEBODY WE WANT TO SEE AGAIN.
EVEN YOU, RIGHT? WON'T YOU FIGHT FOR THAT PERSON?
NO...
I DON'T CARE ...
I DON'T CARE ABOUT ANYTHING ANYMORE!!

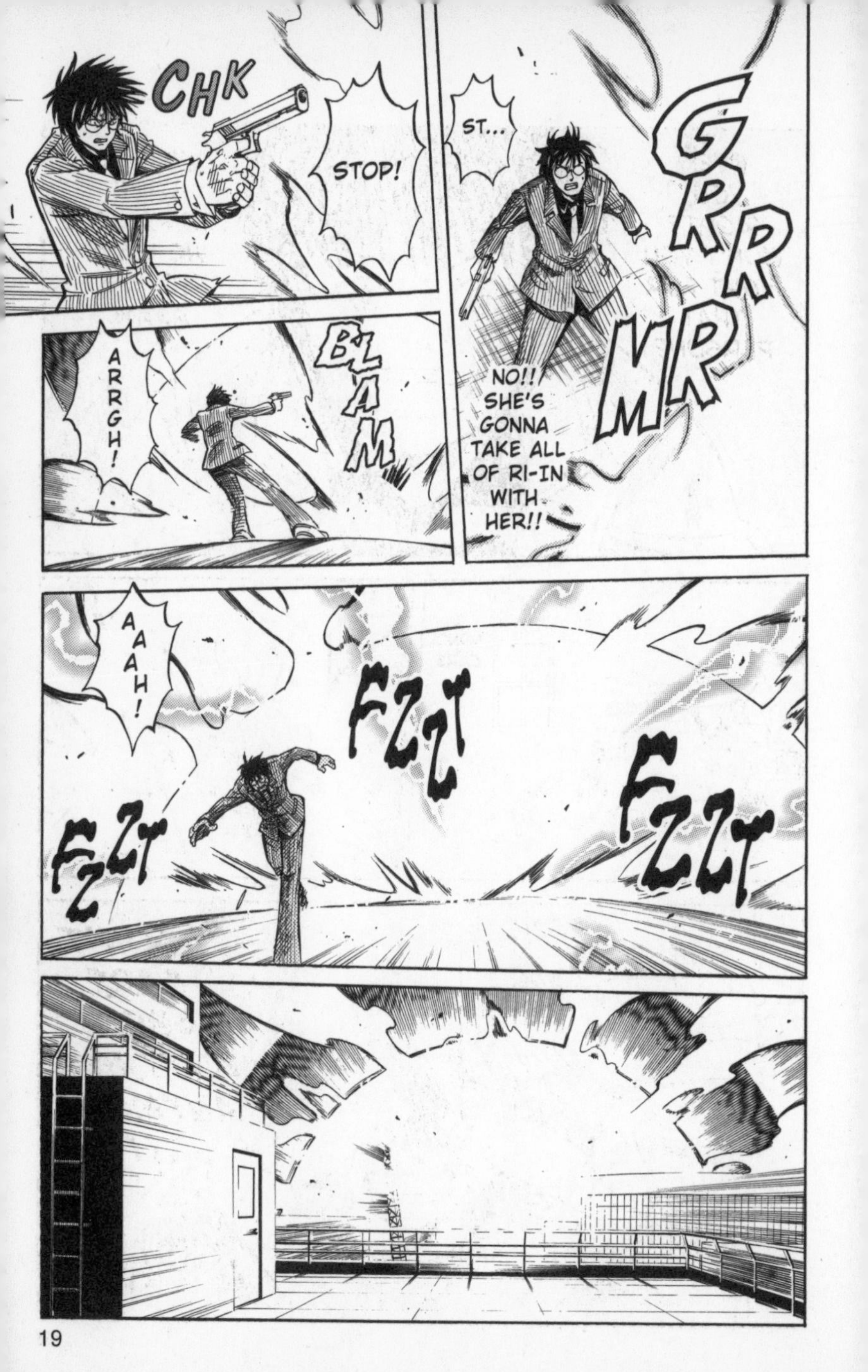
ST...
GRRR
MR
NO!! SHE'S GONNA TAKE ALL OF RI-IN WITH HER!!
CHK
STOP!
BLAM
ARRGH!
FZZT
FZZT
FZZT
AAAH!

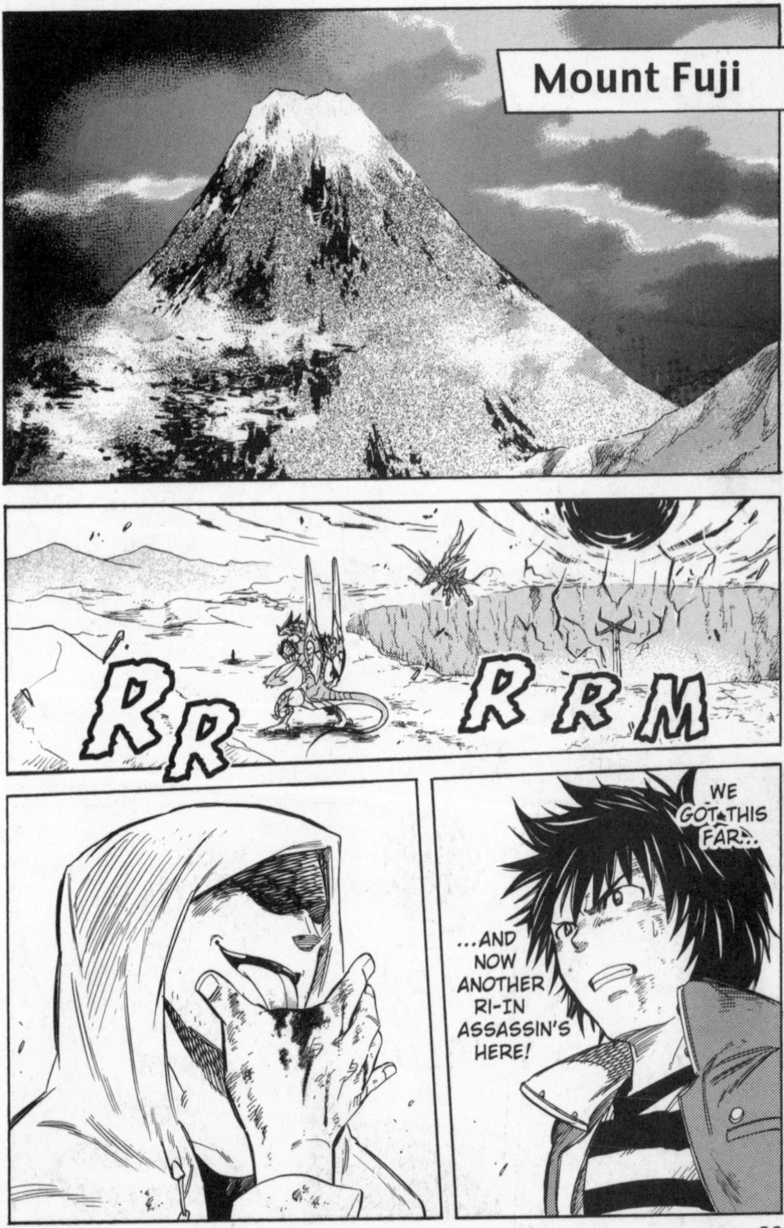
Mount Fuji
RRRRRM
WE GOT THIS FAR...
...AND NOW ANOTHER RI-IN ASSASSIN'S HERE!

READ THIS WAY

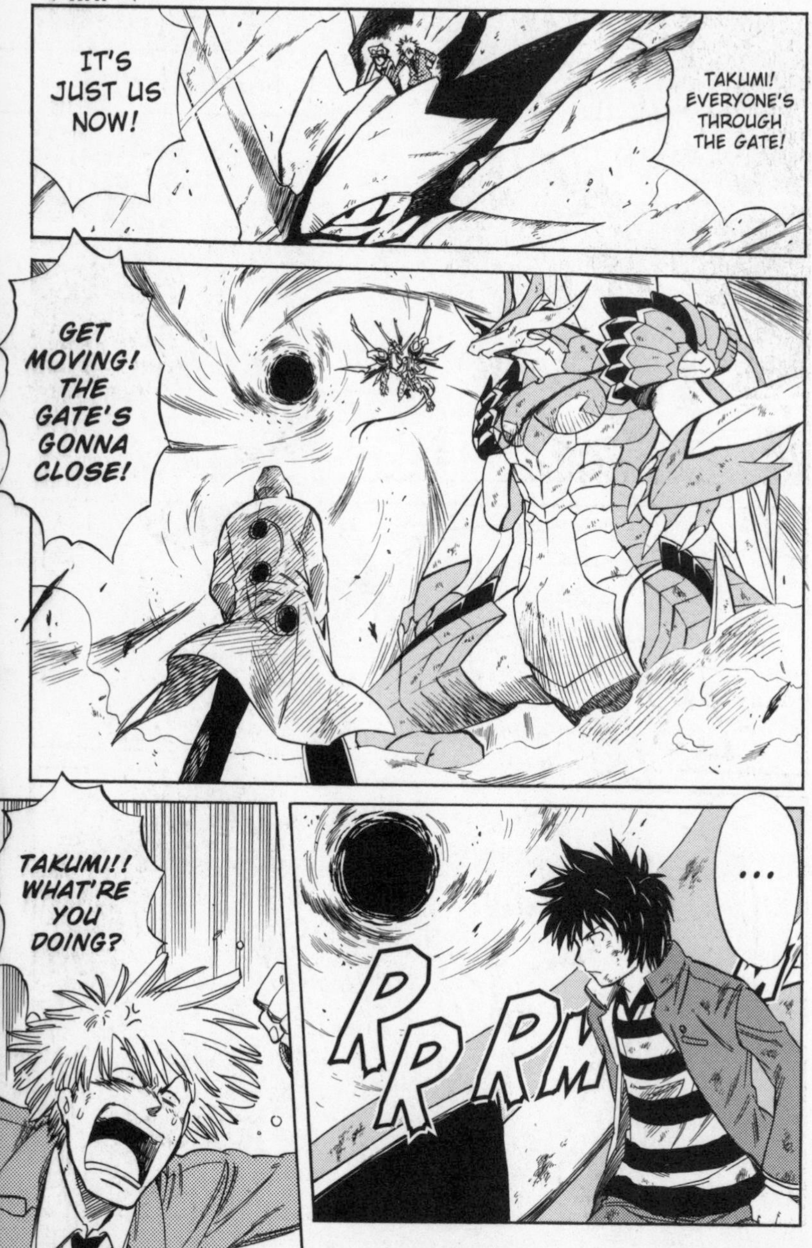
TAKUMI! EVERYONE'S THROUGH THE GATE!
IT'S JUST US NOW!
GET MOVING! THE GATE'S GONNA CLOSE!
...
RRRM
TAKUMI!! WHAT'RE YOU DOING?

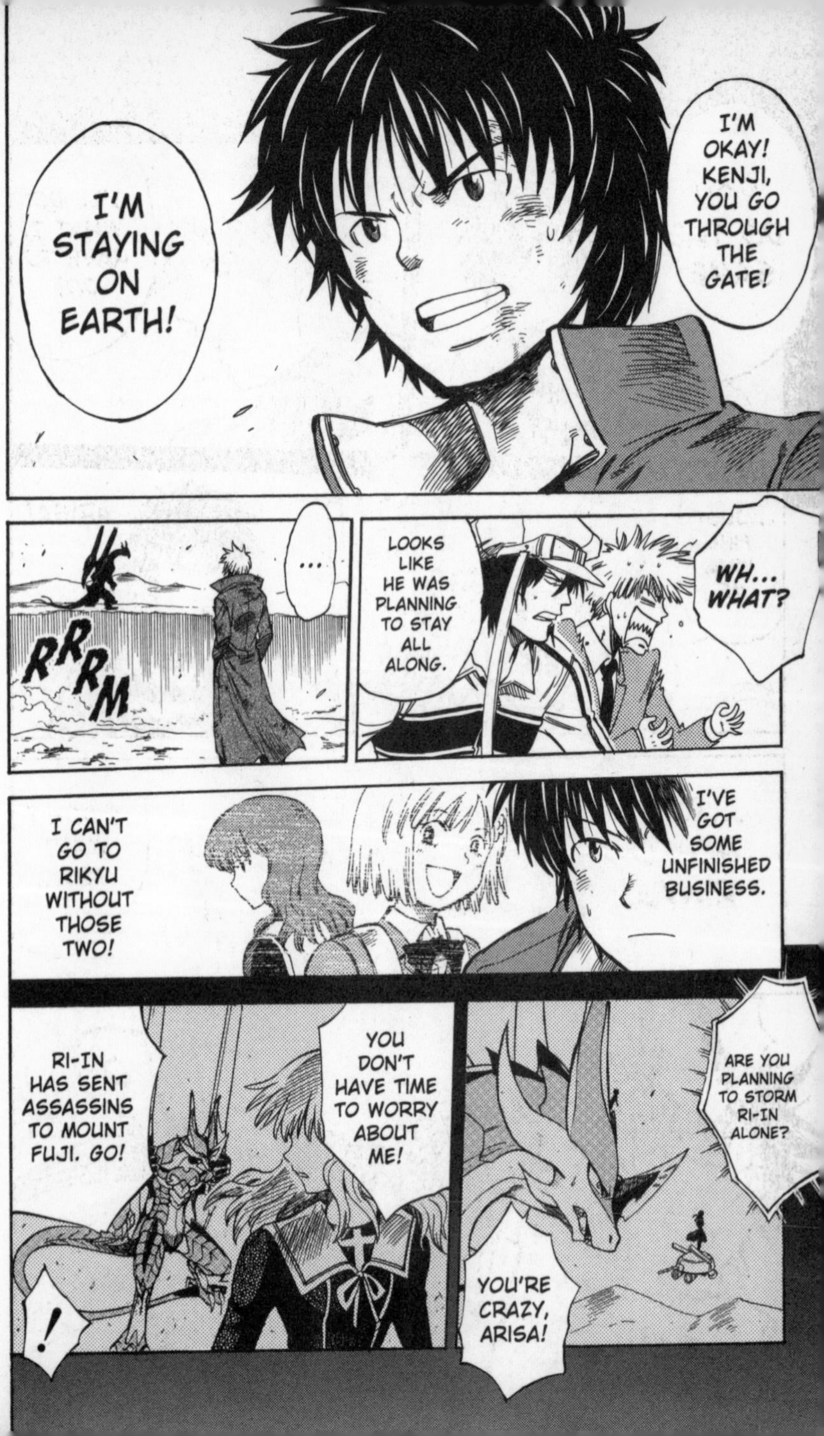
I'M OKAY! KENJI, YOU GO THROUGH THE GATE!
I'M STAYING ON EARTH!
WH... WHAT?
LOOKS LIKE HE WAS PLANNING TO STAY ALL ALONG.
...
RRRM
I'VE GOT SOME UNFINISHED BUSINESS.
I CAN'T GO TO RIKYU WITHOUT THOSE TWO!
ARE YOU PLANNING TO STORM RI-IN ALONE?
YOU'RE CRAZY, ARISA!
YOU DON'T HAVE TIME TO WORRY ABOUT ME!
RI-IN HAS SENT ASSASSINS TO MOUNT FUJI. GO!
!

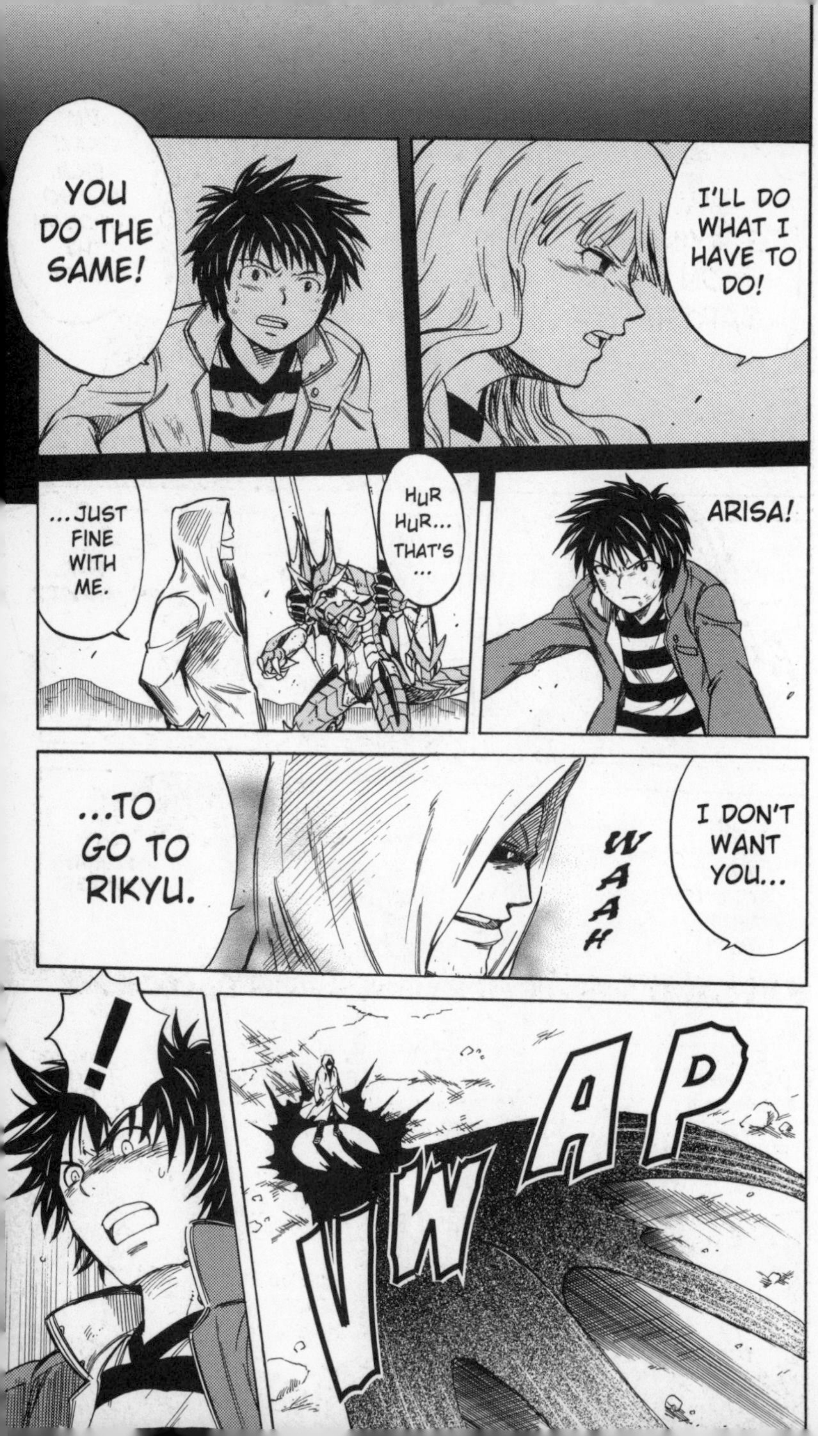
I'LL DO WHAT I HAVE TO DO!
YOU DO THE SAME!
ARISA!
HUR HUR... THAT'S...
...JUST FINE WITH ME.
I DON'T WANT YOU...
WAAH
...TO GO TO RIKYU.
VWAP
!

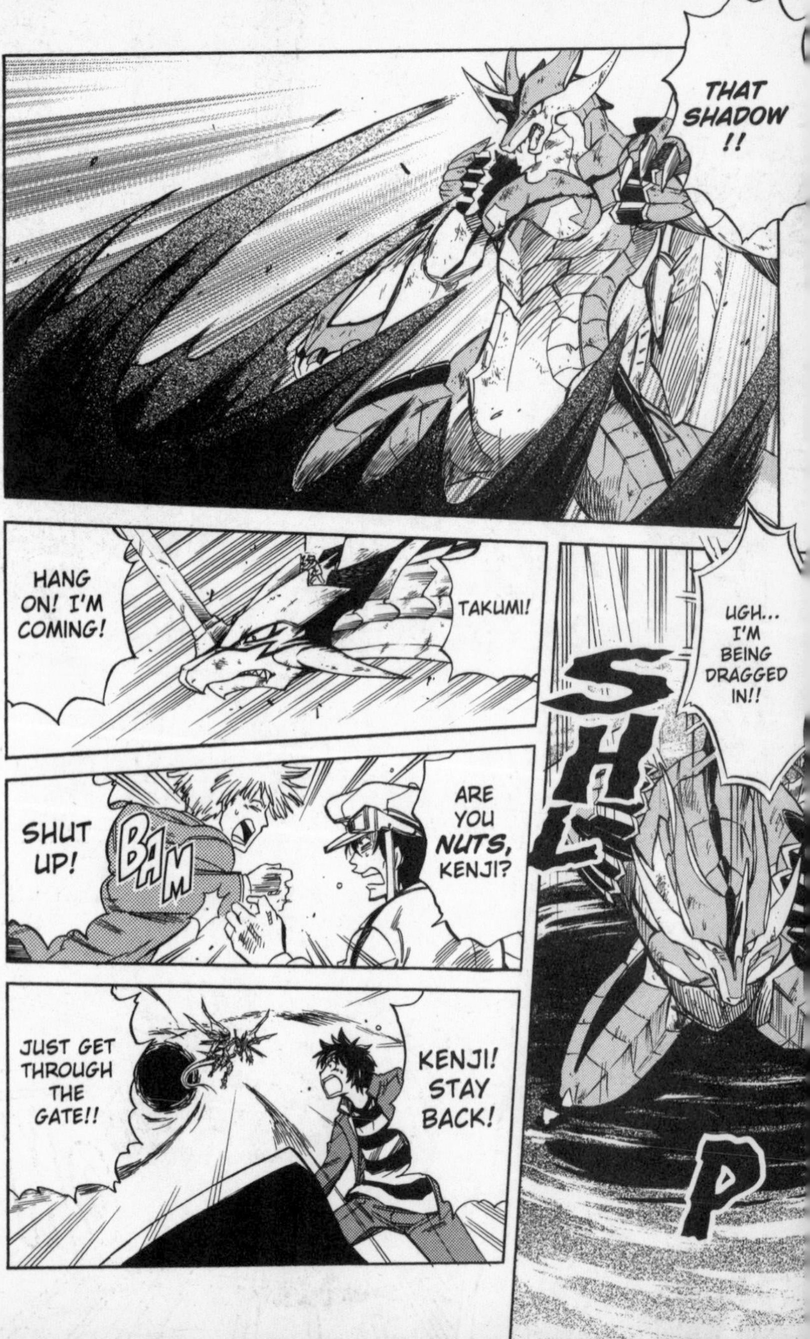
THAT SHADOW!!
UGH... I'M BEING DRAGGED IN!!
SH
P
TAKUMI!
HANG ON! I'M COMING!
ARE YOU NUTS, KENJI?
SHUT UP!
BAM
KENJI! STAY BACK!
JUST GET THROUGH THE GATE!!

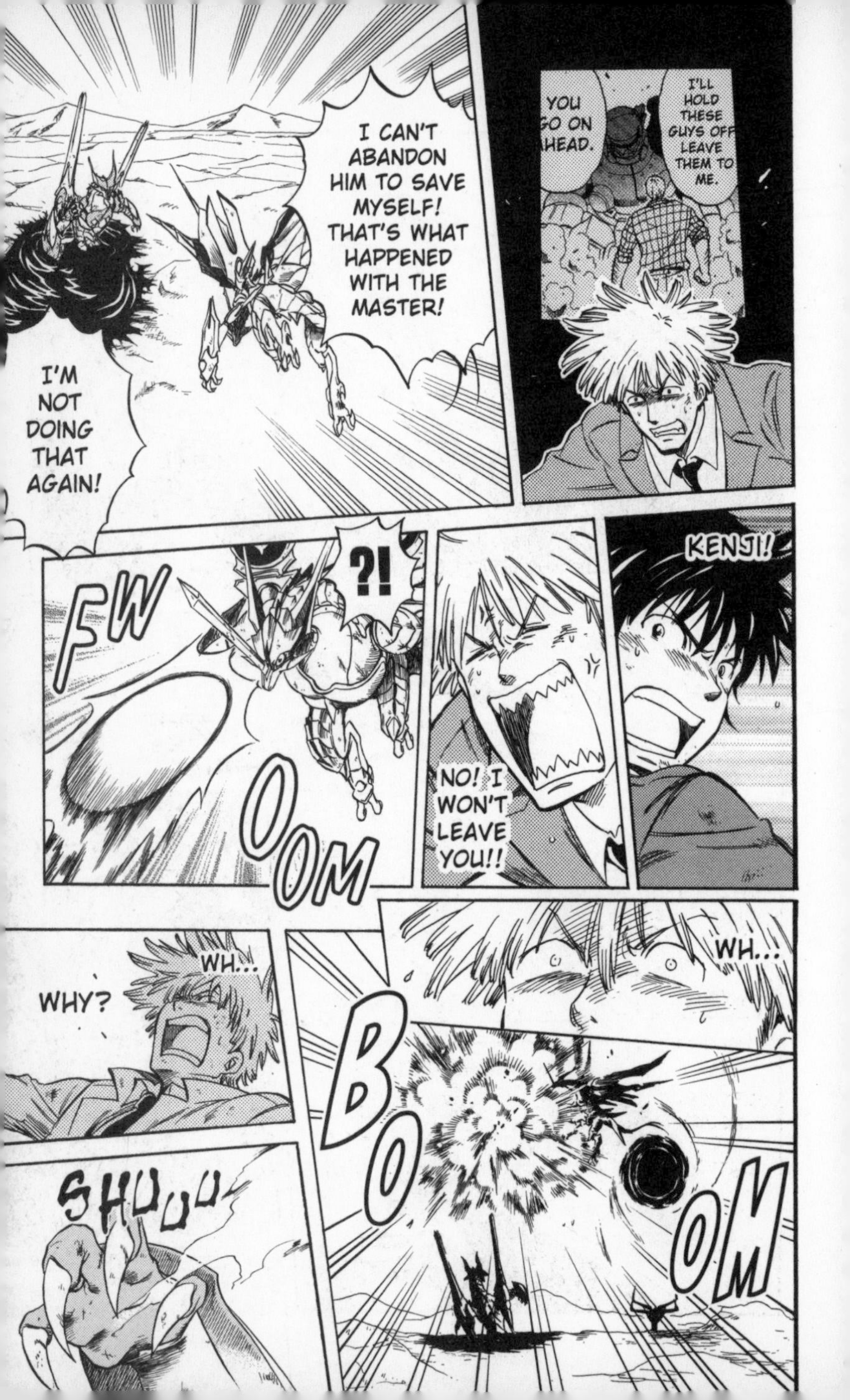
I'LL HOLD THESE GUYS OFF LEAVE THEM TO ME.
YOU GO ON AHEAD.
I CAN'T ABANDON HIM TO SAVE MYSELF! THAT'S WHAT HAPPENED WITH THE MASTER!
I'M NOT DOING THAT AGAIN!
KENJI!
NO! I WON'T LEAVE YOU!!
?!
FW
OOOM
WH...
BOOOM
WH...
WHY?
SHUUU

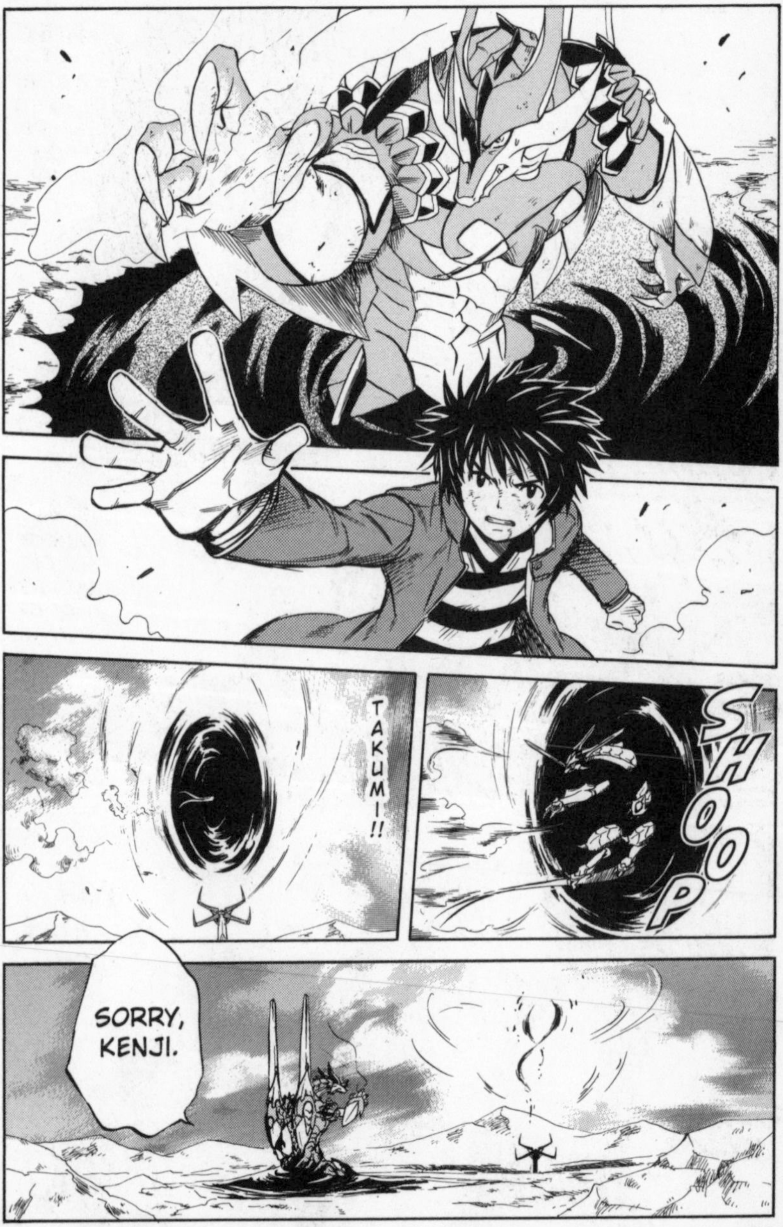
SHOOP
TAKUMI!!
SORRY, KENJI.

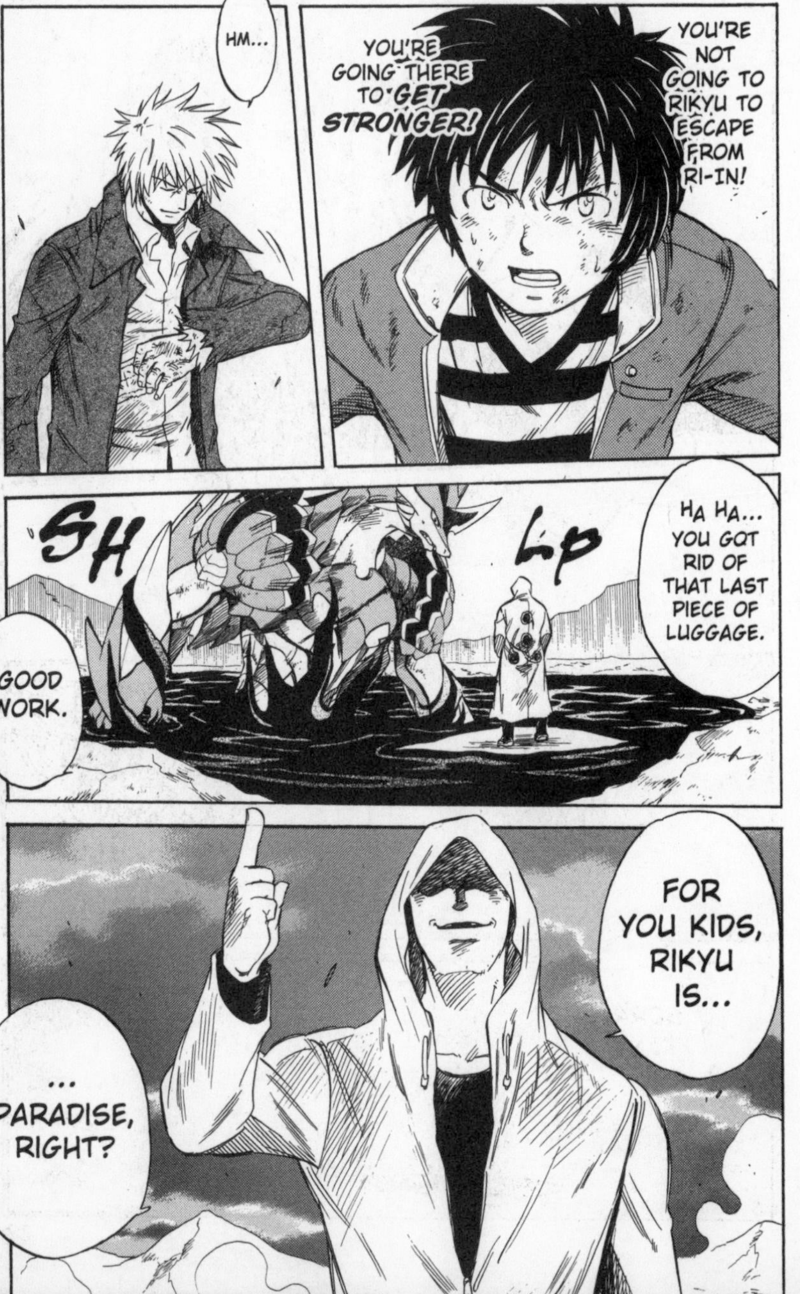
YOU'RE NOT GOING TO RIKYU TO ESCAPE FROM RI-IN!
YOU'RE GOING THERE TO GET STRONGER!
HM...
SHLP
HA HA... YOU GOT RID OF THAT LAST PIECE OF LUGGAGE.
GOOD WORK.
FOR YOU KIDS, RIKYU IS...
...PARADISE, RIGHT?

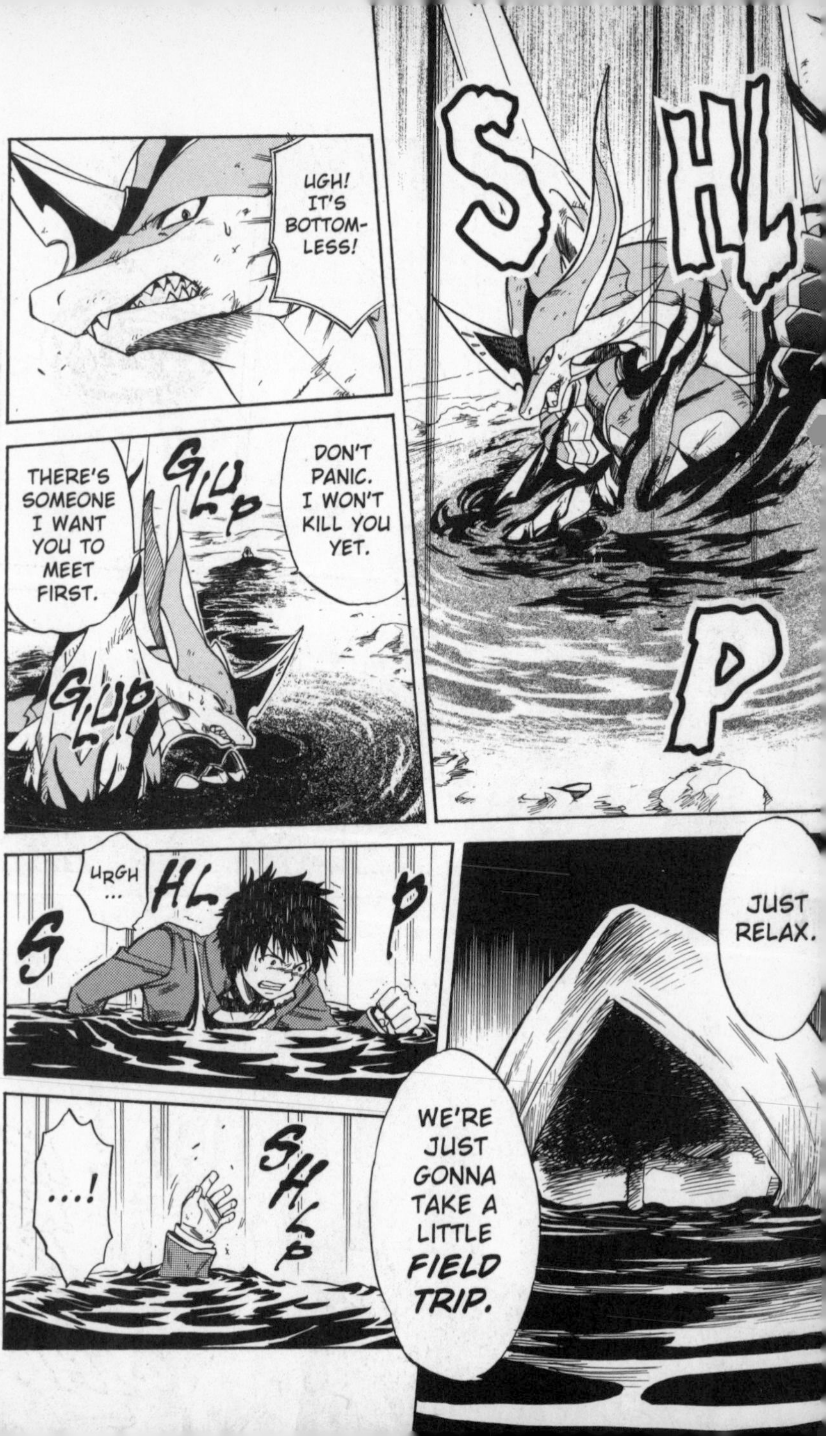
SHLP
UGH! IT'S BOTTOM-LESS!
DON'T PANIC. I WON'T KILL YOU YET.
THERE'S SOMEONE I WANT YOU TO MEET FIRST.
GLUP
GLUP
JUST RELAX.
WE'RE JUST GONNA TAKE A LITTLE FIELD TRIP.
URGH...
SHLP
...!
SHLP

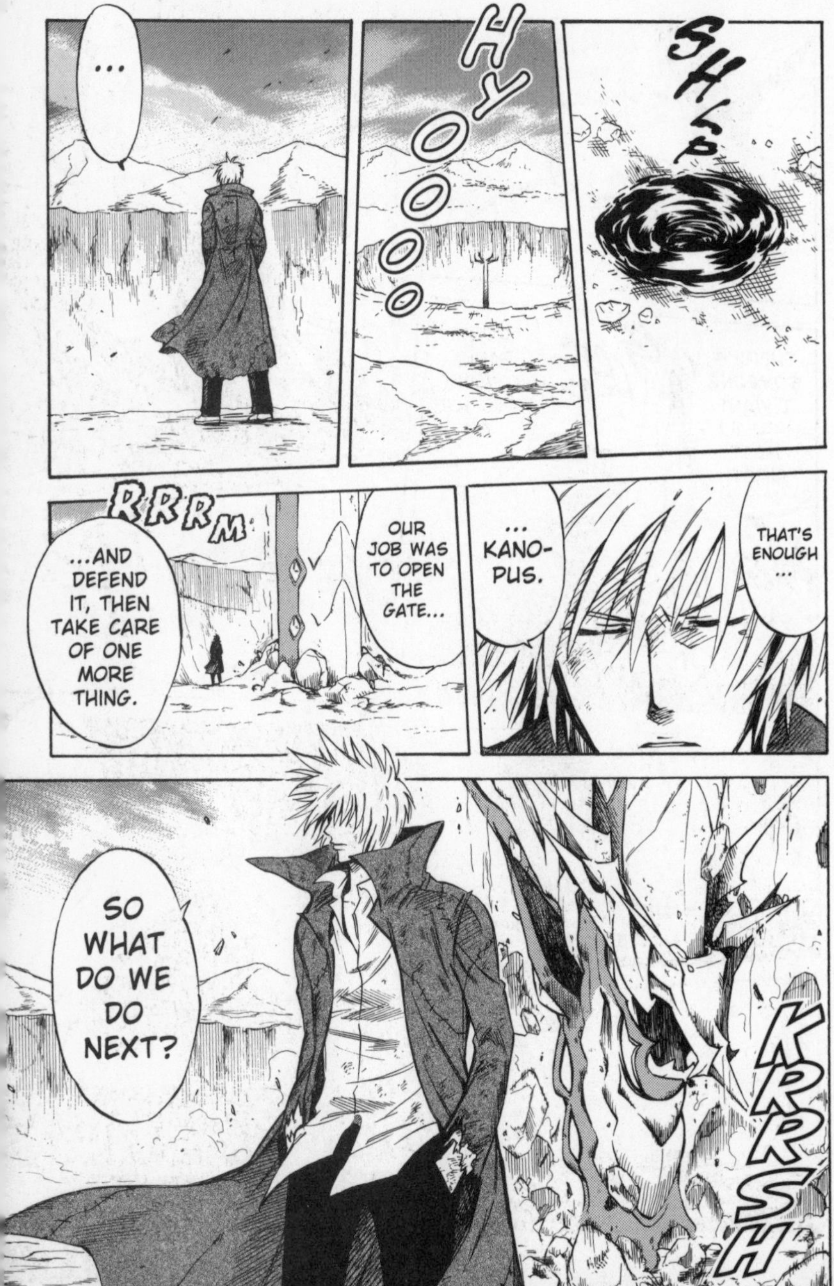
SHLP
HYOOOO
...
THAT'S ENOUGH ...
... KANO-PUS.
OUR JOB WAS TO OPEN THE GATE...
...AND DEFEND IT, THEN TAKE CARE OF ONE MORE THING.
RRRM
KRRSH
SO WHAT DO WE DO NEXT?

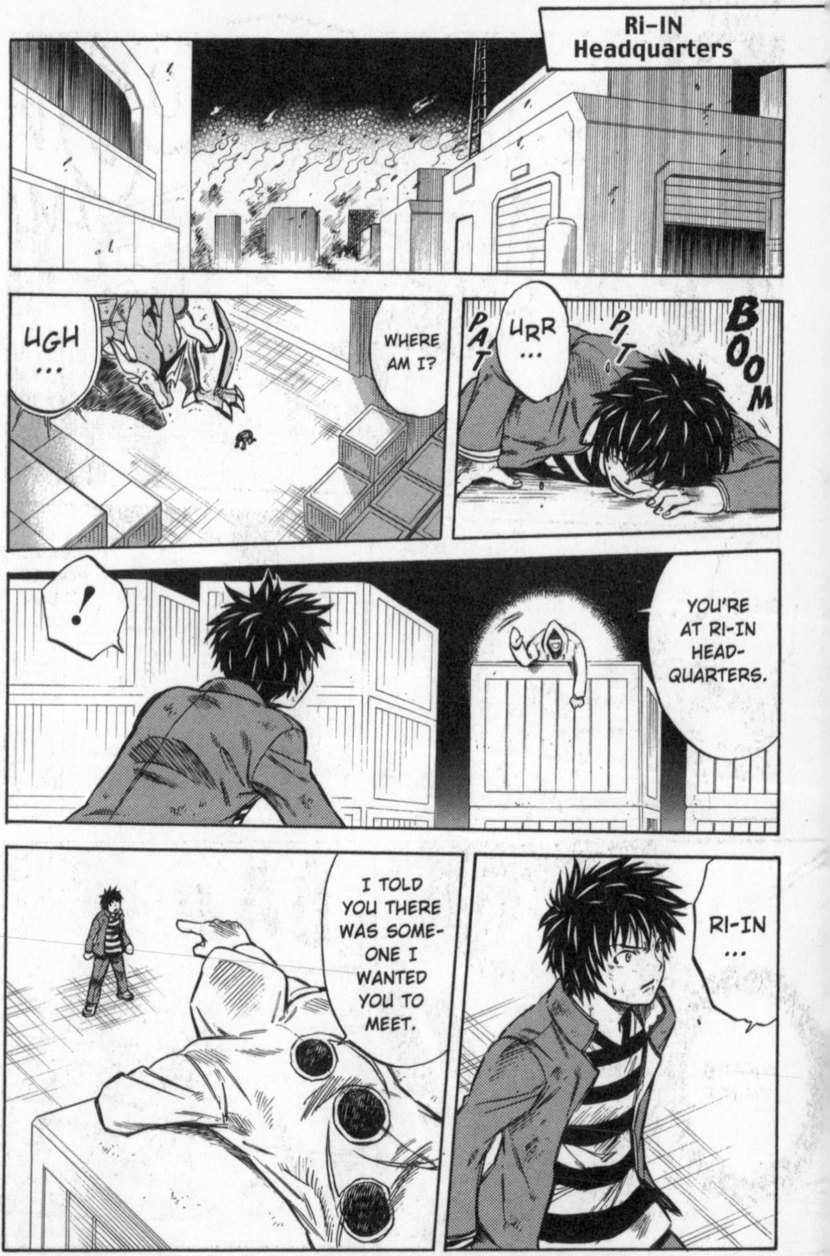

Ri-IN Headquarters
BOOM
PIT
URR ...
PAT
WHERE AM I?
UGH ...
YOU'RE AT RI-IN HEAD-QUARTERS.
!
RI-IN ...
I TOLD YOU THERE WAS SOME-ONE I WANTED YOU TO MEET.

READ THIS WAY

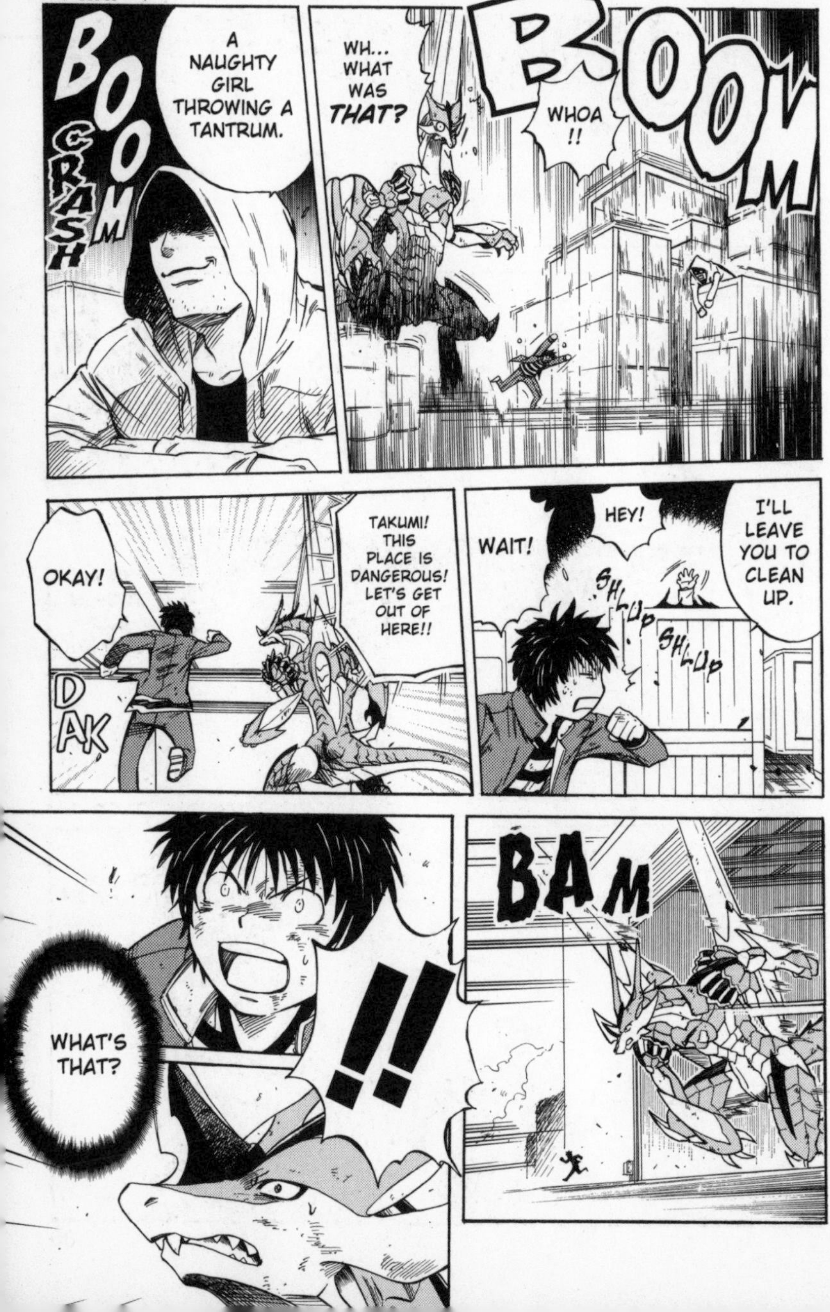
BOOOM
WHOA !!
WH... WHAT WAS *THAT?*
A NAUGHTY GIRL THROWING A TANTRUM.
BOOOM
CRASH
I'LL LEAVE YOU TO CLEAN UP.
HEY!
WAIT!
SHLUP
SHLUP
TAKUMI! THIS PLACE IS DANGEROUS! LET'S GET OUT OF HERE!!
OKAY!
DAK
BAM
!!
WHAT'S THAT?

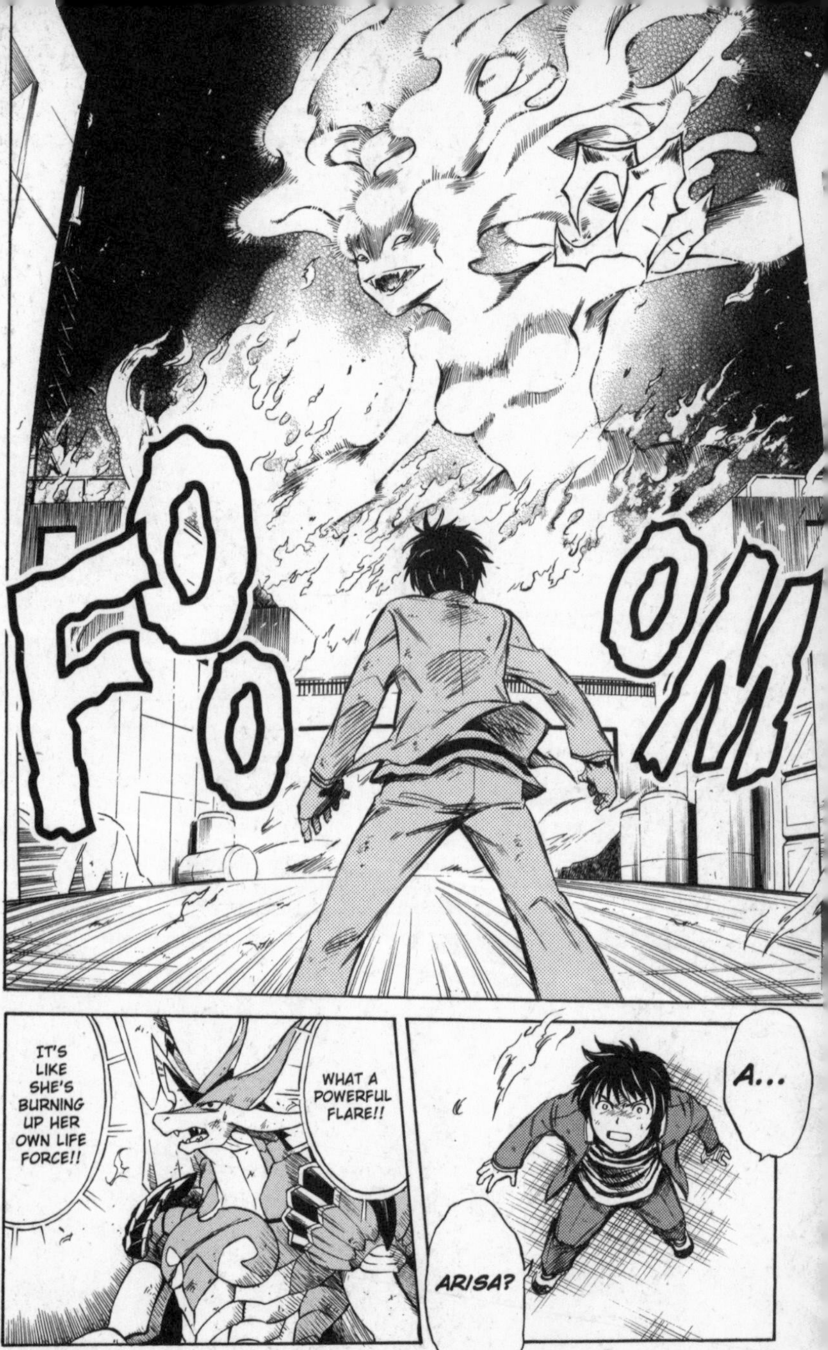
FOOOM
A...
ARISA?
WHAT A POWERFUL FLARE!!
IT'S LIKE SHE'S BURNING UP HER OWN LIFE FORCE!!

READ THIS WAY

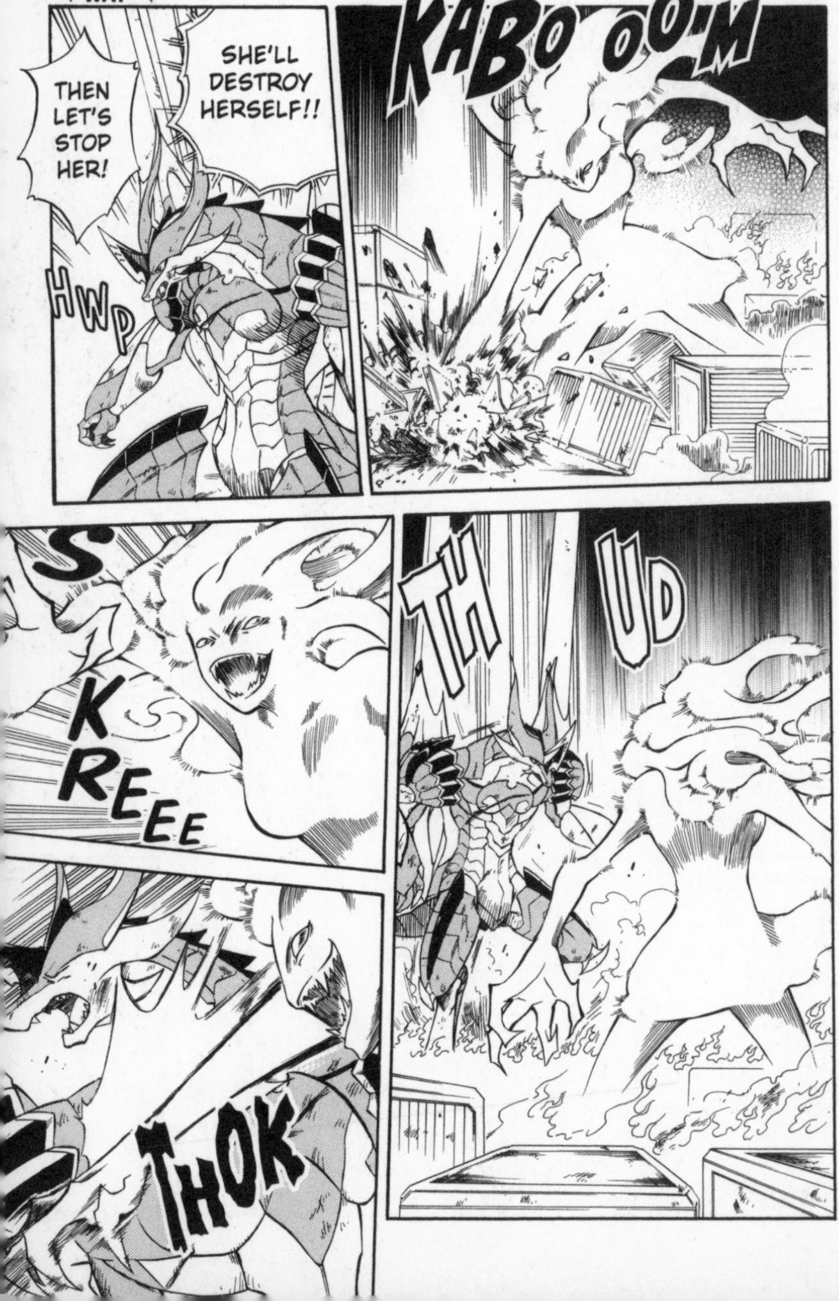
KABOOOM
SHE'LL DESTROY HERSELF!!
THEN LET'S STOP HER!
HWP
THUD
SKREEE
THOK

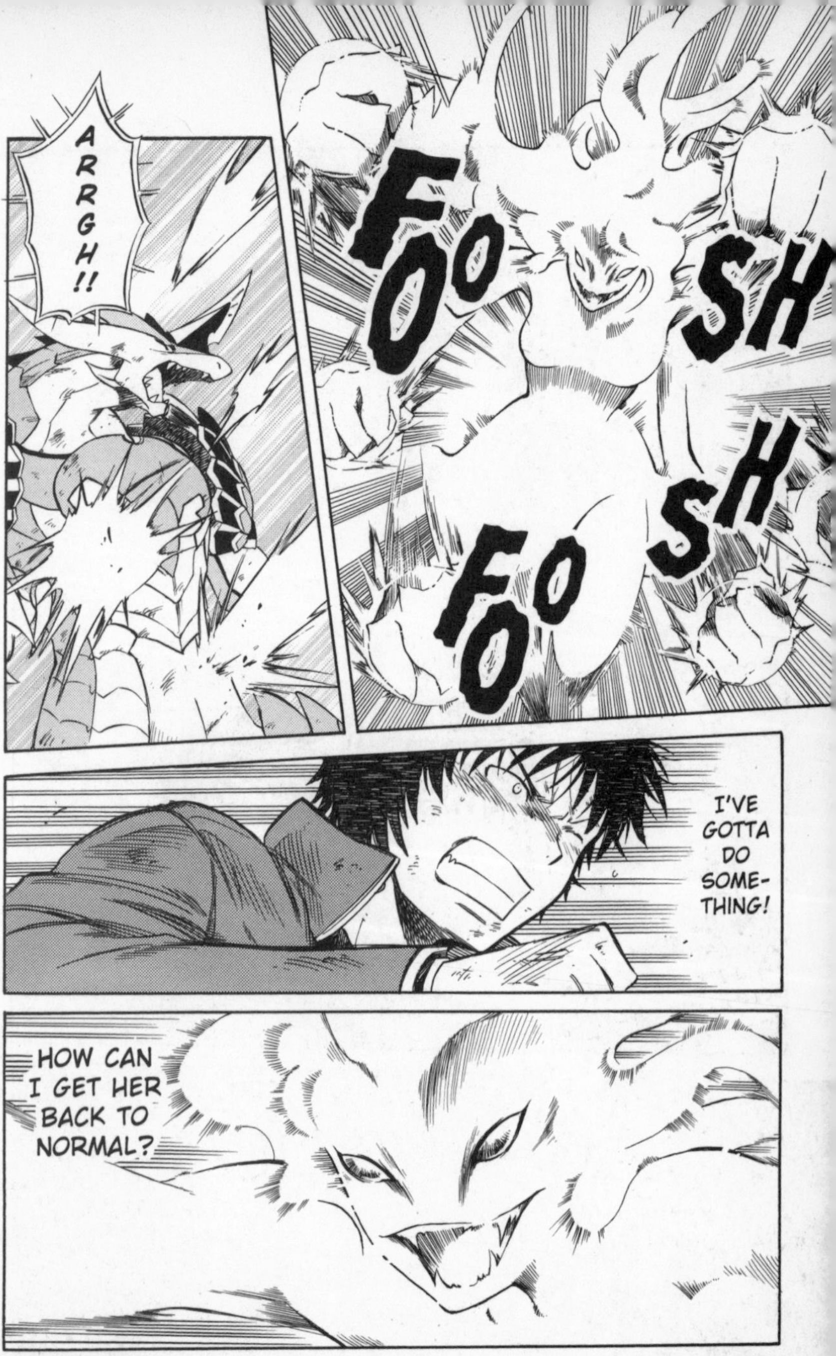
FOOSH
FOOSH
ARRGH!!
I'VE GOTTA DO SOMETHING!
HOW CAN I GET HER BACK TO NORMAL?

READ THIS WAY

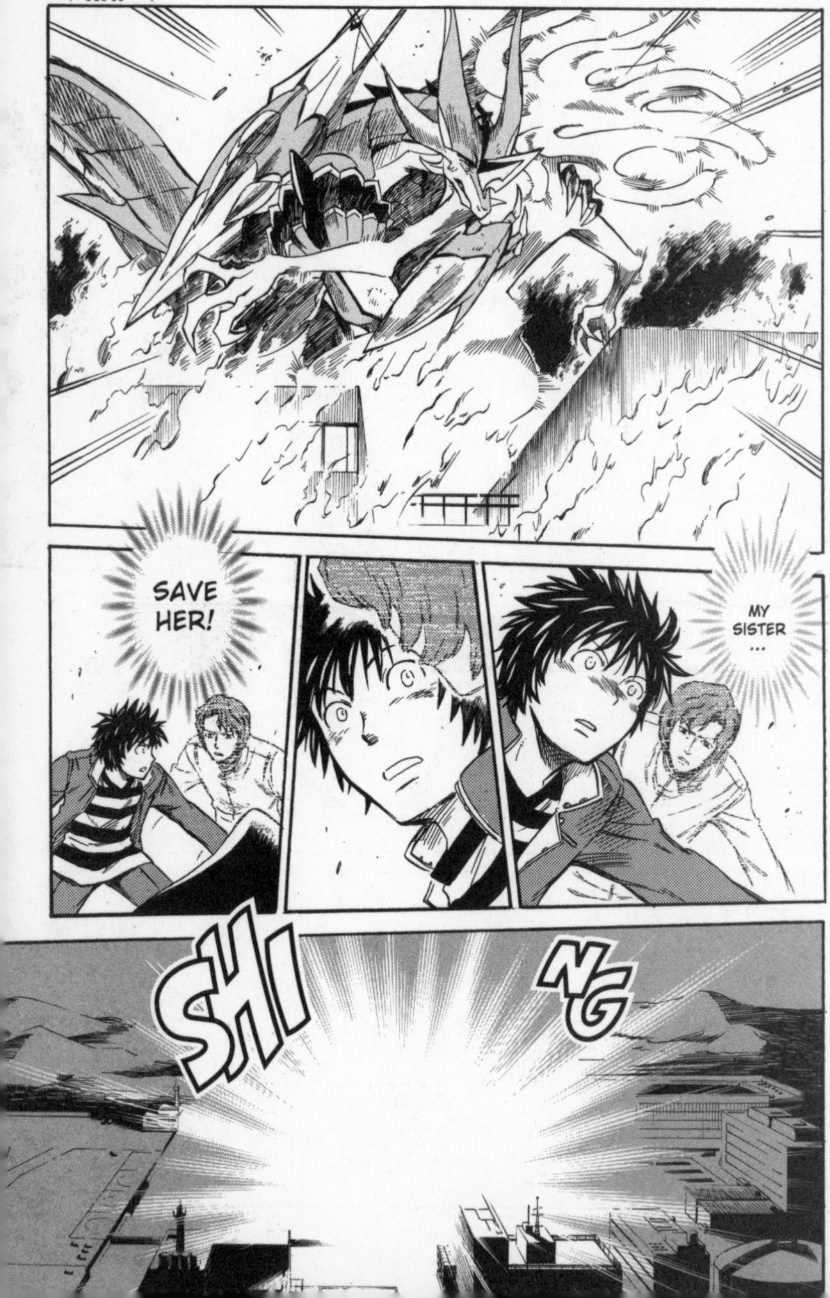
MY SISTER ...
SAVE HER!
SHING

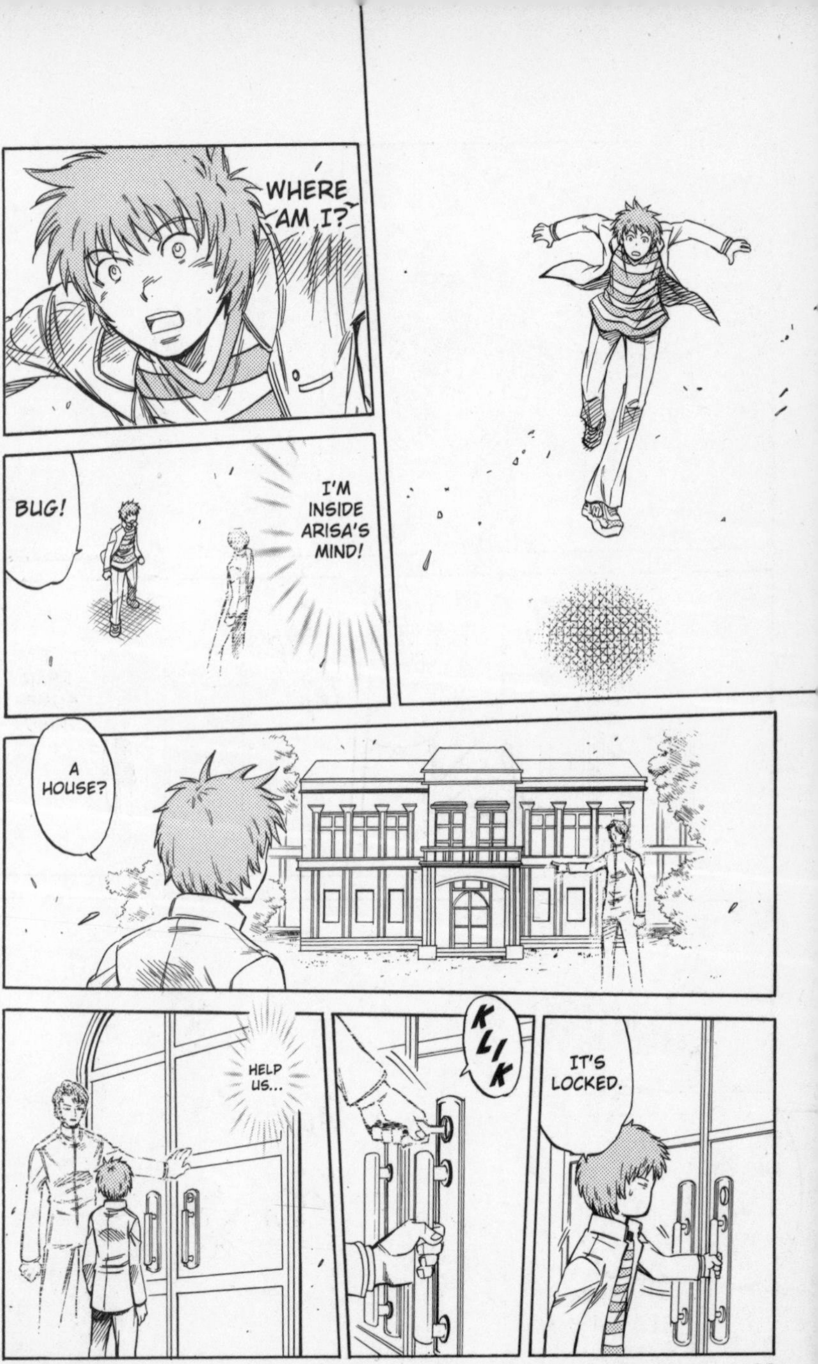
WHERE AM I?
I'M INSIDE ARISA'S MIND!
BUG!
A HOUSE?
IT'S LOCKED.
KLIK
HELP US...

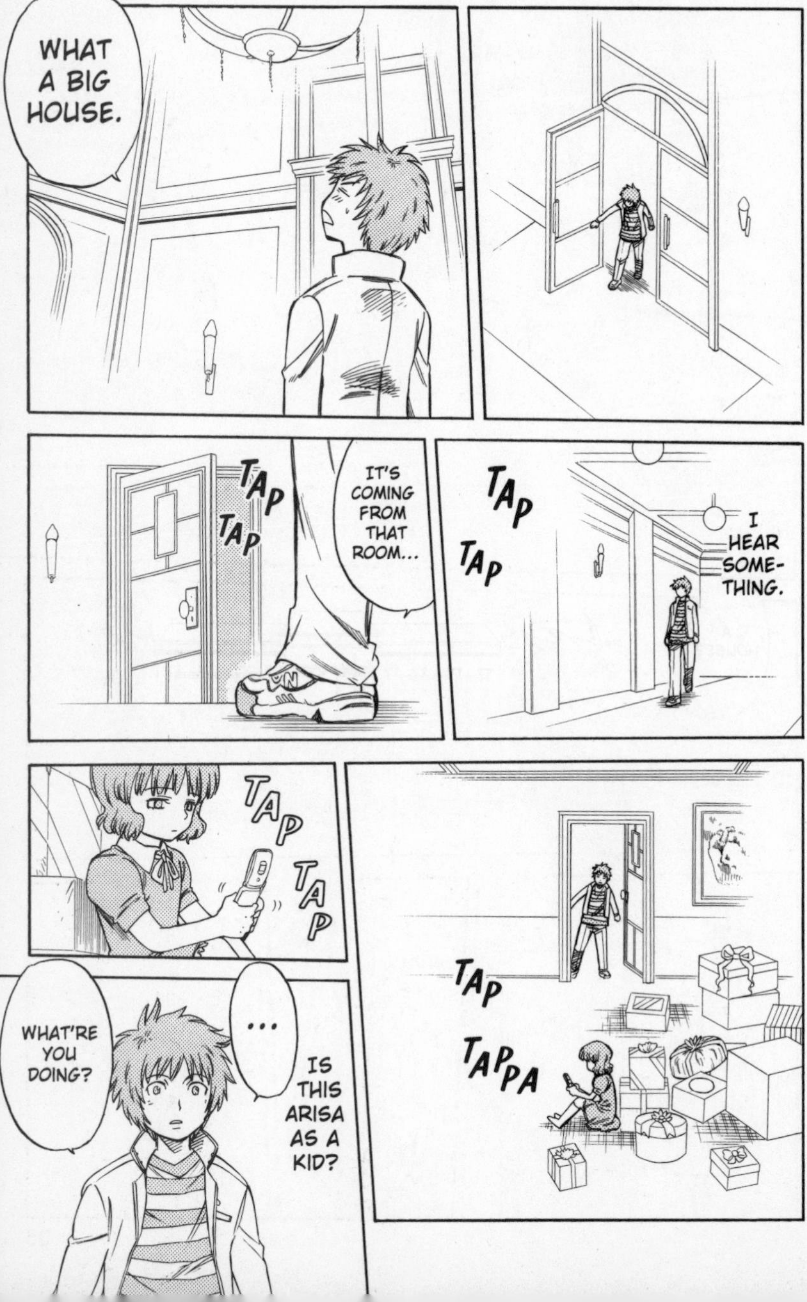
WHAT A BIG HOUSE.
TAP
TAP
I HEAR SOMETHING.
TAP
TAP
IT'S COMING FROM THAT ROOM...
TAP
TAPPA
TAP
TAP
...
IS THIS ARISA AS A KID?
WHAT'RE YOU DOING?

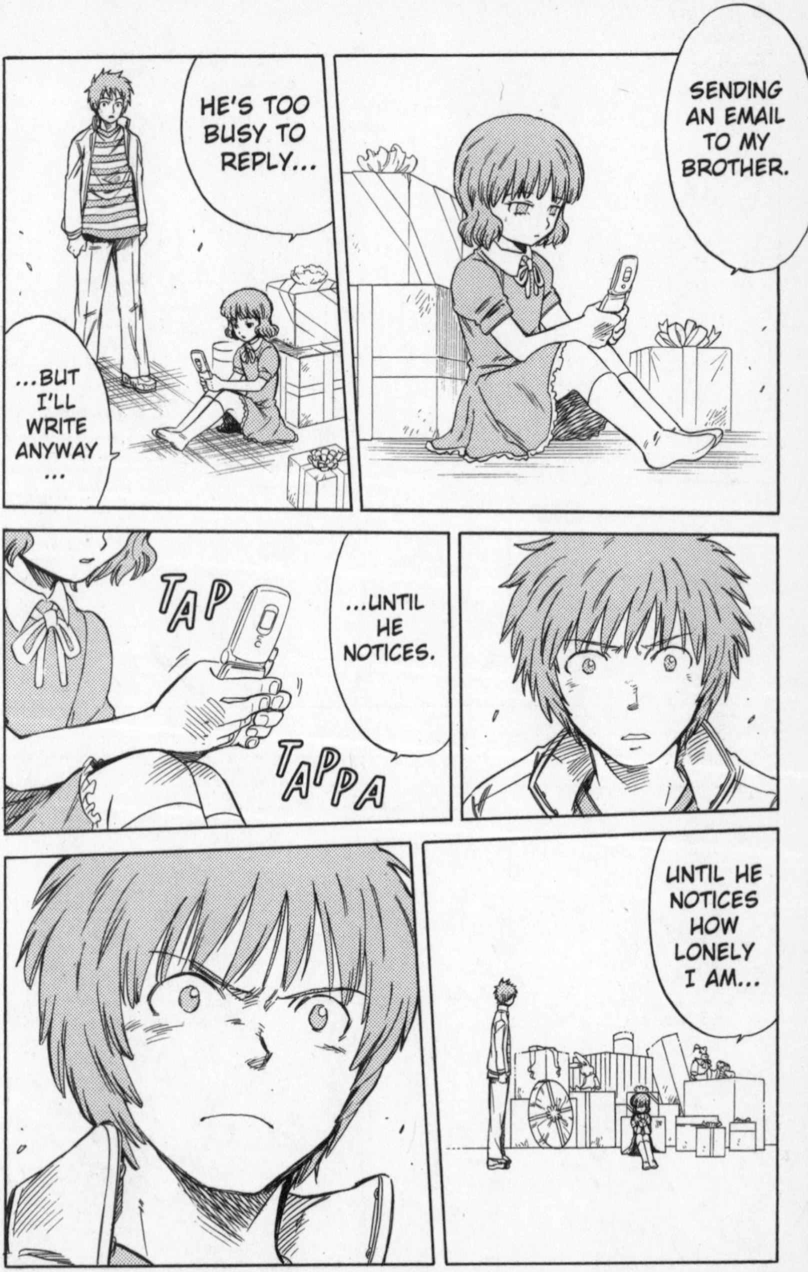
SENDING AN EMAIL TO MY BROTHER.
HE'S TOO BUSY TO REPLY...
...BUT I'LL WRITE ANYWAY...
...UNTIL HE NOTICES.
TAP
TAPPA
UNTIL HE NOTICES HOW LONELY I AM...

READ THIS WAY

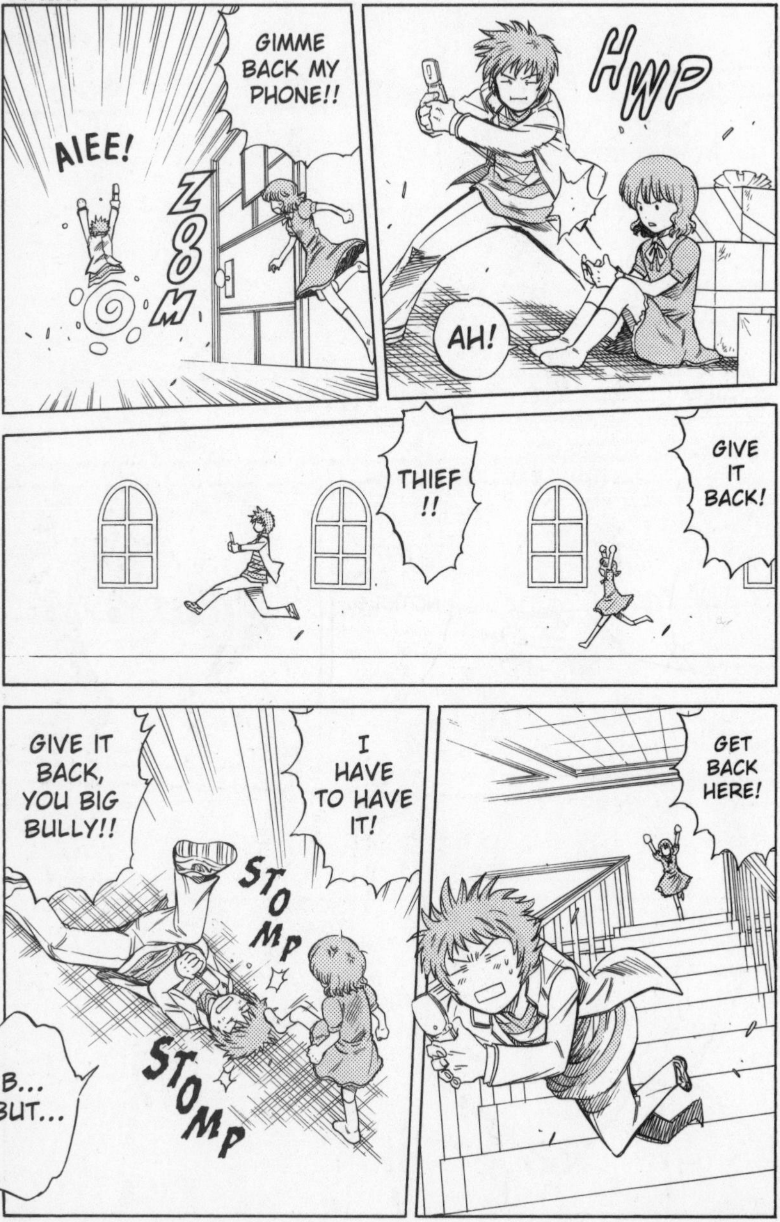
HWP
AH!
GIMME BACK MY PHONE!!
ZOOM
AIEE!
GIVE IT BACK!
THIEF !!
GET BACK HERE!
I HAVE TO HAVE IT!
GIVE IT BACK, YOU BIG BULLY!!
STOMP
STOMP
B... BUT...

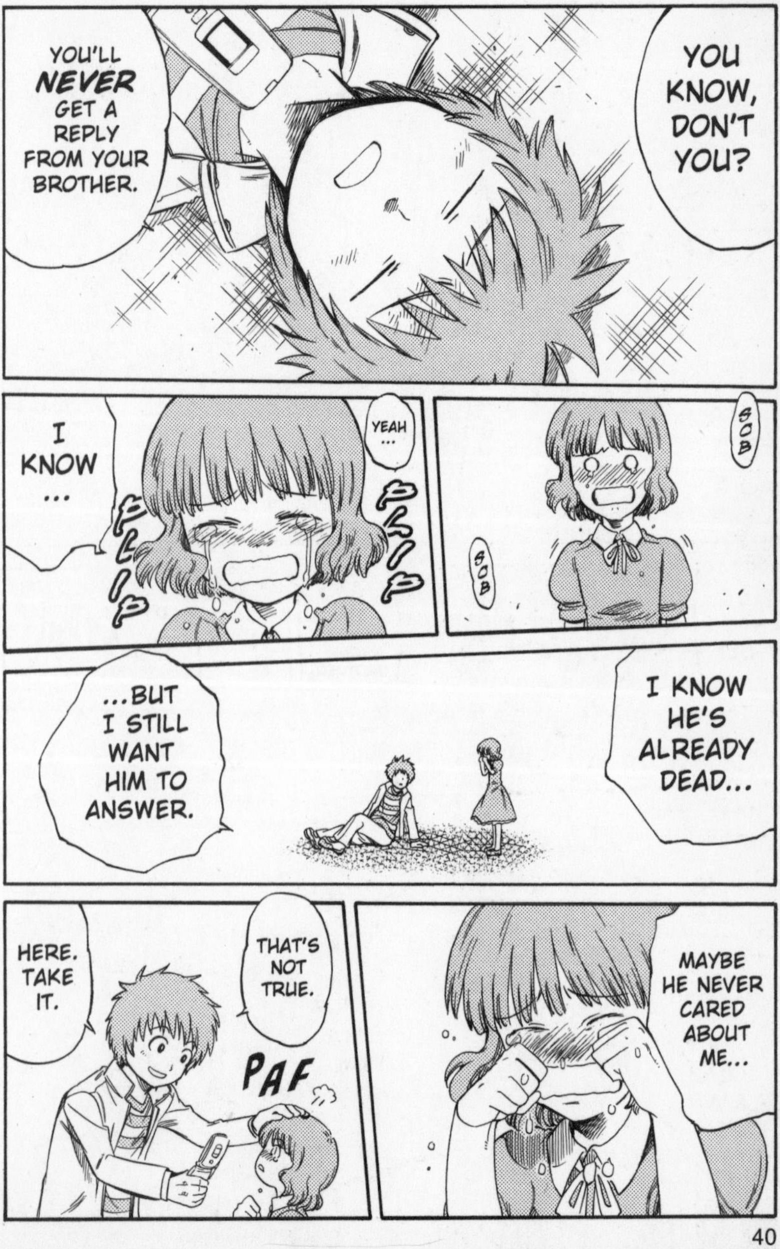
YOU KNOW, DON'T YOU?
YOU'LL NEVER GET A REPLY FROM YOUR BROTHER.
SOB
SOB
YEAH...
I KNOW...
I KNOW HE'S ALREADY DEAD...
...BUT I STILL WANT HIM TO ANSWER.
MAYBE HE NEVER CARED ABOUT ME...
THAT'S NOT TRUE.
PAF
HERE. TAKE IT.

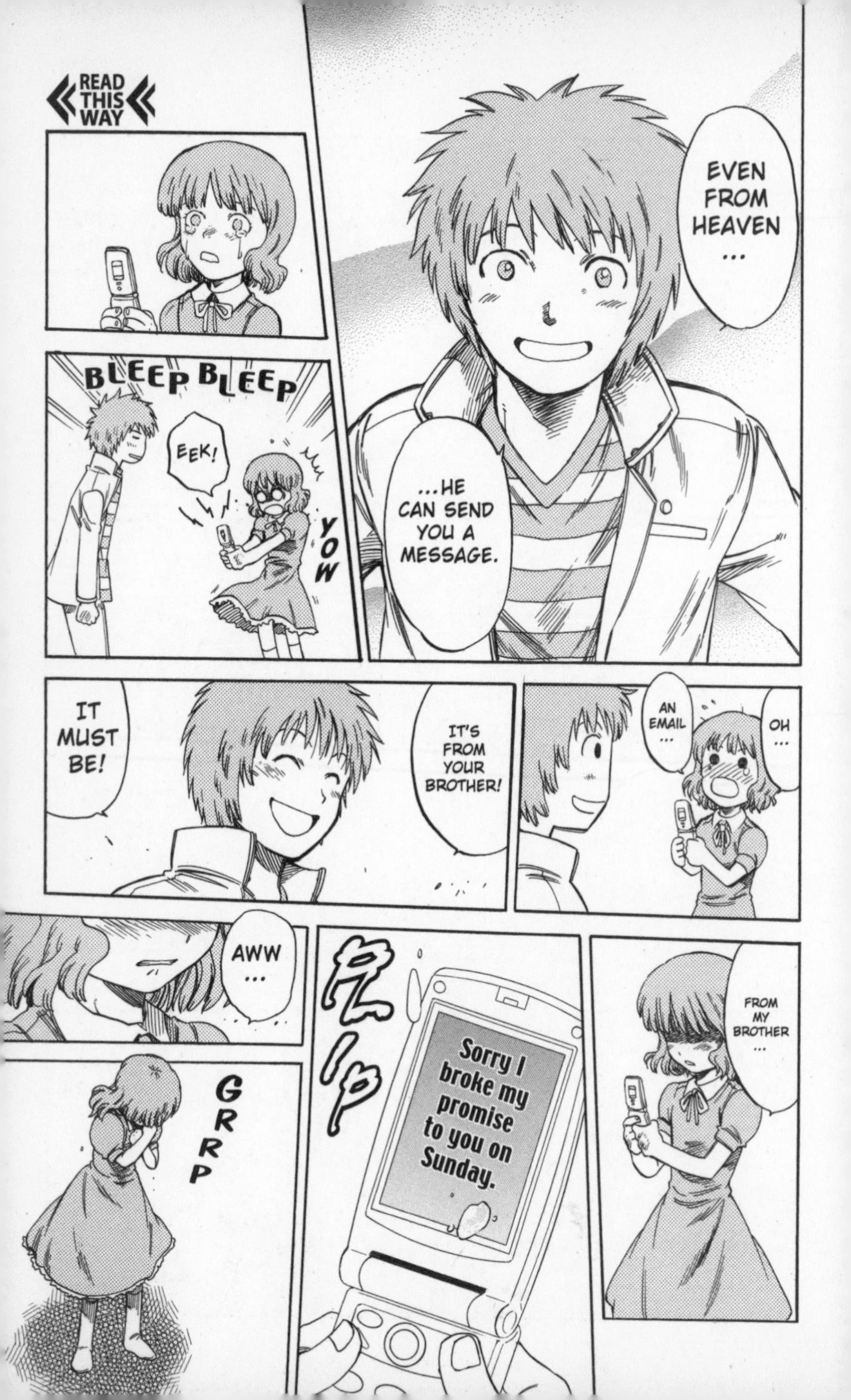
READ THIS WAY
EVEN FROM HEAVEN...
...HE CAN SEND YOU A MESSAGE.
BLEEP BLEEP
EEK!
YOW
OH...
AN EMAIL...
IT'S FROM YOUR BROTHER!
IT MUST BE!
FROM MY BROTHER...
Sorry I broke my promise to you on Sunday.
AWW...
GRRP

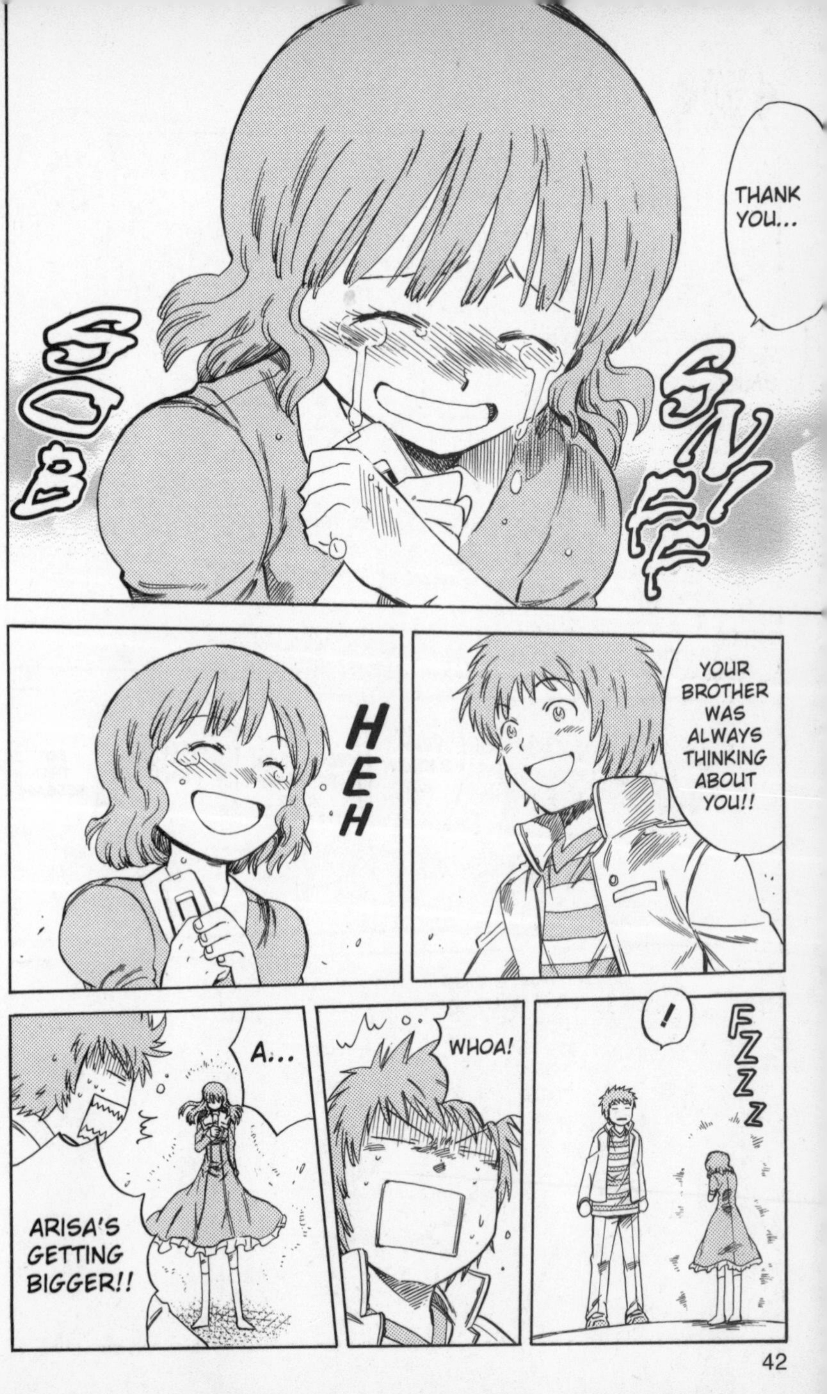
THANK YOU...
SNIFF
SOB
YOUR BROTHER WAS ALWAYS THINKING ABOUT YOU!!
HEH
!
FZZZ
WHOA!
A...
ARISA'S GETTING BIGGER!!

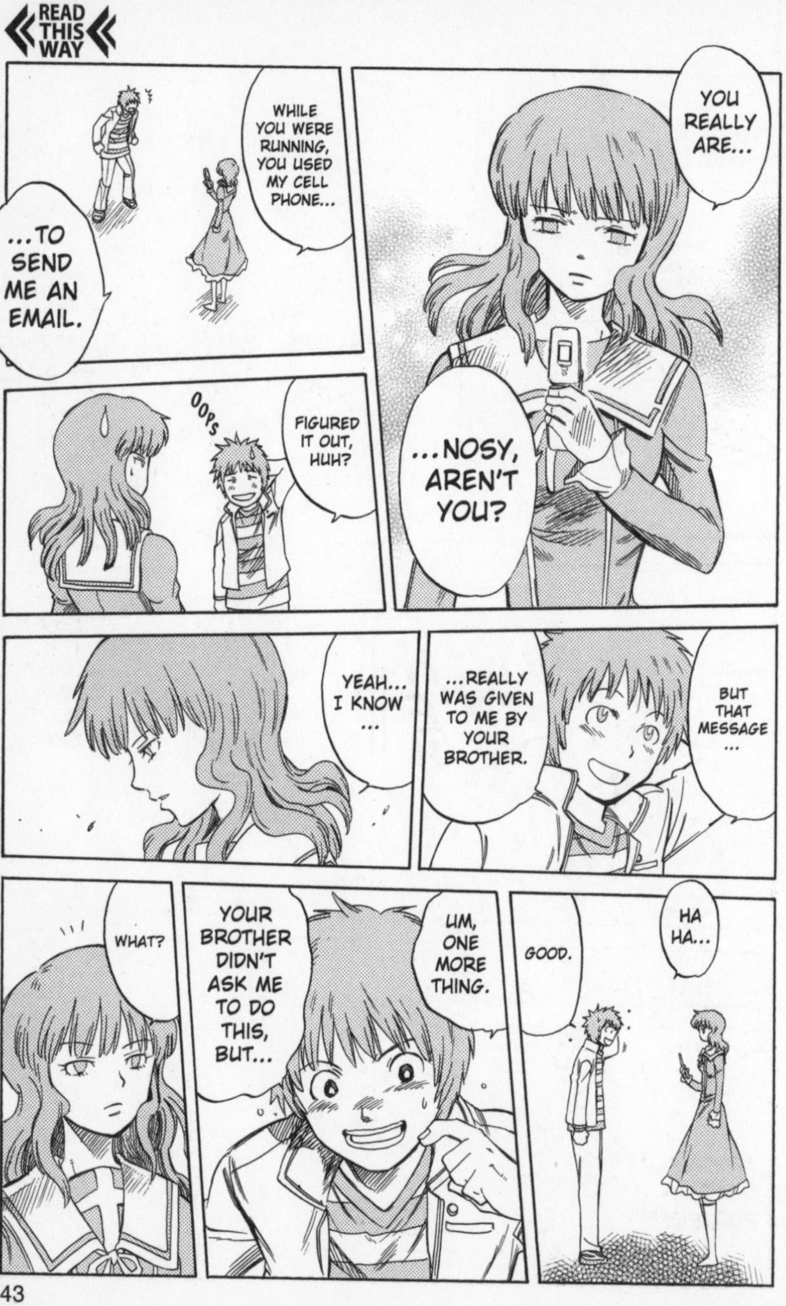
READ THIS WAY
YOU REALLY ARE...
...NOSY, AREN'T YOU?
WHILE YOU WERE RUNNING, YOU USED MY CELL PHONE...
...TO SEND ME AN EMAIL.
OOPS
FIGURED IT OUT, HUH?
BUT THAT MESSAGE ...
...REALLY WAS GIVEN TO ME BY YOUR BROTHER.
YEAH... I KNOW ...
HA HA...
GOOD.
UM, ONE MORE THING.
YOUR BROTHER DIDN'T ASK ME TO DO THIS, BUT...
WHAT?

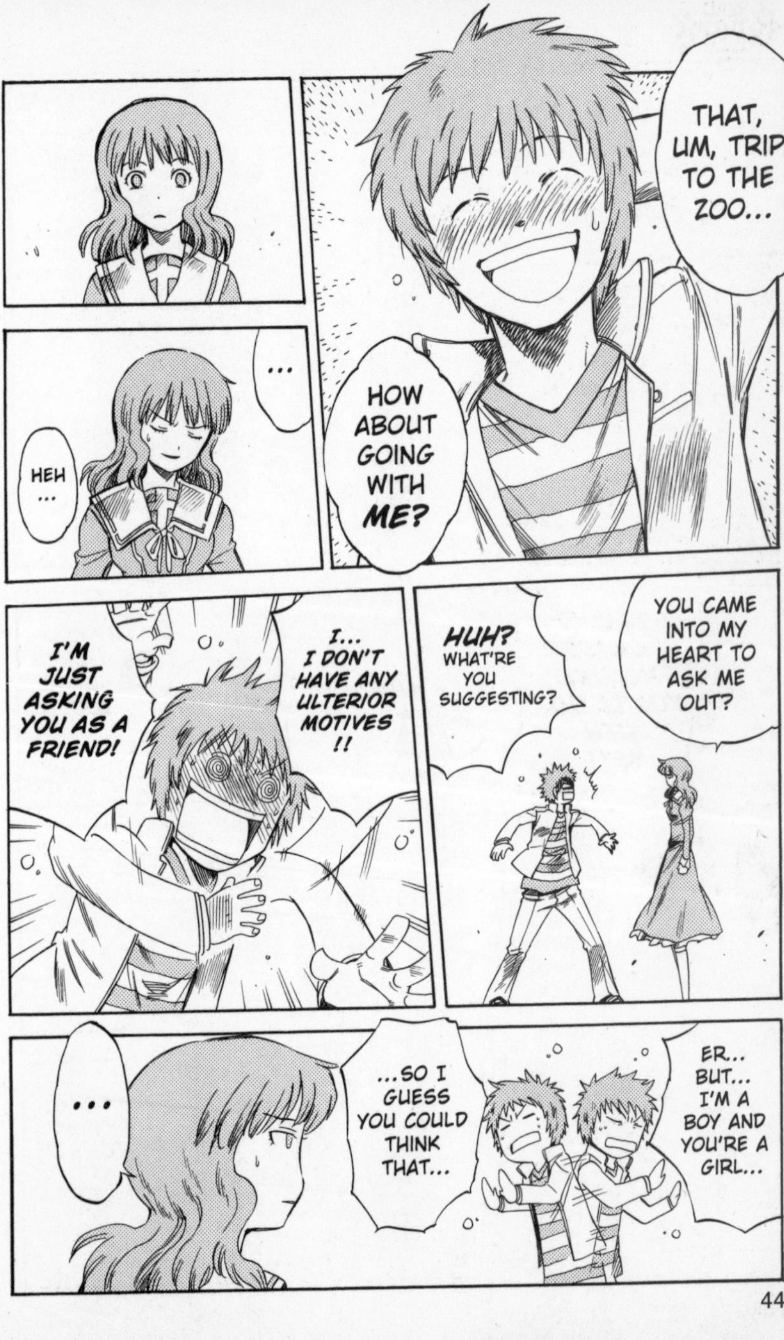
THAT, UM, TRIP TO THE ZOO...
HOW ABOUT GOING WITH ME?
...
HEH...
YOU CAME INTO MY HEART TO ASK ME OUT?
HUH? WHAT'RE YOU SUGGESTING?
I... I DON'T HAVE ANY ULTERIOR MOTIVES !!
I'M JUST ASKING YOU AS A FRIEND!
ER... BUT... I'M A BOY AND YOU'RE A GIRL...
...SO I GUESS YOU COULD THINK THAT...
...

READ THIS WAY

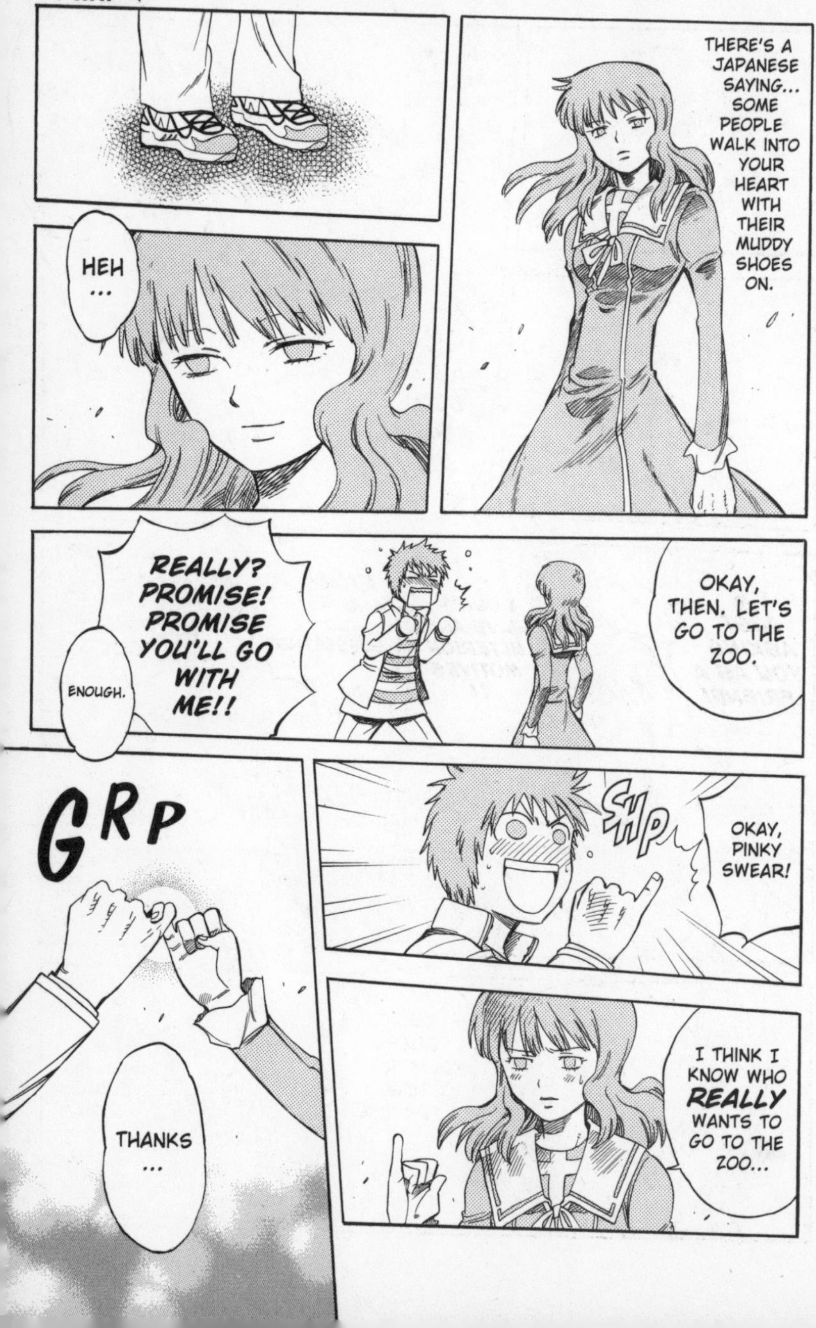
THERE'S A JAPANESE SAYING... SOME PEOPLE WALK INTO YOUR HEART WITH THEIR MUDDY SHOES ON.
HEH ...
OKAY, THEN. LET'S GO TO THE ZOO.
REALLY? PROMISE! PROMISE YOU'LL GO WITH ME!!
ENOUGH.
OKAY, PINKY SWEAR!
SHP
I THINK I KNOW WHO REALLY WANTS TO GO TO THE ZOO...
GRP
THANKS ...

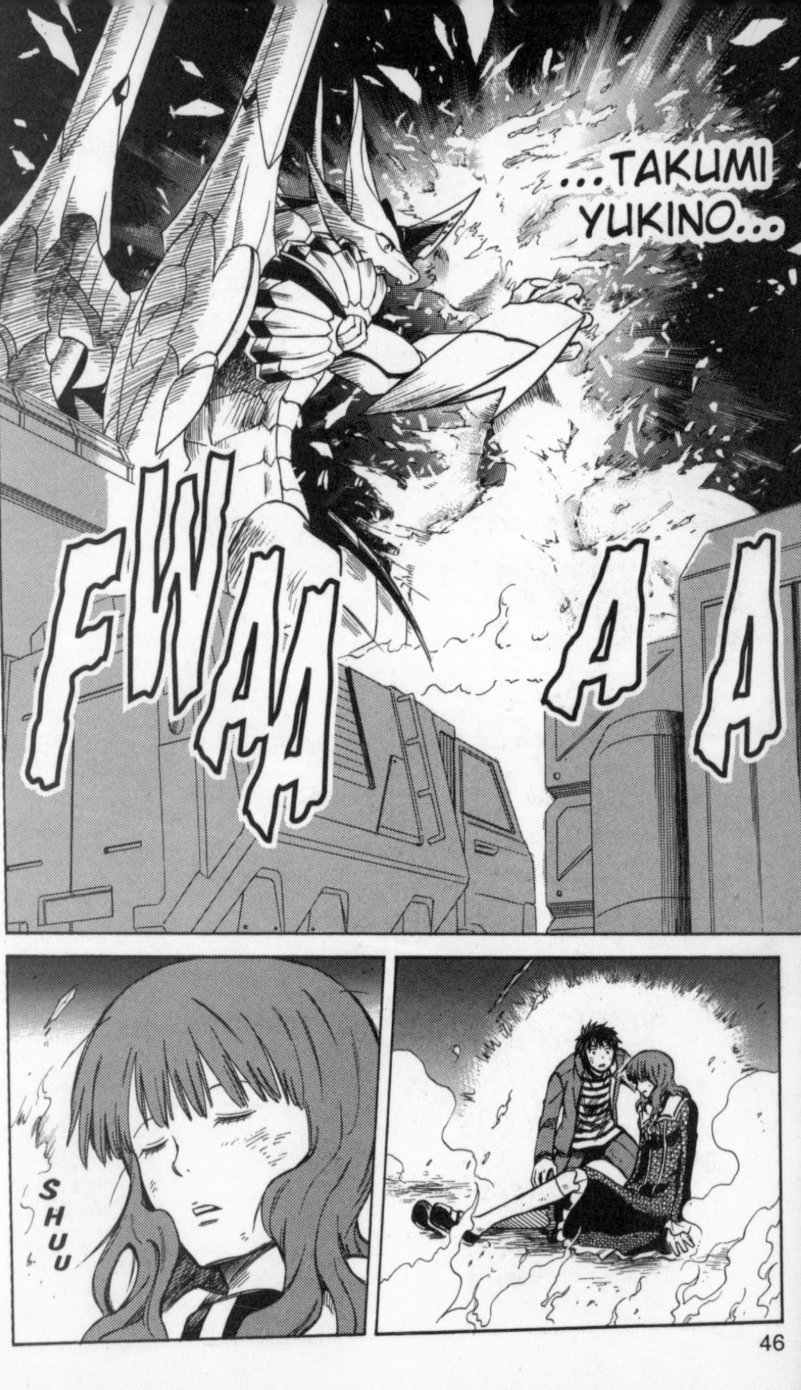
...TAKUMI YUKINO...
FWAAAA
SHUU

READ THIS WAY

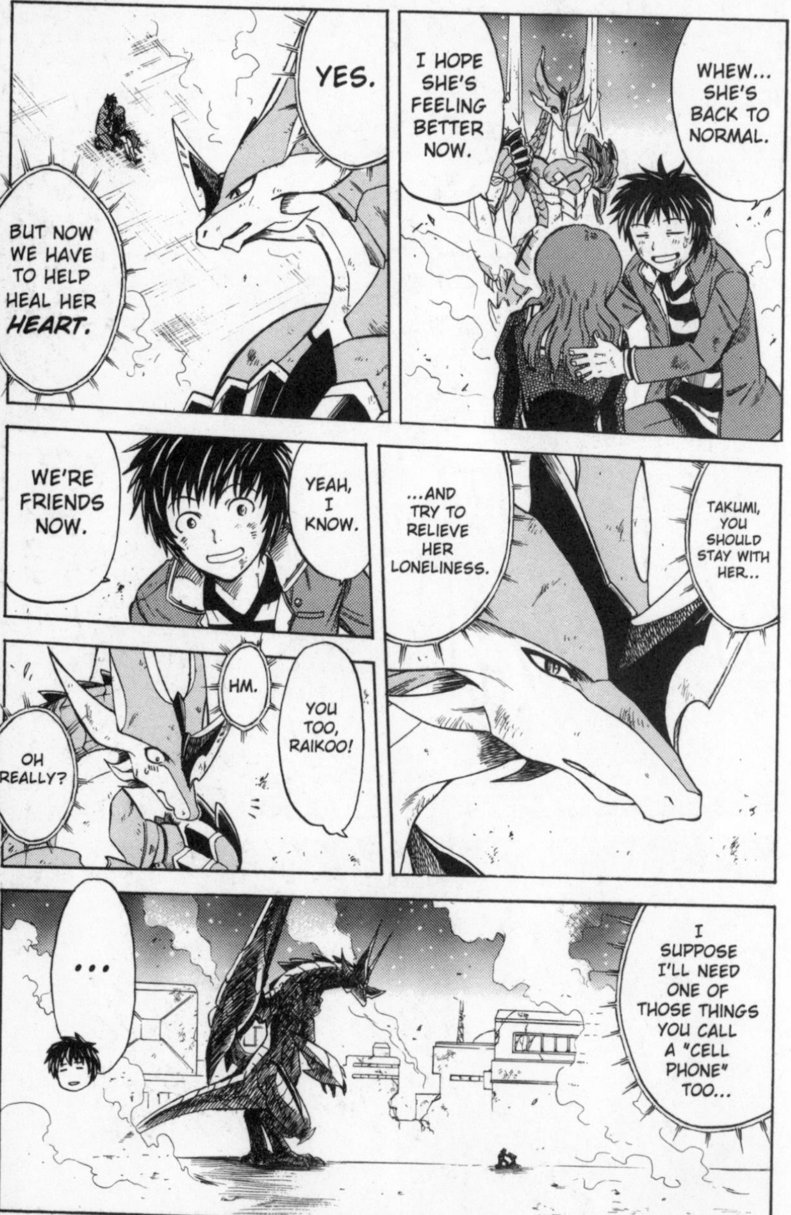

WHEW... SHE'S BACK TO NORMAL.
I HOPE SHE'S FEELING BETTER NOW.
YES.
BUT NOW WE HAVE TO HELP HEAL HER ***HEART.***
TAKUMI, YOU SHOULD STAY WITH HER...
...AND TRY TO RELIEVE HER LONELINESS.
YEAH, I KNOW.
WE'RE FRIENDS NOW.
YOU TOO, RAIKOO!
HM.
OH REALLY?
I SUPPOSE I'LL NEED ONE OF THOSE THINGS YOU CALL A "CELL PHONE" TOO...
...

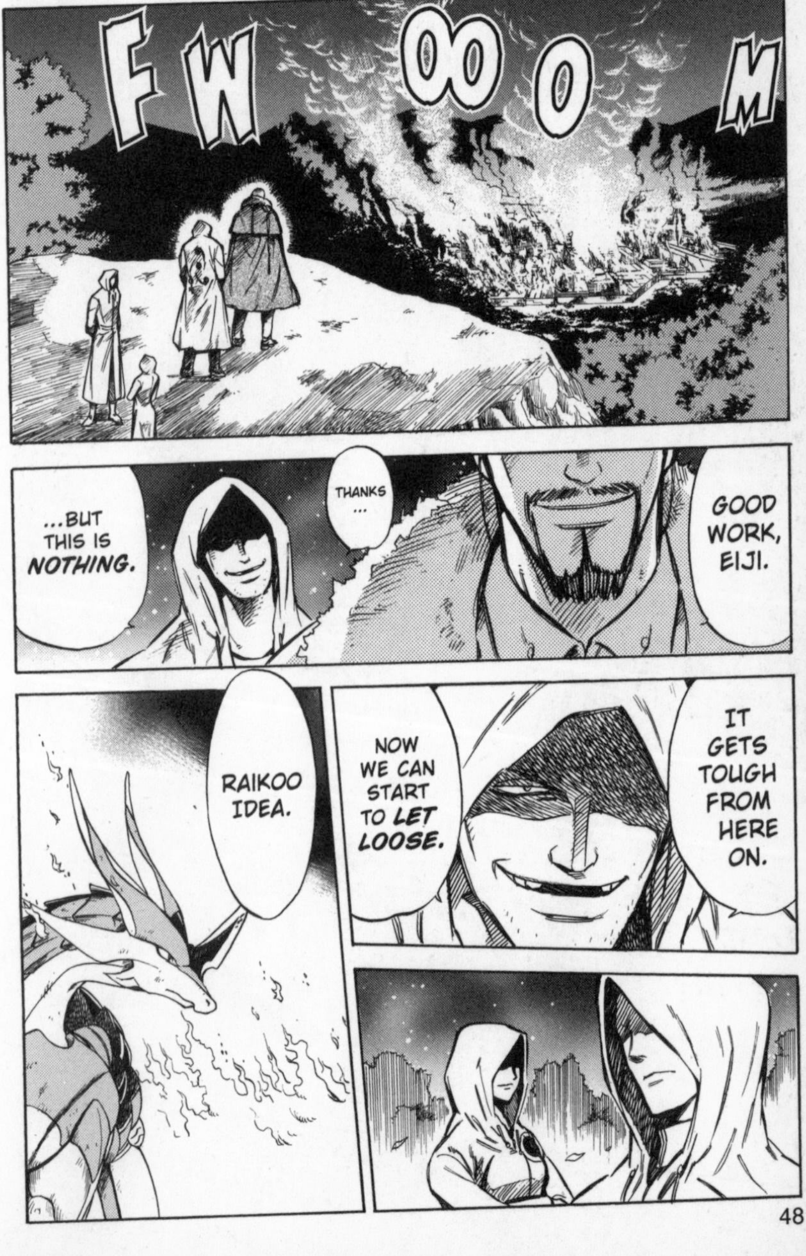
FWOOOM
GOOD WORK, EIJI.
THANKS...
...BUT THIS IS NOTHING.
IT GETS TOUGH FROM HERE ON.
NOW WE CAN START TO LET LOOSE.
RAIKOO IDEA.

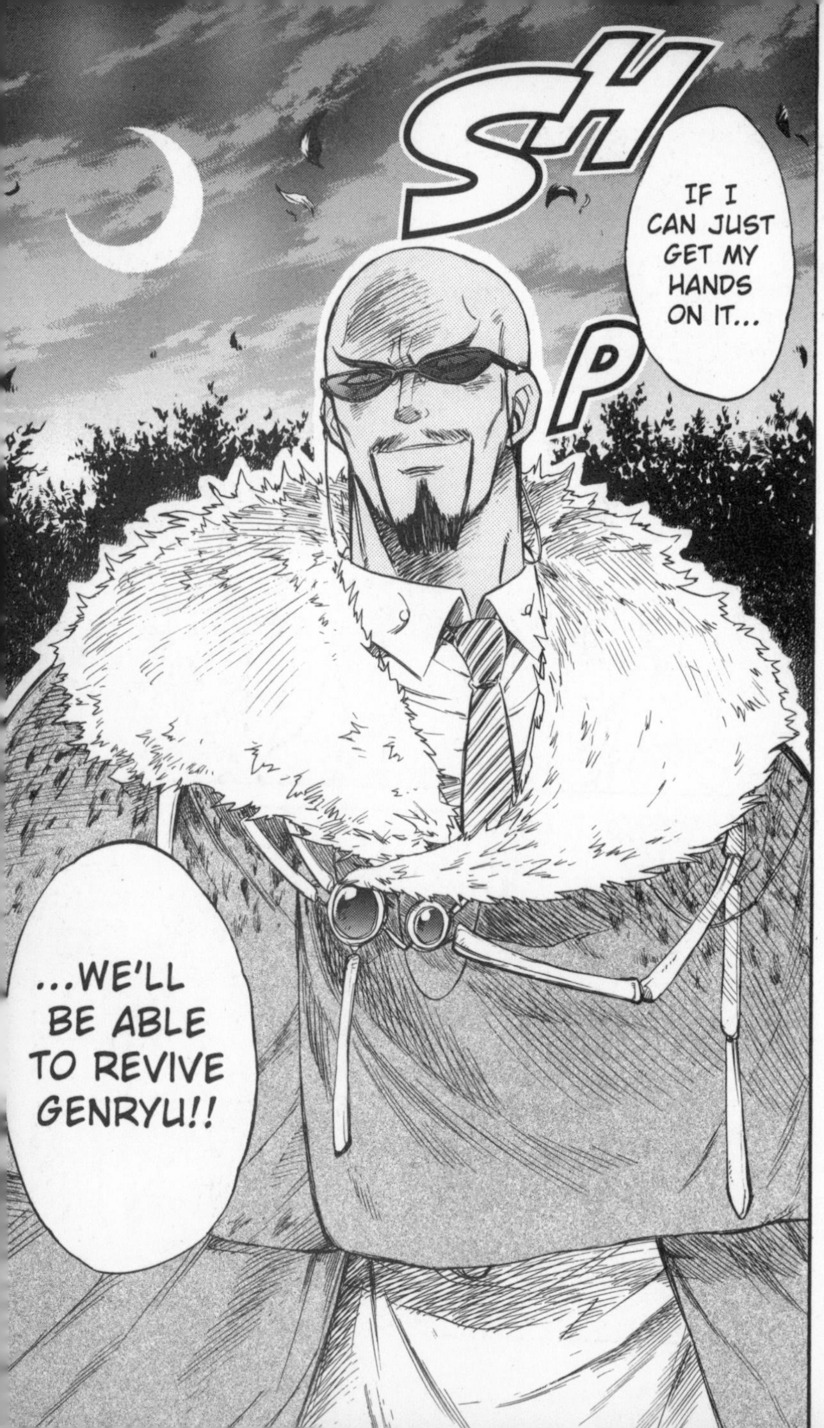
SHP
IF I CAN JUST GET MY HANDS ON IT...
...WE'LL BE ABLE TO REVIVE GENRYU!!

I FOUND THIS NOTE OF SUPPORT ON MY DESK ONE MORNING. IT MAKES ME FEEL SO GOOD...

GO SAKEN!

JUST A LITTLE MORE!

BY KIDOCCHI

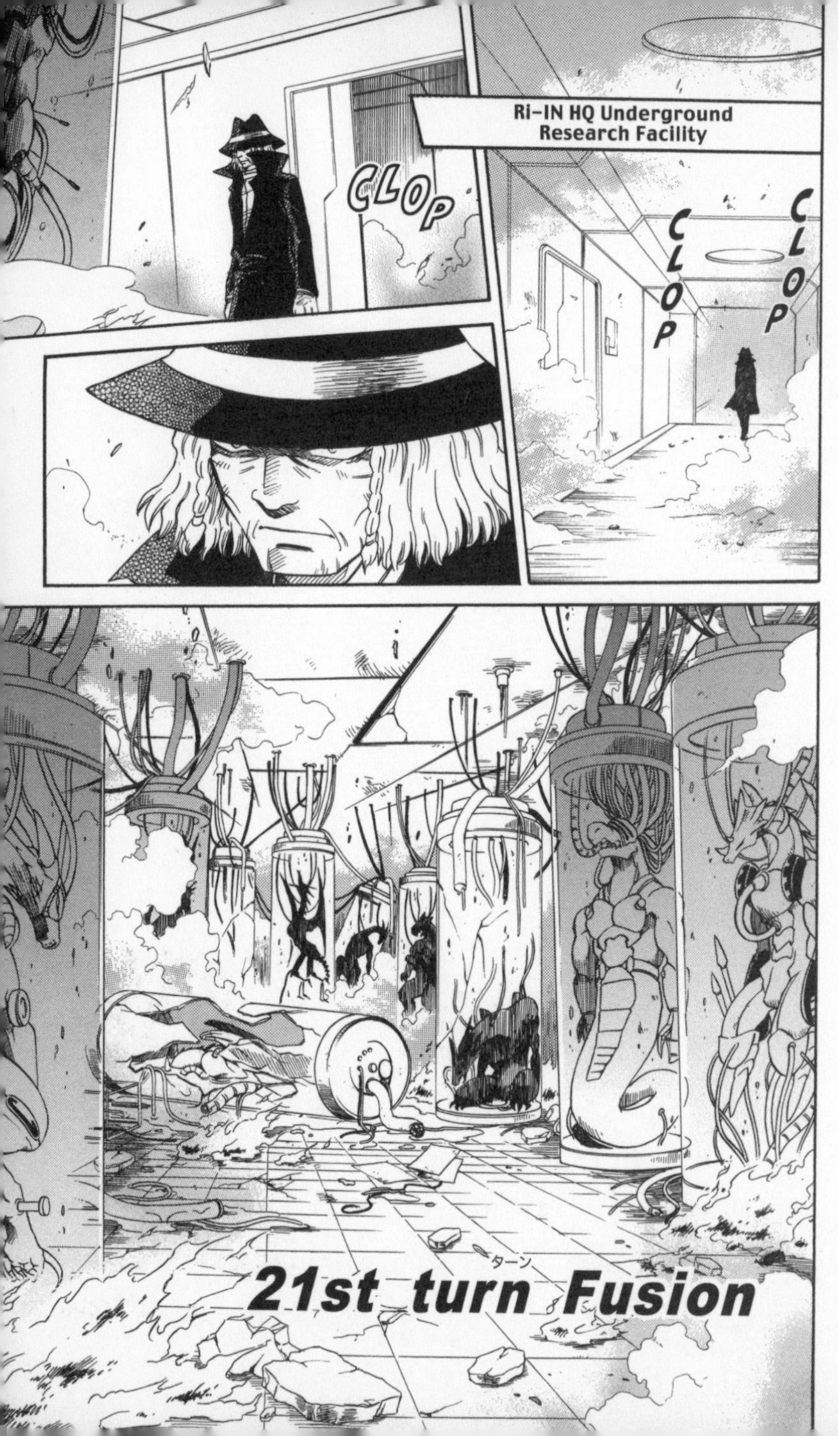
Ri-IN HQ Underground Research Facility
CLOP
CLOP
CLOP
21st turn Fusion

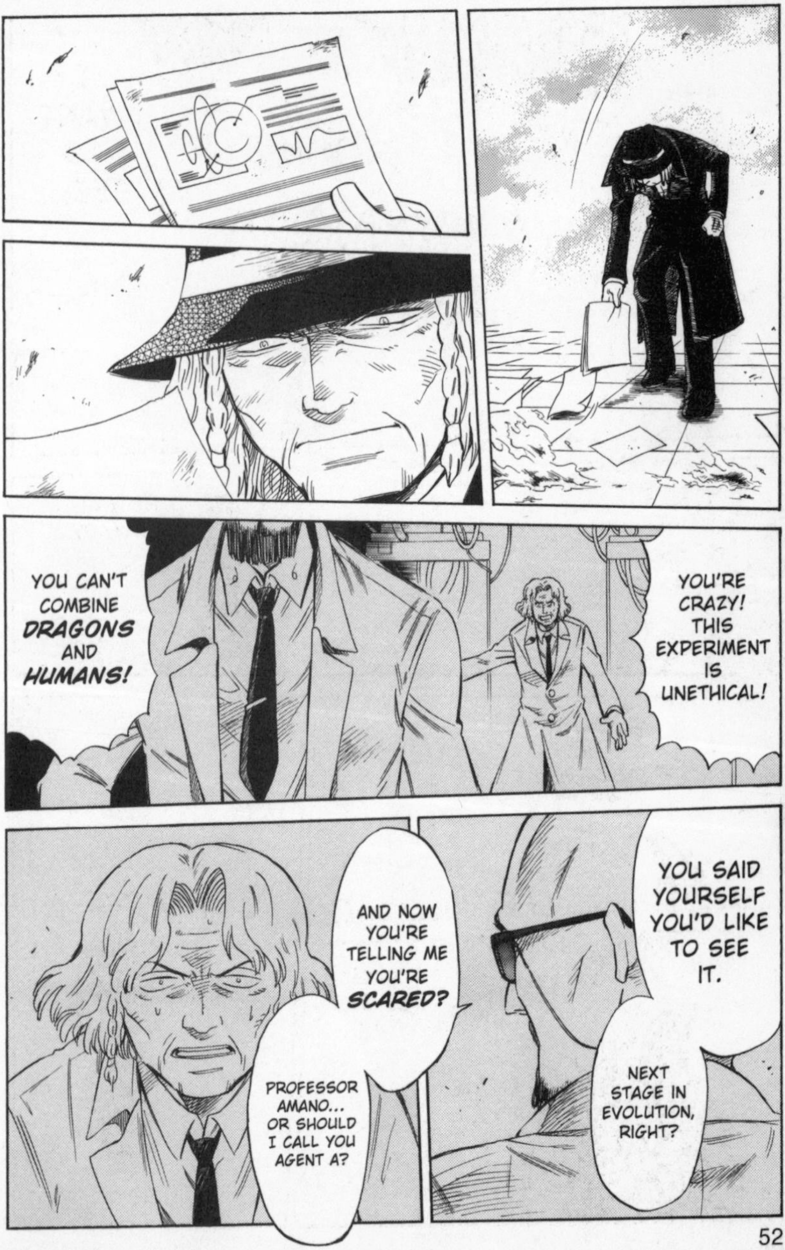
YOU'RE CRAZY! THIS EXPERIMENT IS UNETHICAL!
YOU CAN'T COMBINE DRAGONS AND HUMANS!
YOU SAID YOURSELF YOU'D LIKE TO SEE IT.
NEXT STAGE IN EVOLUTION, RIGHT?
AND NOW YOU'RE TELLING ME YOU'RE SCARED?
PROFESSOR AMANO... OR SHOULD I CALL YOU AGENT A?

READ THIS WAY

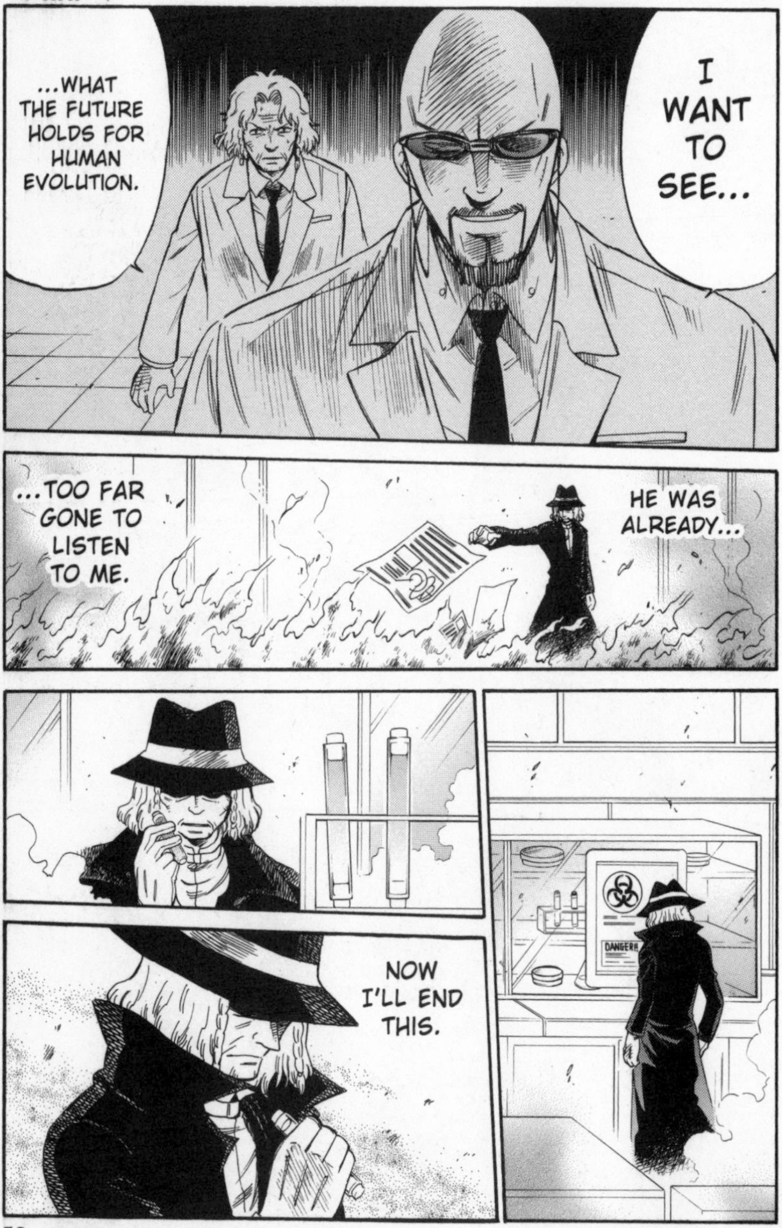
I WANT TO SEE...
...WHAT THE FUTURE HOLDS FOR HUMAN EVOLUTION.
HE WAS ALREADY...
...TOO FAR GONE TO LISTEN TO ME.
DANGER!!
NOW I'LL END THIS.

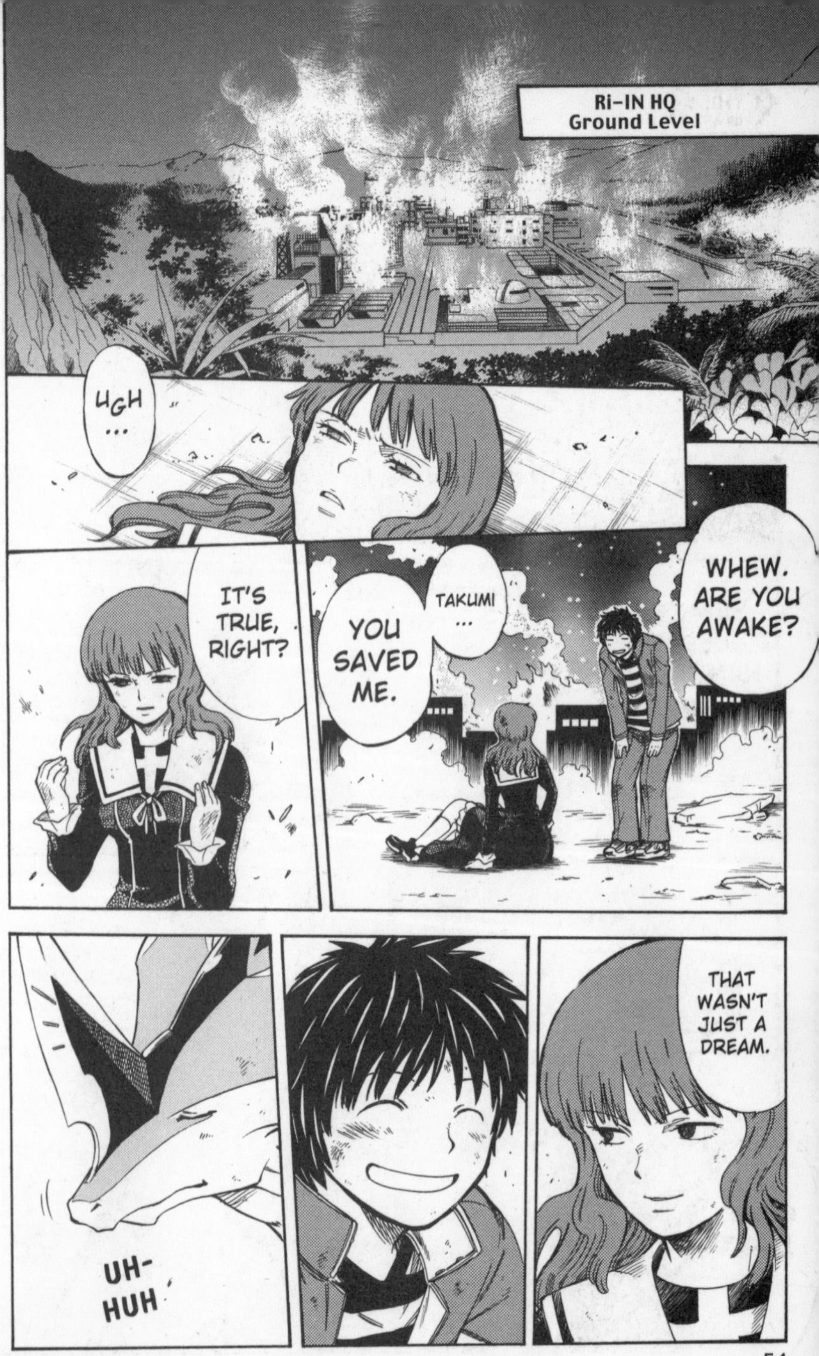
Ri-IN HQ
Ground Level
UGH ...
WHEW. ARE YOU AWAKE?
TAKUMI ...
YOU SAVED ME.
IT'S TRUE, RIGHT?
THAT WASN'T JUST A DREAM.
UH-HUH

READ THIS WAY

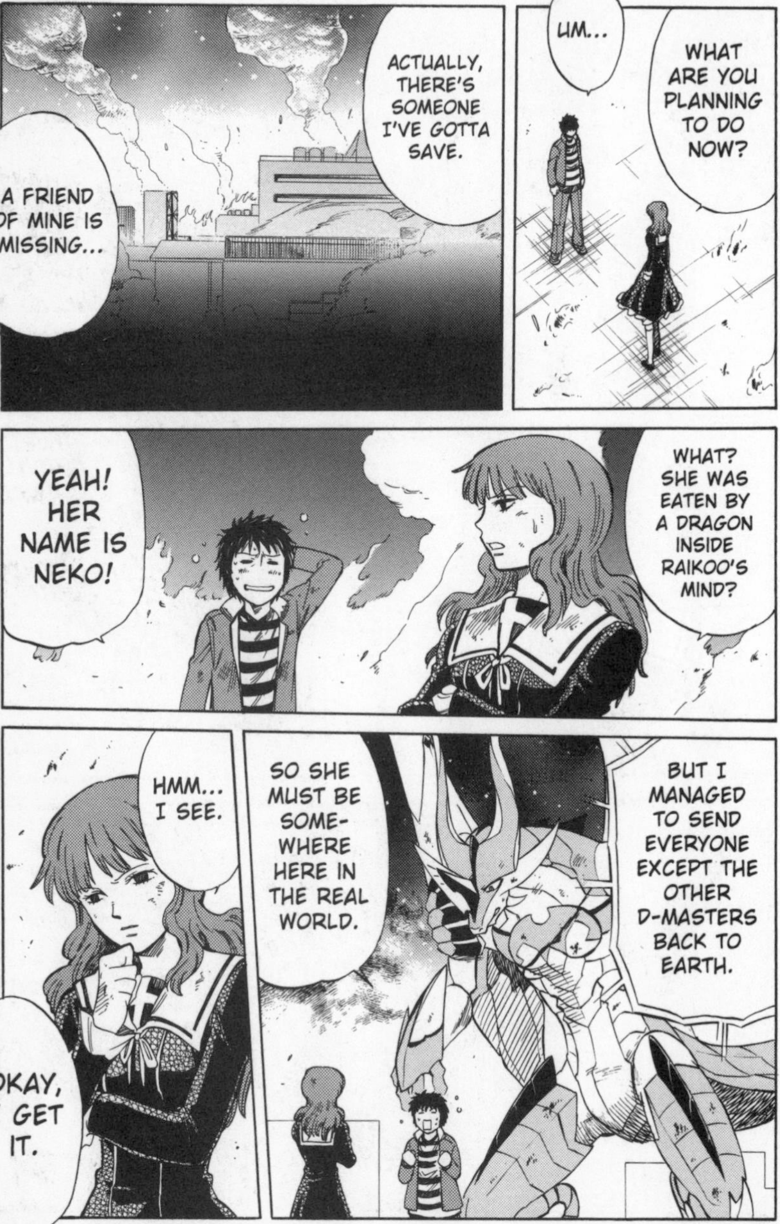
WHAT ARE YOU PLANNING TO DO NOW?
UM...
ACTUALLY, THERE'S SOMEONE I'VE GOTTA SAVE.
A FRIEND OF MINE IS MISSING...
WHAT? SHE WAS EATEN BY A DRAGON INSIDE RAIKOO'S MIND?
YEAH! HER NAME IS NEKO!
BUT I MANAGED TO SEND EVERYONE EXCEPT THE OTHER D-MASTERS BACK TO EARTH.
SO SHE MUST BE SOME-WHERE HERE IN THE REAL WORLD.
HMM... I SEE.
OKAY, I GET IT.

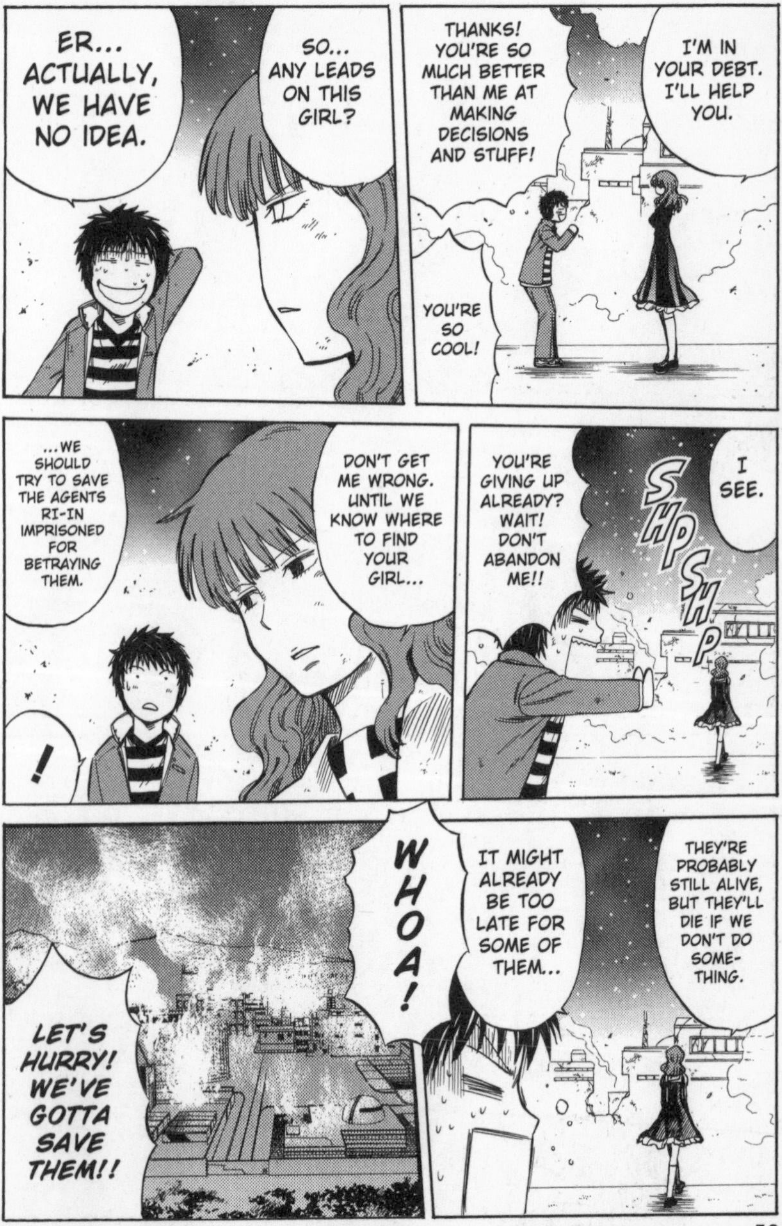
I'M IN YOUR DEBT. I'LL HELP YOU.
THANKS! YOU'RE SO MUCH BETTER THAN ME AT MAKING DECISIONS AND STUFF!
YOU'RE SO COOL!
SO... ANY LEADS ON THIS GIRL?
ER... ACTUALLY, WE HAVE NO IDEA.
I SEE.
SHP SHP
YOU'RE GIVING UP ALREADY? WAIT! DON'T ABANDON ME!!
DON'T GET ME WRONG. UNTIL WE KNOW WHERE TO FIND YOUR GIRL...
...WE SHOULD TRY TO SAVE THE AGENTS RI-IN IMPRISONED FOR BETRAYING THEM.
!
THEY'RE PROBABLY STILL ALIVE, BUT THEY'LL DIE IF WE DON'T DO SOME-THING.
IT MIGHT ALREADY BE TOO LATE FOR SOME OF THEM...
WHOA!
LET'S HURRY! WE'VE GOTTA SAVE THEM!!

READ THIS WAY

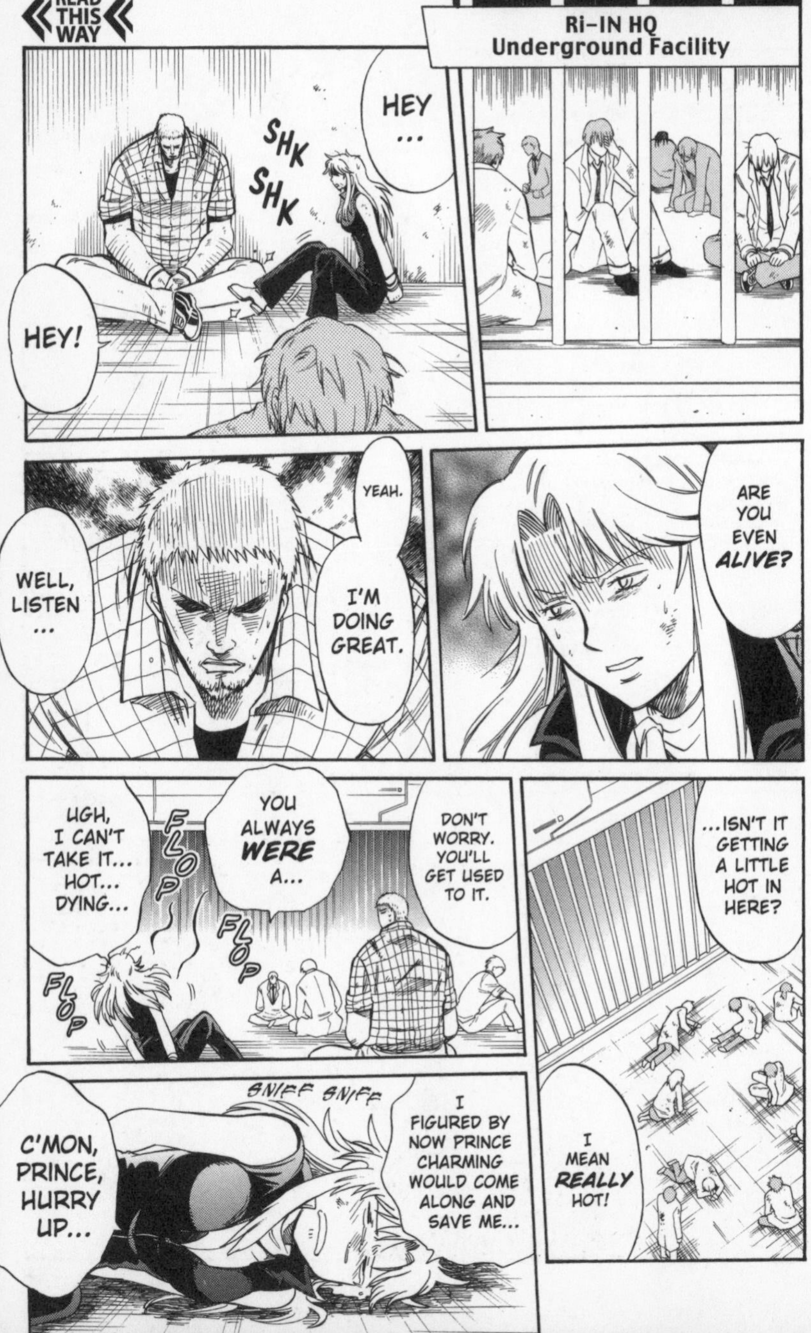
Ri-IN HQ Underground Facility
HEY...
SHK SHK
HEY!
ARE YOU EVEN ALIVE?
YEAH.
I'M DOING GREAT.
WELL, LISTEN...
...ISN'T IT GETTING A LITTLE HOT IN HERE?
I MEAN REALLY HOT!
DON'T WORRY. YOU'LL GET USED TO IT.
YOU ALWAYS WERE A...
UGH, I CAN'T TAKE IT... HOT... DYING...
FLOP
FLOP
FLOP
SNIFF SNIFF
I FIGURED BY NOW PRINCE CHARMING WOULD COME ALONG AND SAVE ME...
C'MON, PRINCE, HURRY UP...

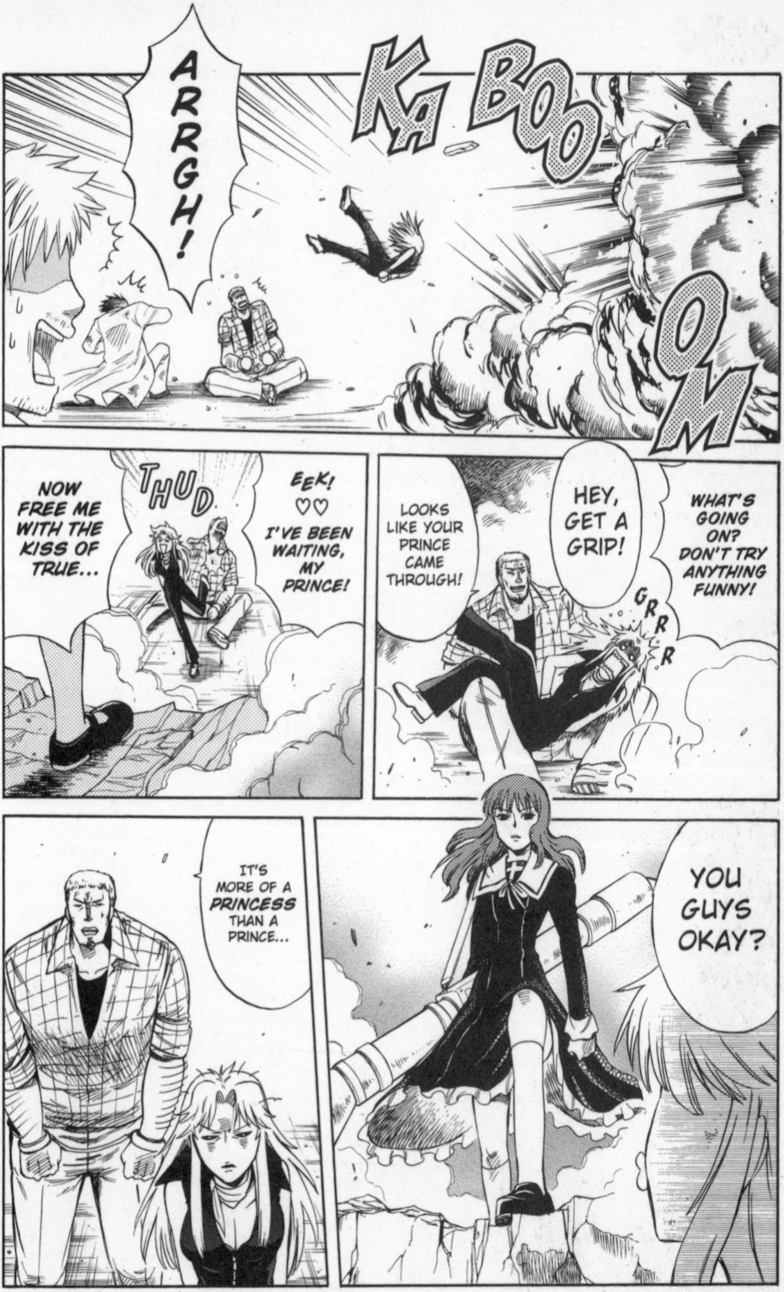
KA-BOOOOM
ARRGH!
WHAT'S GOING ON? DON'T TRY ANYTHING FUNNY!
GRRR
HEY, GET A GRIP!
LOOKS LIKE YOUR PRINCE CAME THROUGH!
EEK! ♡♡
I'VE BEEN WAITING, MY PRINCE!
THUD
NOW FREE ME WITH THE KISS OF TRUE...
YOU GUYS OKAY?
IT'S MORE OF A PRINCESS THAN A PRINCE...

READ THIS WAY

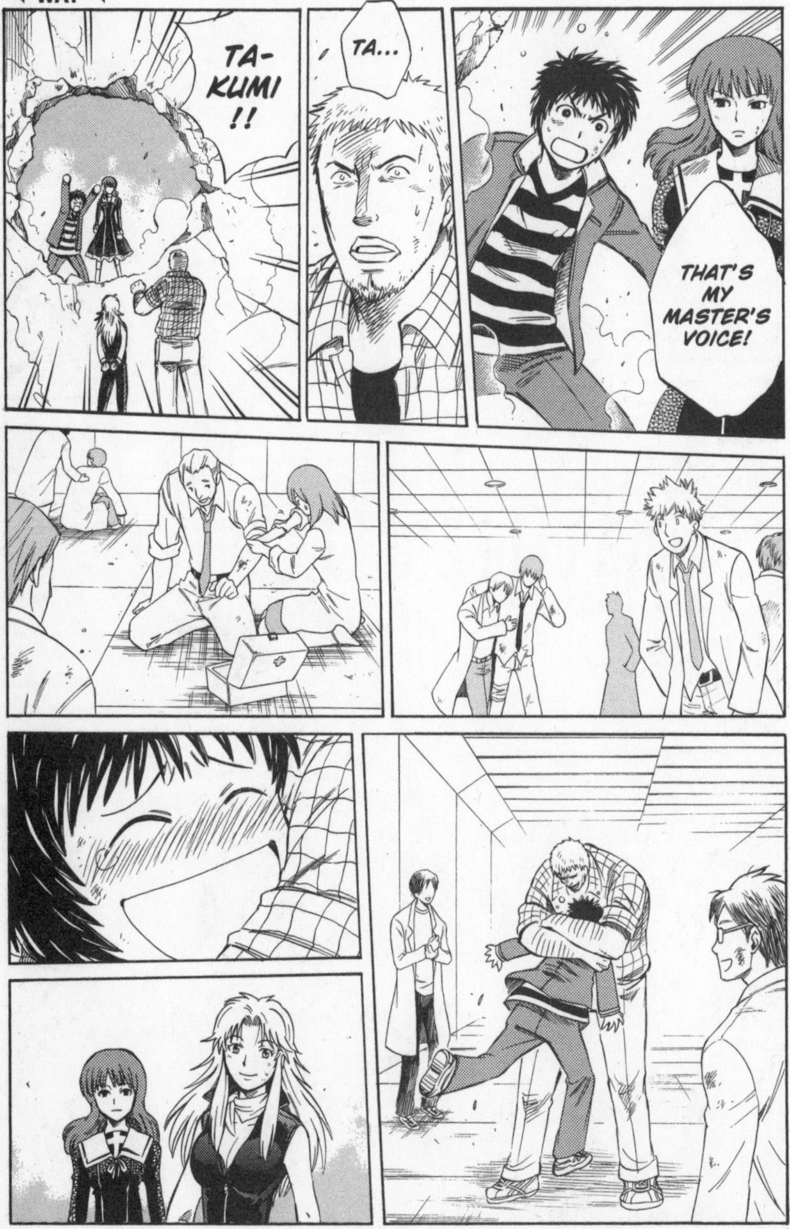
THAT'S MY MASTER'S VOICE!
TA...
TA-KUMI!!

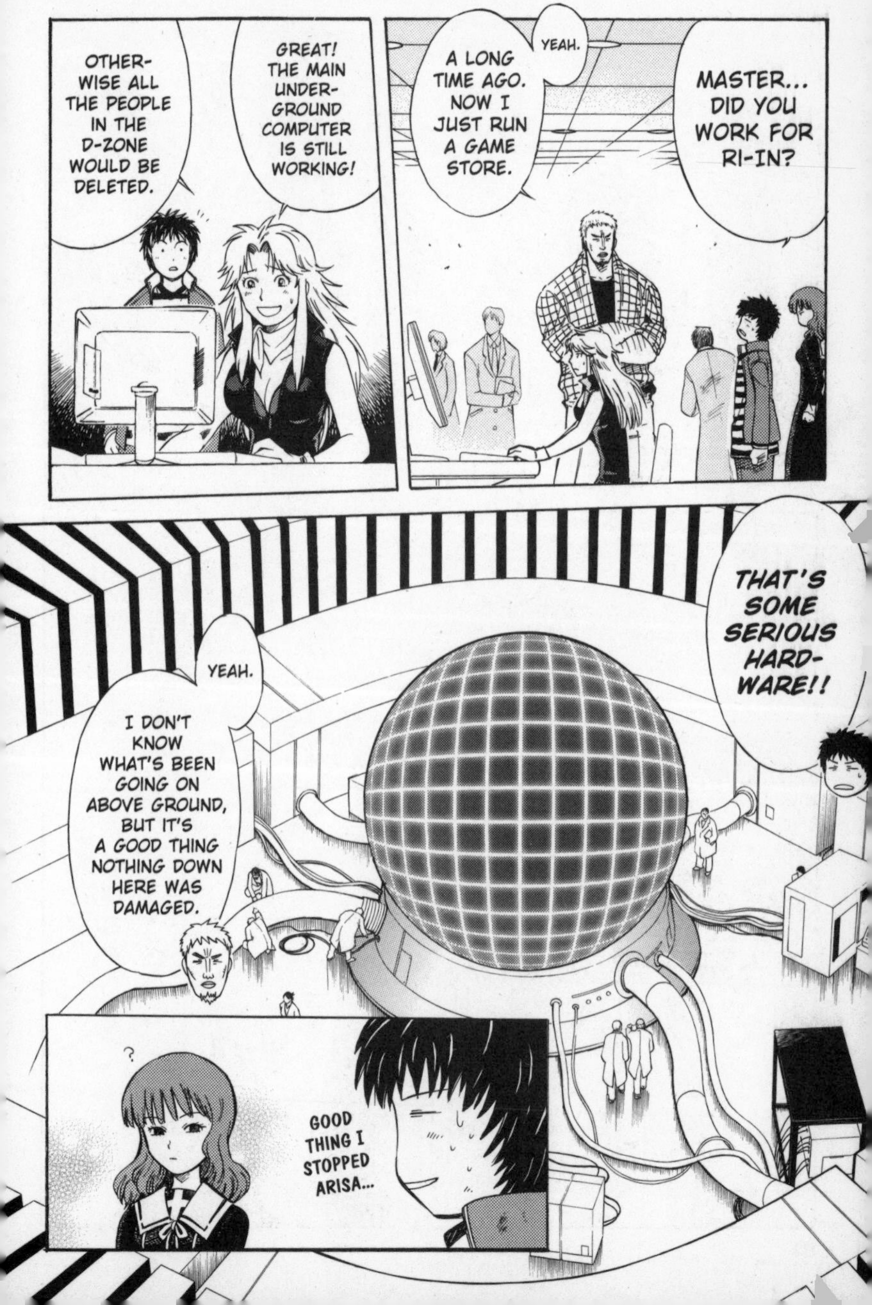
MASTER... DID YOU WORK FOR RI-IN?
YEAH.
A LONG TIME AGO. NOW I JUST RUN A GAME STORE.
GREAT! THE MAIN UNDER-GROUND COMPUTER IS STILL WORKING!
OTHER-WISE ALL THE PEOPLE IN THE D-ZONE WOULD BE DELETED.
THAT'S SOME SERIOUS HARD-WARE!!
YEAH.
I DON'T KNOW WHAT'S BEEN GOING ON ABOVE GROUND, BUT IT'S A GOOD THING NOTHING DOWN HERE WAS DAMAGED.
GOOD THING I STOPPED ARISA...

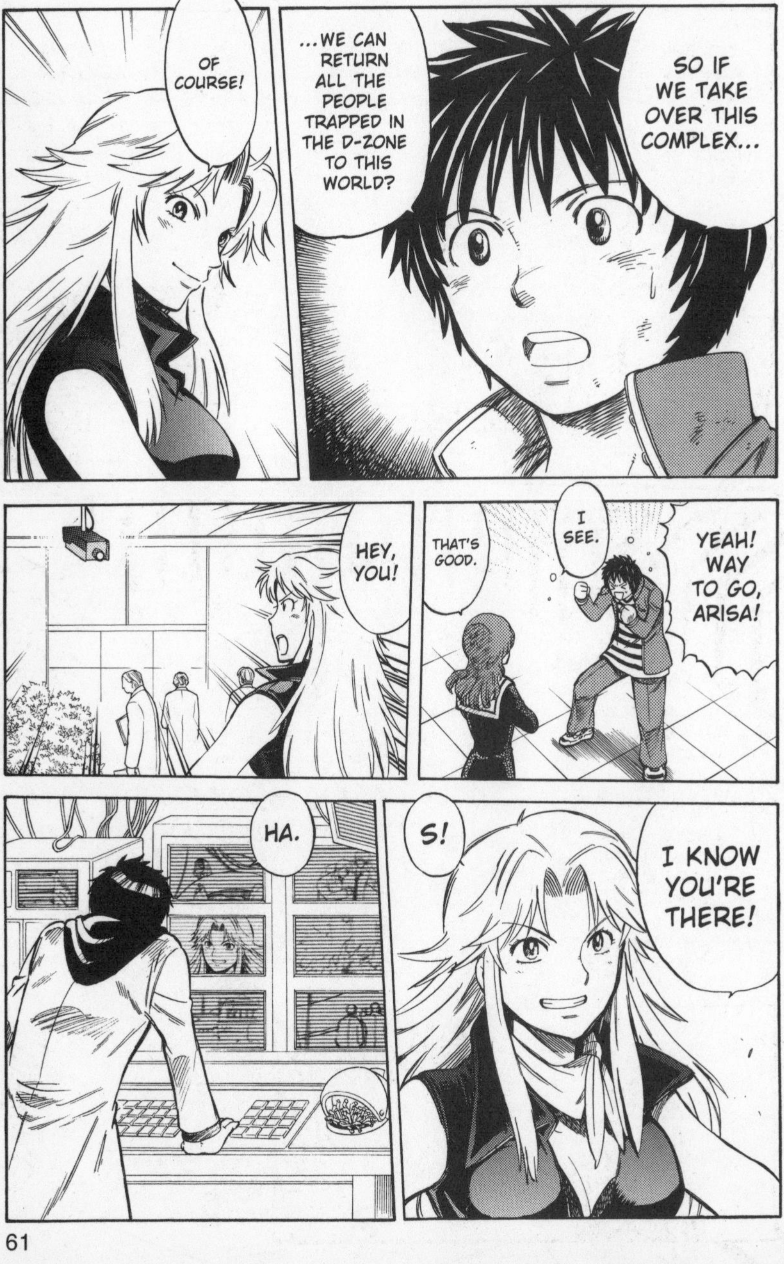
SO IF WE TAKE OVER THIS COMPLEX...
...WE CAN RETURN ALL THE PEOPLE TRAPPED IN THE D-ZONE TO THIS WORLD?
OF COURSE!
YEAH! WAY TO GO, ARISA!
I SEE.
THAT'S GOOD.
HEY, YOU!
I KNOW YOU'RE THERE!
S!
HA.

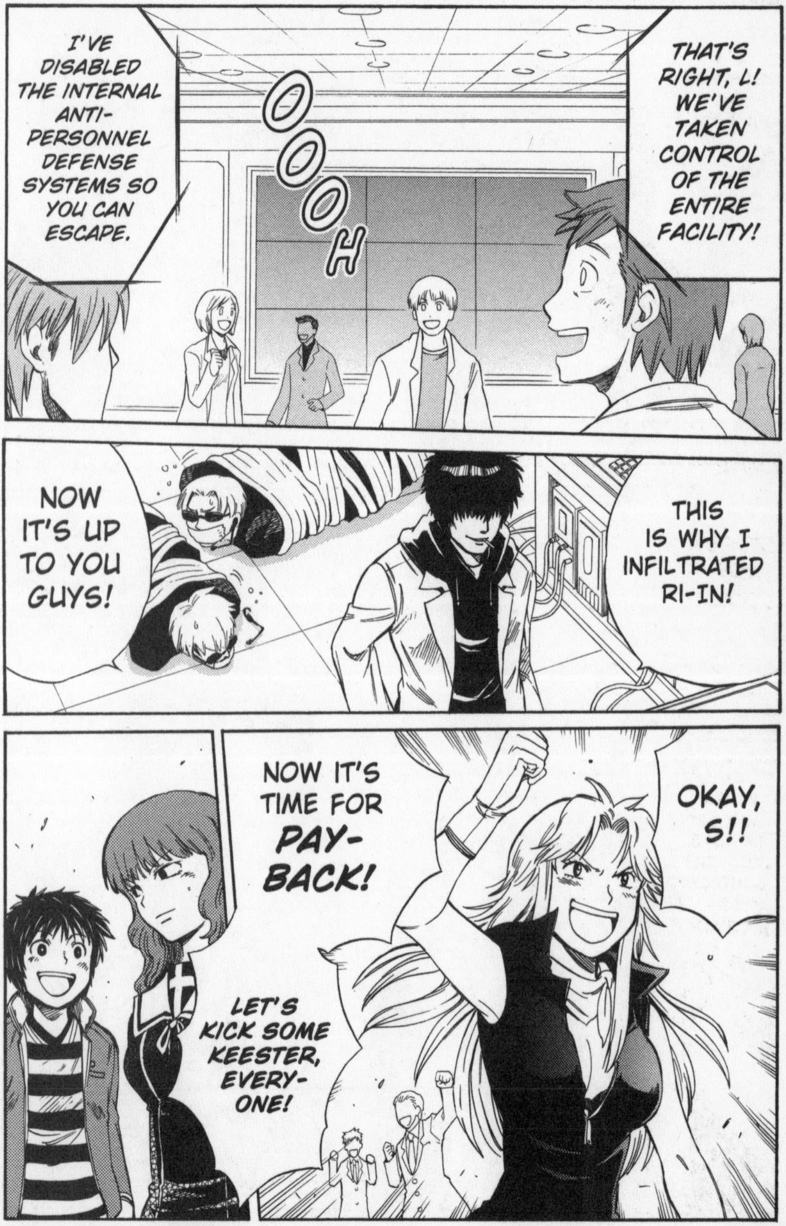
THAT'S RIGHT, L! WE'VE TAKEN CONTROL OF THE ENTIRE FACILITY!
OOOOH
I'VE DISABLED THE INTERNAL ANTI-PERSONNEL DEFENSE SYSTEMS SO YOU CAN ESCAPE.
THIS IS WHY I INFILTRATED RI-IN!
NOW IT'S UP TO YOU GUYS!
OKAY, S!!
NOW IT'S TIME FOR PAY-BACK!
LET'S KICK SOME KEESTER, EVERY-ONE!

READ THIS WAY

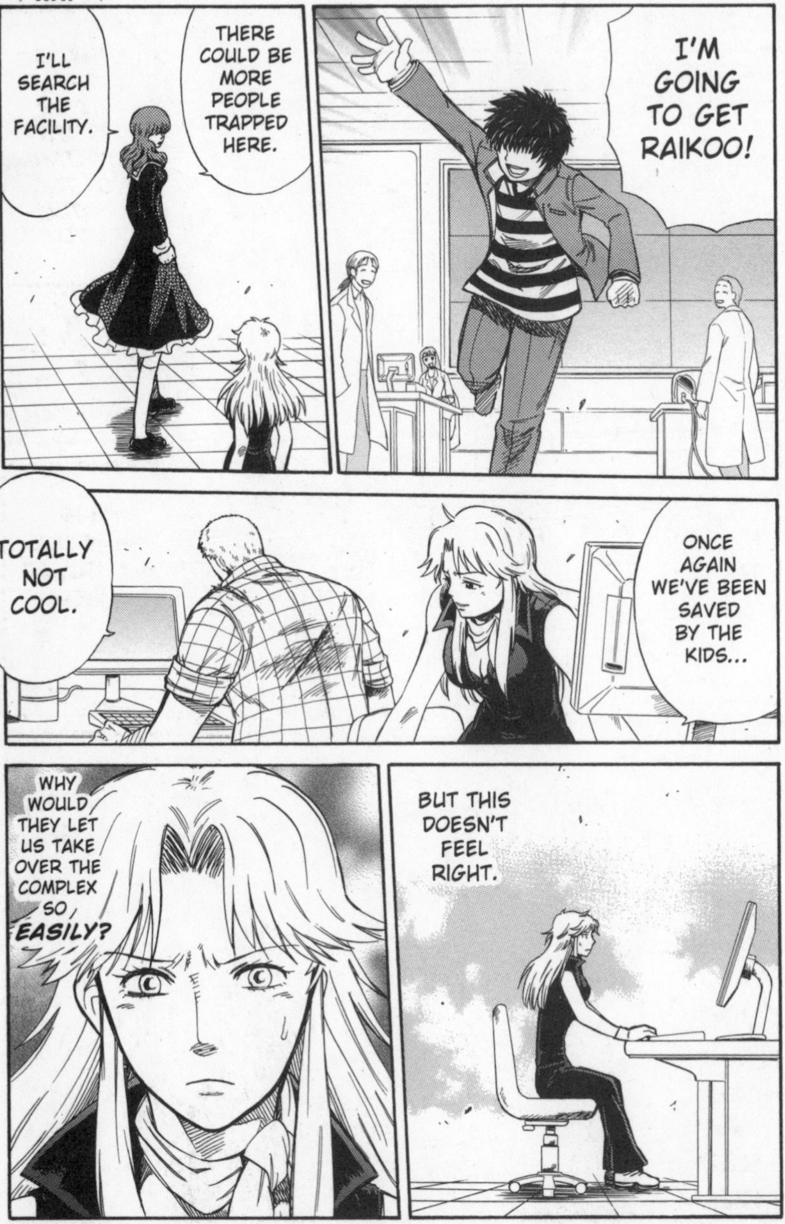

I'M GOING TO GET RAIKOO!
THERE COULD BE MORE PEOPLE TRAPPED HERE.
I'LL SEARCH THE FACILITY.
ONCE AGAIN WE'VE BEEN SAVED BY THE KIDS...
TOTALLY NOT COOL.
BUT THIS DOESN'T FEEL RIGHT.
WHY WOULD THEY LET US TAKE OVER THE COMPLEX SO *EASILY?*

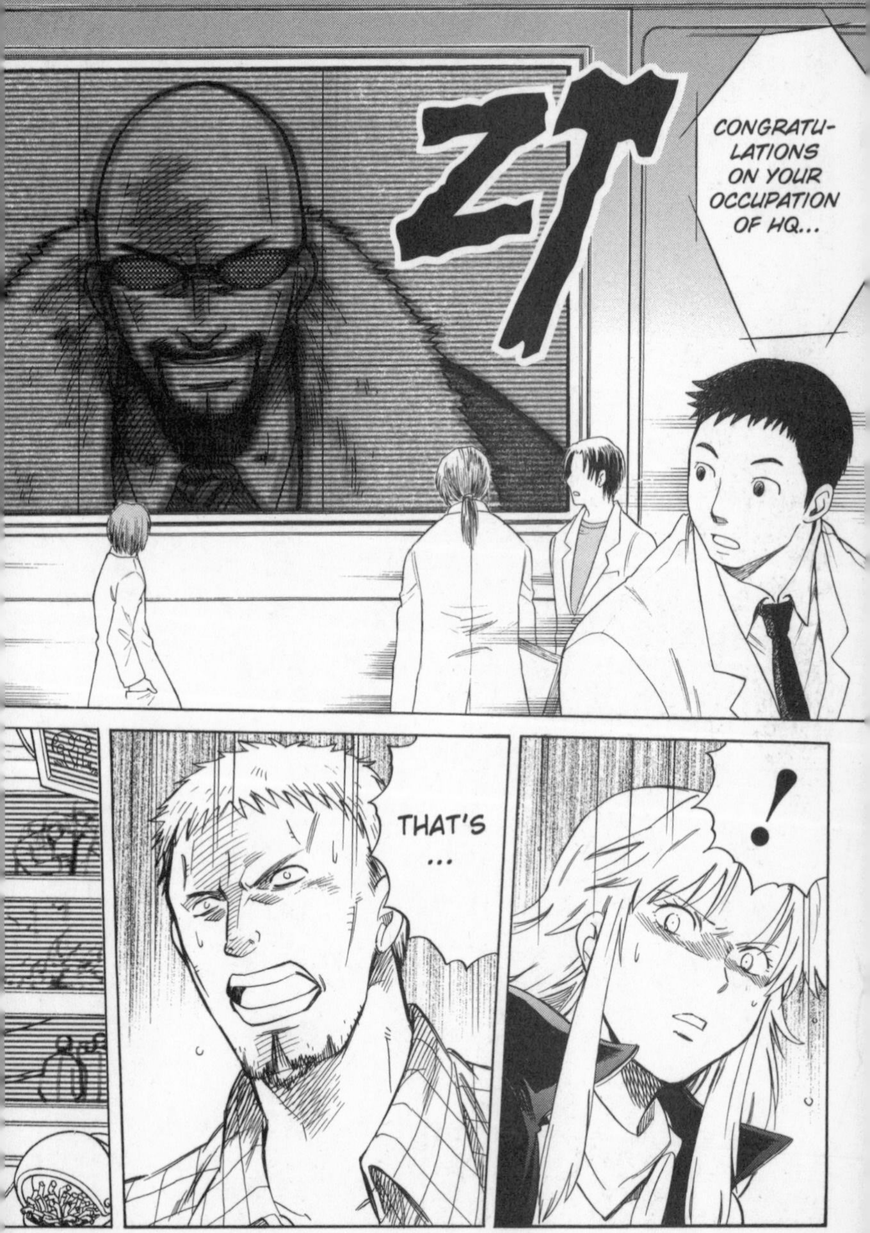
CONGRATU-
LATIONS
ON YOUR
OCCUPATION
OF HQ...
ZT
!
THAT'S
...

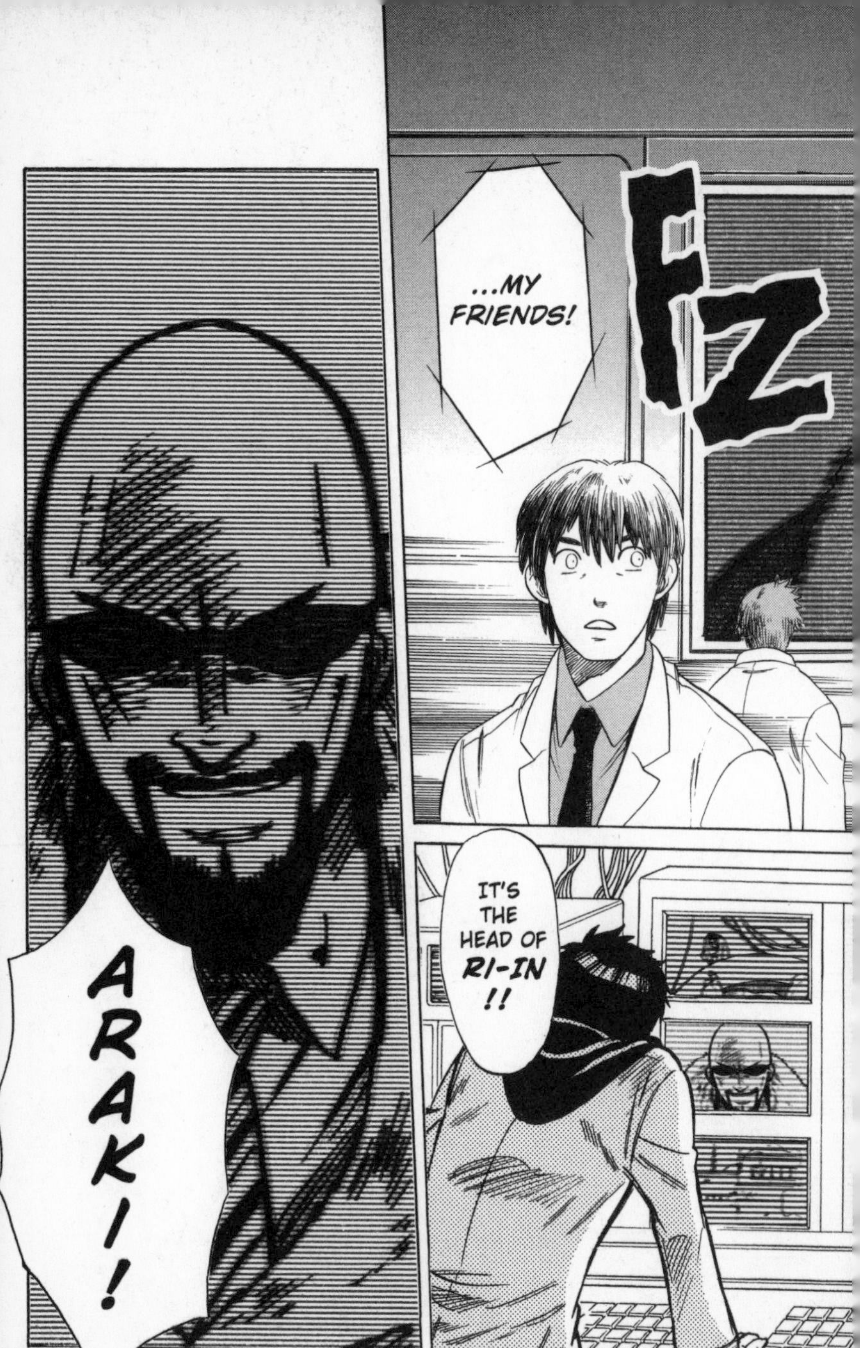
...MY FRIENDS!
FZ
IT'S THE HEAD OF RI-IN!!
ARAKI!

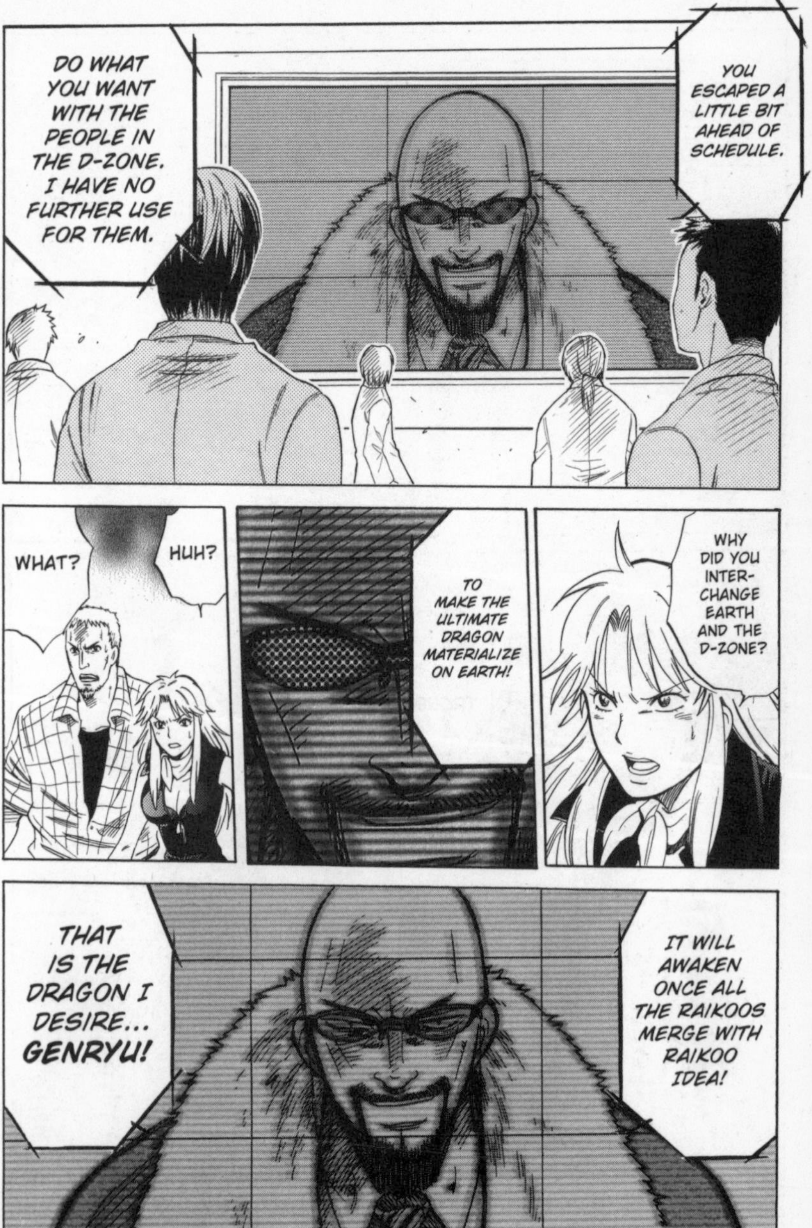
YOU ESCAPED A LITTLE BIT AHEAD OF SCHEDULE.
DO WHAT YOU WANT WITH THE PEOPLE IN THE D-ZONE. I HAVE NO FURTHER USE FOR THEM.
WHY DID YOU INTER-CHANGE EARTH AND THE D-ZONE?
TO MAKE THE ULTIMATE DRAGON MATERIALIZE ON EARTH!
HUH?
WHAT?
IT WILL AWAKEN ONCE ALL THE RAIKOOS MERGE WITH RAIKOO IDEA!
THAT IS THE DRAGON I DESIRE... GENRYU!

READ THIS WAY

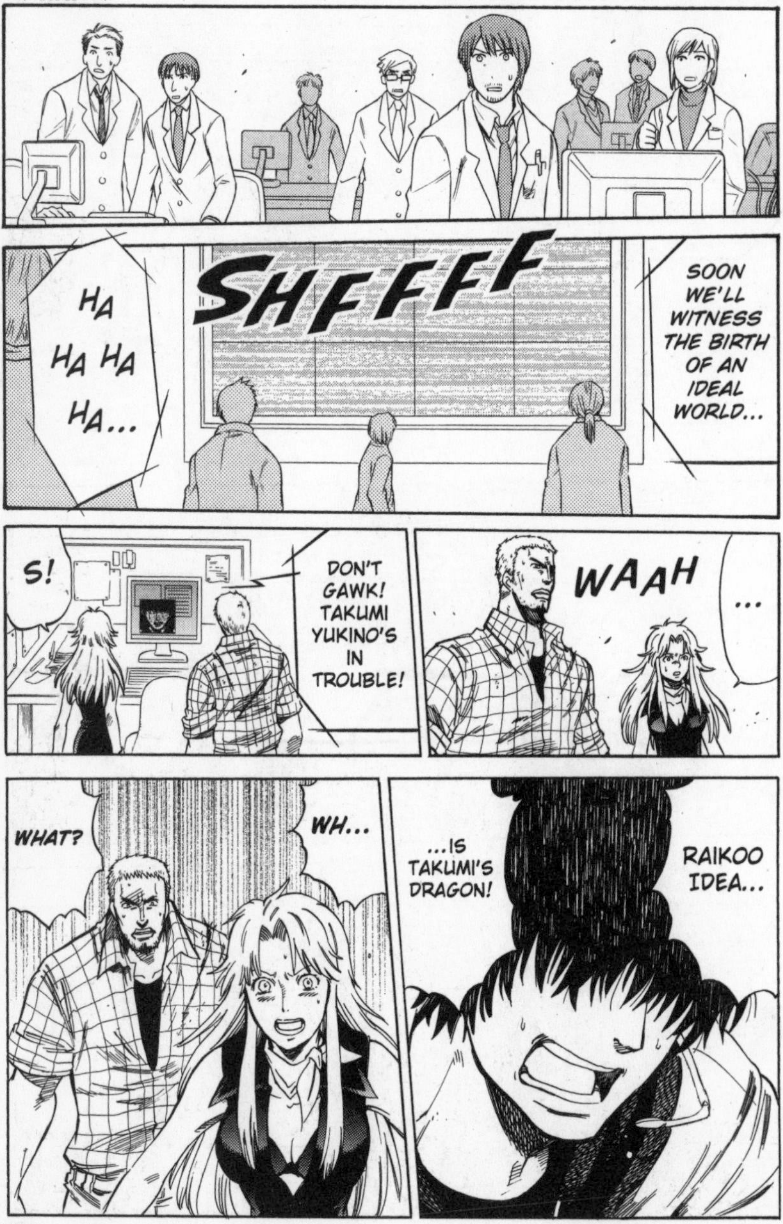
SOON WE'LL WITNESS THE BIRTH OF AN IDEAL WORLD...
SHFFFF
HA HA HA HA...
...
WAAH
DON'T GAWK! TAKUMI YUKINO'S IN TROUBLE!
S!
RAIKOO IDEA...
...IS TAKUMI'S DRAGON!
WH...
WHAT?

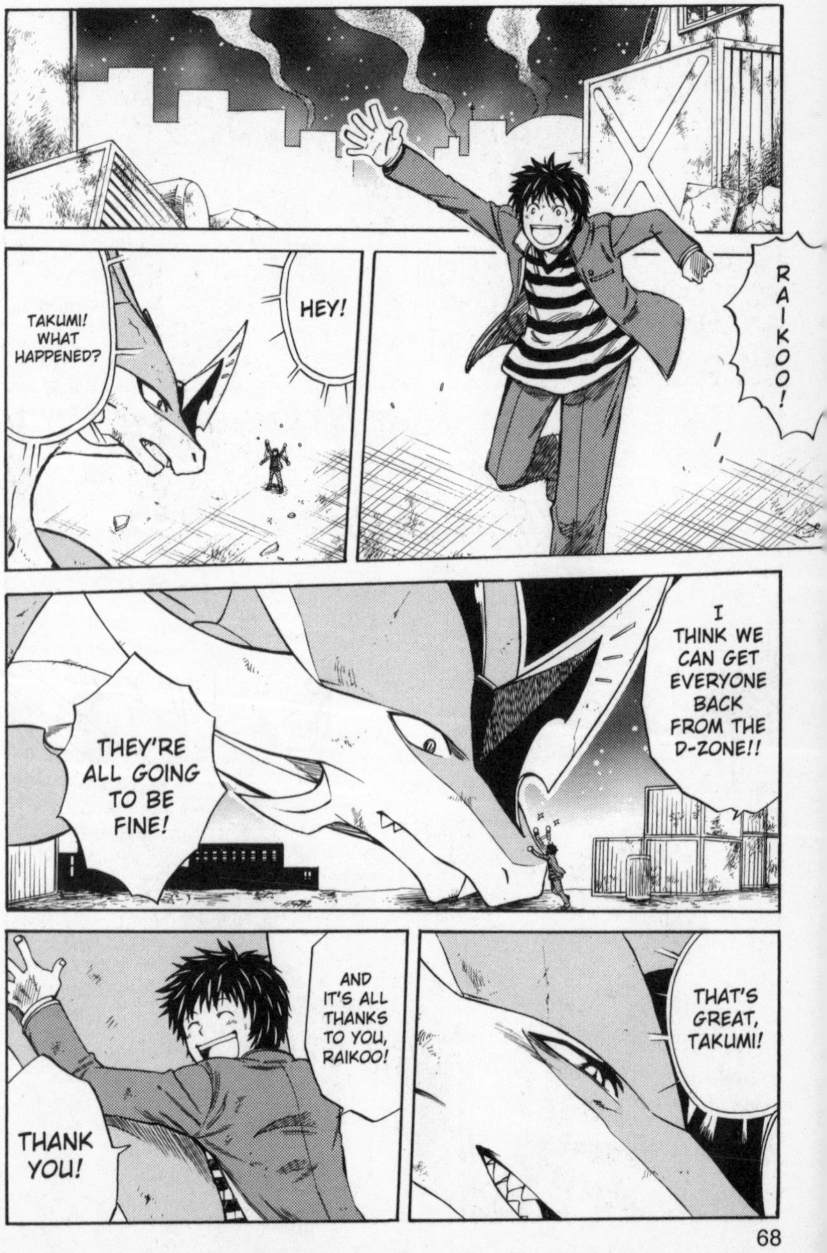
RAIKOO!
HEY!
TAKUMI! WHAT HAPPENED?
I THINK WE CAN GET EVERYONE BACK FROM THE D-ZONE!!
THEY'RE ALL GOING TO BE FINE!
THAT'S GREAT, TAKUMI!
AND IT'S ALL THANKS TO YOU, RAIKOO!
THANK YOU!

READ THIS WAY

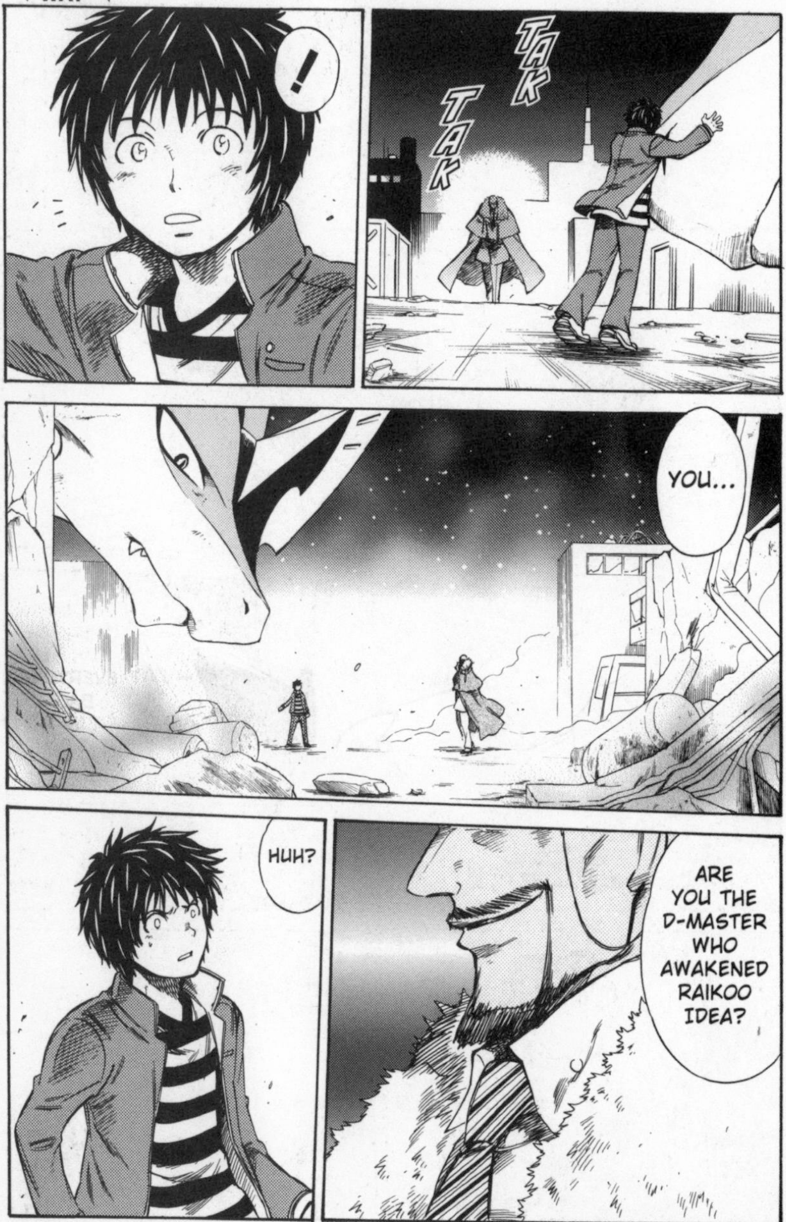
TAK
TAK
!
YOU...
ARE YOU THE D-MASTER WHO AWAKENED RAIKOO IDEA?
HUH?

RI...

...IN
!!

I AM ARAKI, PRESIDENT OF RI-IN.

I'VE COME TO RETRIEVE IDEA.

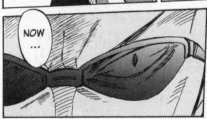

NOW...

WE CREATED IDEA. HE'S OURS.

...COME TO ME, RAIKOO IDEA!

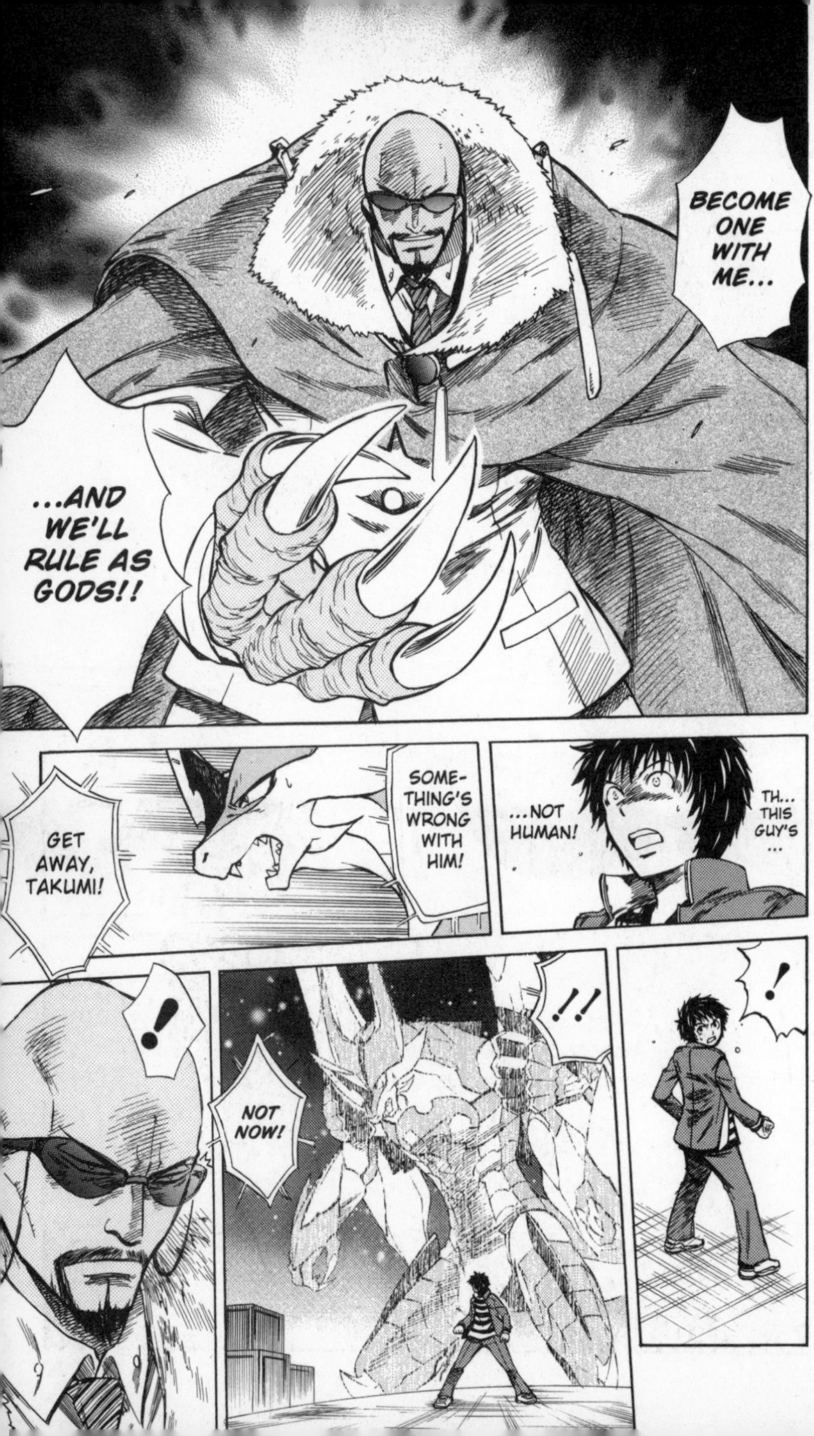
BECOME ONE WITH ME...
...AND WE'LL RULE AS GODS!!
TH... THIS GUY'S ...
...NOT HUMAN!
SOME-THING'S WRONG WITH HIM!
GET AWAY, TAKUMI!
!
!!
NOT NOW!
!

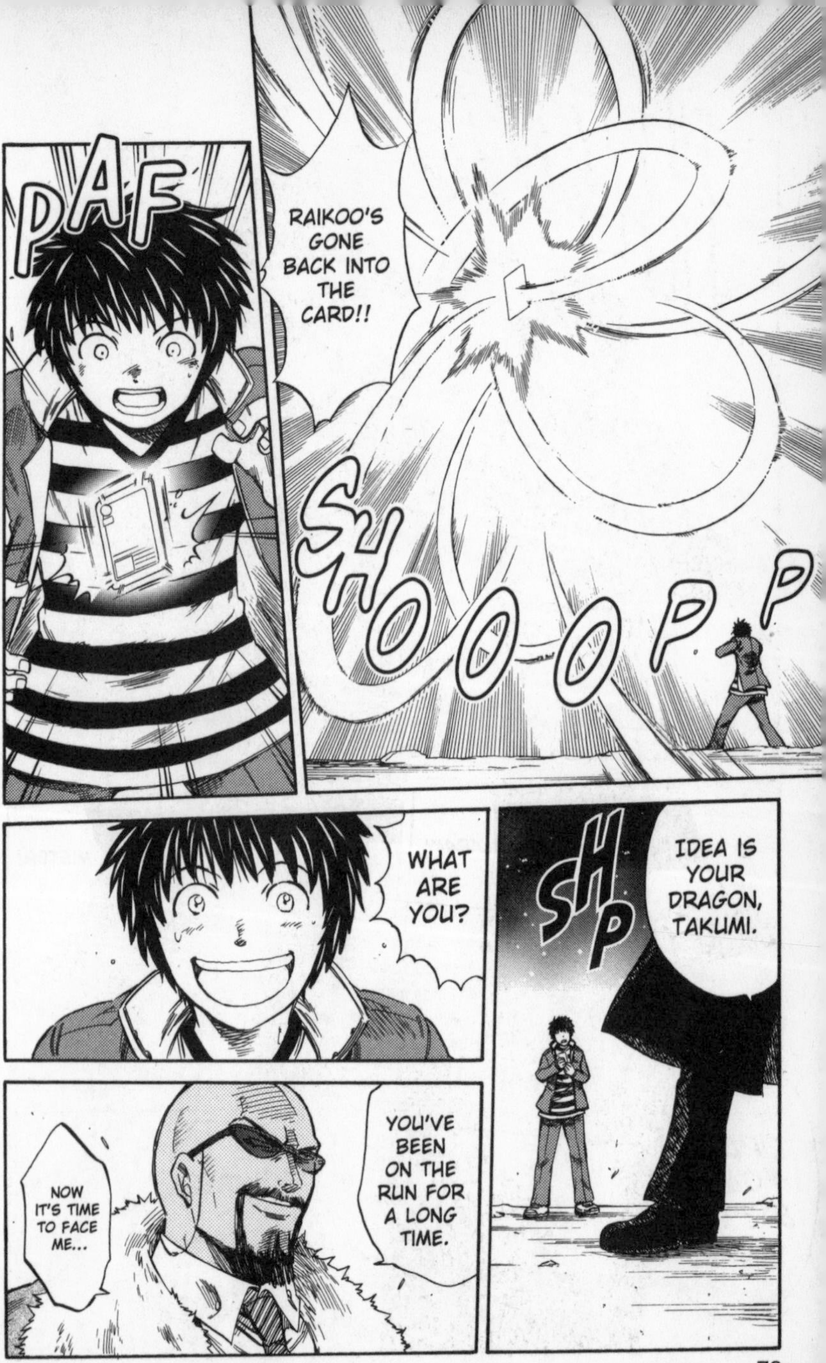
RAIKOO'S GONE BACK INTO THE CARD!!
SHOOOPP
PAF
IDEA IS YOUR DRAGON, TAKUMI.
SHP
WHAT ARE YOU?
YOU'VE BEEN ON THE RUN FOR A LONG TIME.
NOW IT'S TIME TO FACE ME...

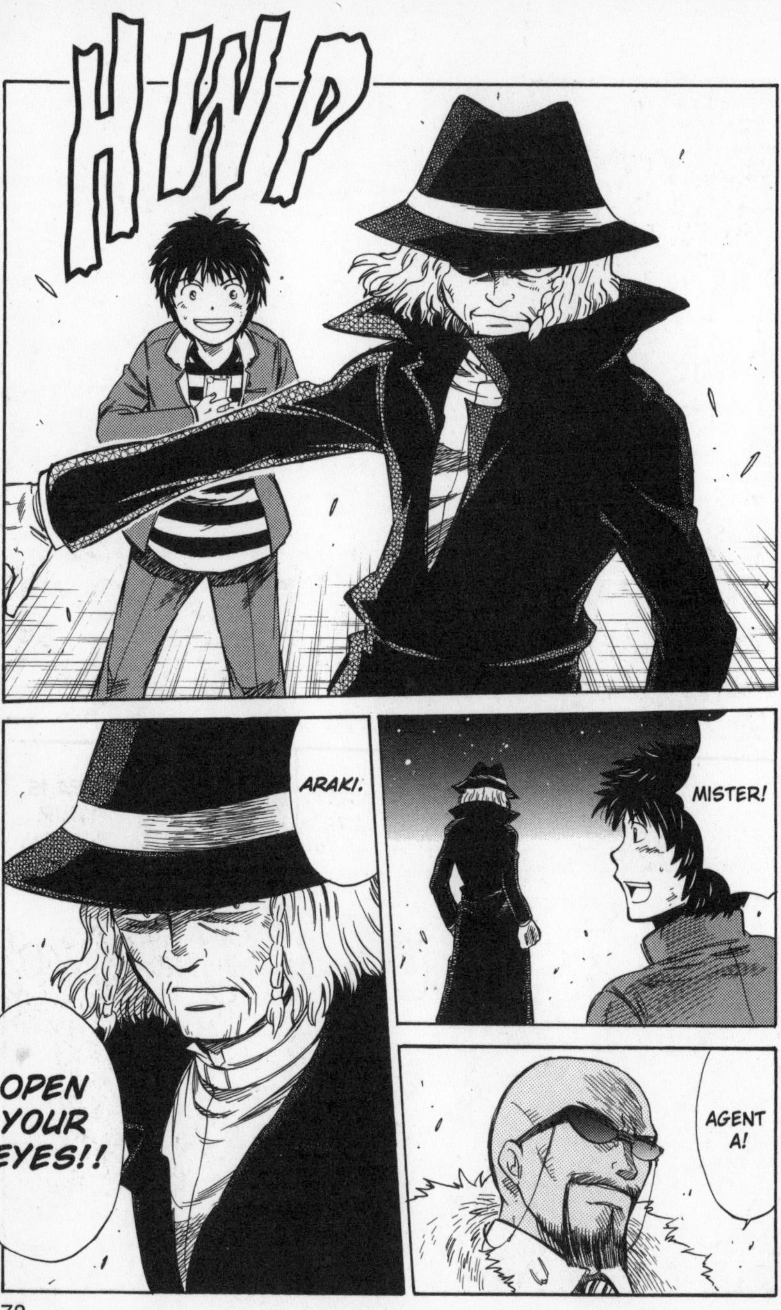
HWP
MISTER!
AGENT A!
ARAKI.
OPEN YOUR EYES!!

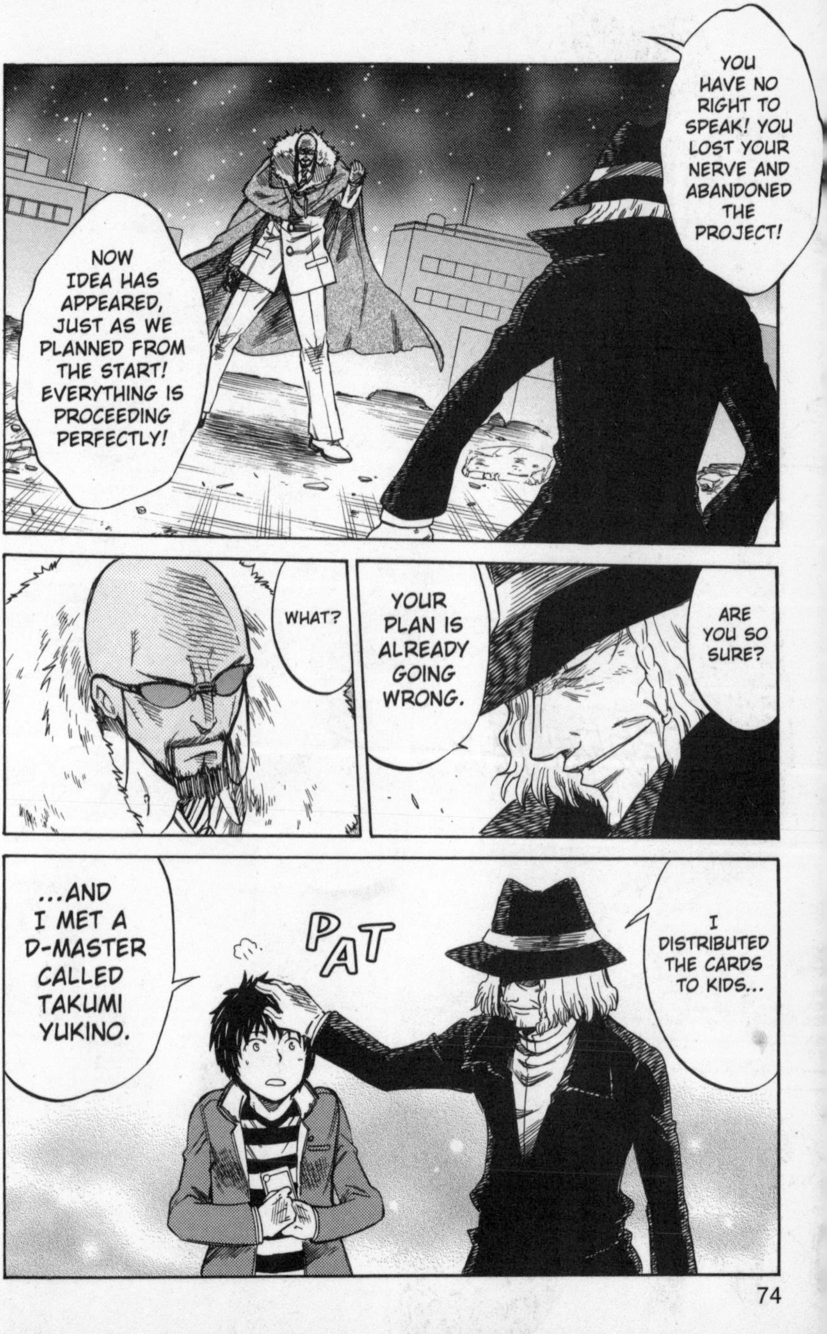
YOU HAVE NO RIGHT TO SPEAK! YOU LOST YOUR NERVE AND ABANDONED THE PROJECT!
NOW IDEA HAS APPEARED, JUST AS WE PLANNED FROM THE START! EVERYTHING IS PROCEEDING PERFECTLY!
ARE YOU SO SURE?
YOUR PLAN IS ALREADY GOING WRONG.
WHAT?
I DISTRIBUTED THE CARDS TO KIDS...
PAT
...AND I MET A D-MASTER CALLED TAKUMI YUKINO.

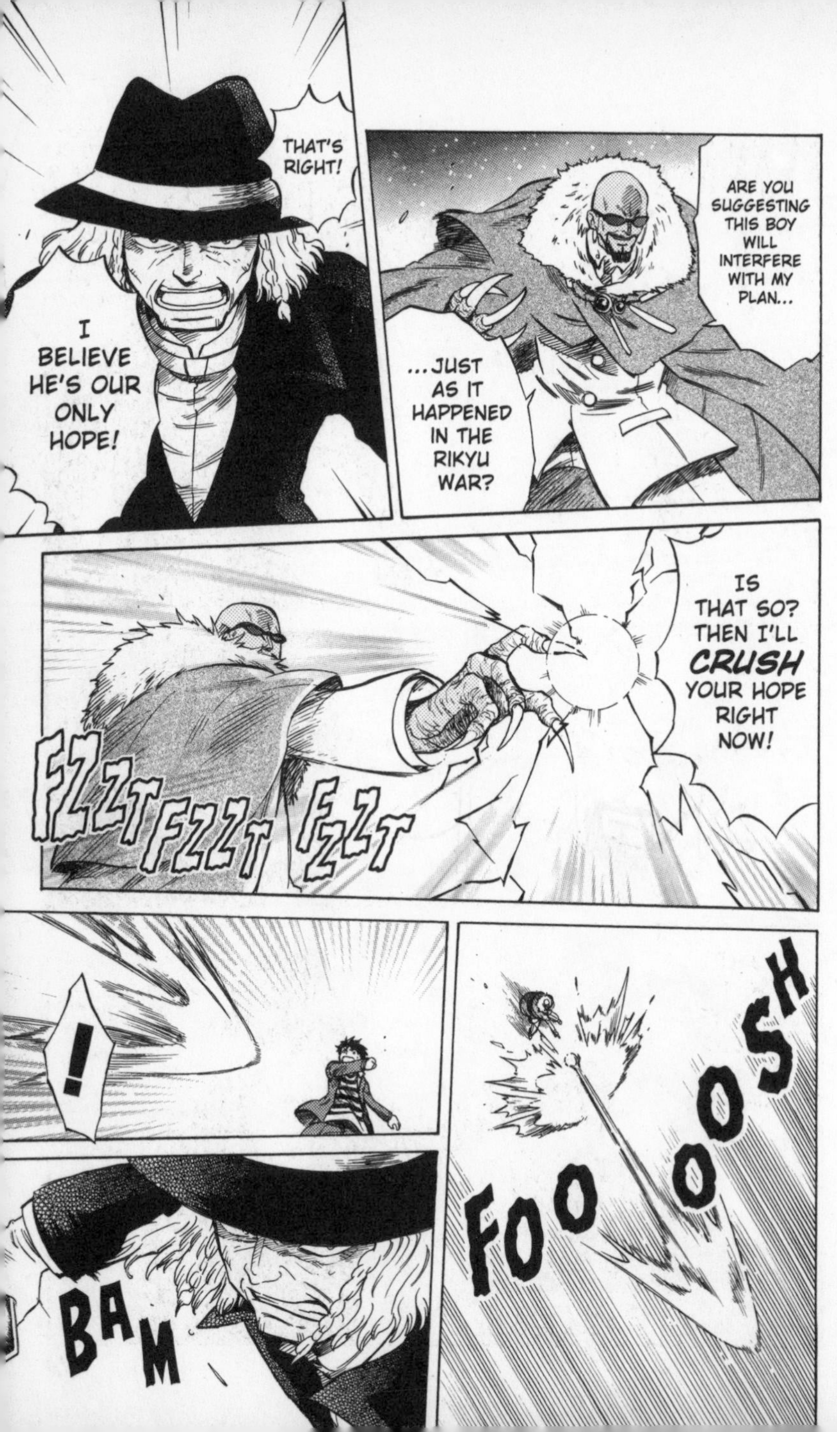
ARE YOU SUGGESTING THIS BOY WILL INTERFERE WITH MY PLAN...
...JUST AS IT HAPPENED IN THE RIKYU WAR?
THAT'S RIGHT!
I BELIEVE HE'S OUR ONLY HOPE!
IS THAT SO? THEN I'LL CRUSH YOUR HOPE RIGHT NOW!
FZZT FZZT FZZT
FOOOOSH
!
BAM

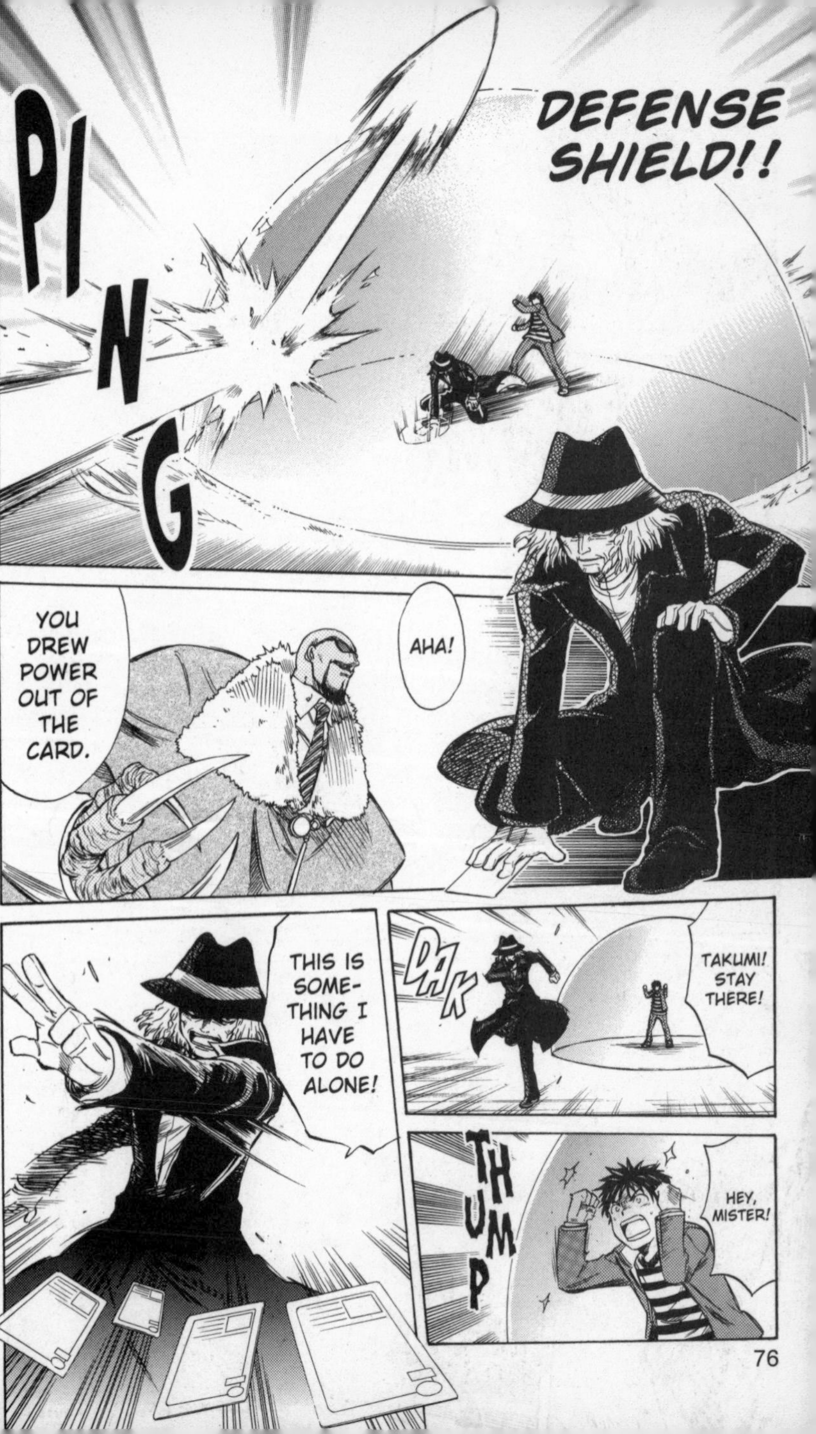
DEFENSE SHIELD!!
PING
AHA!
YOU DREW POWER OUT OF THE CARD.
TAKUMI! STAY THERE!
DAK
HEY, MISTER!
THUMP
THIS IS SOME-THING I HAVE TO DO ALONE!

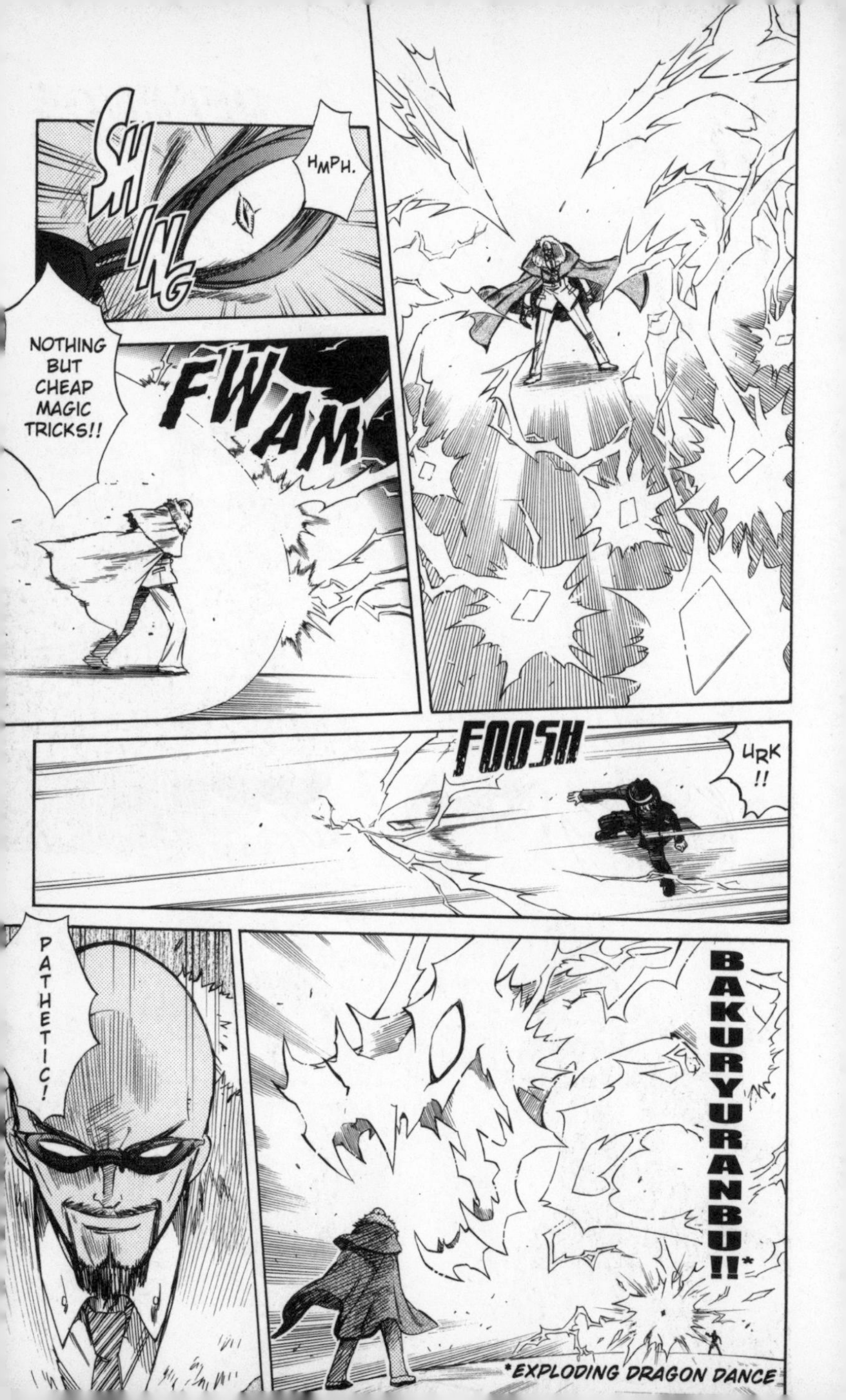
SHING
HMPH.
FWAM
NOTHING BUT CHEAP MAGIC TRICKS!!
FOOSH
URK!!
BAKURYURANBU!!*
PATHETIC!
*EXPLODING DRAGON DANCE

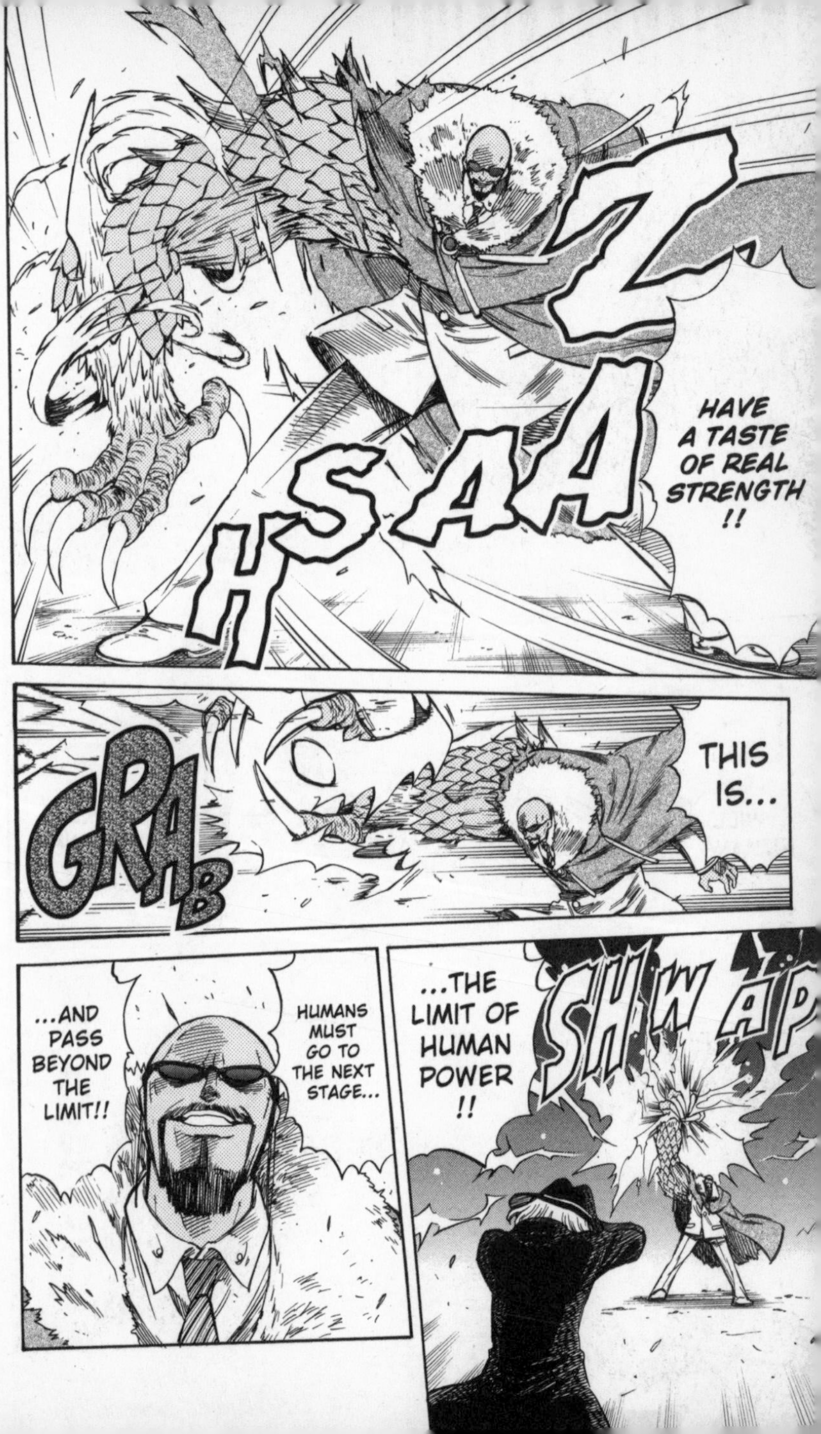
HSAAZ
HAVE A TASTE OF REAL STRENGTH!!
THIS IS...
GRAB
SHWAP
...THE LIMIT OF HUMAN POWER!!
HUMANS MUST GO TO THE NEXT STAGE...
...AND PASS BEYOND THE LIMIT!!

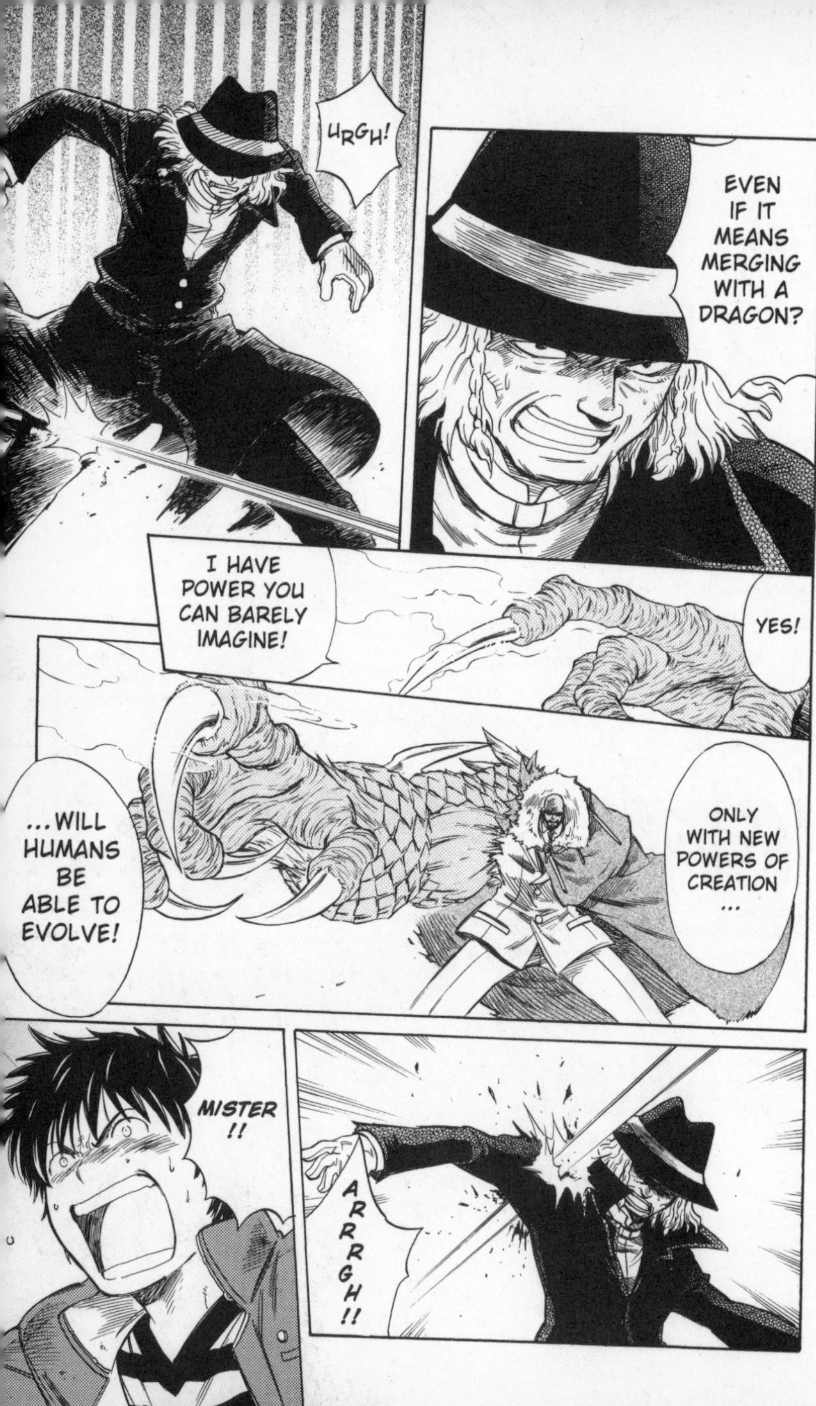
EVEN IF IT MEANS MERGING WITH A DRAGON?
URGH!
YES!
I HAVE POWER YOU CAN BARELY IMAGINE!
ONLY WITH NEW POWERS OF CREATION ...
...WILL HUMANS BE ABLE TO EVOLVE!
ARRRGH!!
MISTER!!

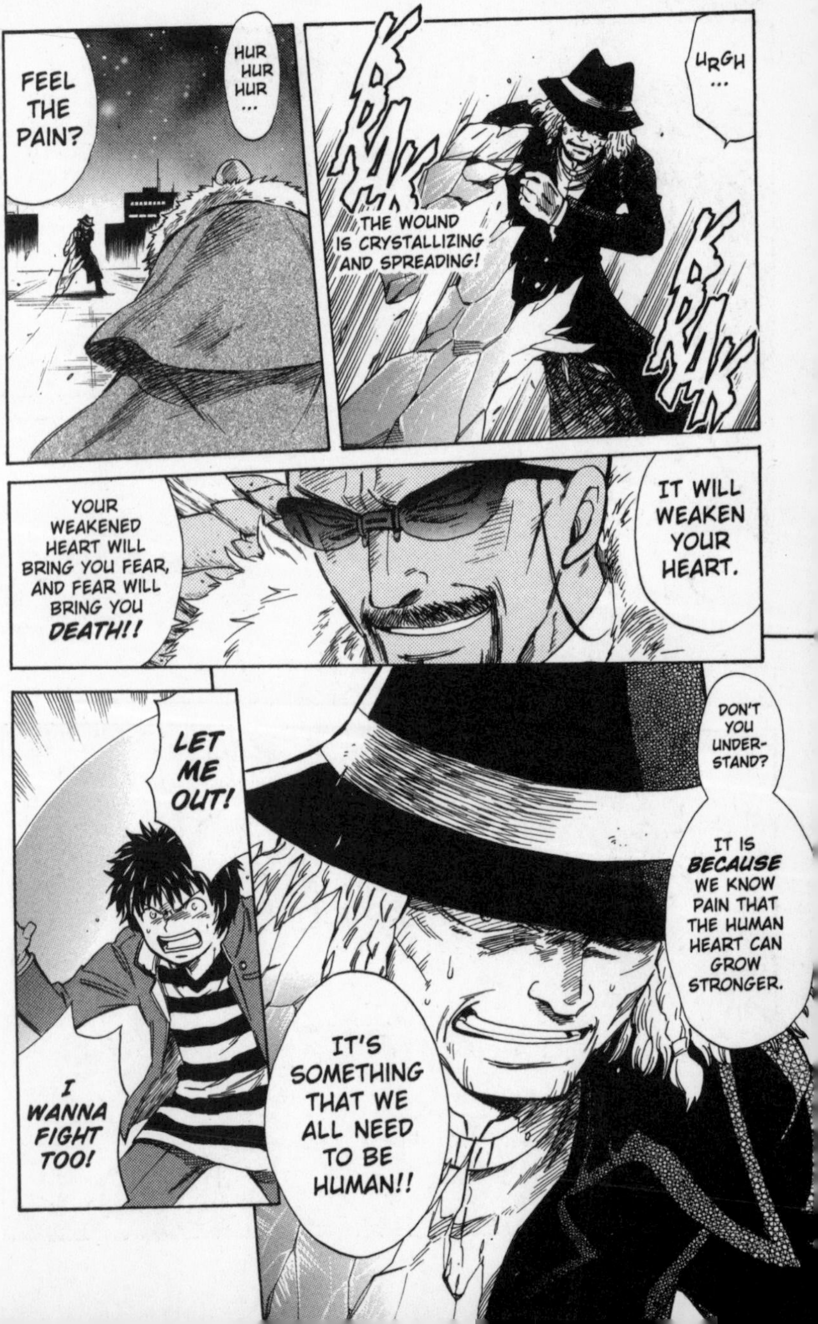
URGH ...
KRAK
KRAK
THE WOUND IS CRYSTALLIZING AND SPREADING!
HUR HUR HUR ...
FEEL THE PAIN?
IT WILL WEAKEN YOUR HEART.
YOUR WEAKENED HEART WILL BRING YOU FEAR, AND FEAR WILL BRING YOU *DEATH!!*
DON'T YOU UNDER-STAND?
IT IS *BECAUSE* WE KNOW PAIN THAT THE HUMAN HEART CAN GROW STRONGER.
IT'S SOMETHING THAT WE ALL NEED TO BE HUMAN!!
LET ME OUT!
I WANNA FIGHT TOO!

READ THIS WAY

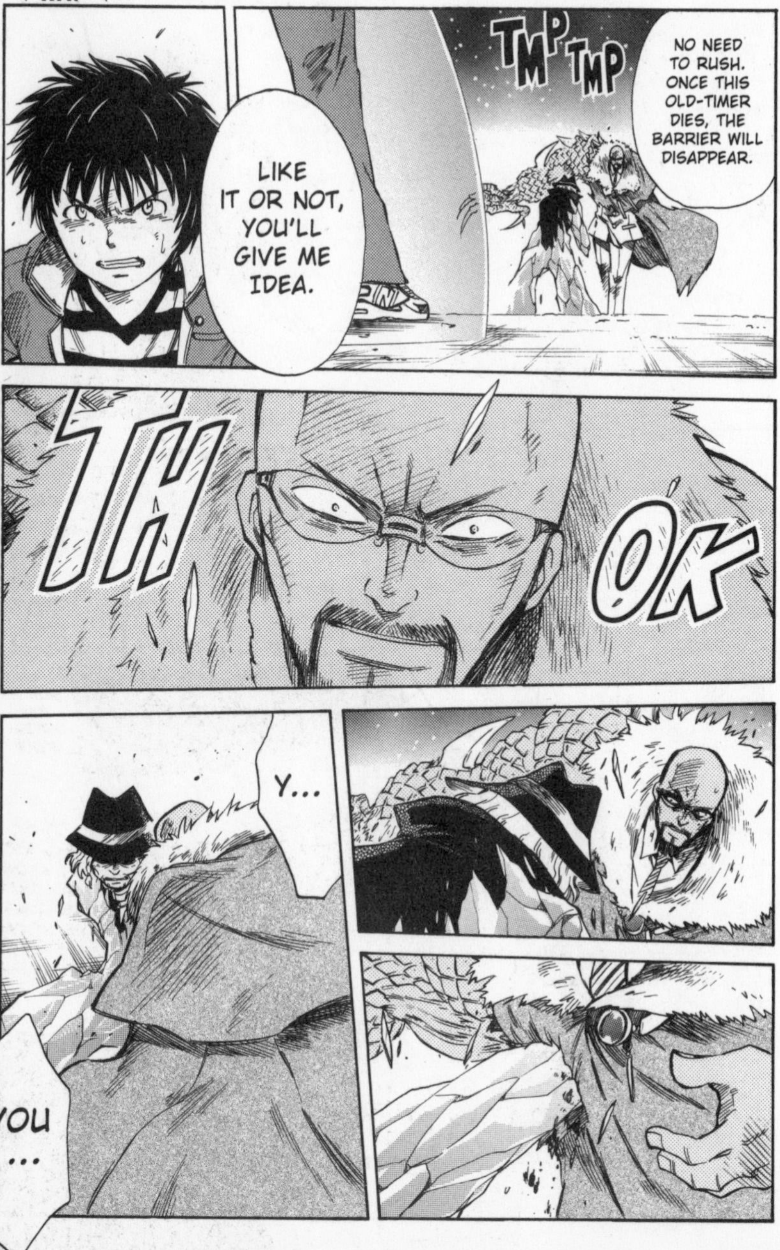
NO NEED TO RUSH. ONCE THIS OLD-TIMER DIES, THE BARRIER WILL DISAPPEAR.
TMP TMP TMP
LIKE IT OR NOT, YOU'LL GIVE ME IDEA.
TH
OK
Y...
YOU ...

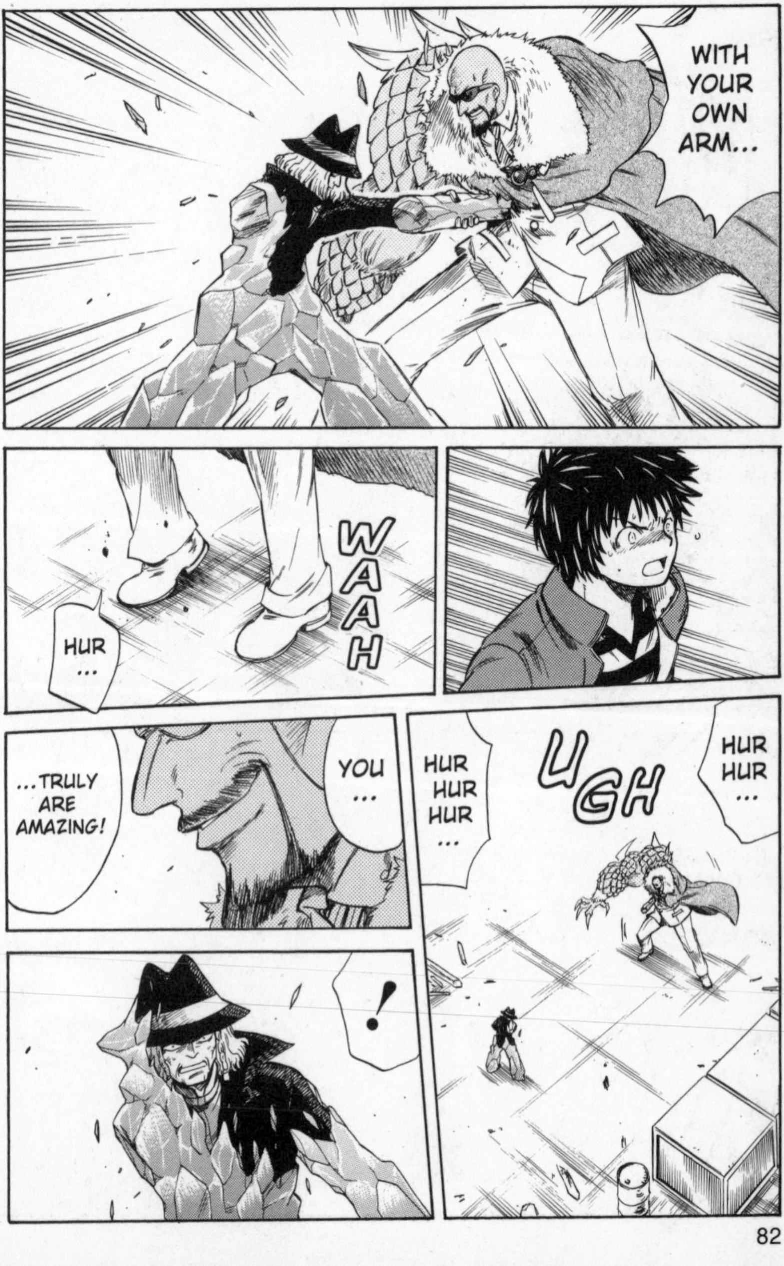
WITH YOUR OWN ARM...
WAAAH
HUR...
HUR HUR...
UGH
HUR HUR HUR...
YOU...
...TRULY ARE AMAZING!
!

READ THIS WAY

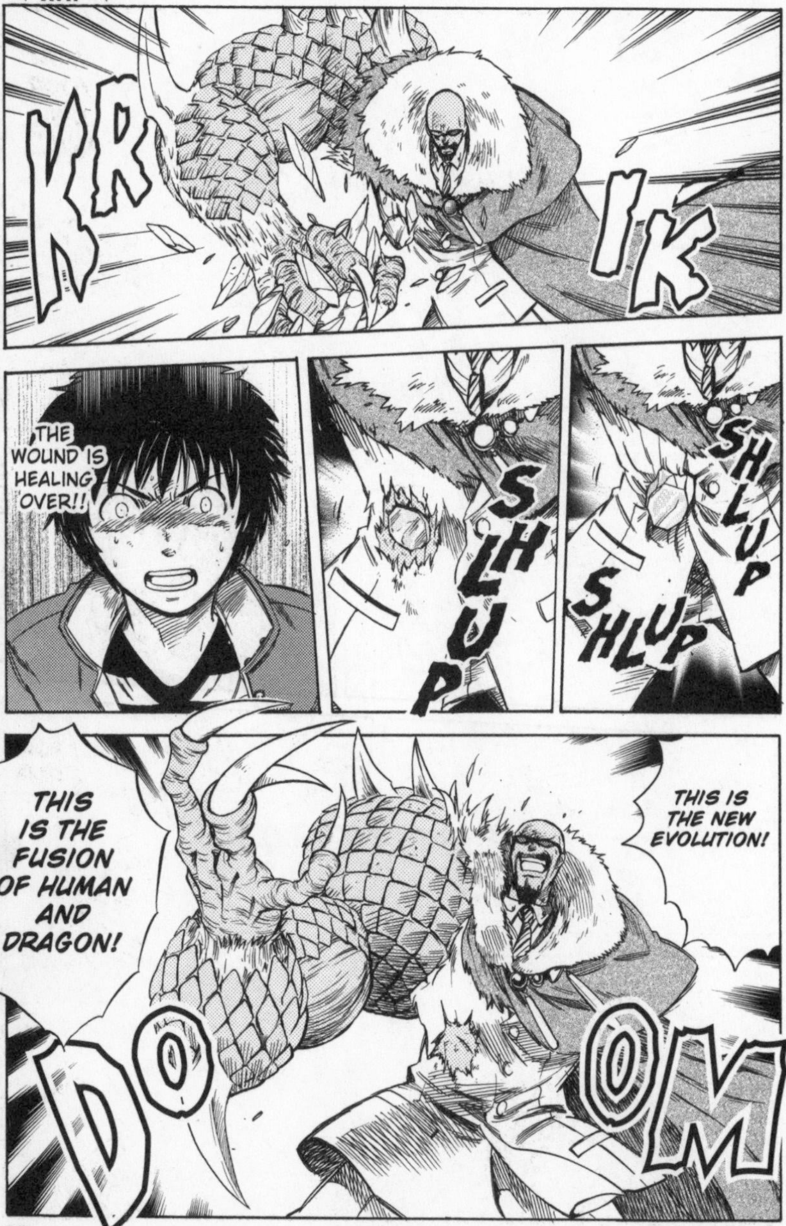

KRIK
SHLUP
SHLUP
SHLUP
THE WOUND IS HEALING OVER!!
THIS IS THE NEW EVOLUTION!
THIS IS THE FUSION OF HUMAN AND DRAGON!
DOOM

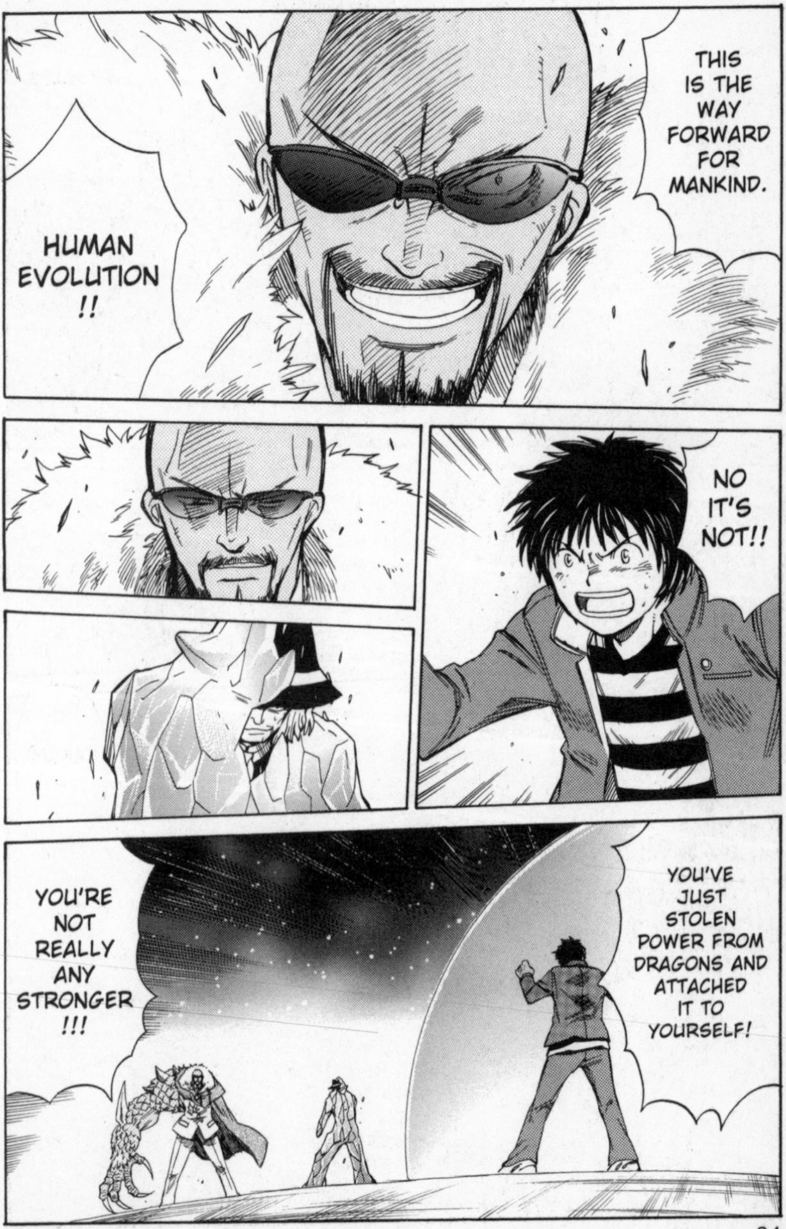
THIS IS THE WAY FORWARD FOR MANKIND.
HUMAN EVOLUTION !!
NO IT'S NOT!!
YOU'VE JUST STOLEN POWER FROM DRAGONS AND ATTACHED IT TO YOURSELF!
YOU'RE NOT REALLY ANY STRONGER !!!

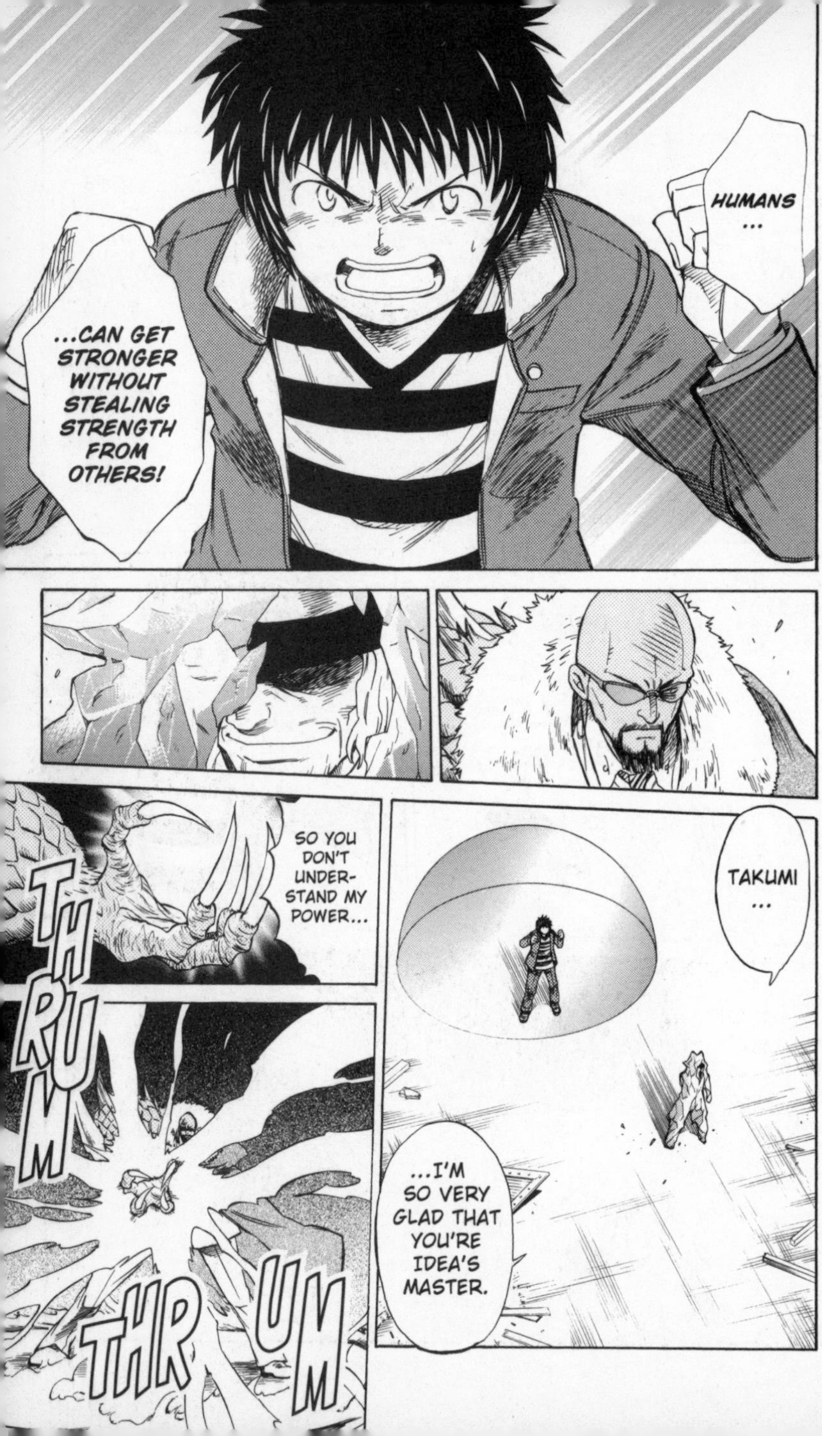
HUMANS ...
...CAN GET STRONGER WITHOUT STEALING STRENGTH FROM OTHERS!
TAKUMI ...
...I'M SO VERY GLAD THAT YOU'RE IDEA'S MASTER.
SO YOU DON'T UNDER-STAND MY POWER...
THRUM
THRUM

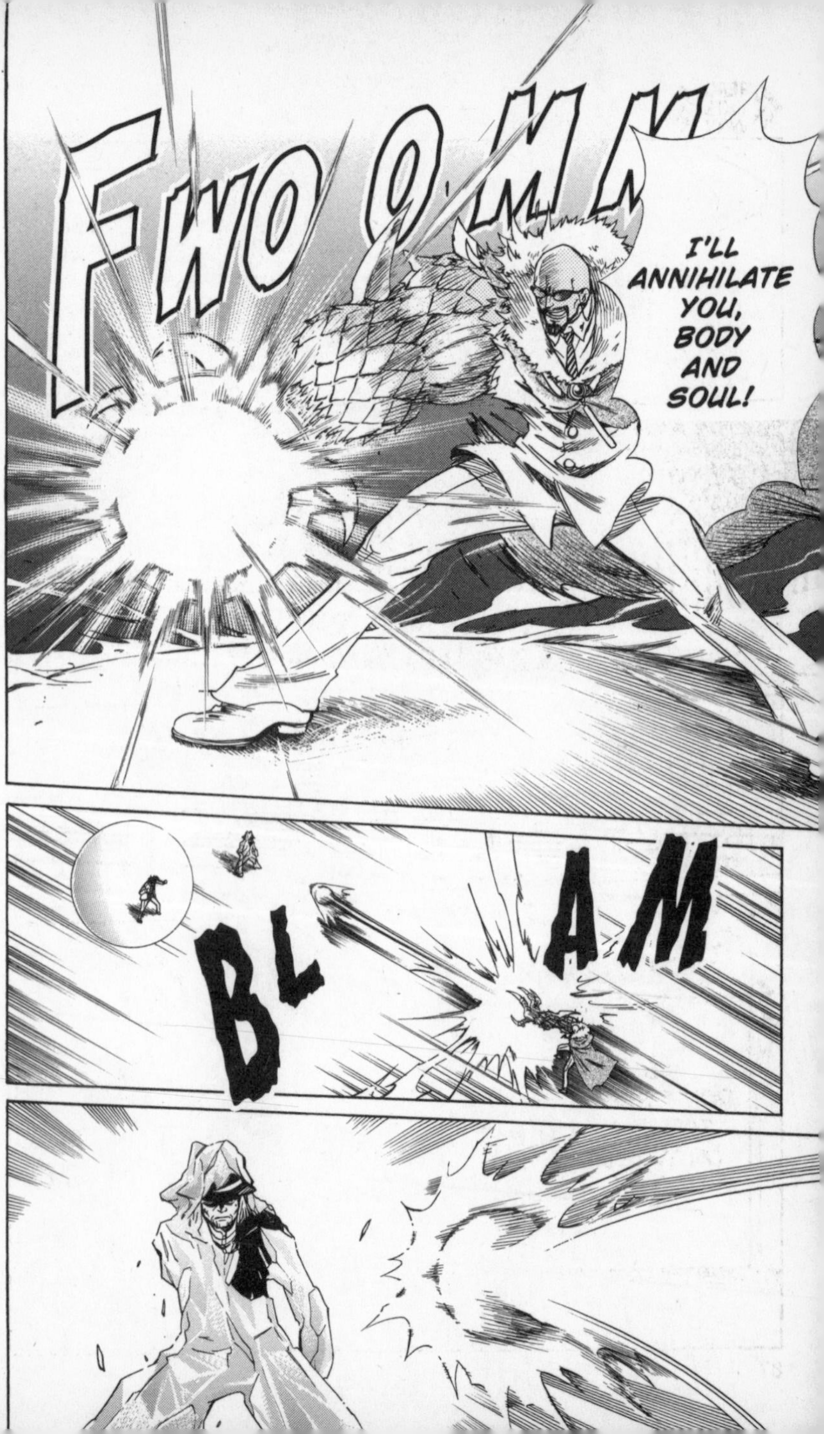
FWOOMM
I'LL ANNIHILATE YOU, BODY AND SOUL!
BLAM

READ THIS WAY

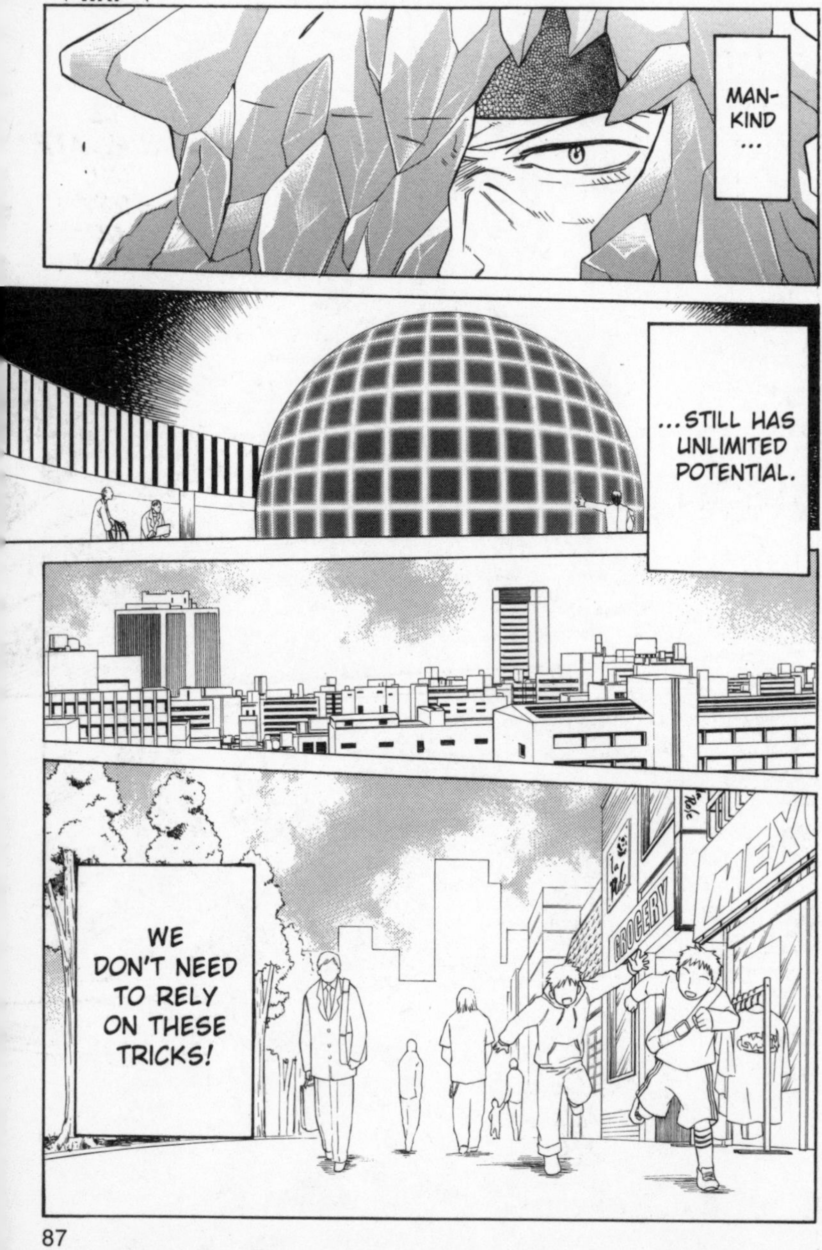
MAN-KIND ...
...STILL HAS UNLIMITED POTENTIAL.
WE DON'T NEED TO RELY ON THESE TRICKS!
GROCERY

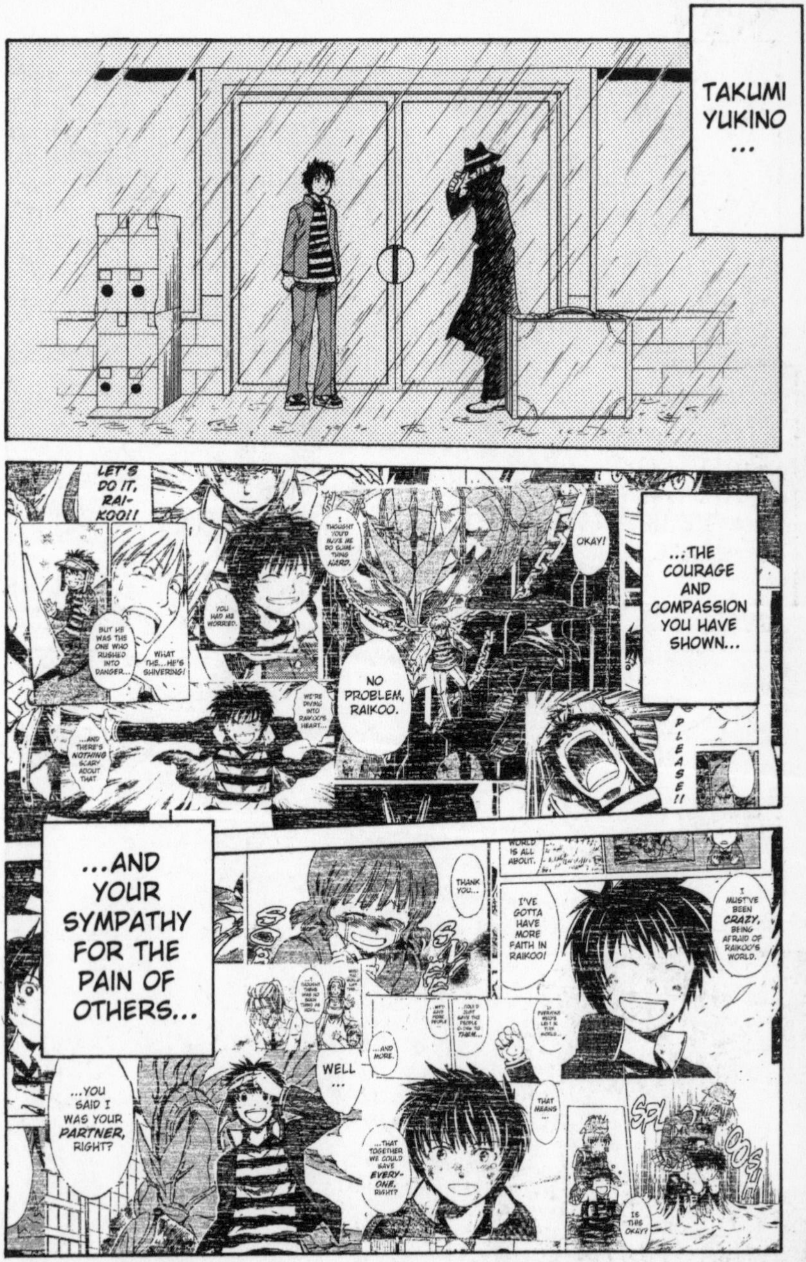
TAKUMI YUKINO ...
...THE COURAGE AND COMPASSION YOU HAVE SHOWN...
PLEASE!!
OKAY!
I THOUGHT YOU'D HAVE ME DO SOME-THING HARD.
NO PROBLEM, RAIKOO.
YOU HAD ME WORRIED.
LET'S DO IT, RAI-KOO!!
WHAT THE...HE'S SHIVERING!
BUT HE WAS THE ONE WHO RUSHED INTO DANGER...
WE'RE DIVING INTO RAIKOO'S HEART...
...AND THERE'S NOTHING SCARY ABOUT THAT
WORLD IS ALL ABOUT.
I MUST'VE BEEN CRAZY, BEING AFRAID OF RAIKOO'S WORLD.
I'VE GOTTA HAVE MORE FAITH IN RAIKOO!
THANK YOU...
...AND YOUR SYMPATHY FOR THE PAIN OF OTHERS...
...AND MORE.
WELL ...
SPLOOSH
IS THIS OKAY?
THAT MEANS ...
...THAT TOGETHER WE COULD SAVE EVERY-ONE, RIGHT?
...YOU SAID I WAS YOUR PARTNER, RIGHT?

READ THIS WAY

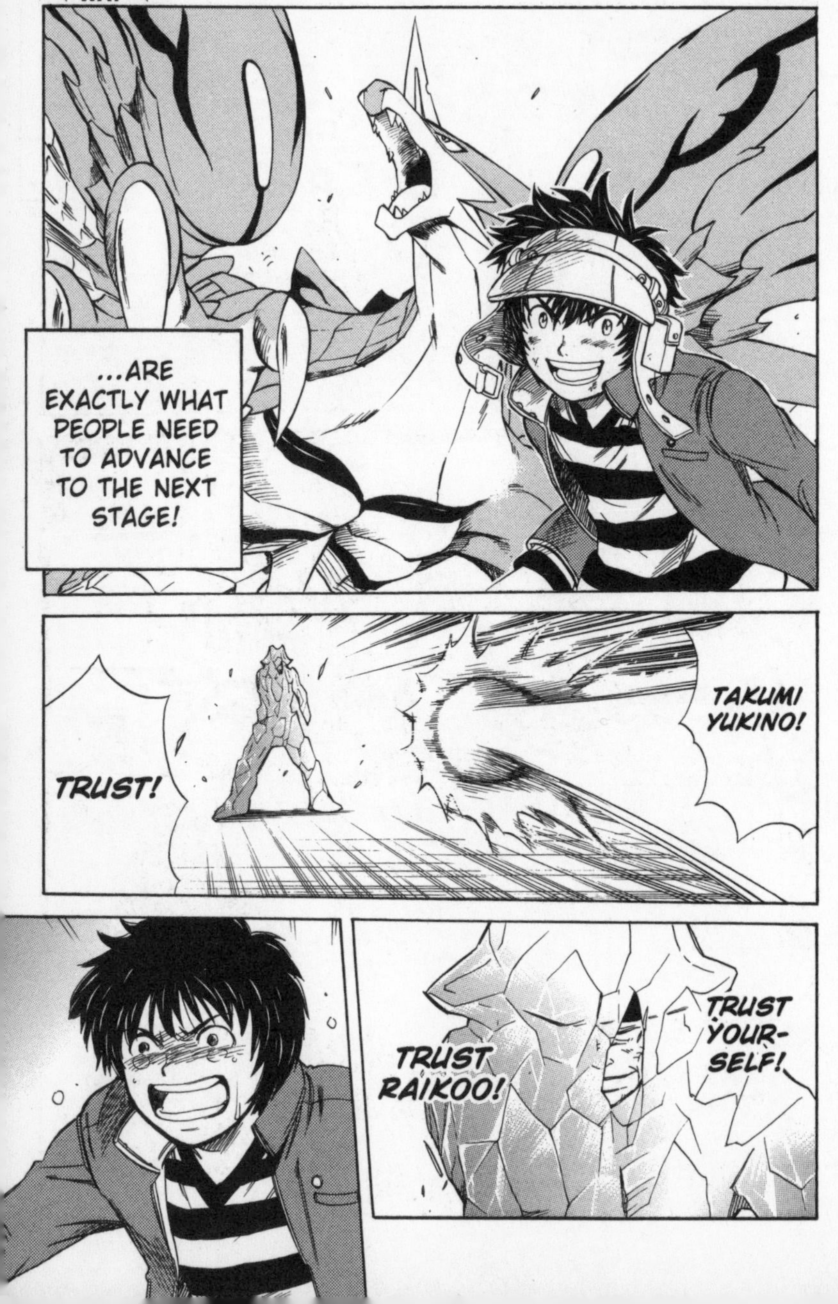
...ARE EXACTLY WHAT PEOPLE NEED TO ADVANCE TO THE NEXT STAGE!
TAKUMI YUKINO!
TRUST!
TRUST YOUR-SELF!
TRUST RAIKOO!

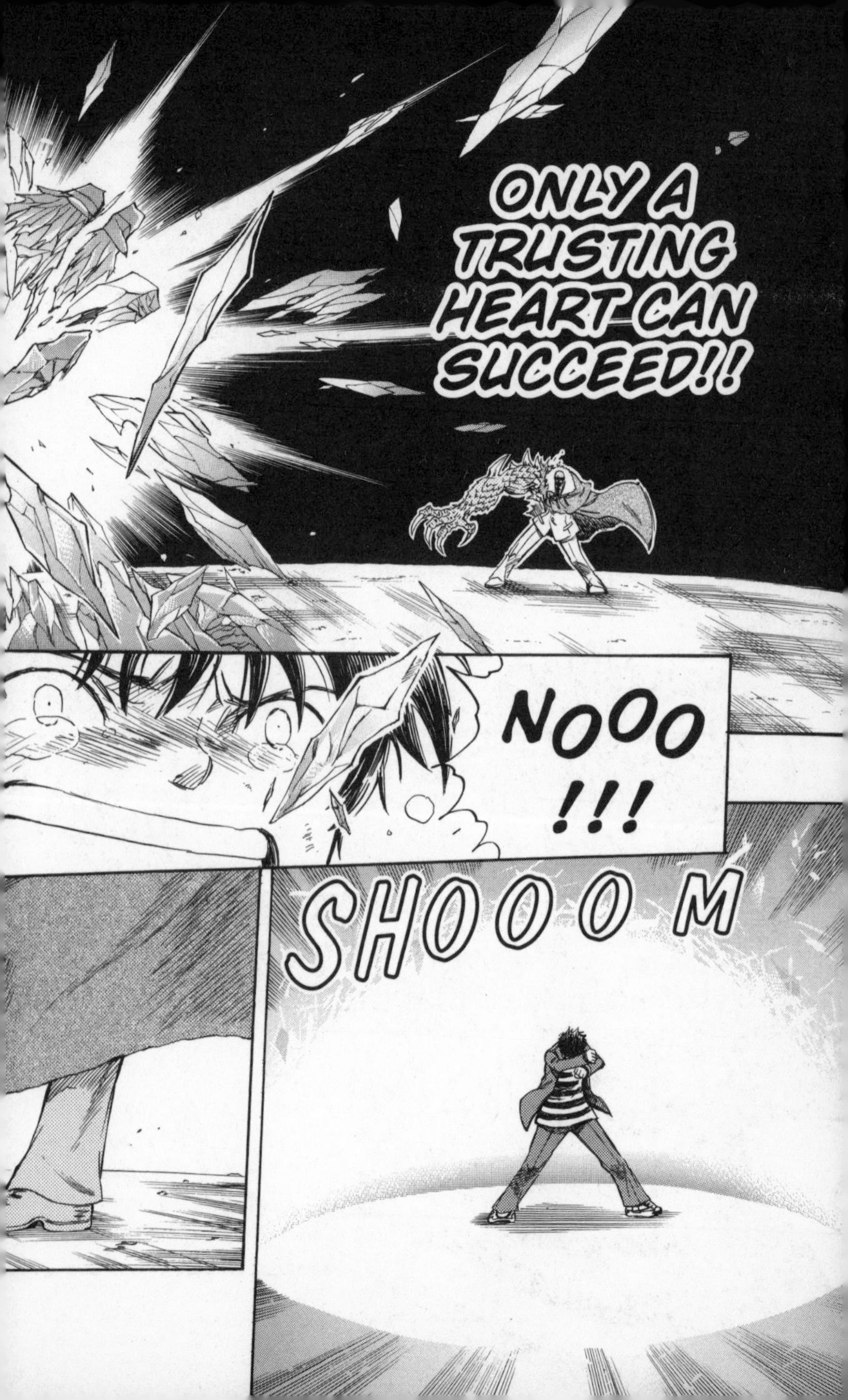
ONLY A TRUSTING HEART CAN SUCCEED!!
NOOO!!!
SHOOOM

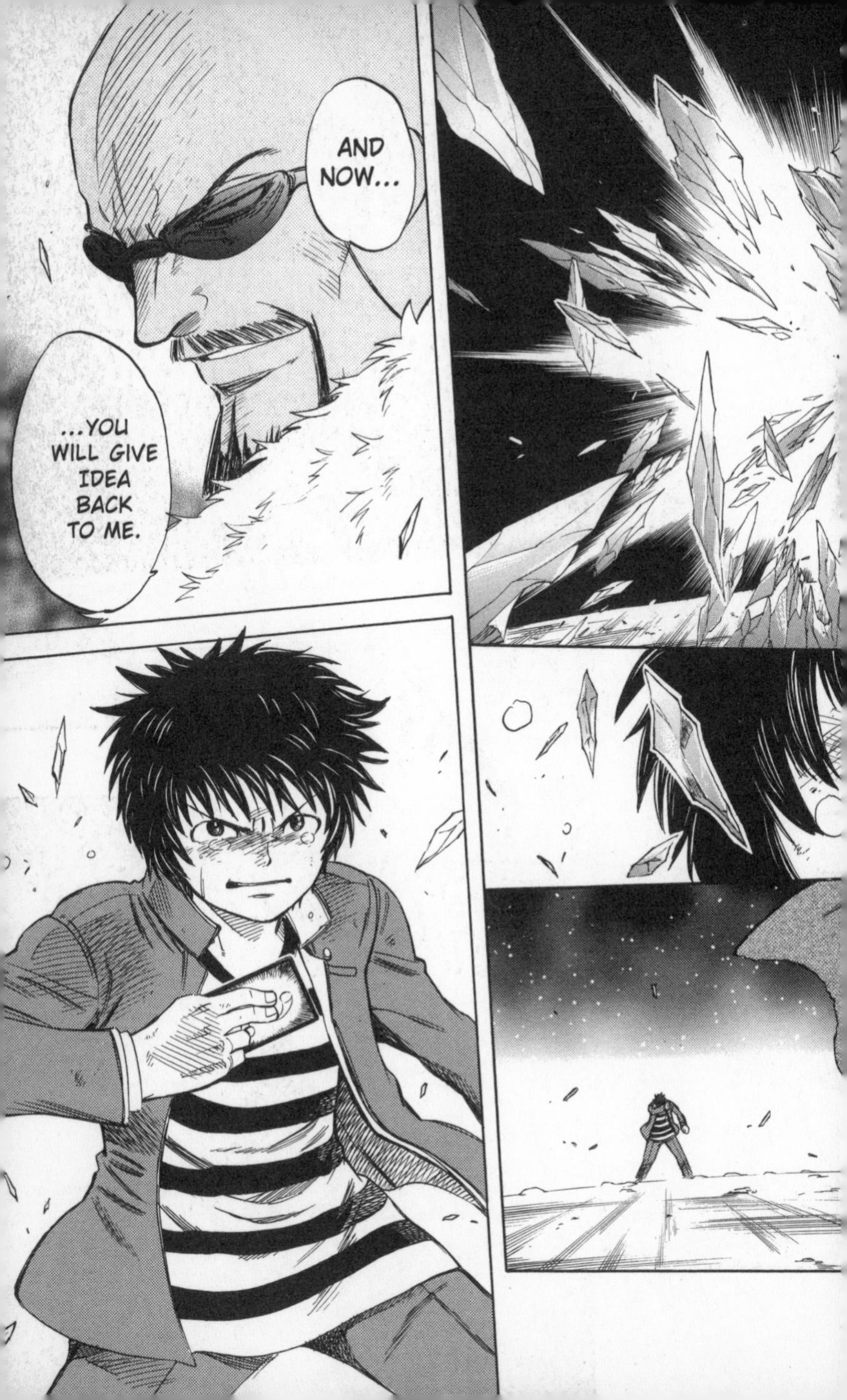
AND NOW...
...YOU WILL GIVE IDEA BACK TO ME.

BY NAGI

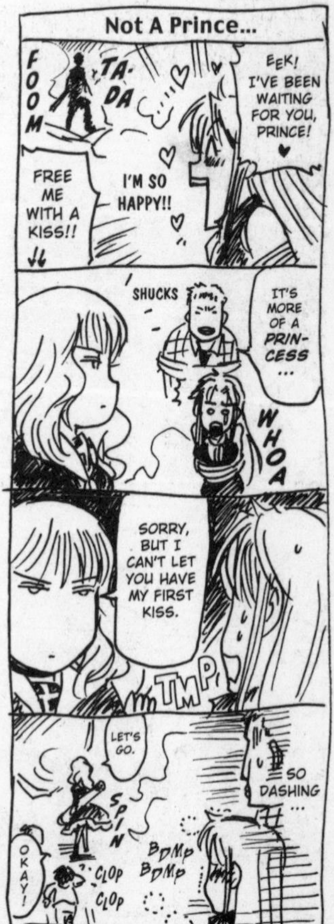
Not A Prince...
FOOM
TA-DA
EEK! I'VE BEEN WAITING FOR YOU, PRINCE!
I'M SO HAPPY!!
FREE ME WITH A KISS!!
IT'S MORE OF A PRINCESS...
WHOA
SHUCKS
SORRY, BUT I CAN'T LET YOU HAVE MY FIRST KISS.
TMP
SO DASHING...
BDMP BDMP
LET'S GO.
SPIN
CLOP CLOP
OKAY!

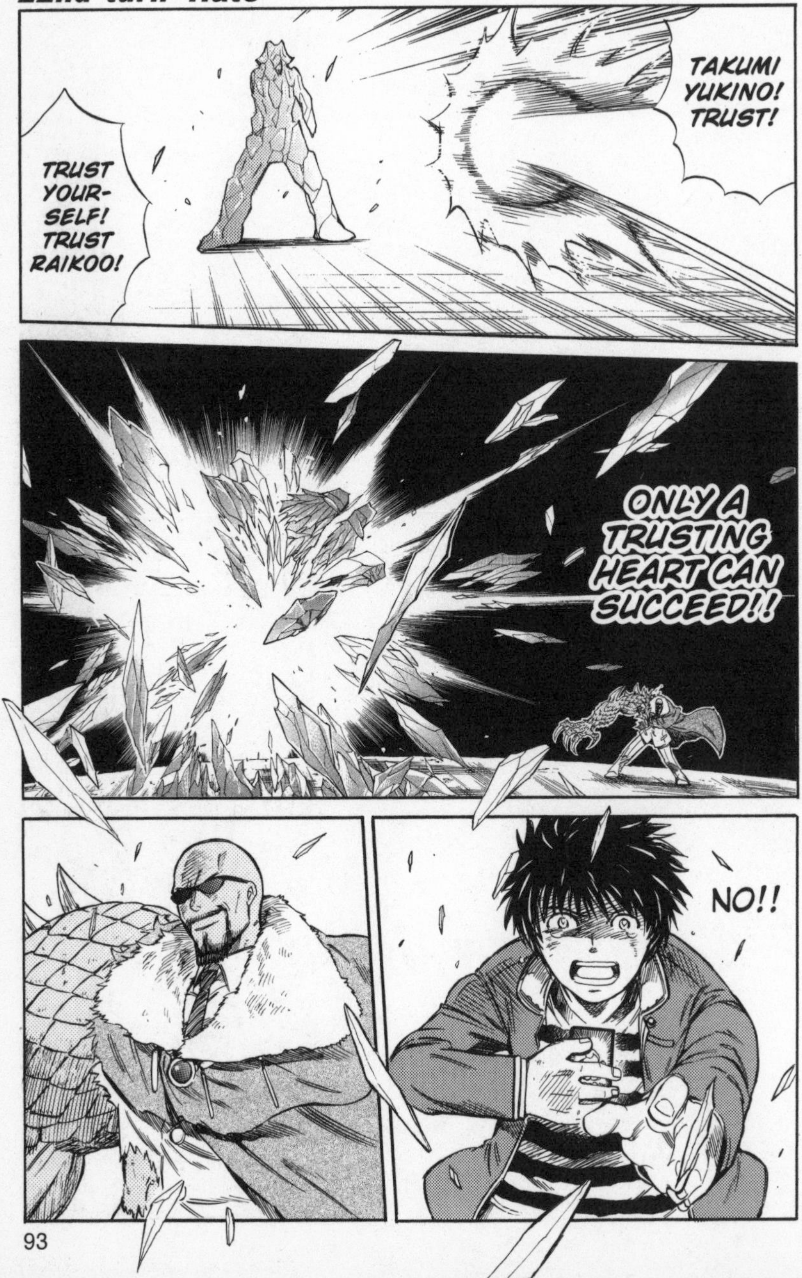
TAKUMI YUKINO! TRUST!
TRUST YOUR-SELF! TRUST RAIKOO!
ONLY A TRUSTING HEART CAN SUCCEED!!
NO!!

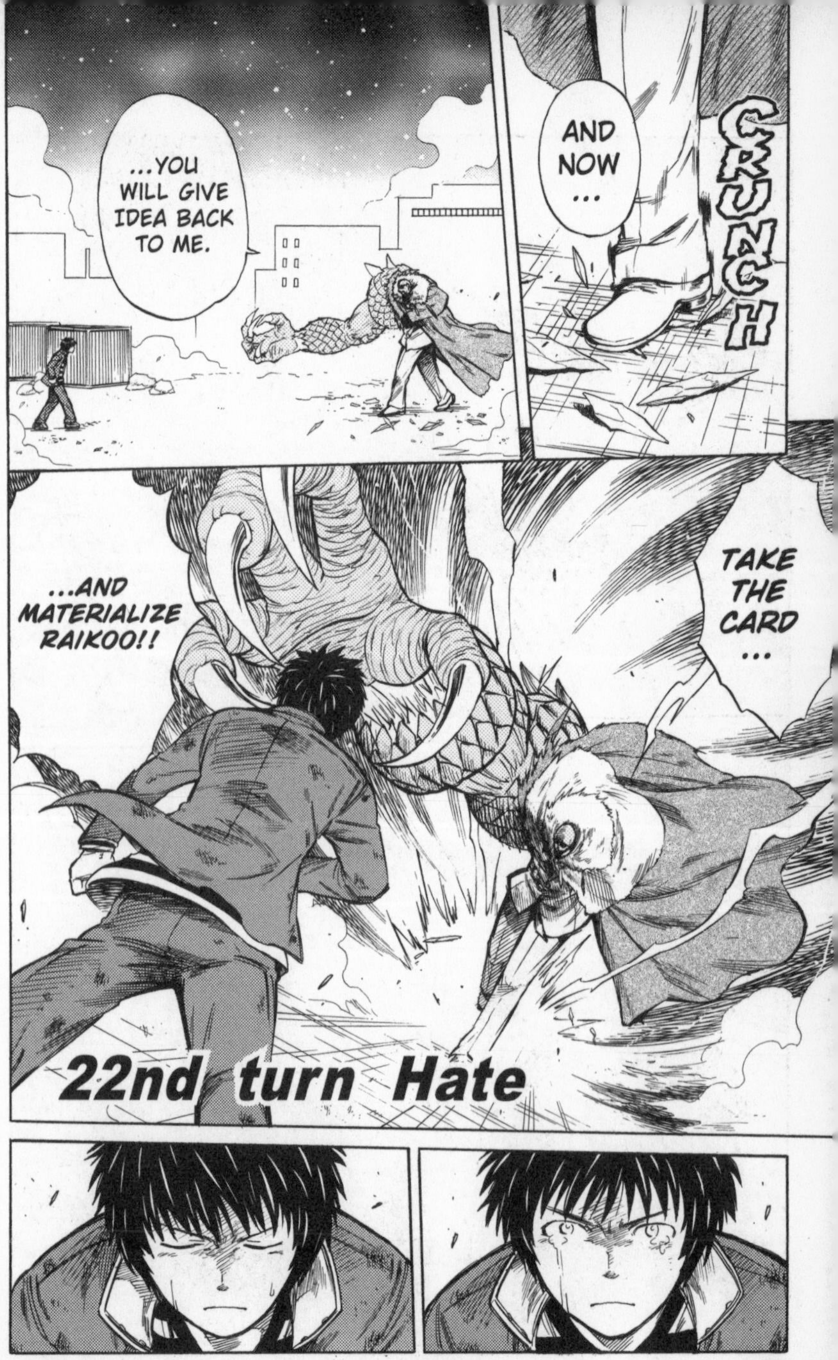
AND NOW ...
CRUNCH
...YOU WILL GIVE IDEA BACK TO ME.
TAKE THE CARD ...
...AND MATERIALIZE RAIKOO!!
22nd turn Hate

READ THIS WAY

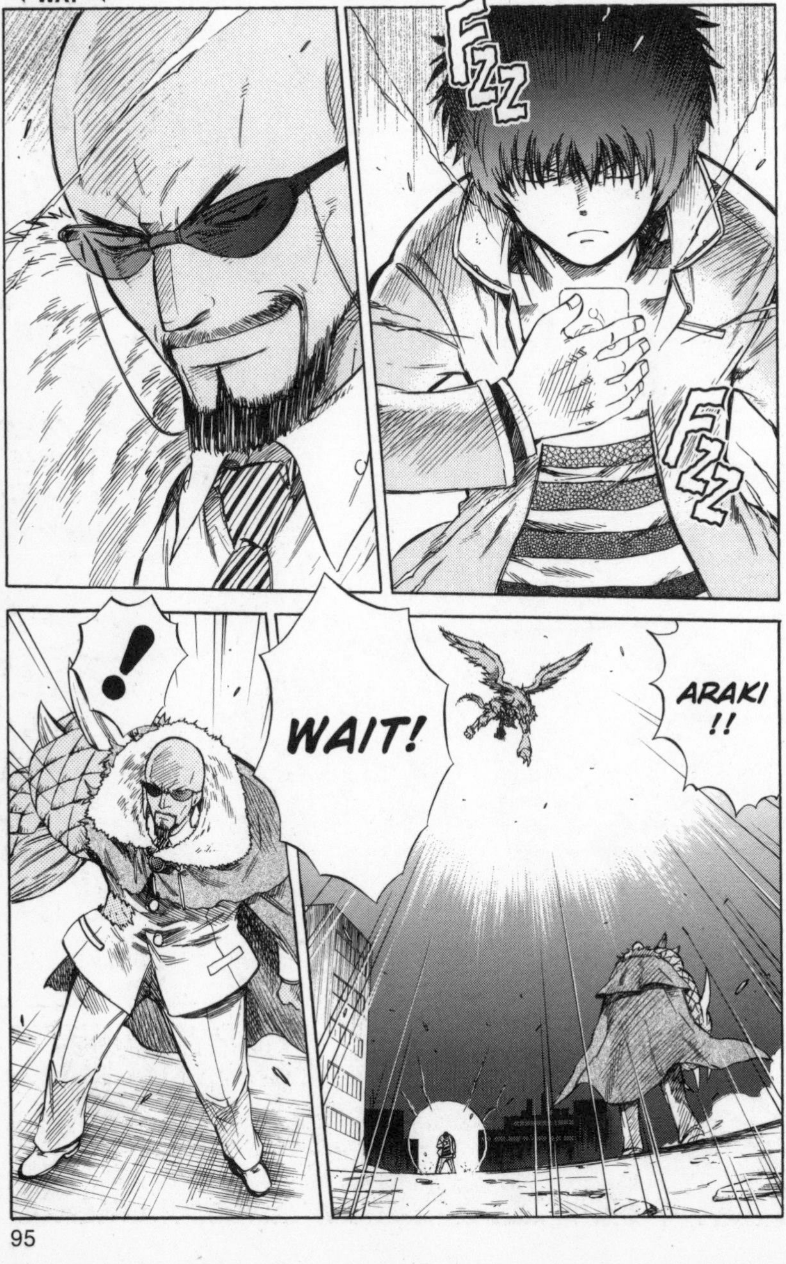
FZZ
FZZ
ARAKI !!
WAIT!
!

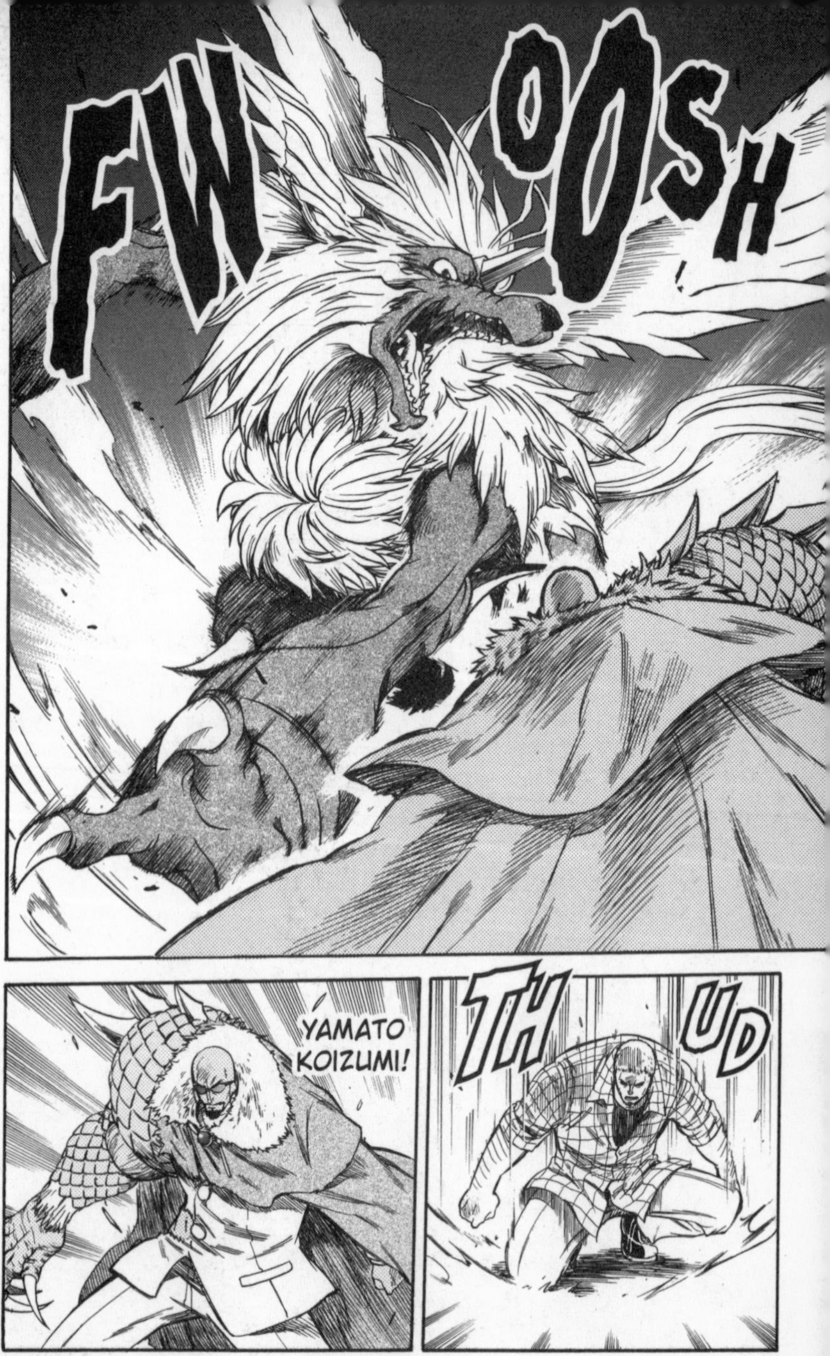
FWOOSH
THUD
YAMATO KOIZUMI!

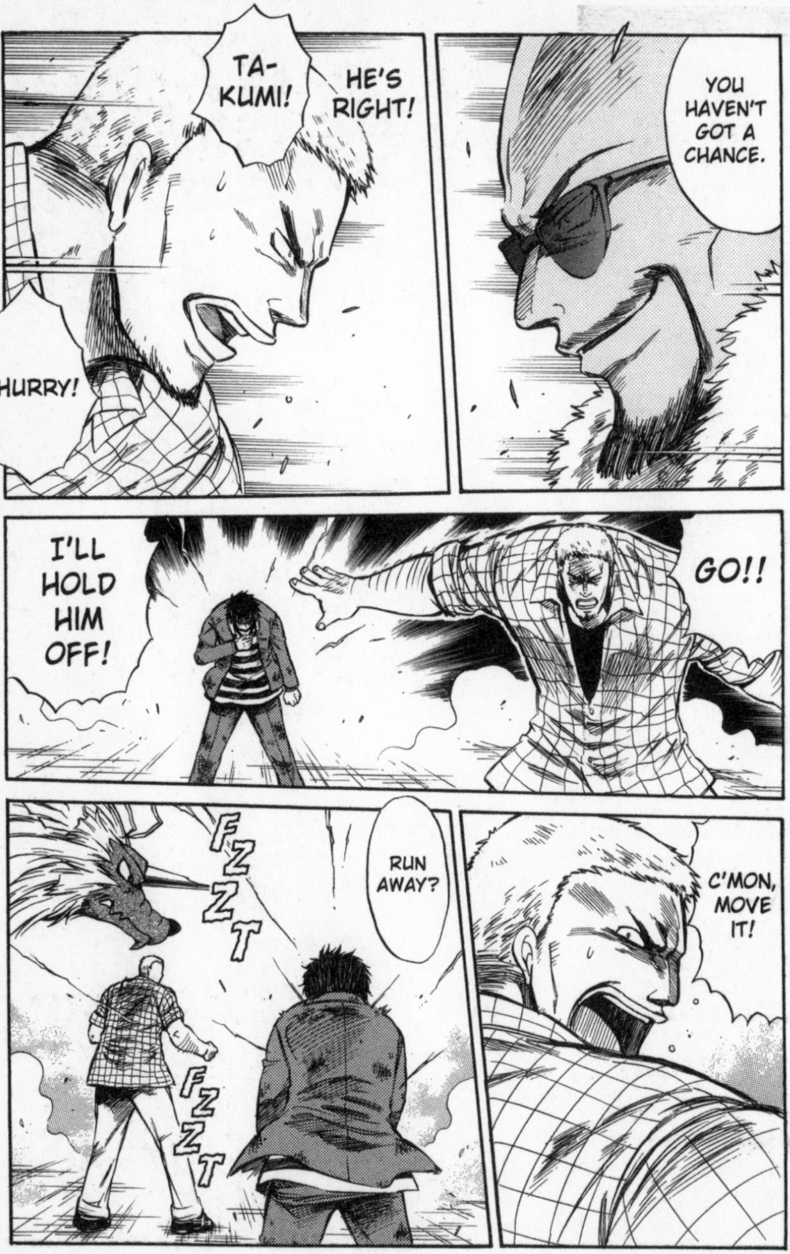
YOU HAVEN'T GOT A CHANCE.
TA-KUMI!
HE'S RIGHT!
HURRY!
GO!!
I'LL HOLD HIM OFF!
C'MON, MOVE IT!
RUN AWAY?
FZZT
FZZT

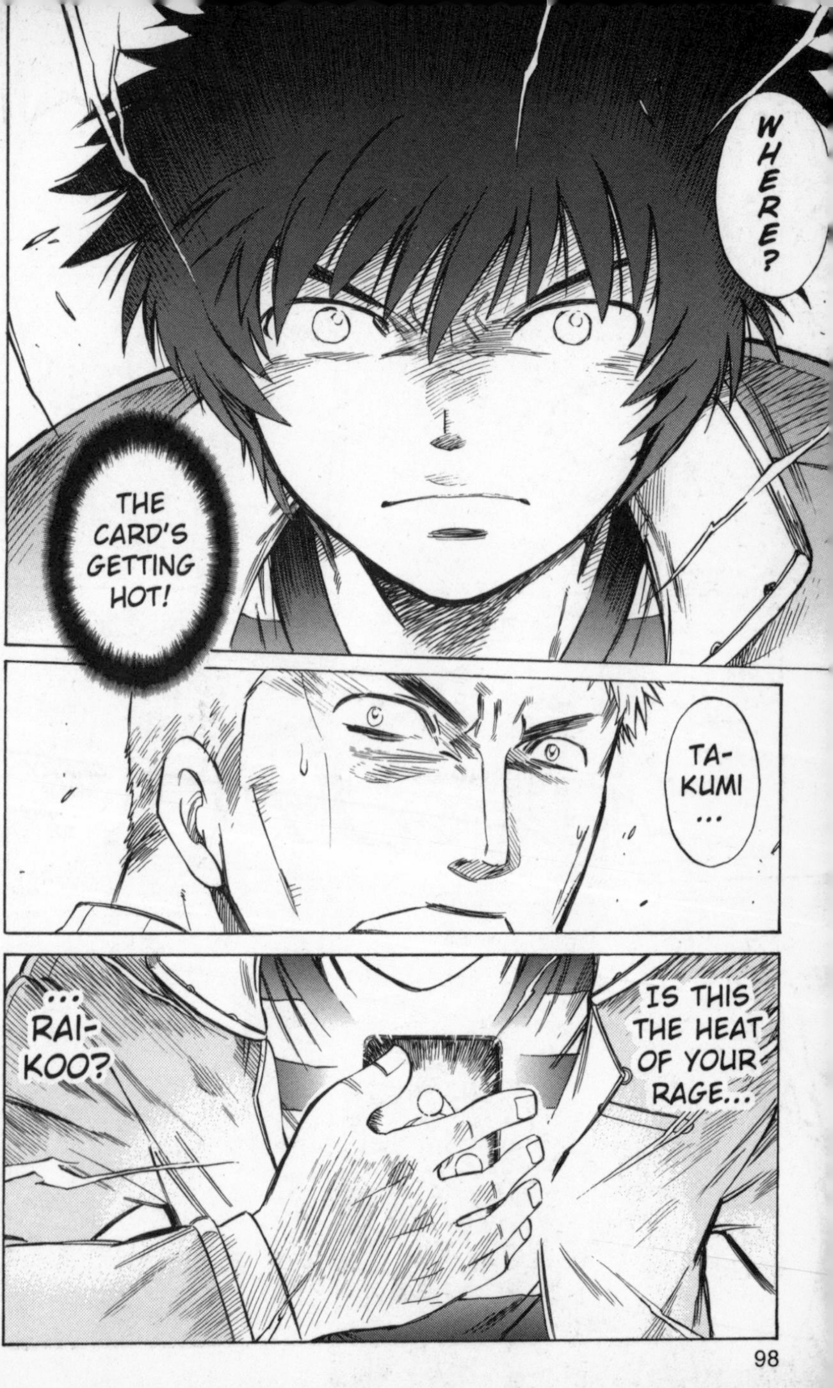
WHERE?
THE CARD'S GETTING HOT!
TA-KUMI ...
IS THIS THE HEAT OF YOUR RAGE...
... RAI-KOO?

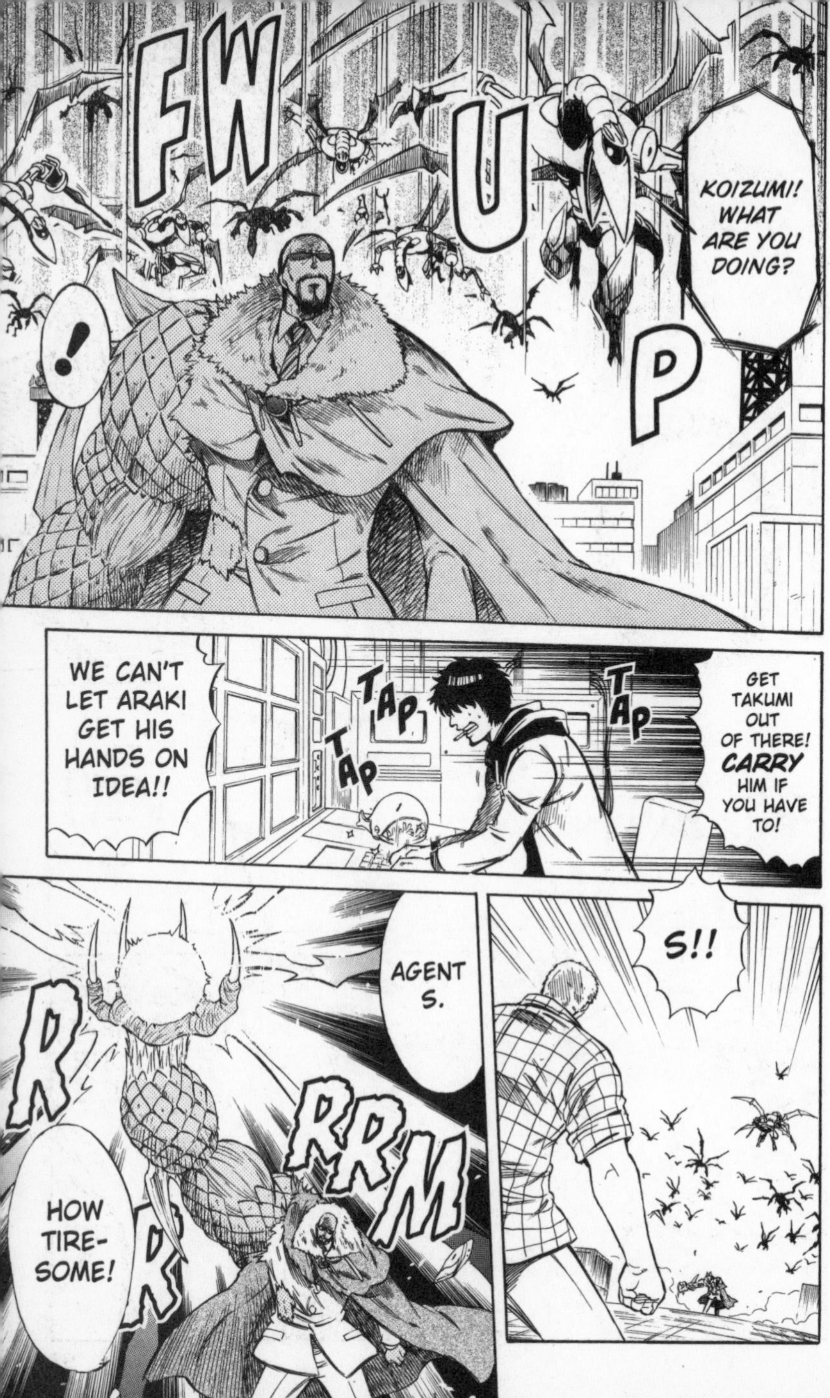
KOIZUMI! WHAT ARE YOU DOING?
FWUP
!
GET TAKUMI OUT OF THERE! **CARRY** HIM IF YOU HAVE TO!
TAP
TAP
TAP
WE CAN'T LET ARAKI GET HIS HANDS ON IDEA!!
S!!
AGENT S.
RRRRM
HOW TIRE-SOME!

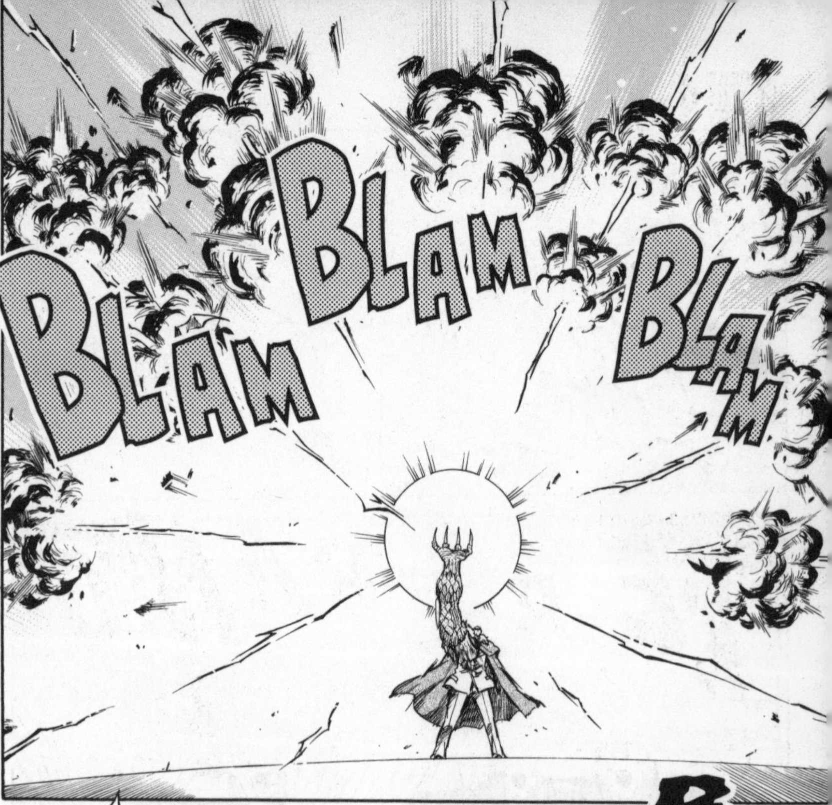
BLAM
BLAM
BLAM
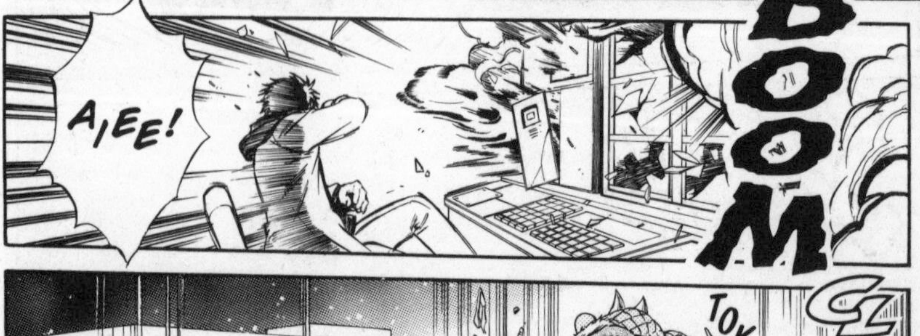
BOOM
AIEE!
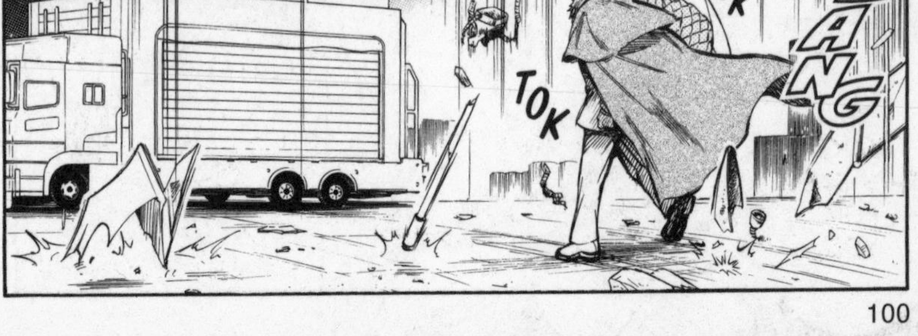
CLANG
TOK
TOK

READ THIS WAY

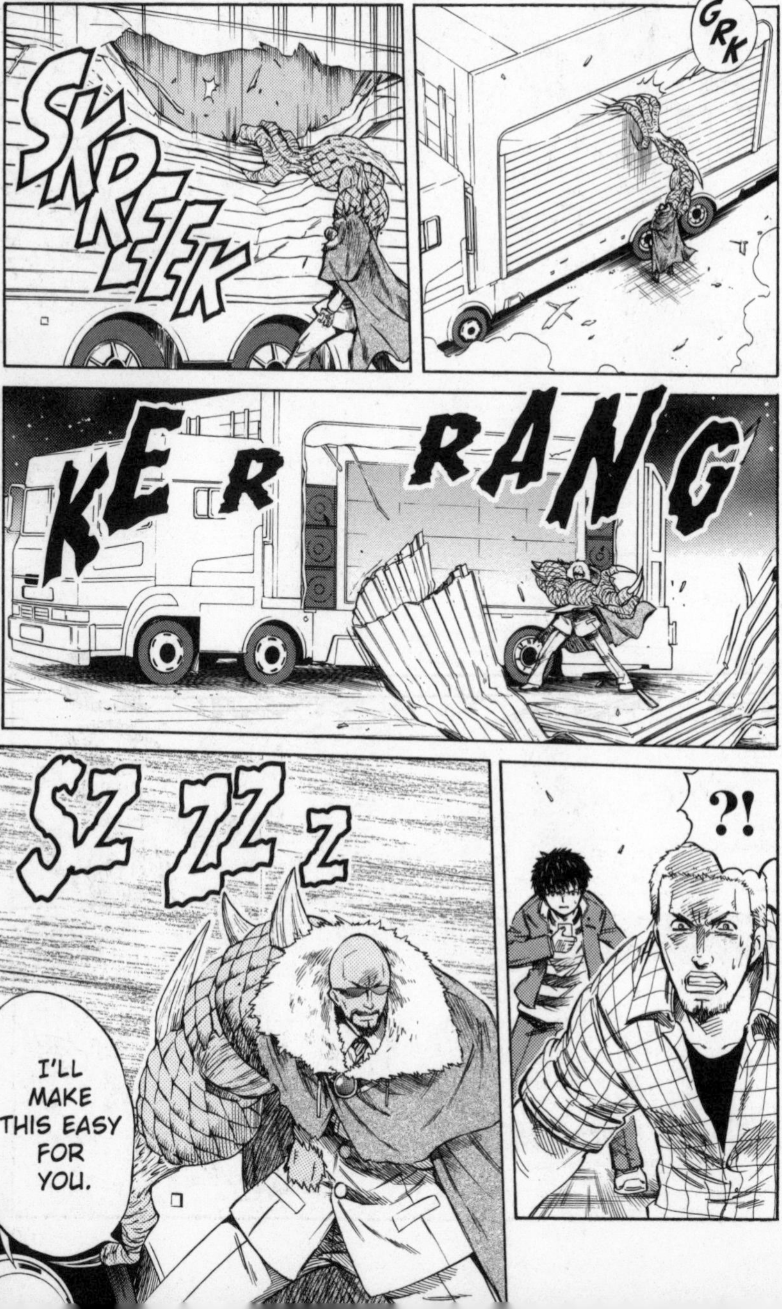
GRK
SKREEK
KERRANG
?!
SZZZZ
I'LL MAKE THIS EASY FOR YOU.

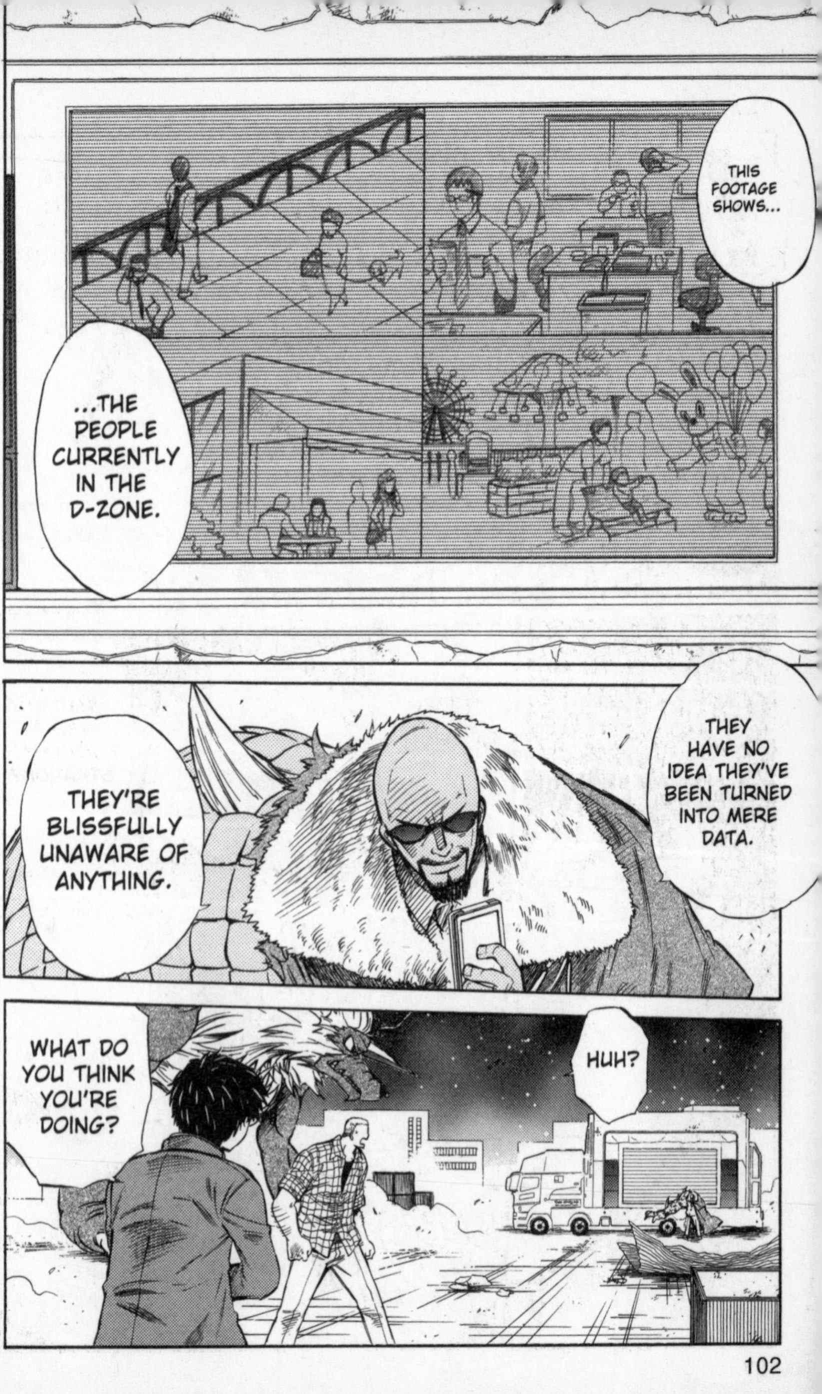
THIS FOOTAGE SHOWS...
...THE PEOPLE CURRENTLY IN THE D-ZONE.
THEY HAVE NO IDEA THEY'VE BEEN TURNED INTO MERE DATA.
THEY'RE BLISSFULLY UNAWARE OF ANYTHING.
HUH?
WHAT DO YOU THINK YOU'RE DOING?

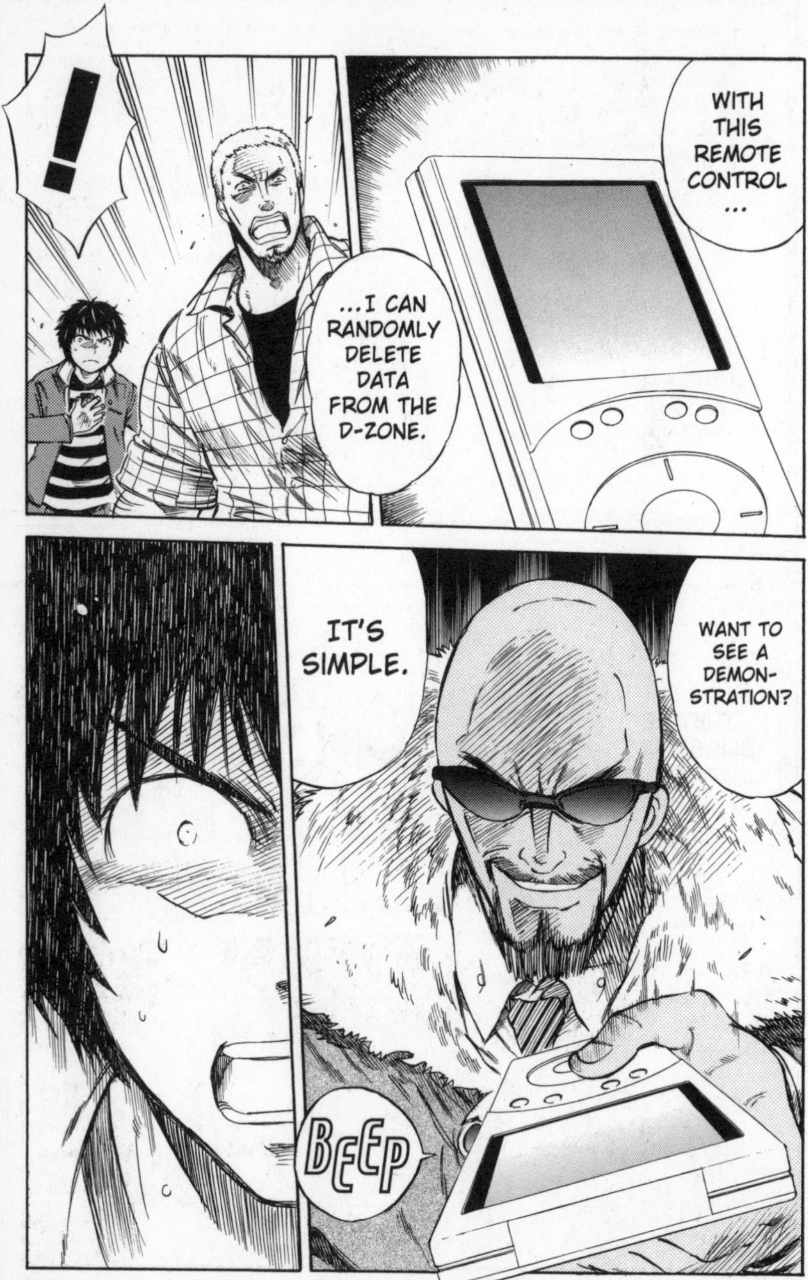
WITH THIS REMOTE CONTROL ...
...I CAN RANDOMLY DELETE DATA FROM THE D-ZONE.
!
WANT TO SEE A DEMON-STRATION?
IT'S SIMPLE.
BEEP

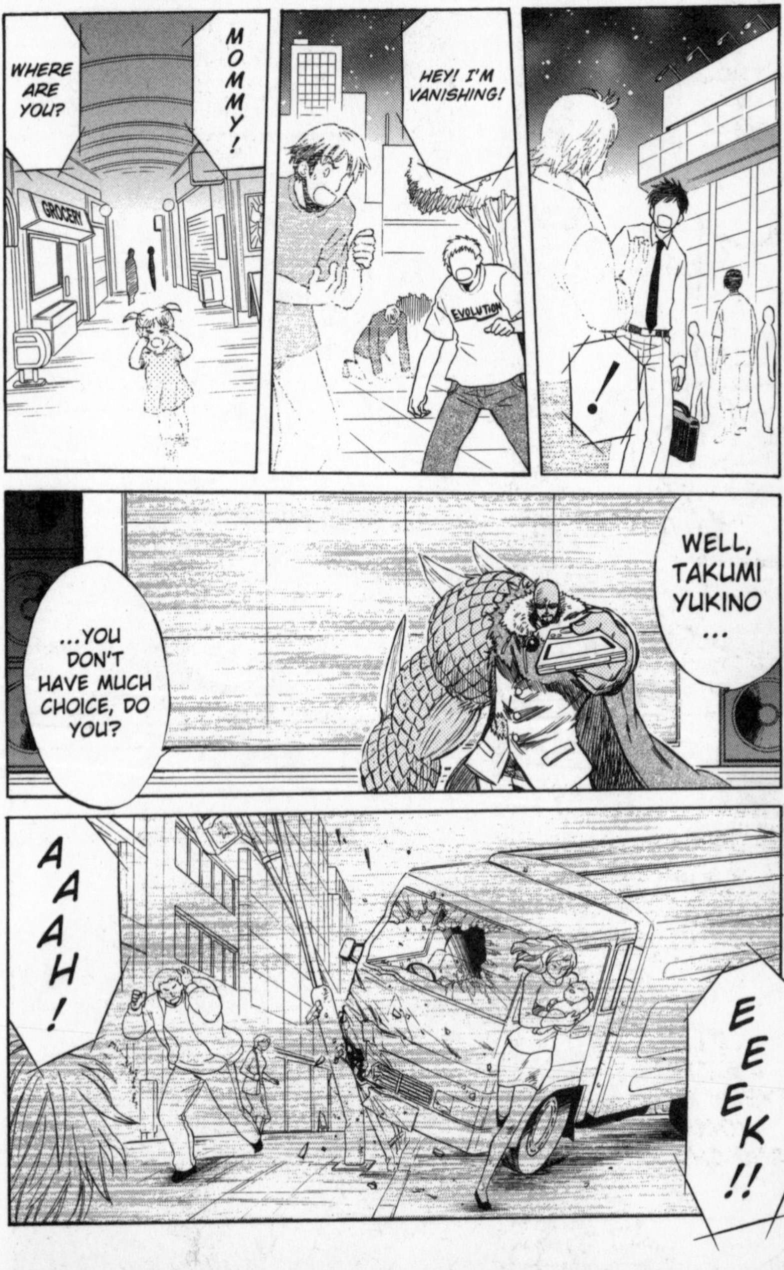
!
HEY! I'M VANISHING!
MOMMY!
WHERE ARE YOU?
GROCERY
EVOLUTION
WELL, TAKUMI YUKINO ...
...YOU DON'T HAVE MUCH CHOICE, DO YOU?
EEEK!!
AAAH!

READ THIS WAY

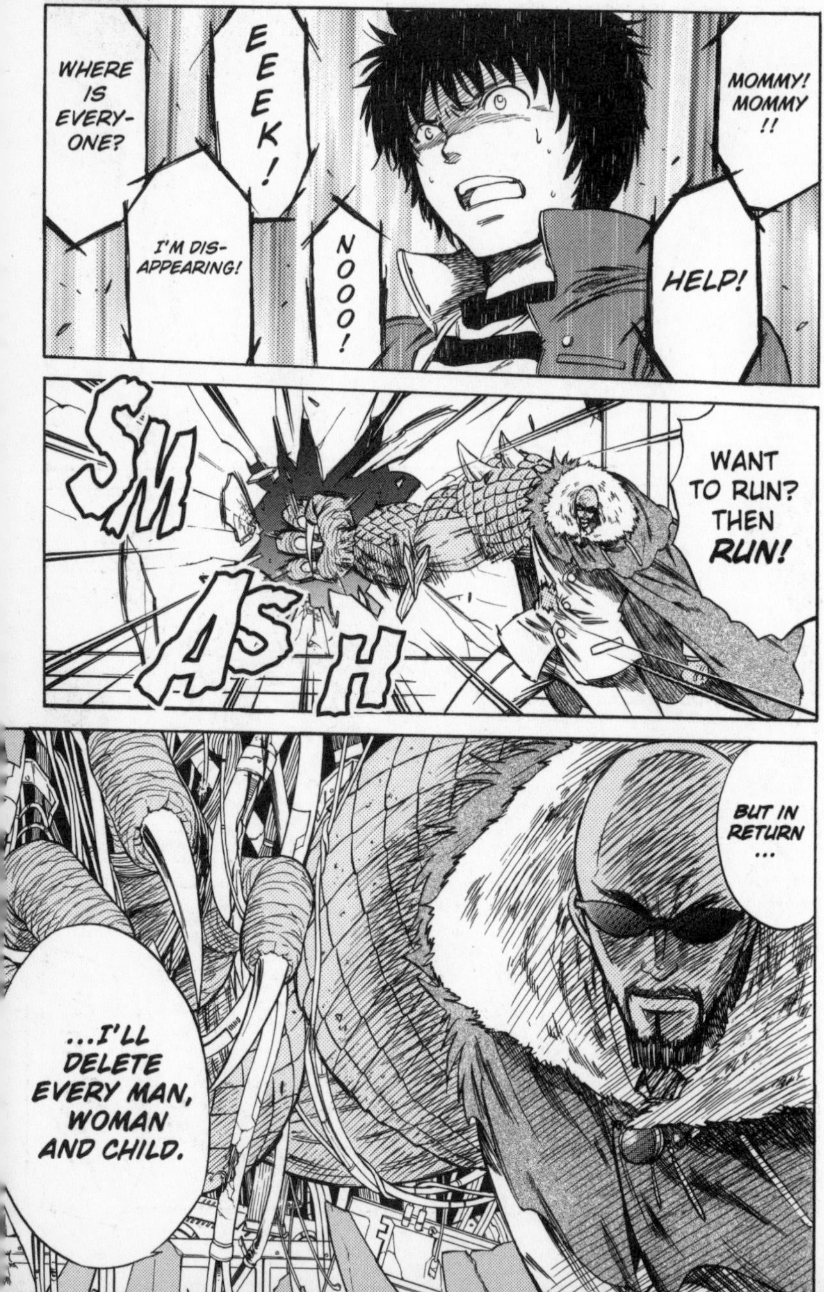
MOMMY! MOMMY!!
HELP!
EEEK!
NOOOO!
WHERE IS EVERY-ONE?
I'M DIS-APPEARING!
WANT TO RUN? THEN RUN!
SMASH
BUT IN RETURN...
...I'LL DELETE EVERY MAN, WOMAN AND CHILD.

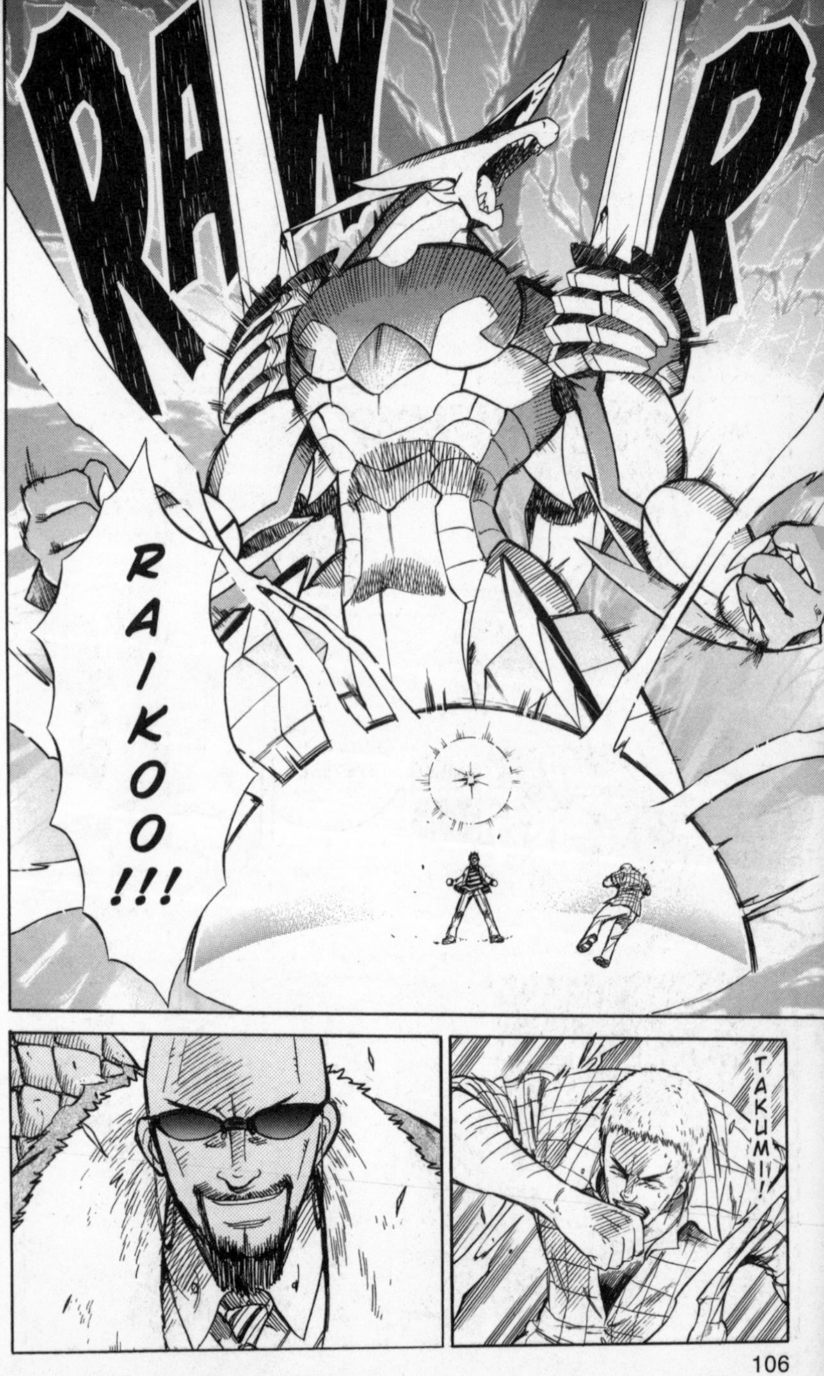
RAWR
RAIKOO!!!
TAKUMI!!

READ THIS WAY

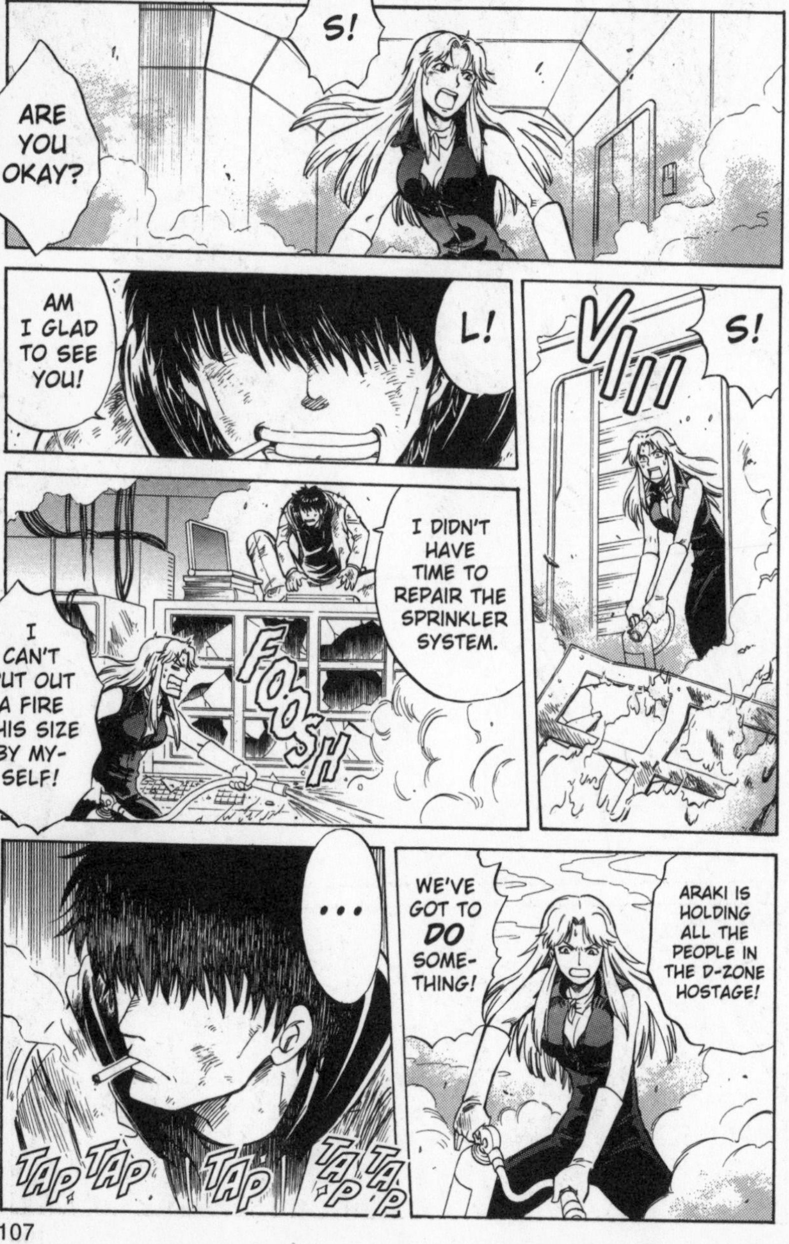
S!
ARE YOU OKAY?
VIII
S!
L!
AM I GLAD TO SEE YOU!
I DIDN'T HAVE TIME TO REPAIR THE SPRINKLER SYSTEM.
FOOSH
I CAN'T PUT OUT A FIRE THIS SIZE BY MY-SELF!
ARAKI IS HOLDING ALL THE PEOPLE IN THE D-ZONE HOSTAGE!
WE'VE GOT TO DO SOMETHING!
...
TAP TAP TAP TAP TAP

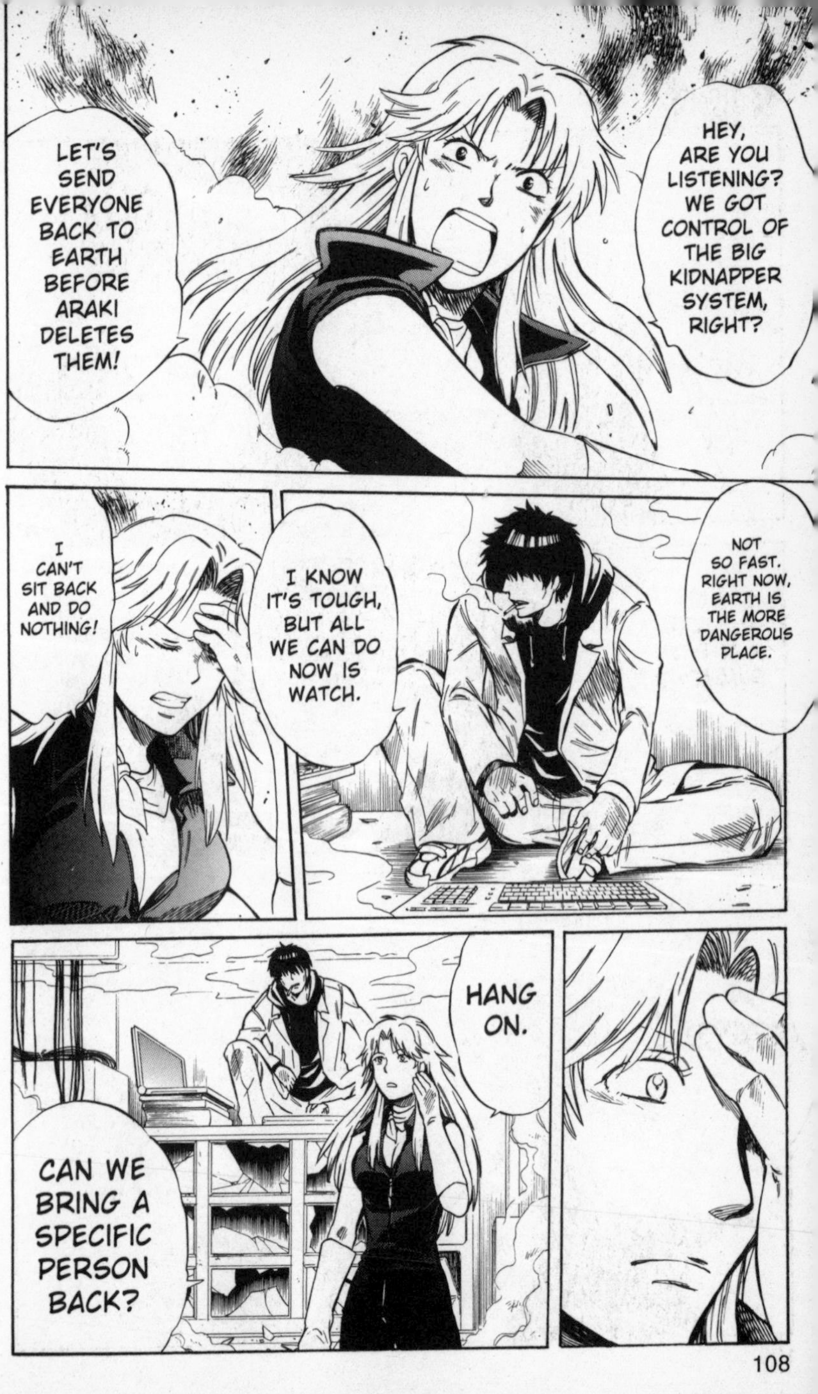
HEY, ARE YOU LISTENING? WE GOT CONTROL OF THE BIG KIDNAPPER SYSTEM, RIGHT?
LET'S SEND EVERYONE BACK TO EARTH BEFORE ARAKI DELETES THEM!
NOT SO FAST. RIGHT NOW, EARTH IS THE MORE DANGEROUS PLACE.
I KNOW IT'S TOUGH, BUT ALL WE CAN DO NOW IS WATCH.
I CAN'T SIT BACK AND DO NOTHING!
HANG ON.
CAN WE BRING A SPECIFIC PERSON BACK?

READ THIS WAY

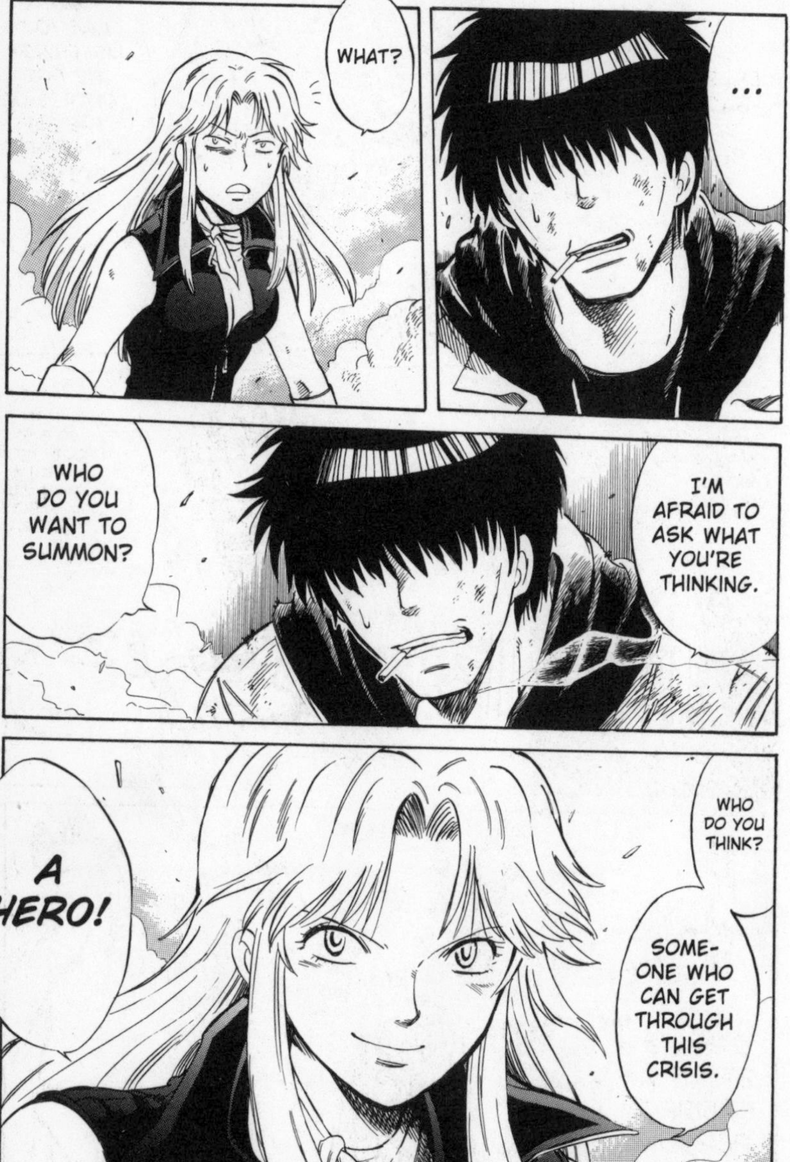

...
WHAT?
I'M AFRAID TO ASK WHAT YOU'RE THINKING.
WHO DO YOU WANT TO SUMMON?
WHO DO YOU THINK?
SOME-ONE WHO CAN GET THROUGH THIS CRISIS.
A HERO!

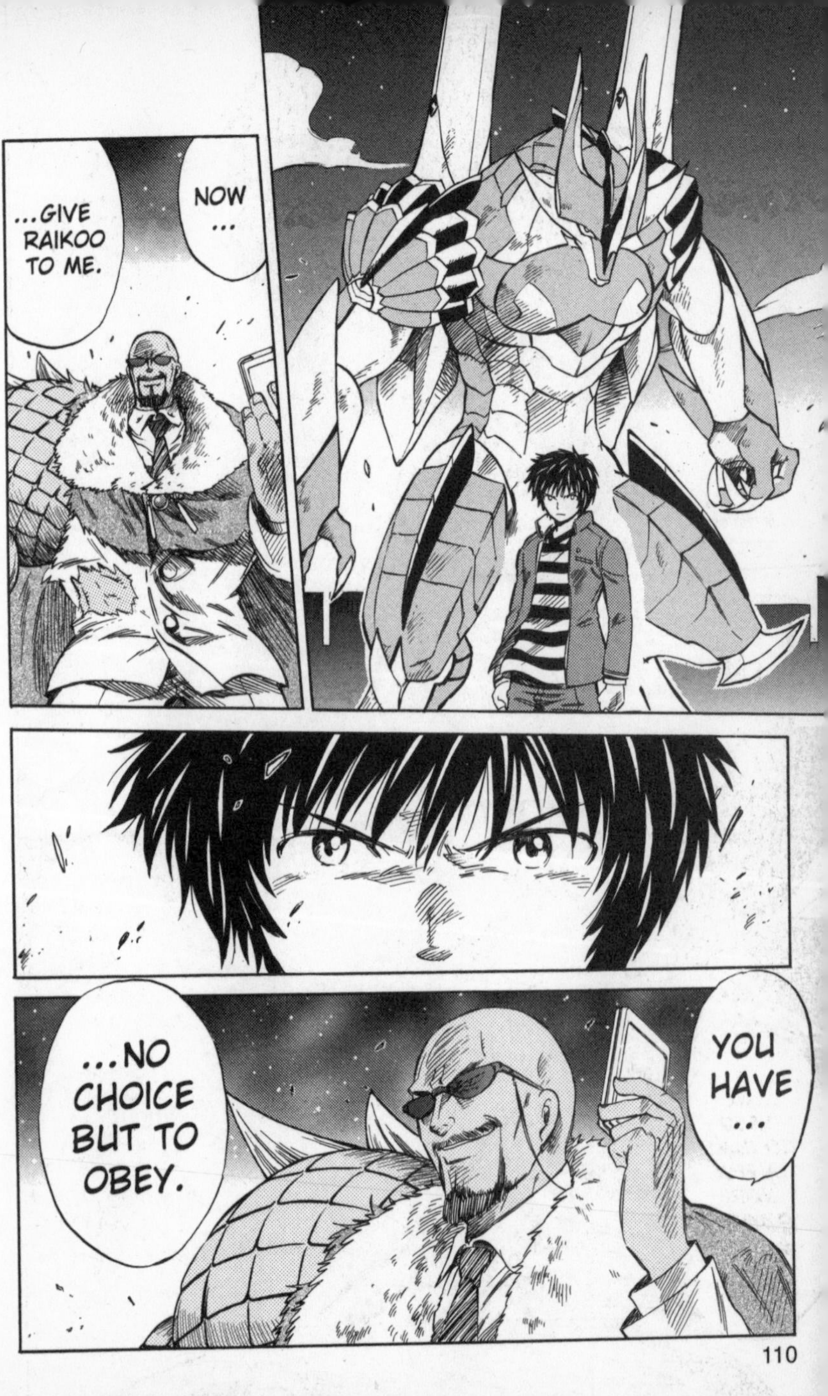
NOW ...
...GIVE RAIKOO TO ME.
YOU HAVE ...
...NO CHOICE BUT TO OBEY.

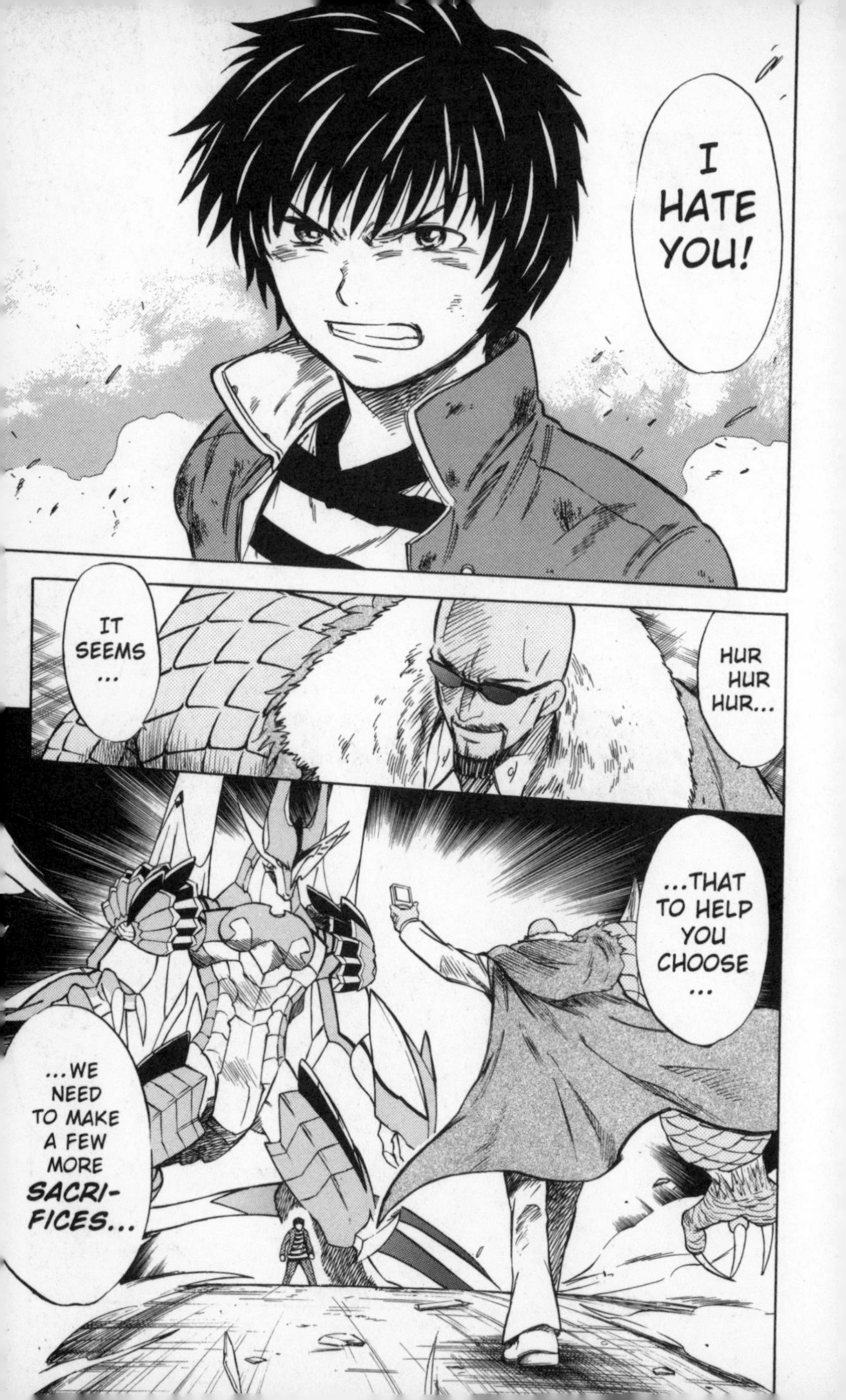
I HATE YOU!
HUR HUR HUR...
IT SEEMS ...
...THAT TO HELP YOU CHOOSE ...
...WE NEED TO MAKE A FEW MORE SACRI-FICES...

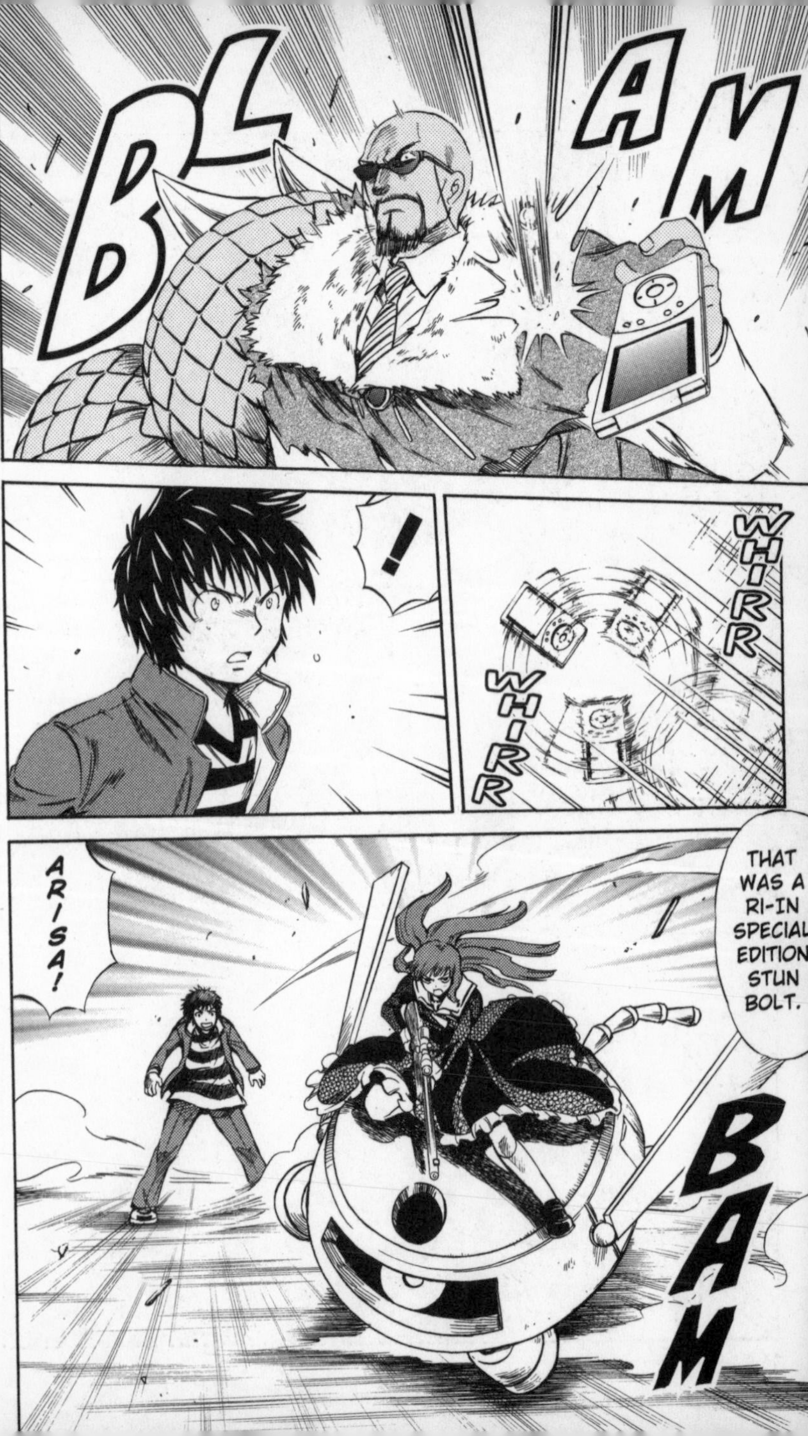
BLAM
WHIRR
WHIRR
!
THAT WAS A RI-IN SPECIAL EDITION STUN BOLT.
BAM
ARISA!

READ THIS WAY

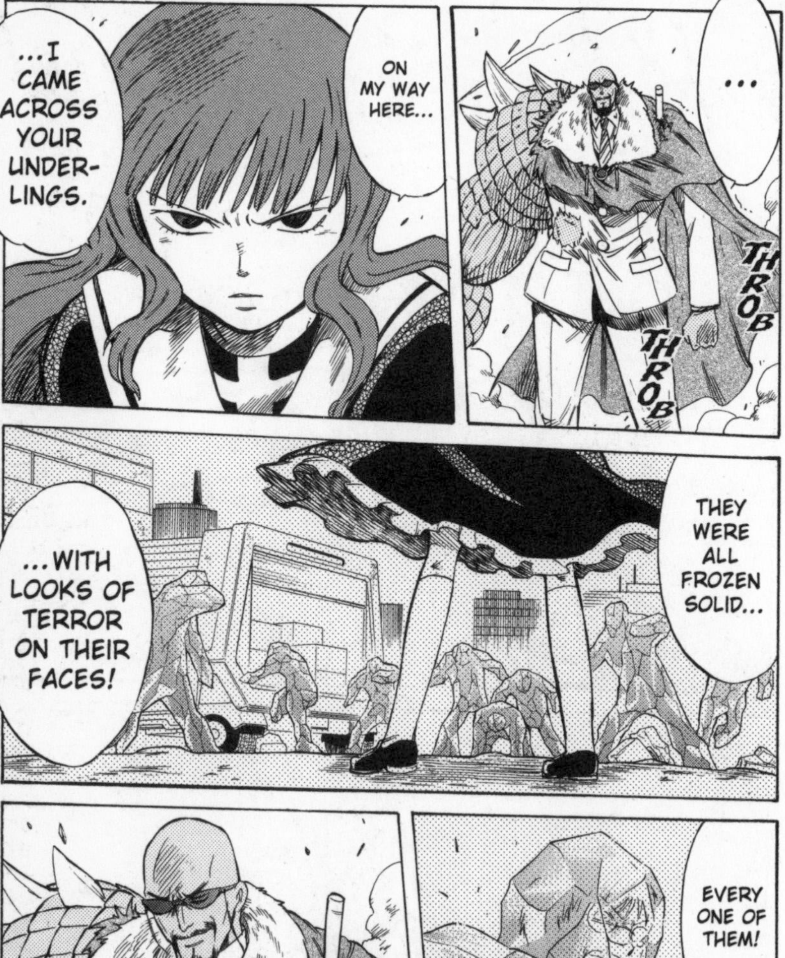
...
THROB THROB
ON MY WAY HERE...
...I CAME ACROSS YOUR UNDER-LINGS.
THEY WERE ALL FROZEN SOLID...
...WITH LOOKS OF TERROR ON THEIR FACES!
EVERY ONE OF THEM!

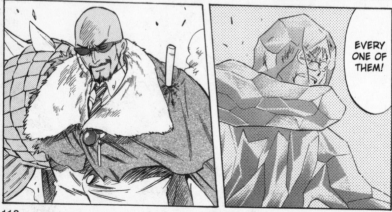

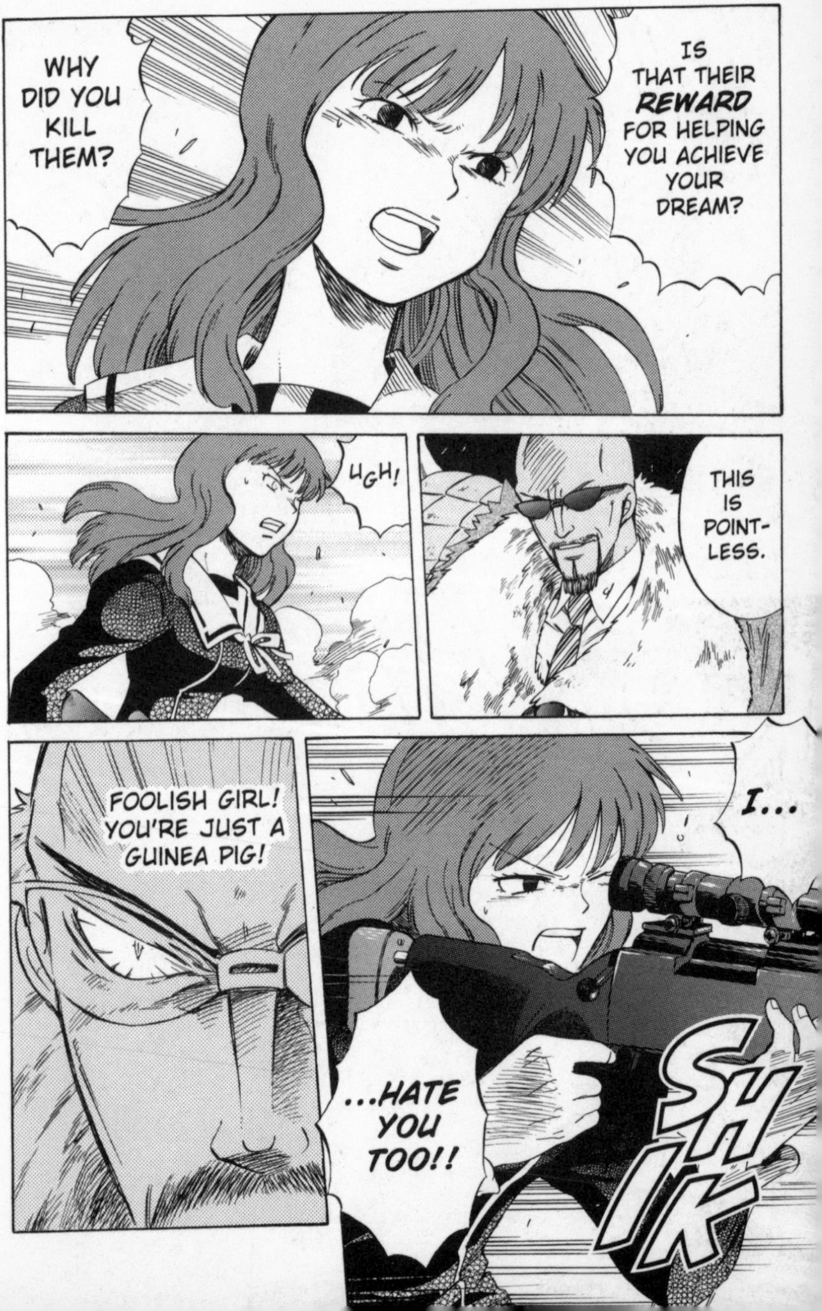
IS THAT THEIR REWARD FOR HELPING YOU ACHIEVE YOUR DREAM?
WHY DID YOU KILL THEM?
THIS IS POINTLESS.
UGH!
I...
...HATE YOU TOO!!
SHIK
FOOLISH GIRL! YOU'RE JUST A GUINEA PIG!

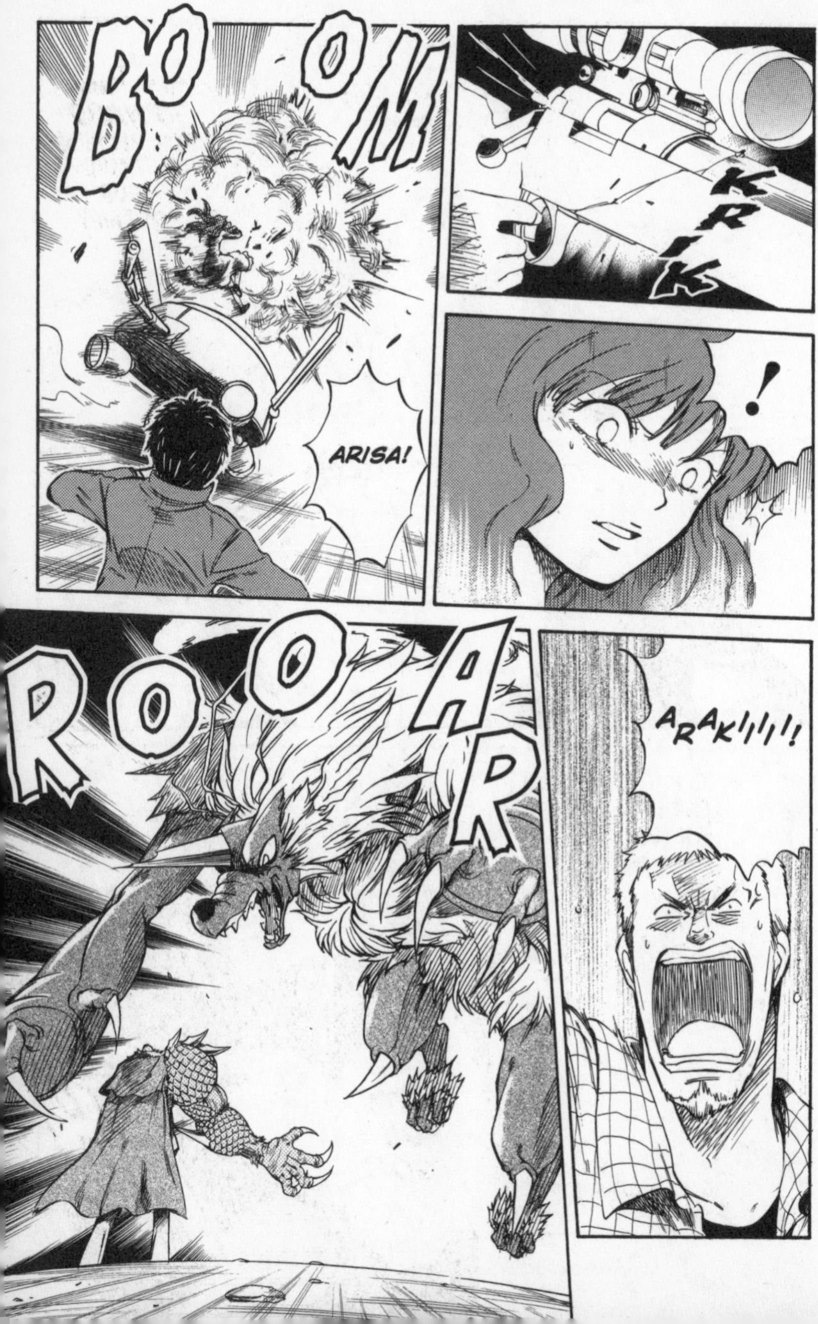
KRIK
!
BOOM
ARISA!
ARAKIIIII!
ROOAR

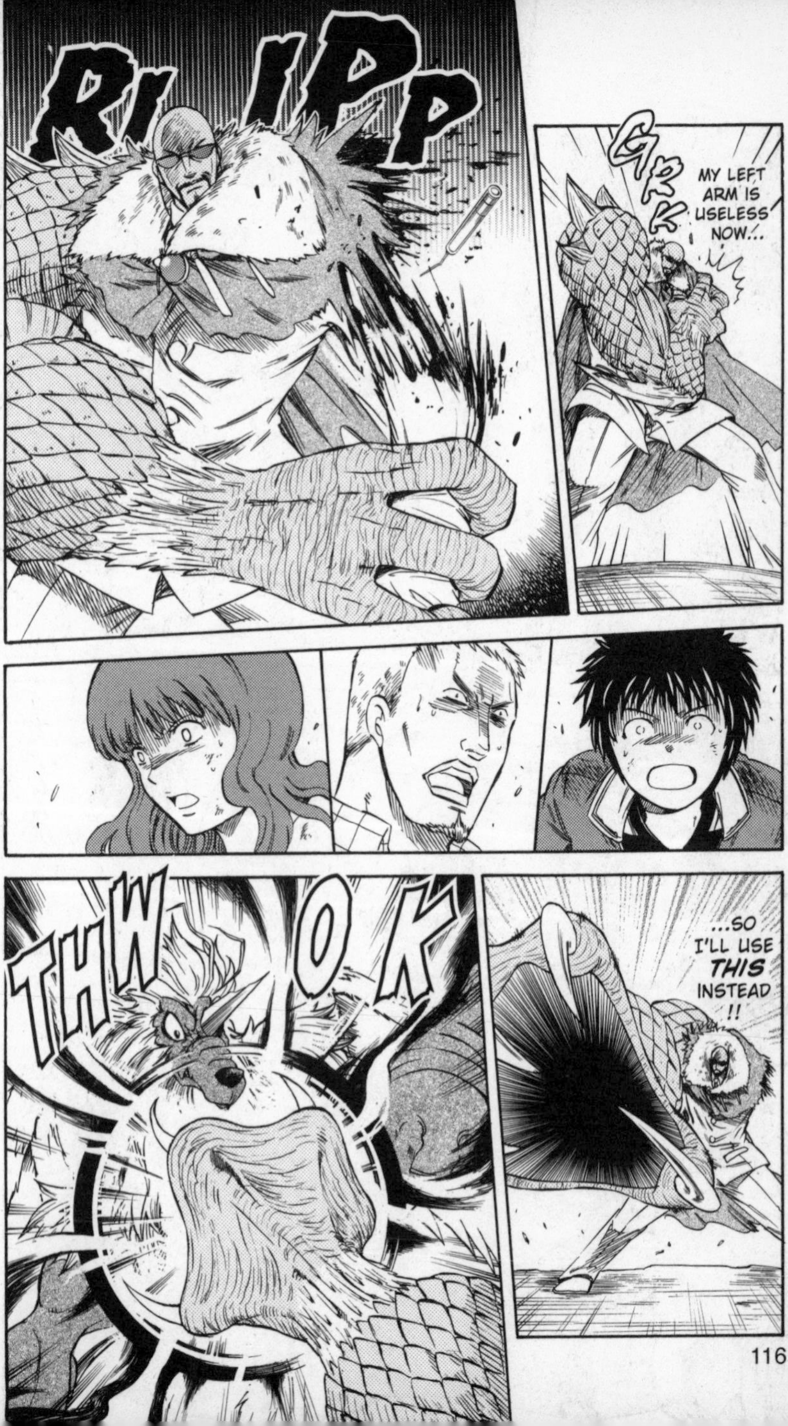
GRK
MY LEFT ARM IS USELESS NOW...
RIIPP
...SO I'LL USE THIS INSTEAD!!
THWOK

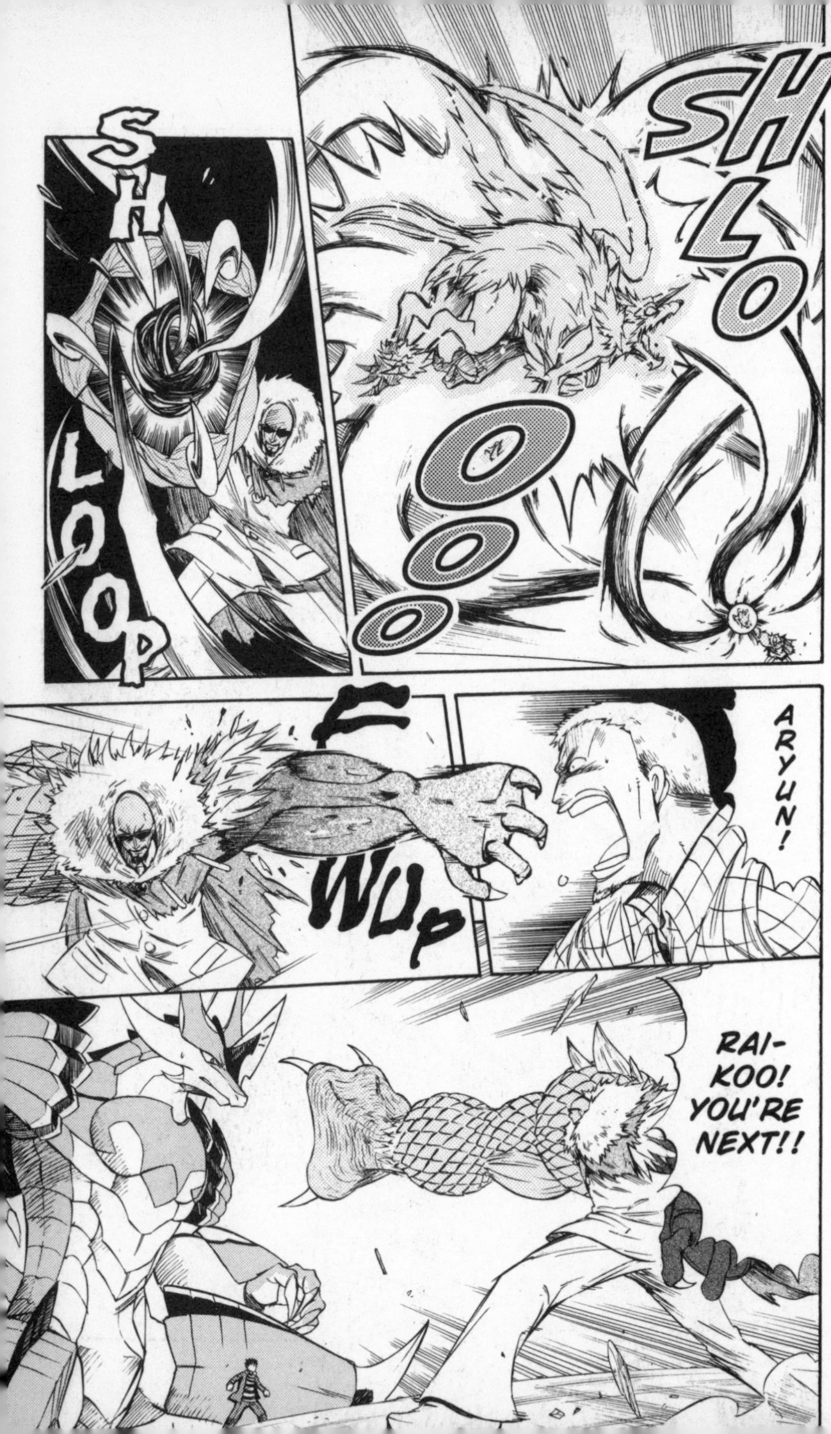
SHLOOOOO
SHLOOP
ARYUN!
FWUP
RAI-KOO! YOU'RE NEXT!!

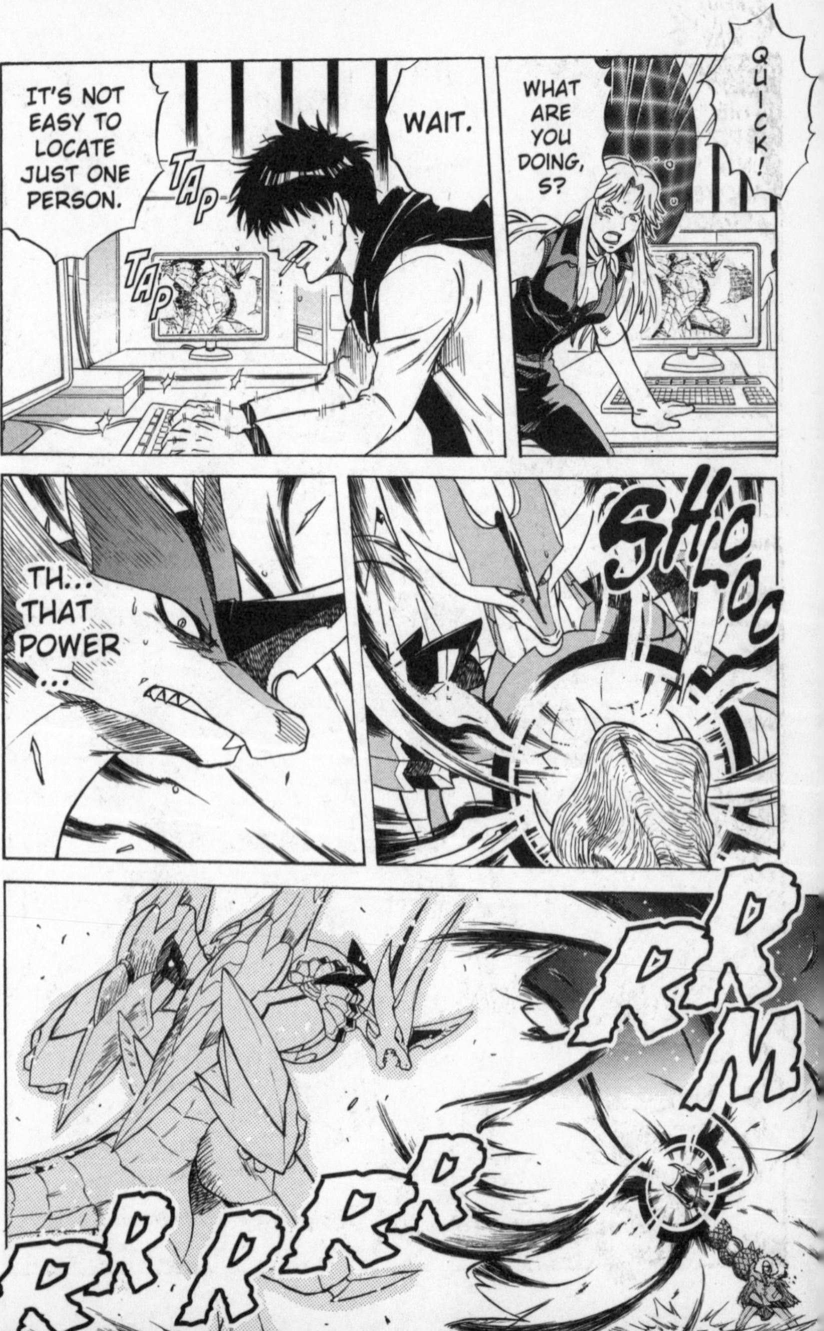
QUICK!
WHAT ARE YOU DOING, S?
WAIT.
IT'S NOT EASY TO LOCATE JUST ONE PERSON.
TAP
TAP
SHLOOO
TH... THAT POWER...
RRRRRRM

READ THIS WAY

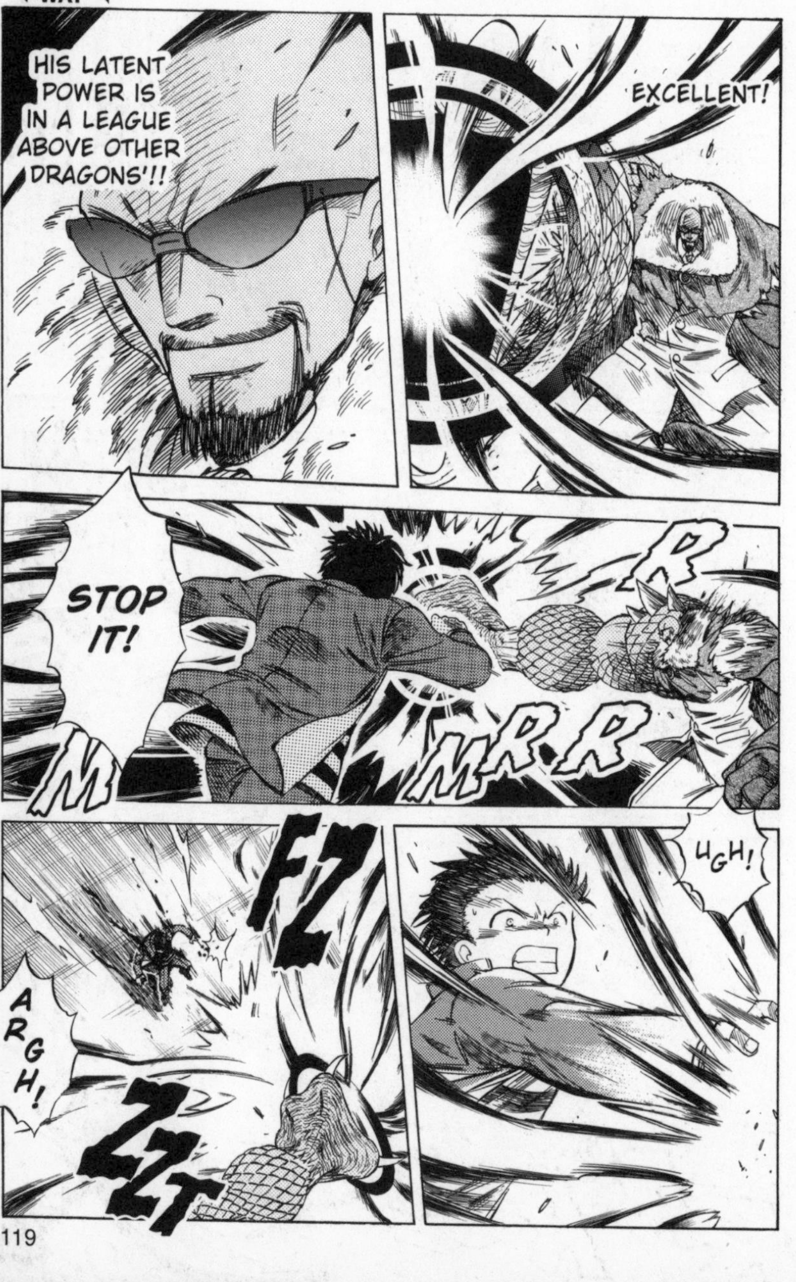
EXCELLENT!
HIS LATENT POWER IS IN A LEAGUE ABOVE OTHER DRAGONS'!!
STOP IT!
R
M
MRR
UGH!
FZ
ARGH!
ZZT

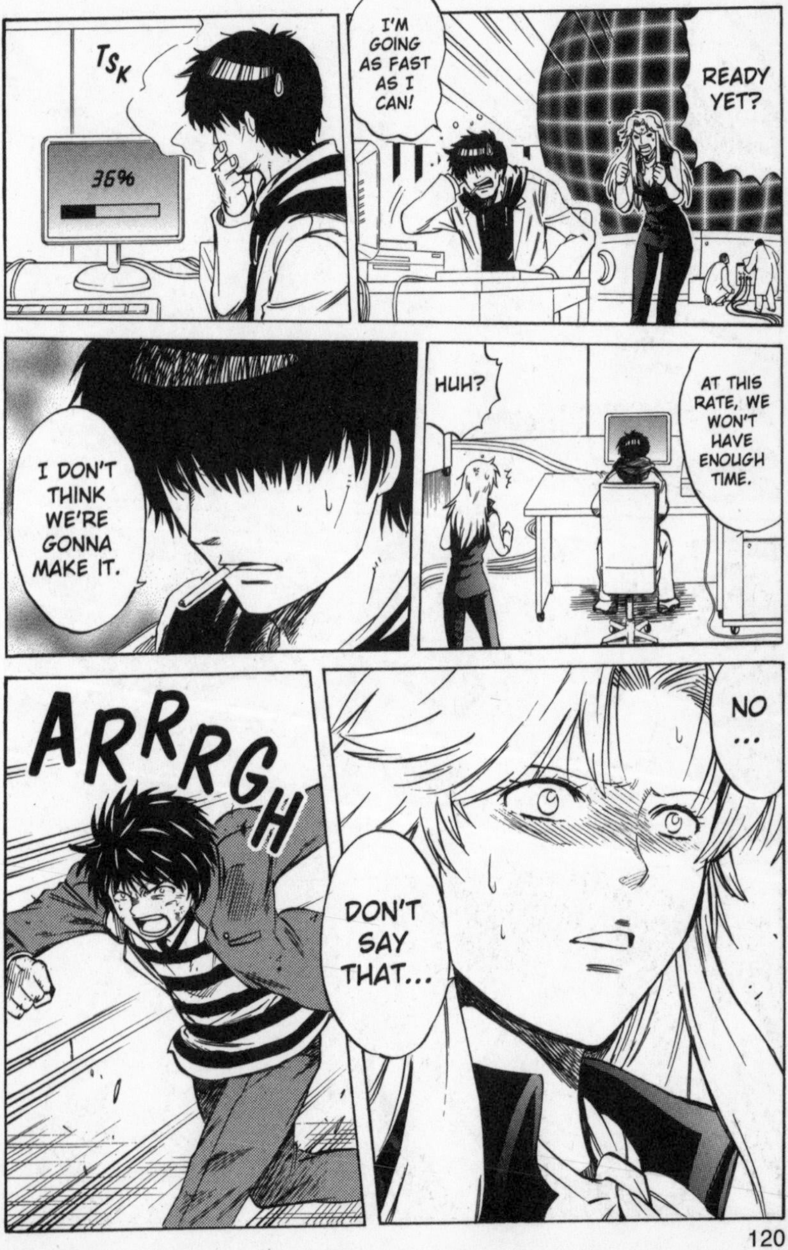
READY YET?
I'M GOING AS FAST AS I CAN!
TSK
36%
AT THIS RATE, WE WON'T HAVE ENOUGH TIME.
HUH?
I DON'T THINK WE'RE GONNA MAKE IT.
NO ...
DON'T SAY THAT...
ARRRGH

READ THIS WAY

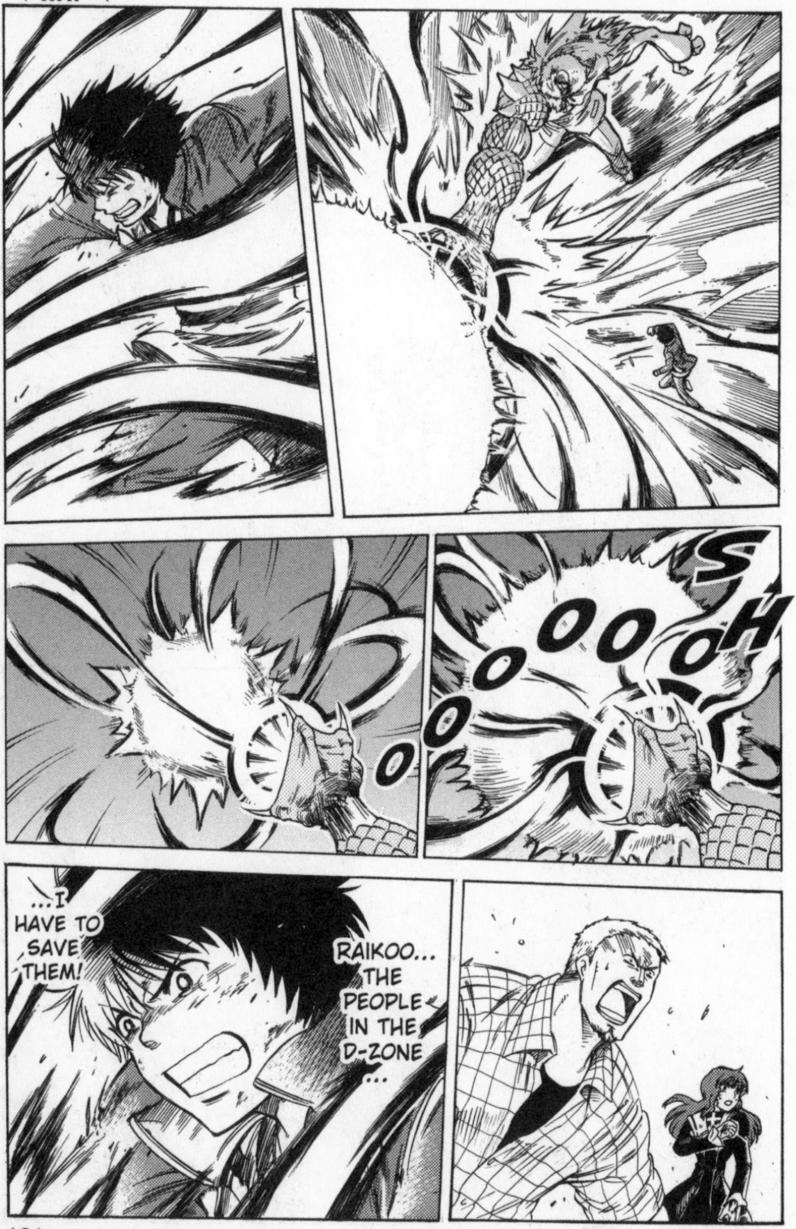
SHOOOOOOO
RAIKOO... THE PEOPLE IN THE D-ZONE...
...I HAVE TO SAVE THEM!

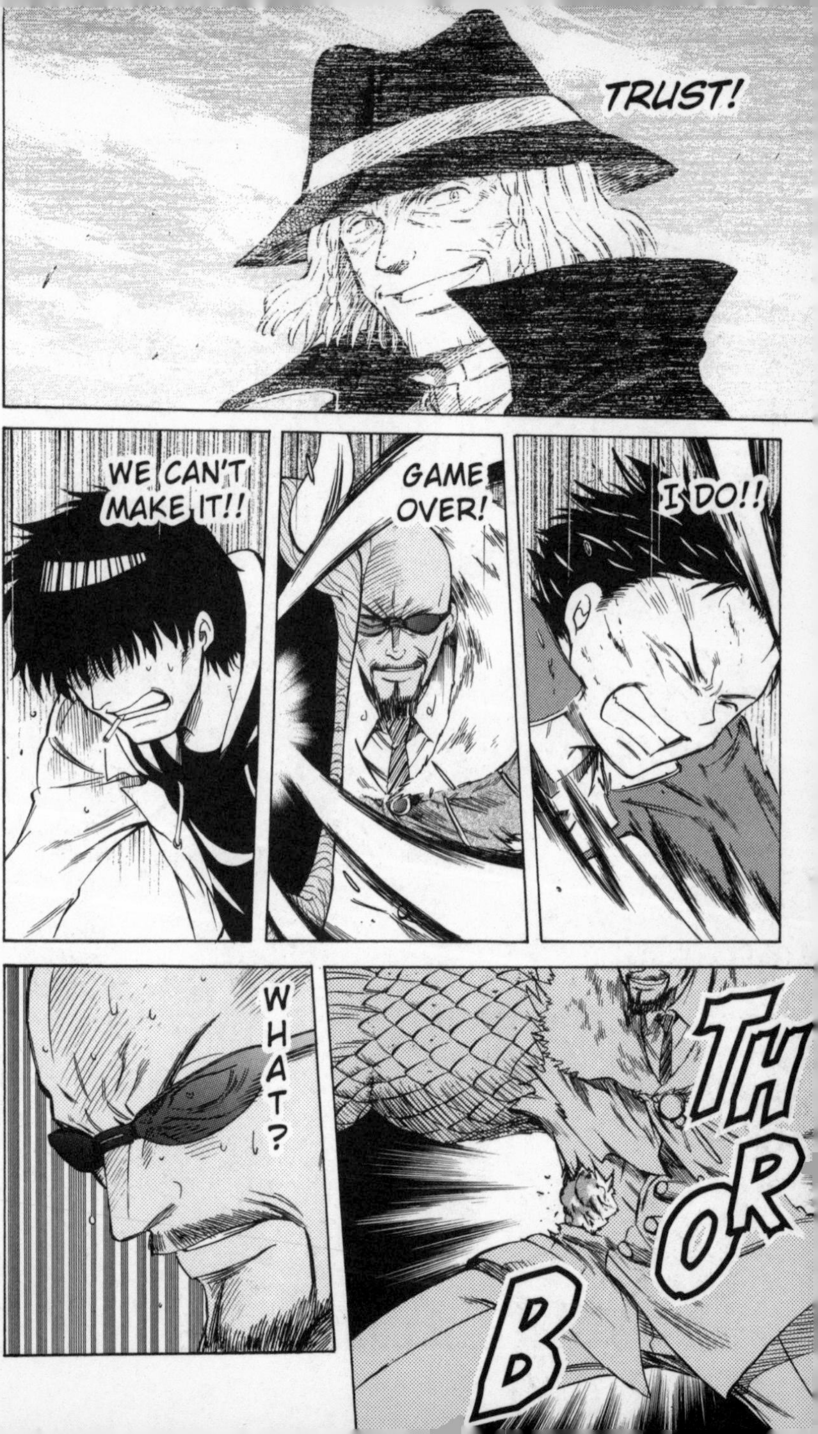
TRUST!
I DO!!
GAME OVER!
WE CAN'T MAKE IT!!
THROB
WHAT?

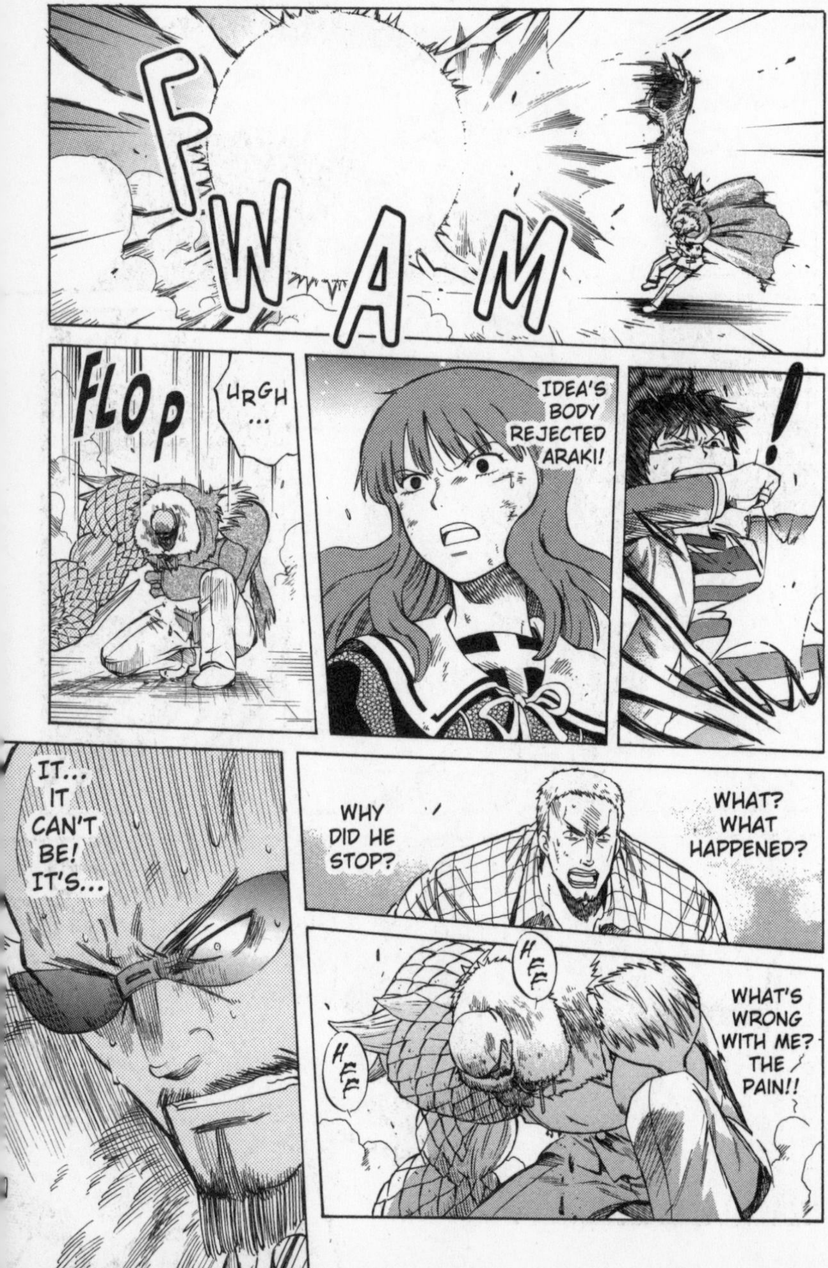
FWAM
!
IDEA'S BODY REJECTED ARAKI!
FLOP
URGH ...
WHAT? WHAT HAPPENED?
WHY DID HE STOP?
WHAT'S WRONG WITH ME? THE PAIN!!
HEF
HEF
IT... IT CAN'T BE! IT'S...

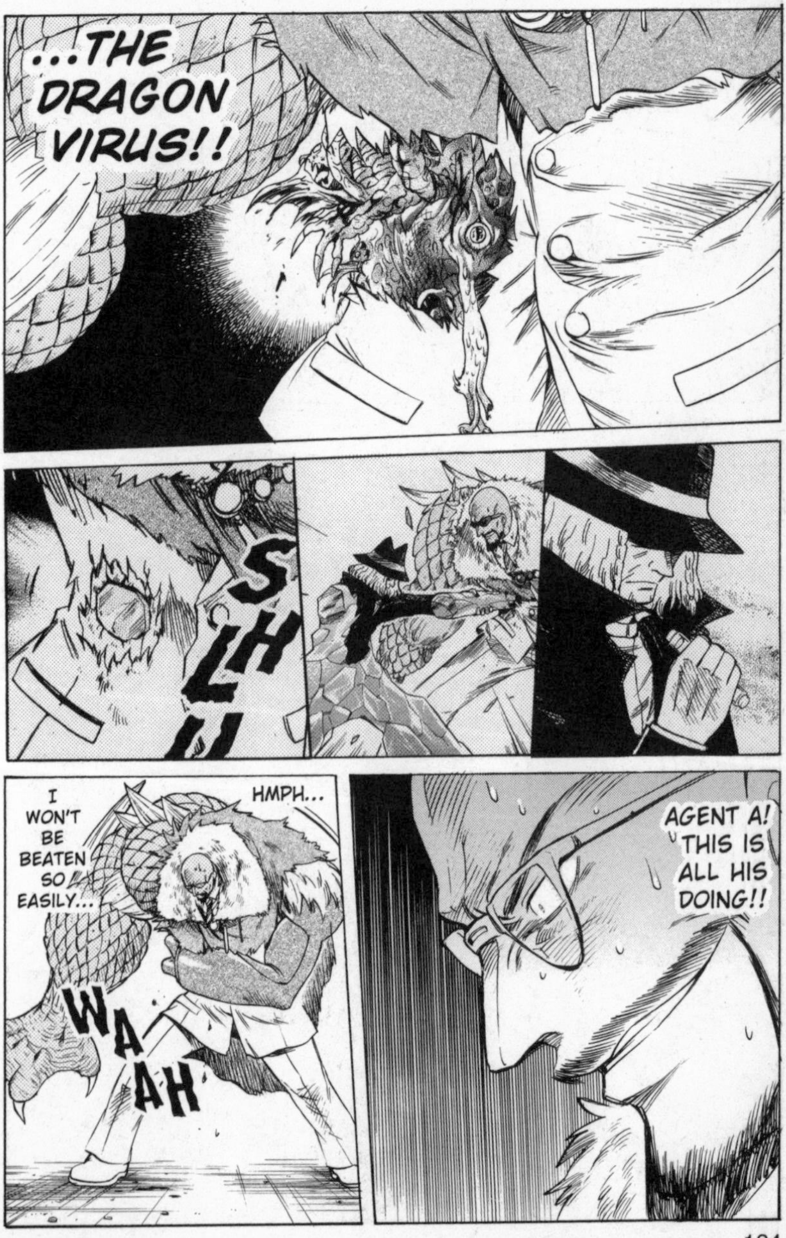
...THE DRAGON VIRUS!!
SHLU
AGENT A! THIS IS ALL HIS DOING!!
HMPH...
I WON'T BE BEATEN SO EASILY...
WAAAH

READ THIS WAY

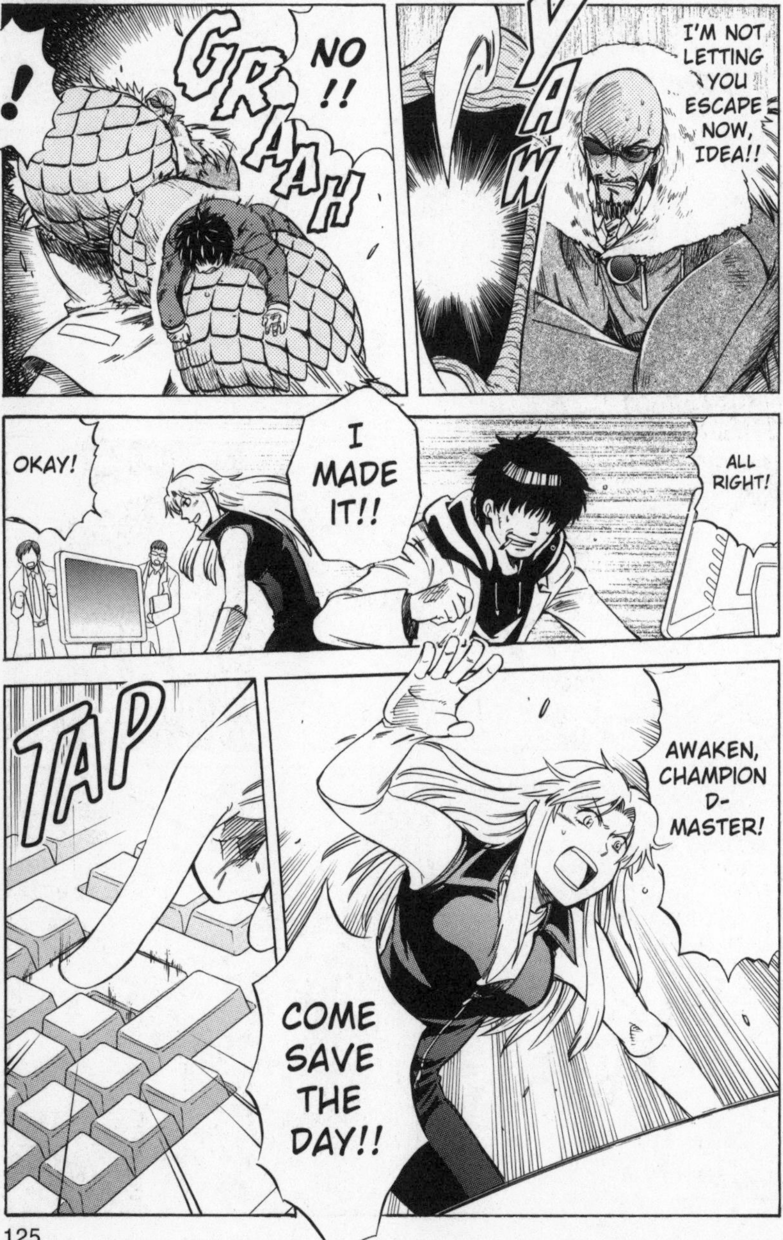
I'M NOT LETTING YOU ESCAPE NOW, IDEA!!
YAWN
NO!!
GRAAH
!
ALL RIGHT!
I MADE IT!!
OKAY!
AWAKEN, CHAMPION D-MASTER!
COME SAVE THE DAY!!
TAP

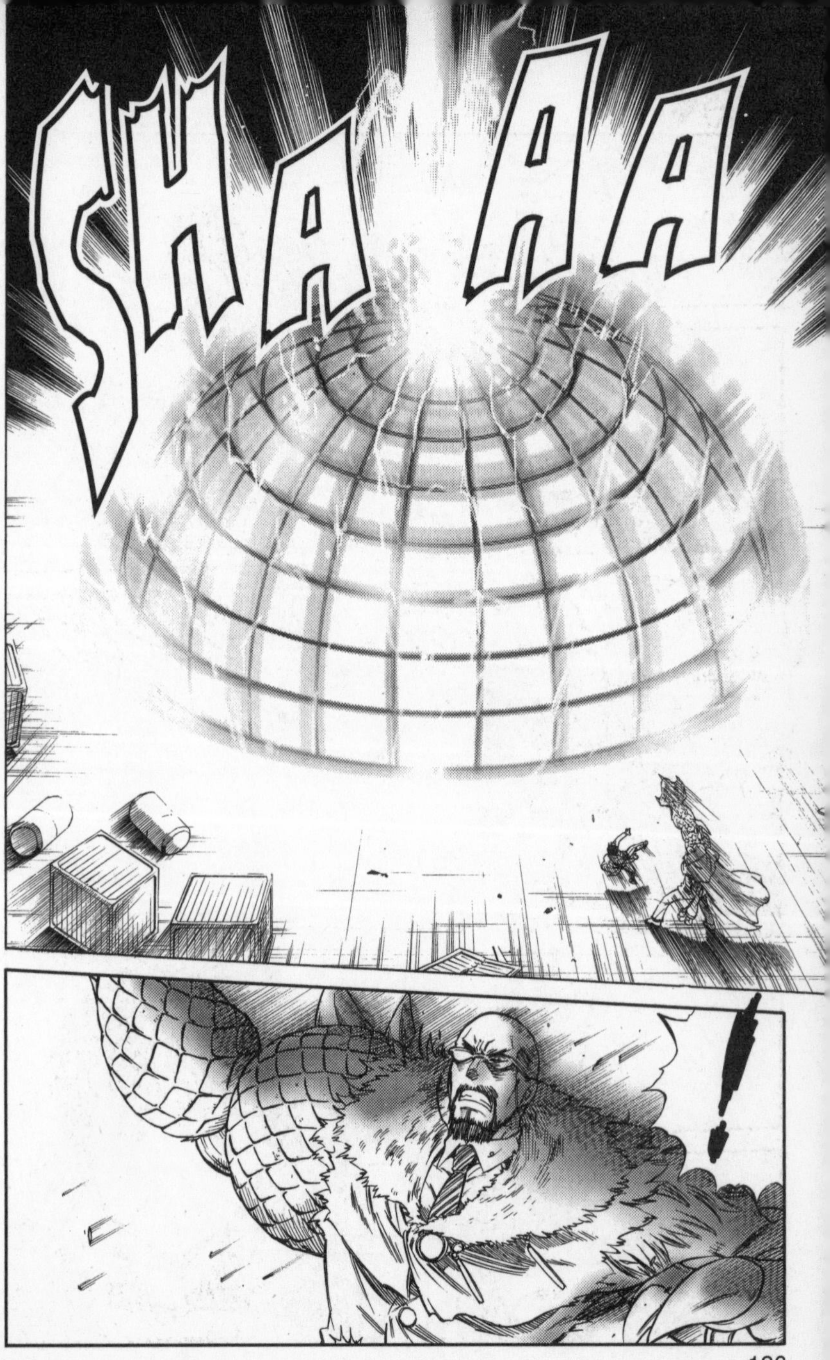
SHA AA
!

READ THIS WAY

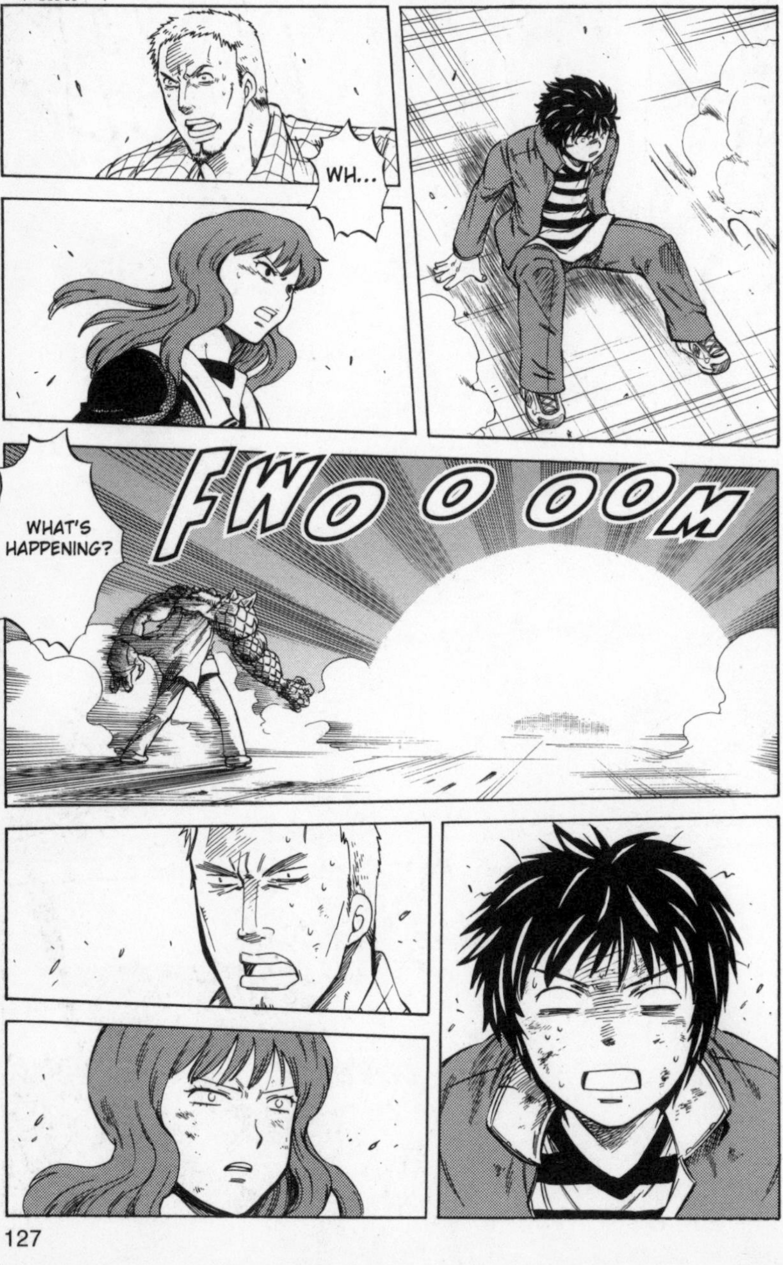
WH...
FWO O OOM
WHAT'S HAPPENING?

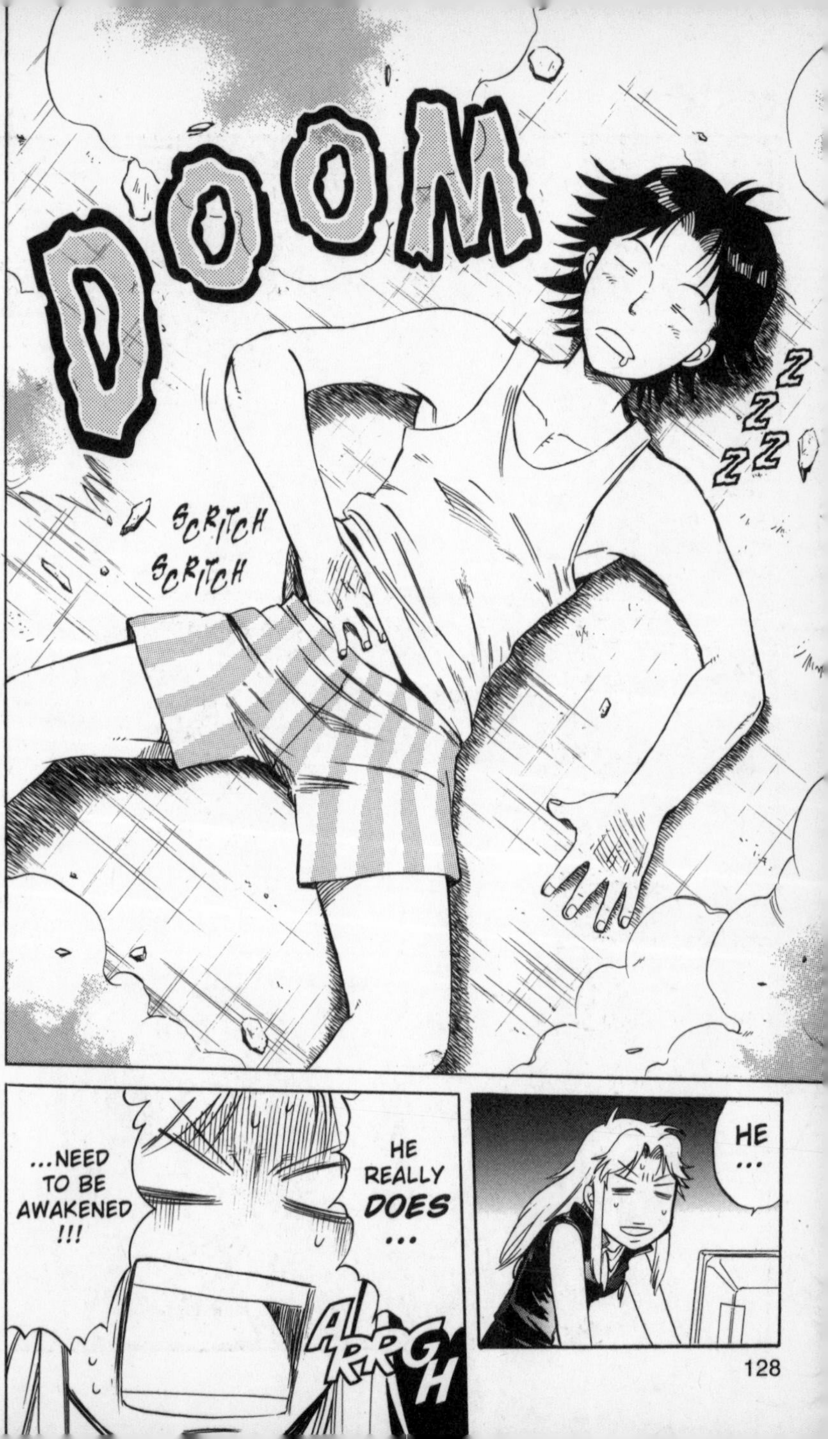
DOOM
ZZZ
SCRITCH SCRITCH
HE ...
HE REALLY DOES ...
...NEED TO BE AWAKENED !!!
ARRGH

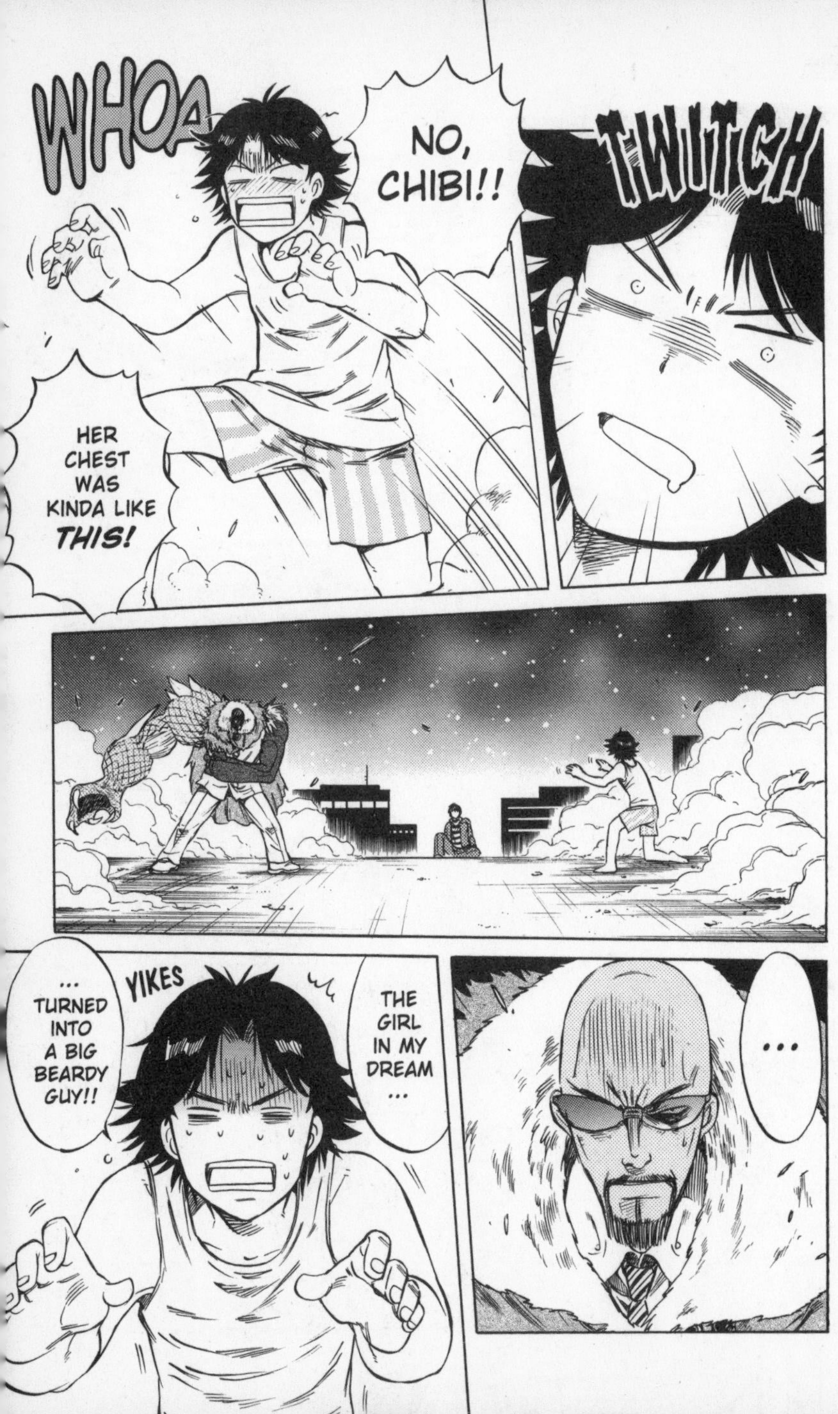
TWITCH
NO, CHIBI!!
WHOA
HER CHEST WAS KINDA LIKE *THIS!*
...
THE GIRL IN MY DREAM ...
YIKES
... TURNED INTO A BIG BEARDY GUY!!

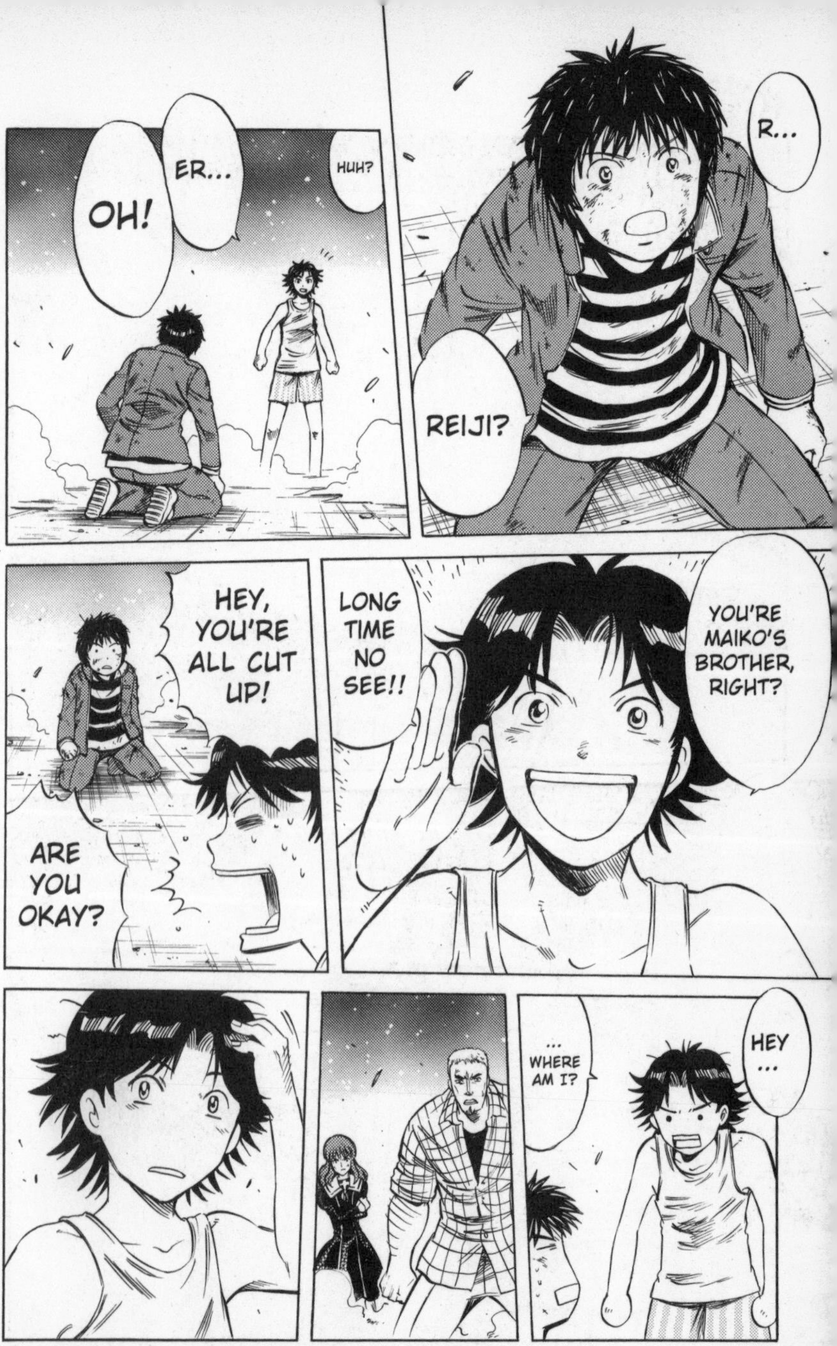
R...
REIJI?
HUH?
ER...
OH!
YOU'RE MAIKO'S BROTHER, RIGHT?
LONG TIME NO SEE!!
HEY, YOU'RE ALL CUT UP!
ARE YOU OKAY?
HEY ...
... WHERE AM I?

READ THIS WAY

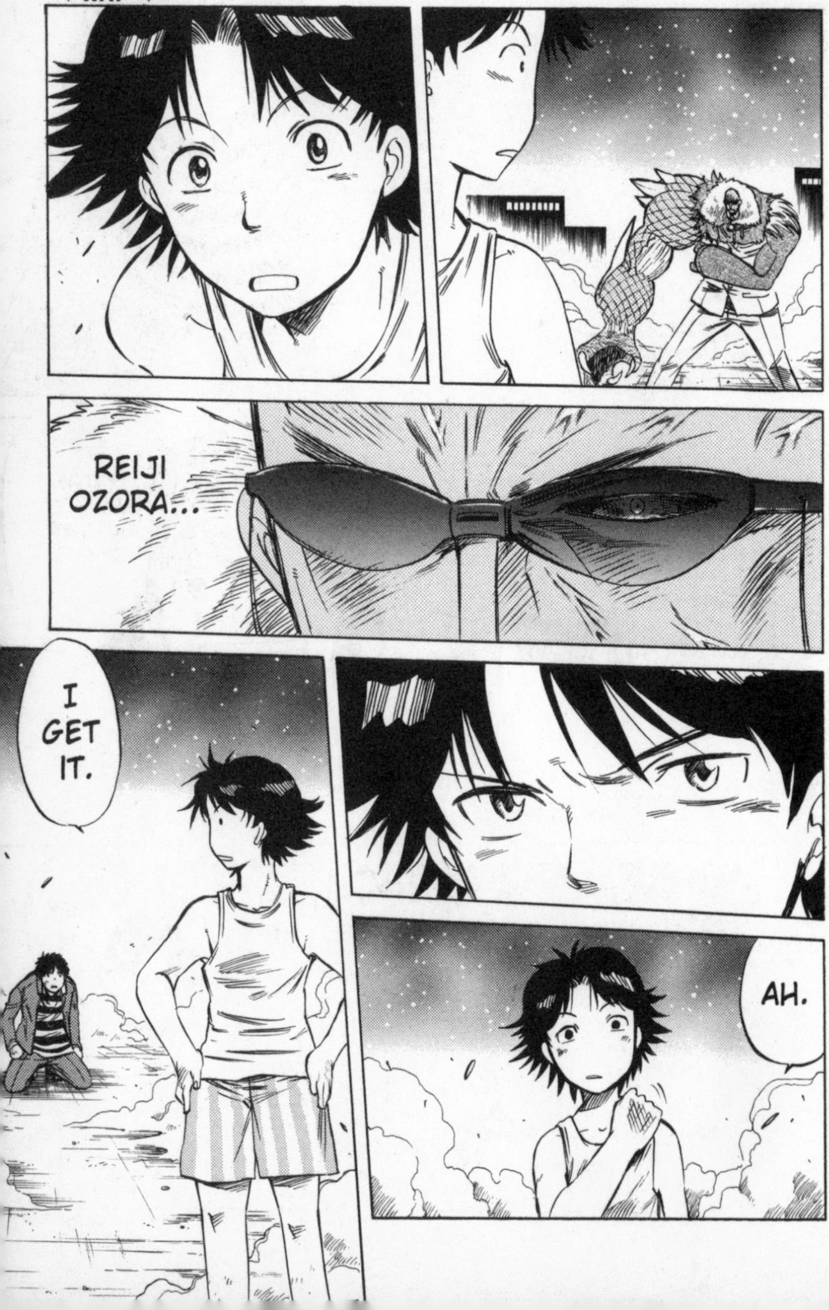
REIJI OZORA...
AH.
I GET IT.

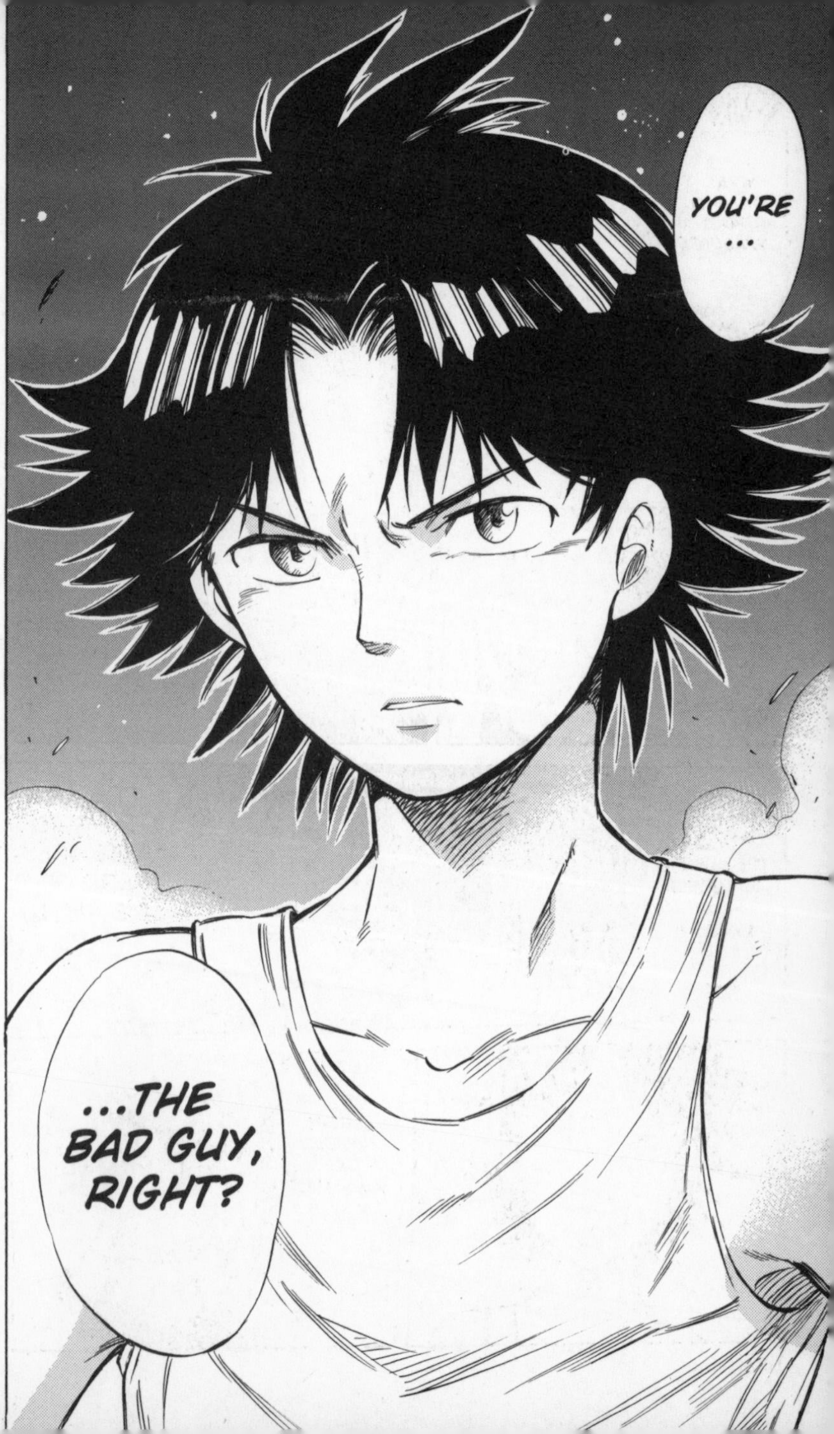
YOU'RE ...
...THE BAD GUY, RIGHT?

READ THIS WAY

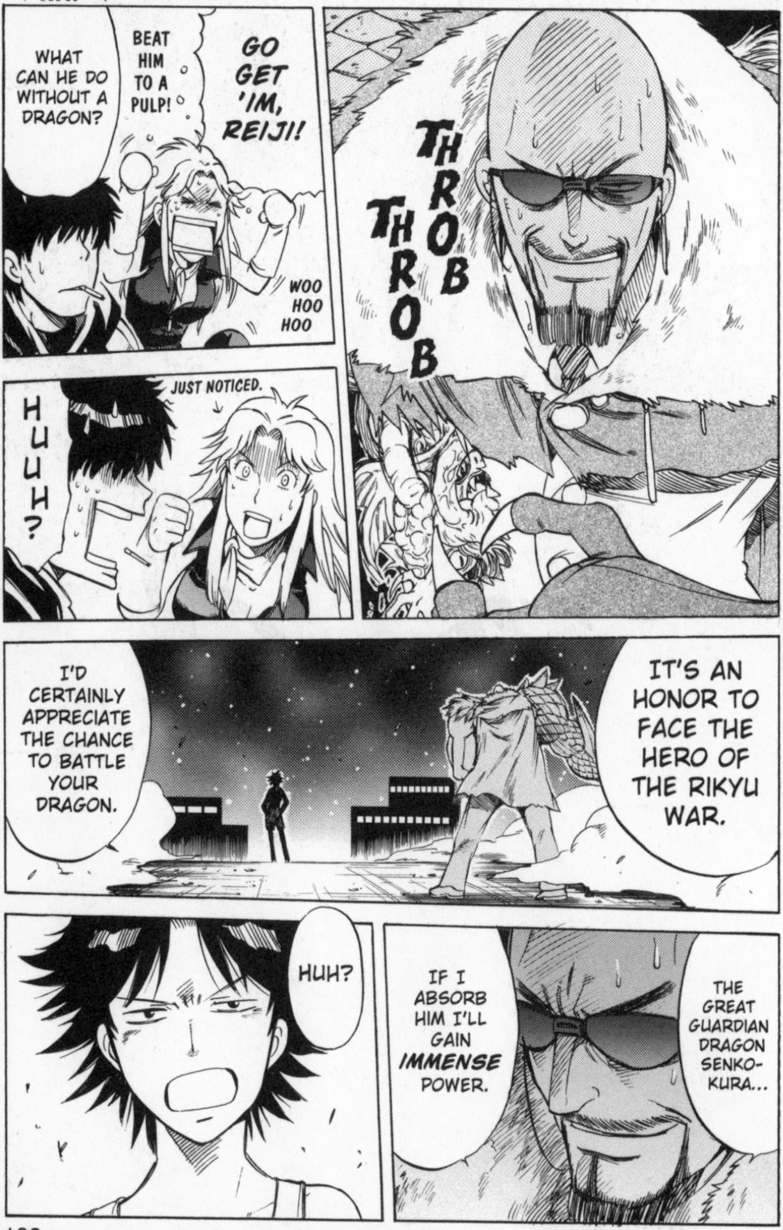
THROB THROB
GO GET 'IM, REIJI!
BEAT HIM TO A PULP!
WHAT CAN HE DO WITHOUT A DRAGON?
WOO HOO HOO
JUST NOTICED.
HUUUH?
IT'S AN HONOR TO FACE THE HERO OF THE RIKYU WAR.
I'D CERTAINLY APPRECIATE THE CHANCE TO BATTLE YOUR DRAGON.
THE GREAT GUARDIAN DRAGON SENKO-KURA...
IF I ABSORB HIM I'LL GAIN *IMMENSE* POWER.
HUH?

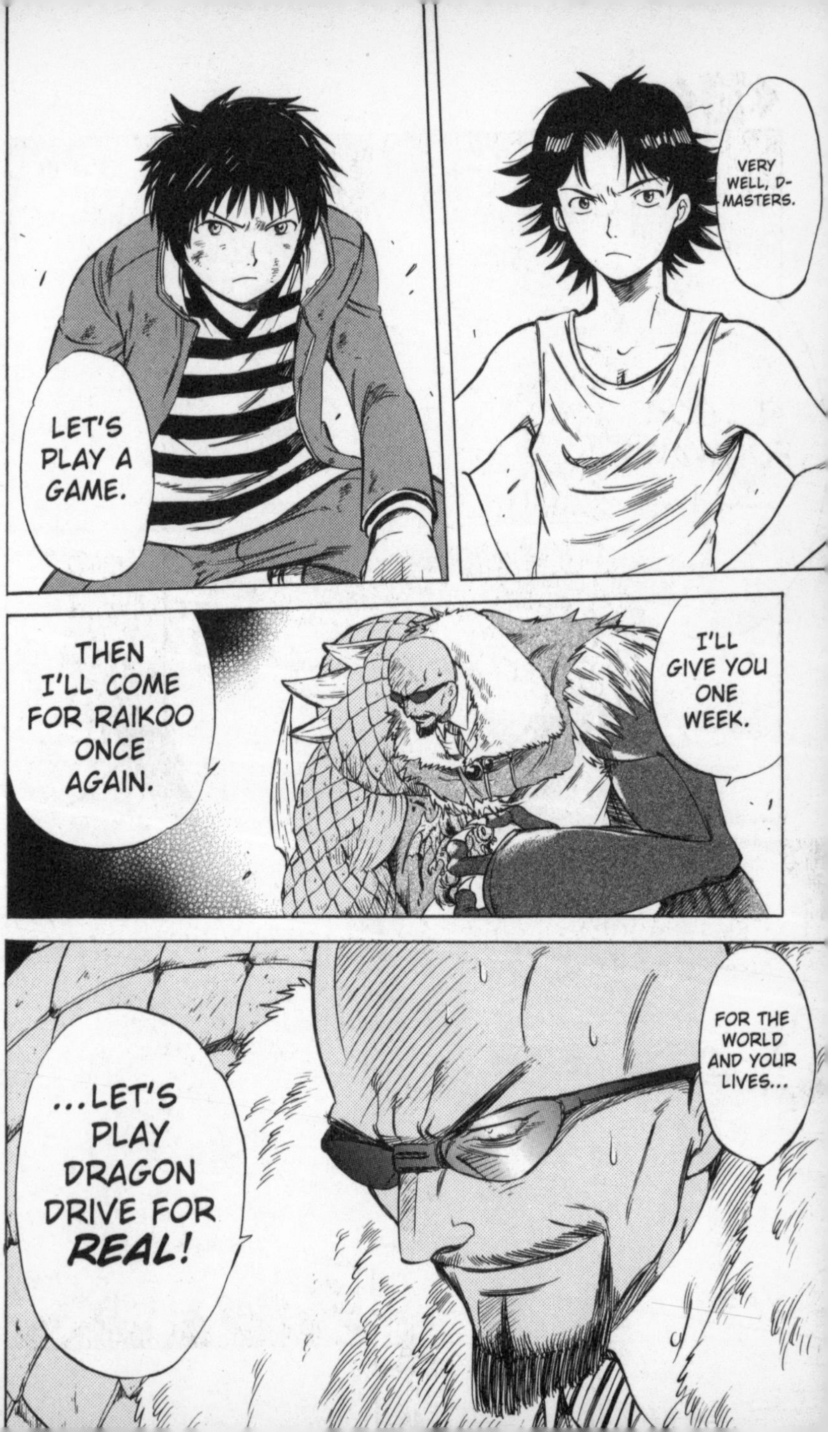
VERY WELL, D-MASTERS.
LET'S PLAY A GAME.
I'LL GIVE YOU ONE WEEK.
THEN I'LL COME FOR RAIKOO ONCE AGAIN.
FOR THE WORLD AND YOUR LIVES...
...LET'S PLAY DRAGON DRIVE FOR REAL!

READ THIS WAY

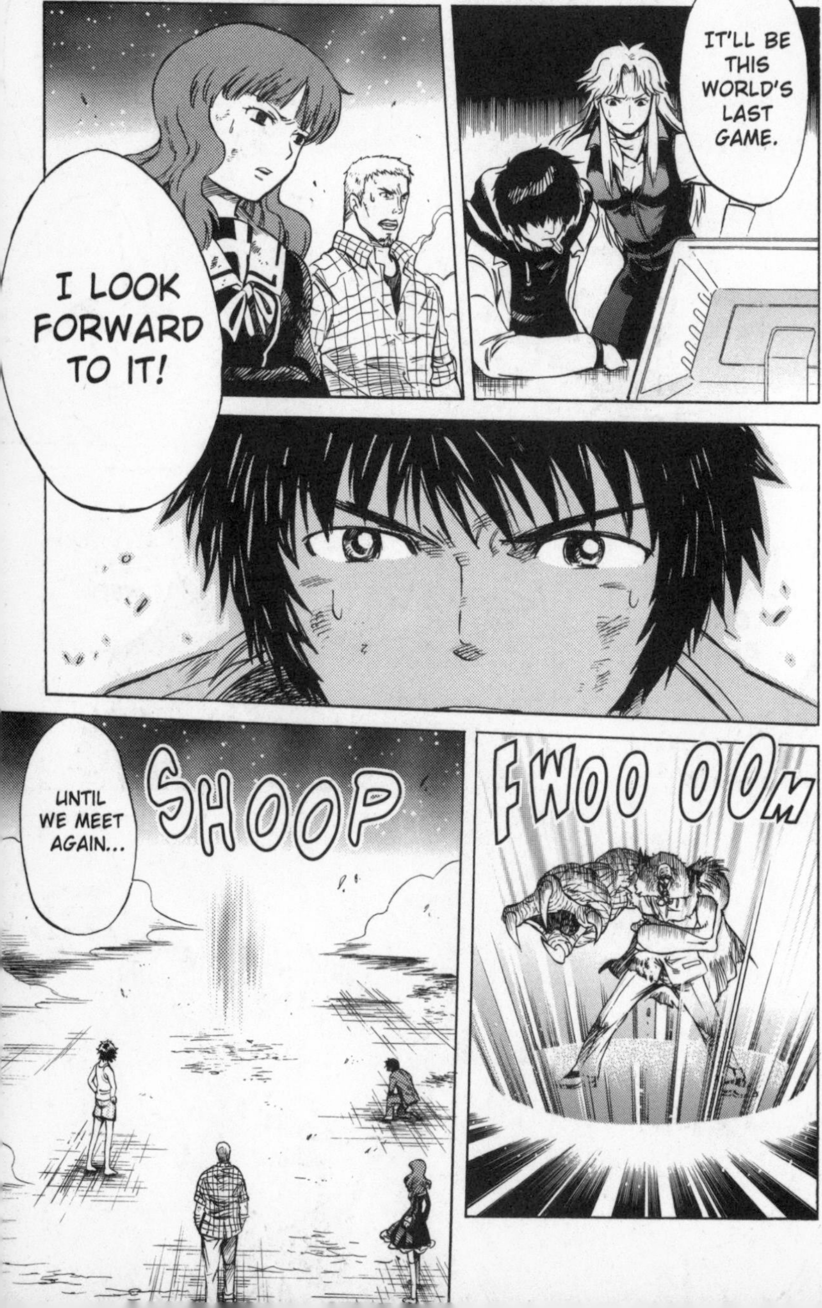
IT'LL BE THIS WORLD'S LAST GAME.
I LOOK FORWARD TO IT!
FWOO OOM
SHOOP
UNTIL WE MEET AGAIN...

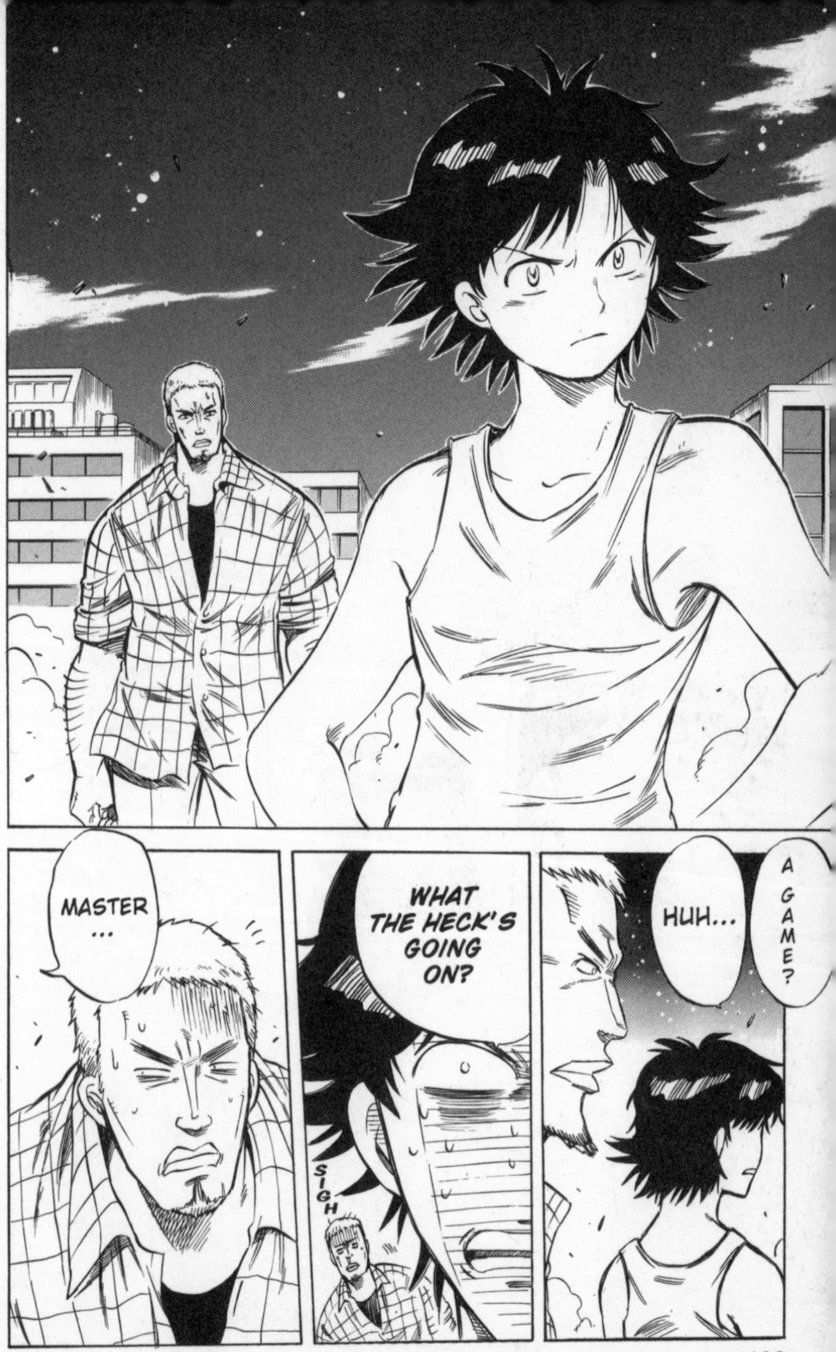
A GAME?
HUH...
WHAT THE HECK'S GOING ON?
SIGH
MASTER ...

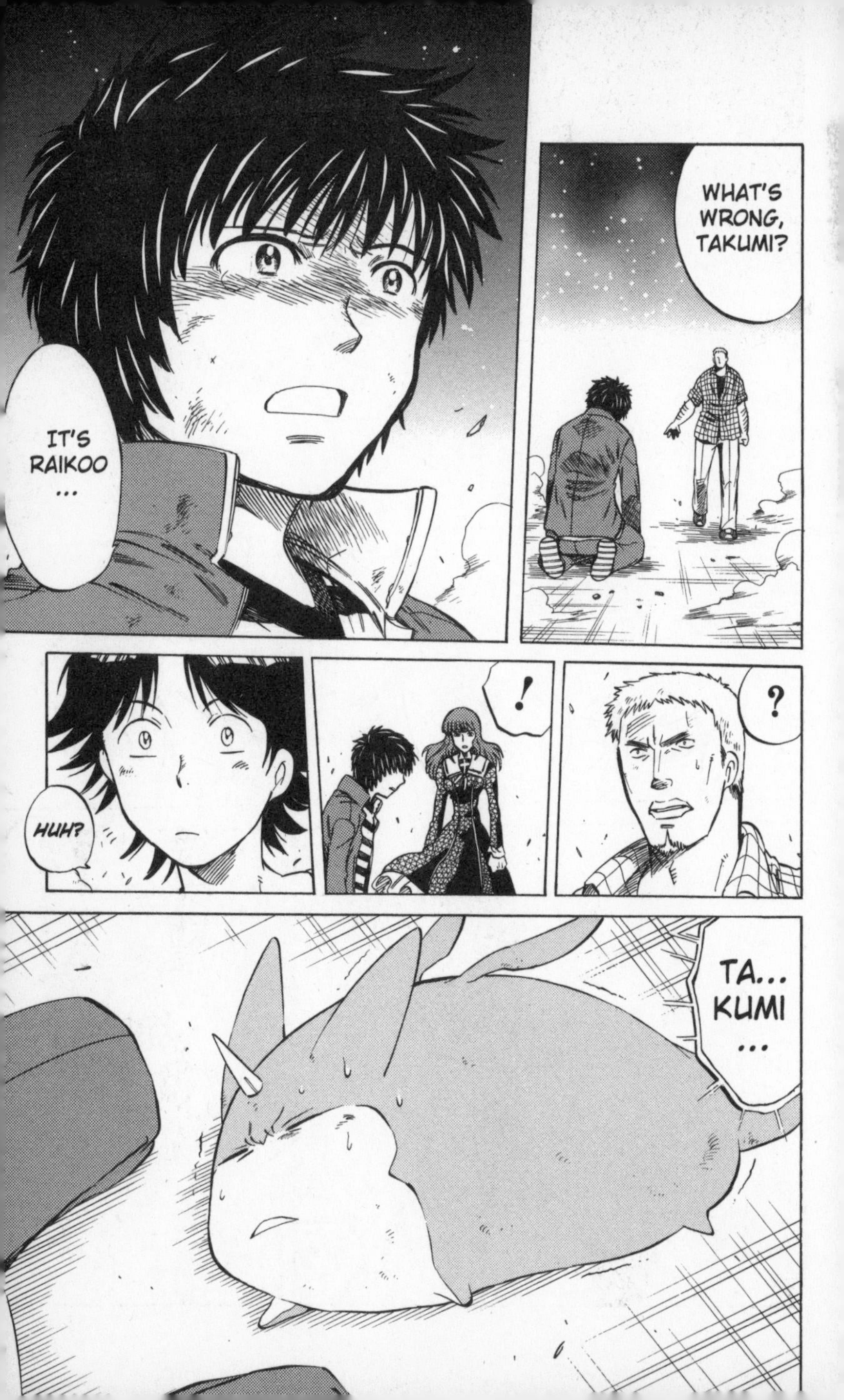
WHAT'S WRONG, TAKUMI?
IT'S RAIKOO ...
?
!
HUH?
TA... KUMI ...

A Storm of Misunderstandings!!

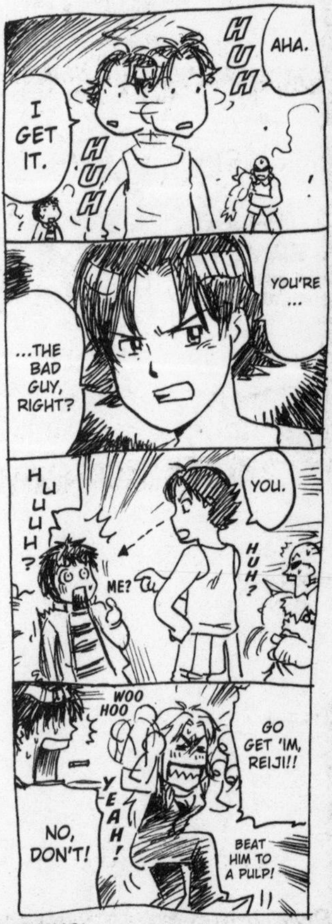
AHA.
HUH
HUH
I GET IT.
HUH
HUH
YOU'RE ...
...THE BAD GUY, RIGHT?
YOU.
HUH?
ME?
HUUUH?
GO GET 'IM, REIJI!!
BEAT HIM TO A PULP!
WOO HOO
YEAH!
NO, DON'T!

BY NAGI

TAKUMI AND LITTLE RAIKOO

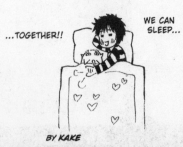

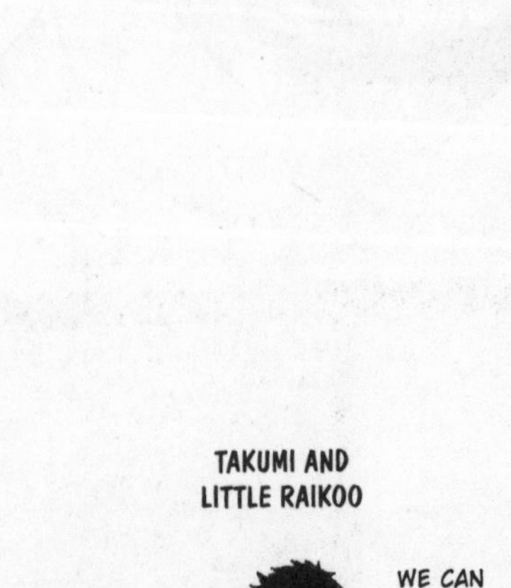
WE CAN SLEEP...
...TOGETHER!!

BY KAKE

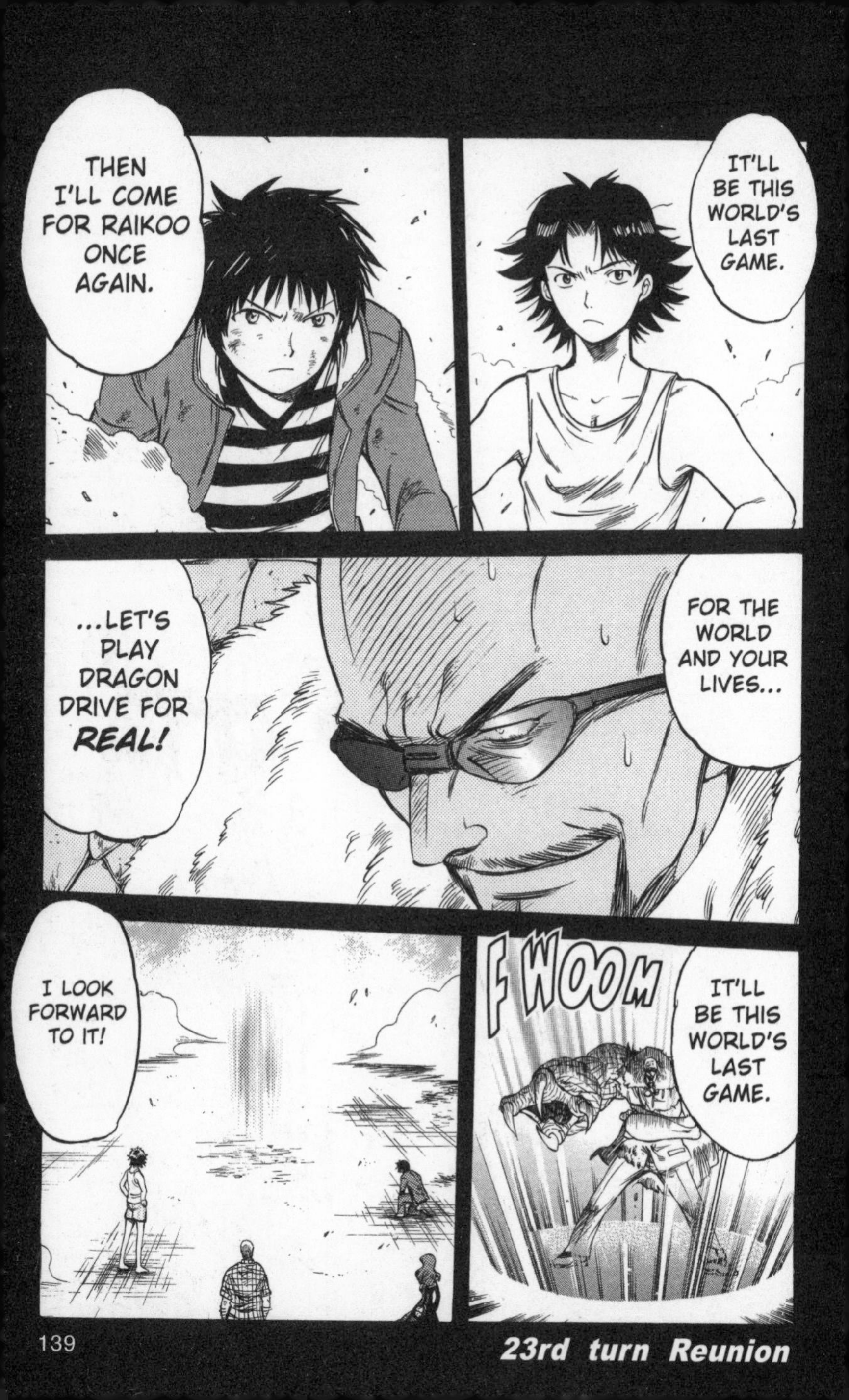
IT'LL BE THIS WORLD'S LAST GAME.
THEN I'LL COME FOR RAIKOO ONCE AGAIN.
FOR THE WORLD AND YOUR LIVES...
...LET'S PLAY DRAGON DRIVE FOR REAL!
FWOOM
IT'LL BE THIS WORLD'S LAST GAME.
I LOOK FORWARD TO IT!

23rd turn Reunion

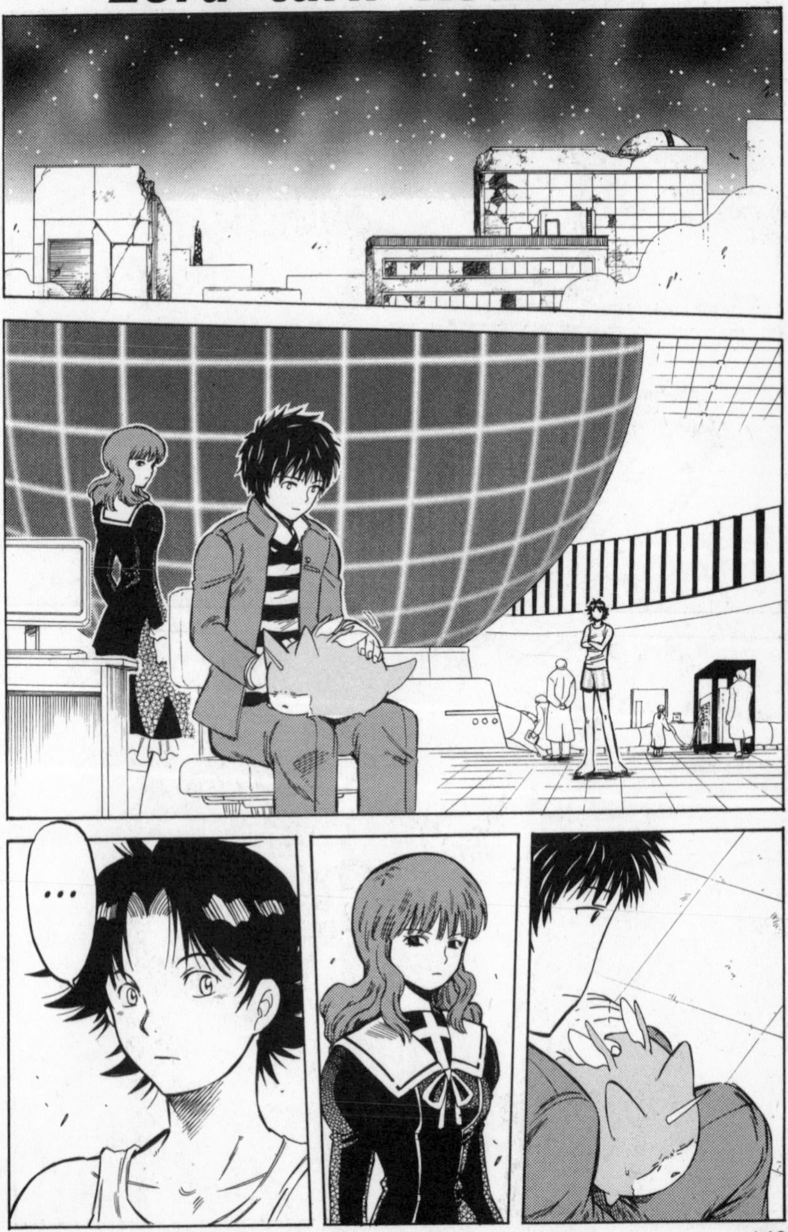
...

READ THIS WAY

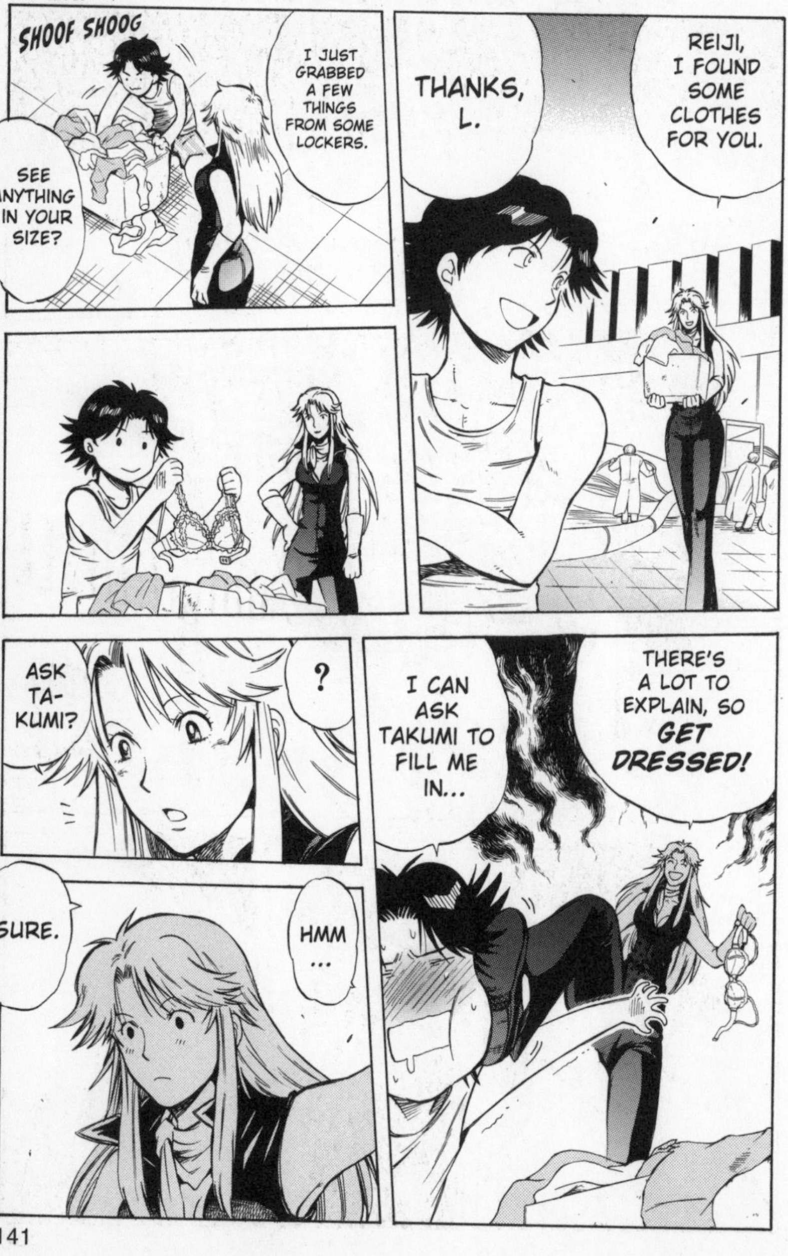

REIJI, I FOUND SOME CLOTHES FOR YOU.
THANKS, L.
I JUST GRABBED A FEW THINGS FROM SOME LOCKERS.
SHOOF SHOOG
SEE ANYTHING IN YOUR SIZE?
THERE'S A LOT TO EXPLAIN, SO **GET DRESSED!**
I CAN ASK TAKUMI TO FILL ME IN...
?
ASK TA-KUMI?
HMM ...
SURE.

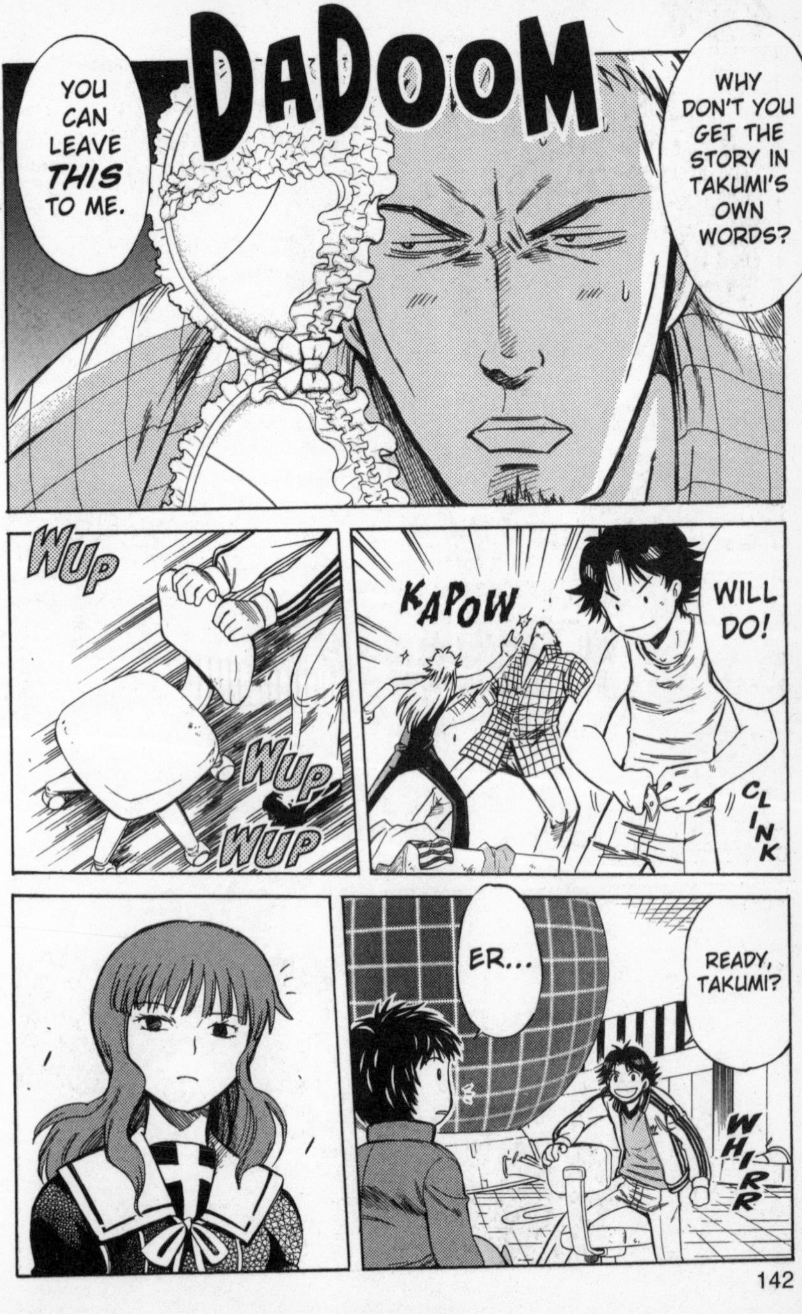
WHY DON'T YOU GET THE STORY IN TAKUMI'S OWN WORDS?
DADOOM
YOU CAN LEAVE *THIS* TO ME.
WILL DO!
KAPOW
CLINK
WUP
WUP
WUP
READY, TAKUMI?
ER...
WHIRR

READ THIS WAY

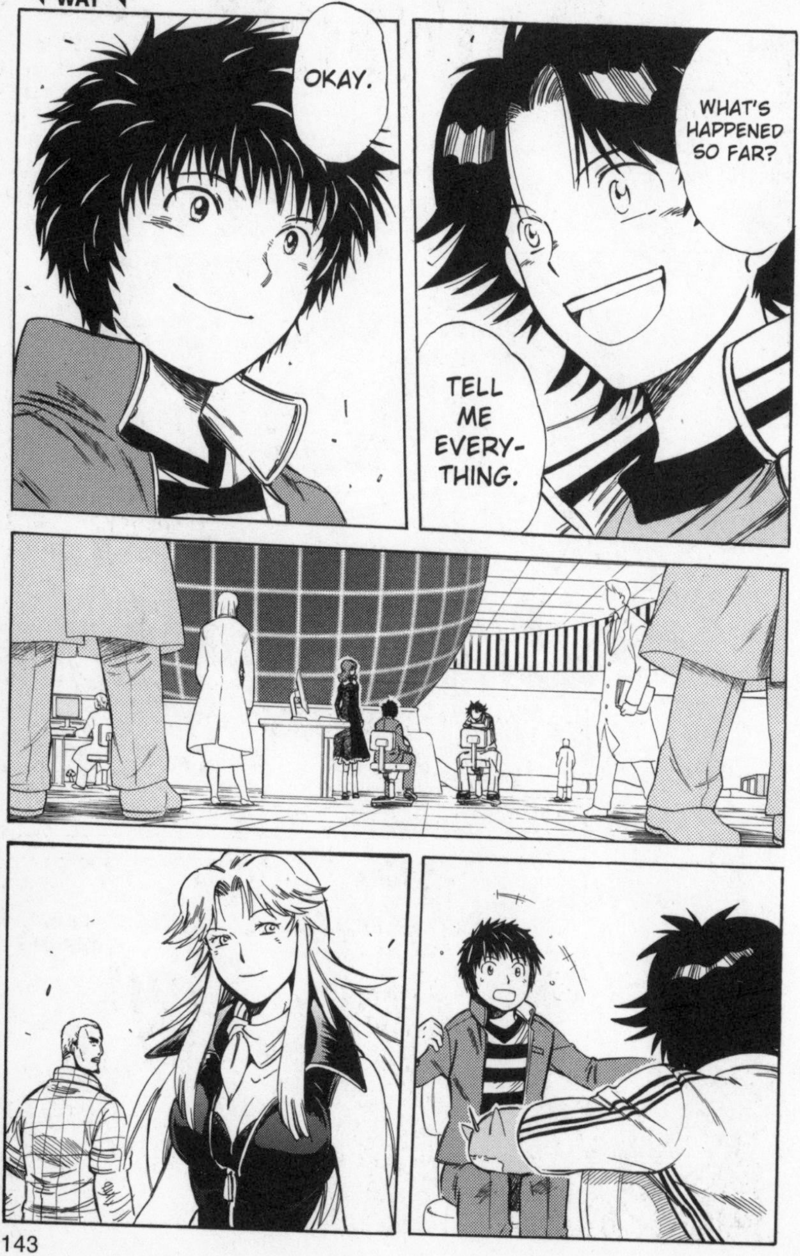
WHAT'S HAPPENED SO FAR?
TELL ME EVERY-THING.
OKAY.

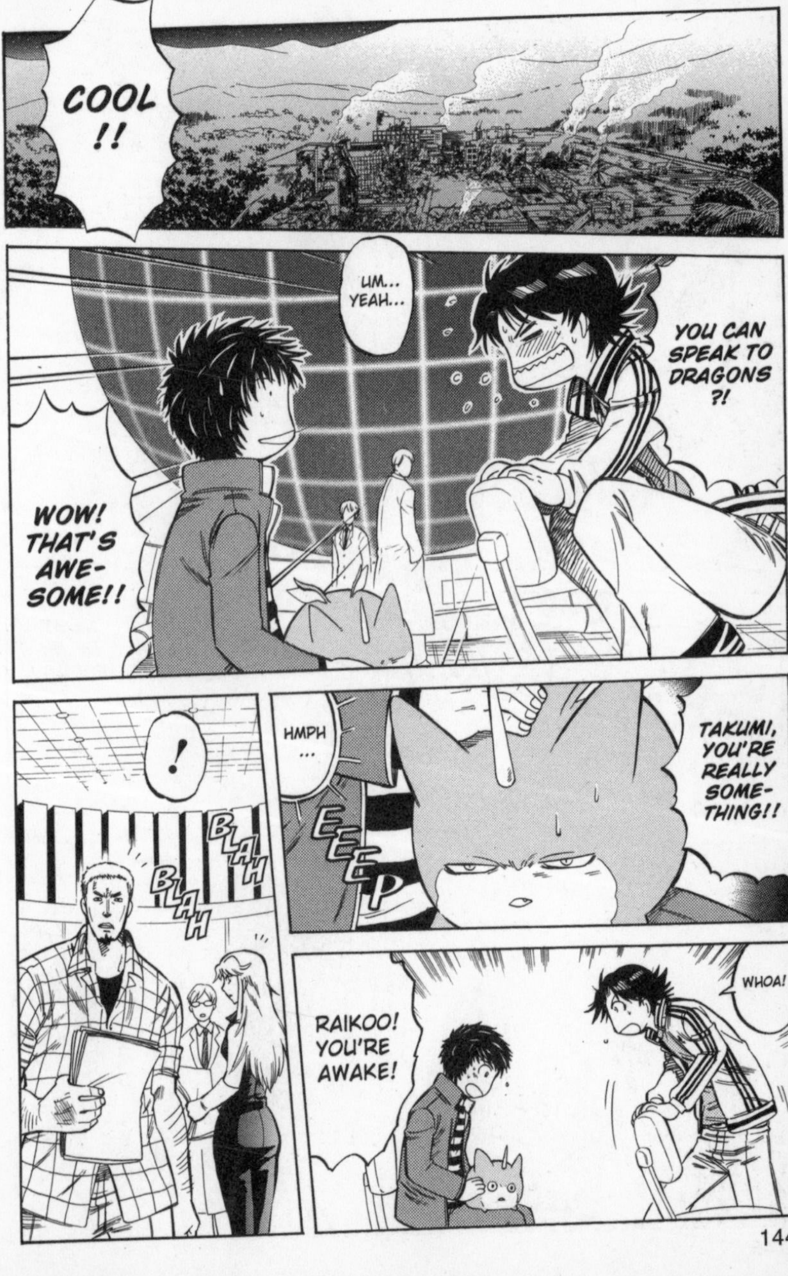
COOL !!
YOU CAN SPEAK TO DRAGONS ?!
UM... YEAH...
WOW! THAT'S AWE-SOME!!
TAKUMI, YOU'RE REALLY SOME-THING!!
HMPH ...
EEEP
WHOA!
RAIKOO! YOU'RE AWAKE!
!
BLAH BLAH

READ THIS WAY

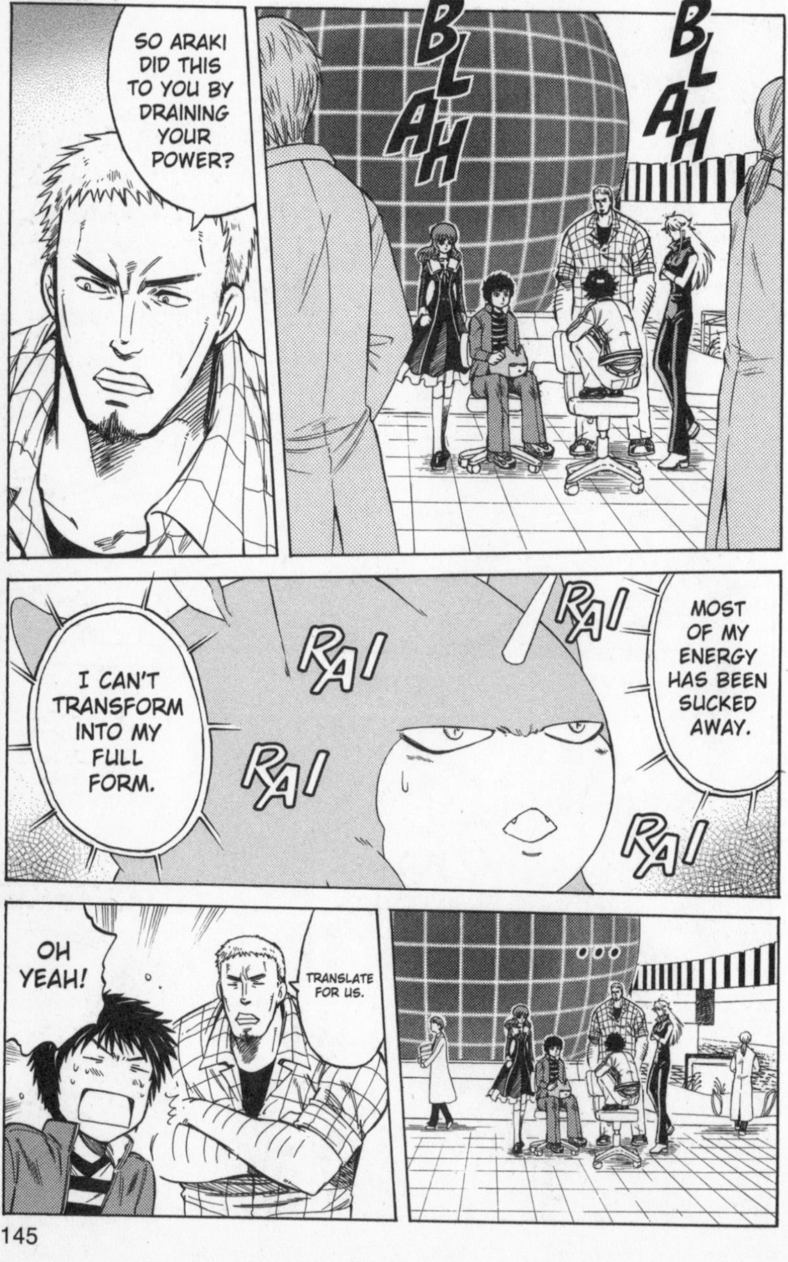
BLAH
BLAH
SO ARAKI DID THIS TO YOU BY DRAINING YOUR POWER?
MOST OF MY ENERGY HAS BEEN SUCKED AWAY.
RAI
RAI
RAI
RAI
I CAN'T TRANSFORM INTO MY FULL FORM.
...
TRANSLATE FOR US.
OH YEAH!

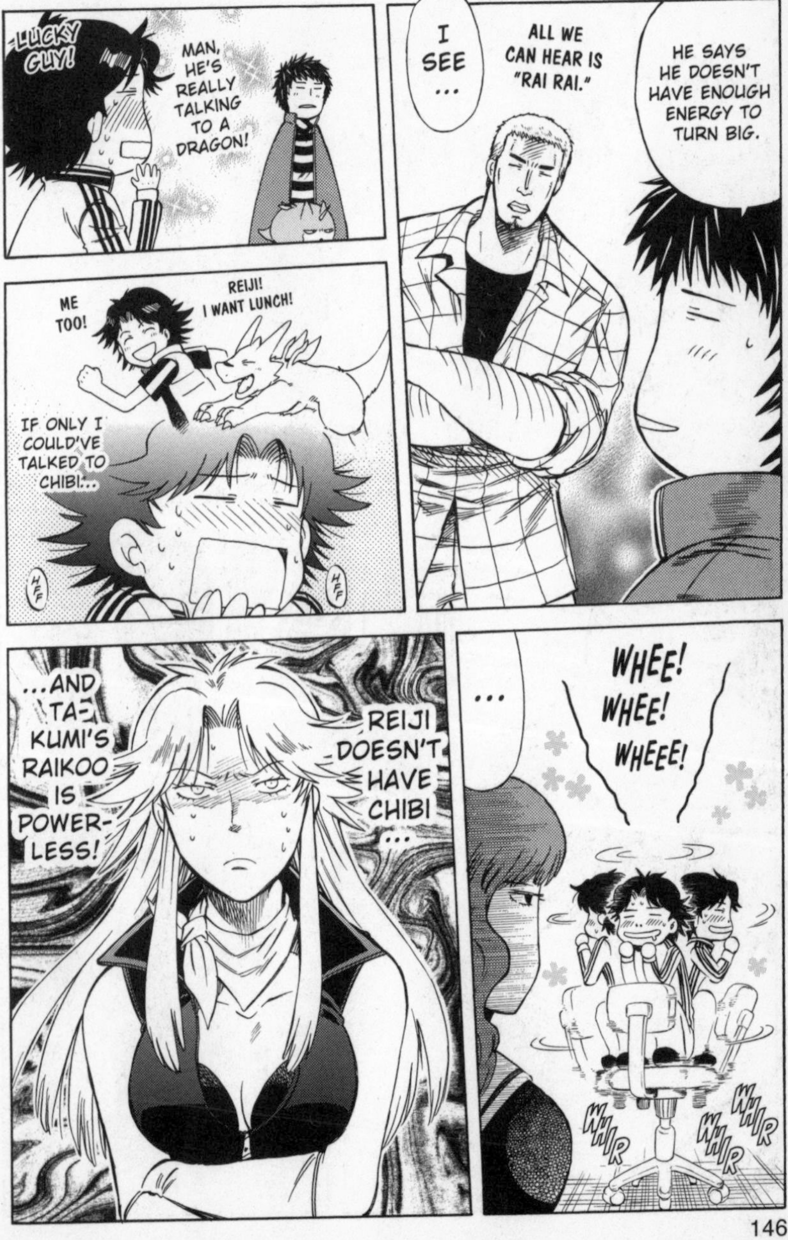
HE SAYS HE DOESN'T HAVE ENOUGH ENERGY TO TURN BIG.
ALL WE CAN HEAR IS "RAI RAI."
I SEE ...
MAN, HE'S REALLY TALKING TO A DRAGON!
LUCKY GUY!
REIJI! I WANT LUNCH!
ME TOO!
IF ONLY I COULD'VE TALKED TO CHIBI...
HFF
HFF
WHEE! WHEE! WHEEE!
...
WHIR
WHIR
WHIR
WHIR
REIJI DOESN'T HAVE CHIBI ...
...AND TAKUMI'S RAIKOO IS POWERLESS!

READ THIS WAY

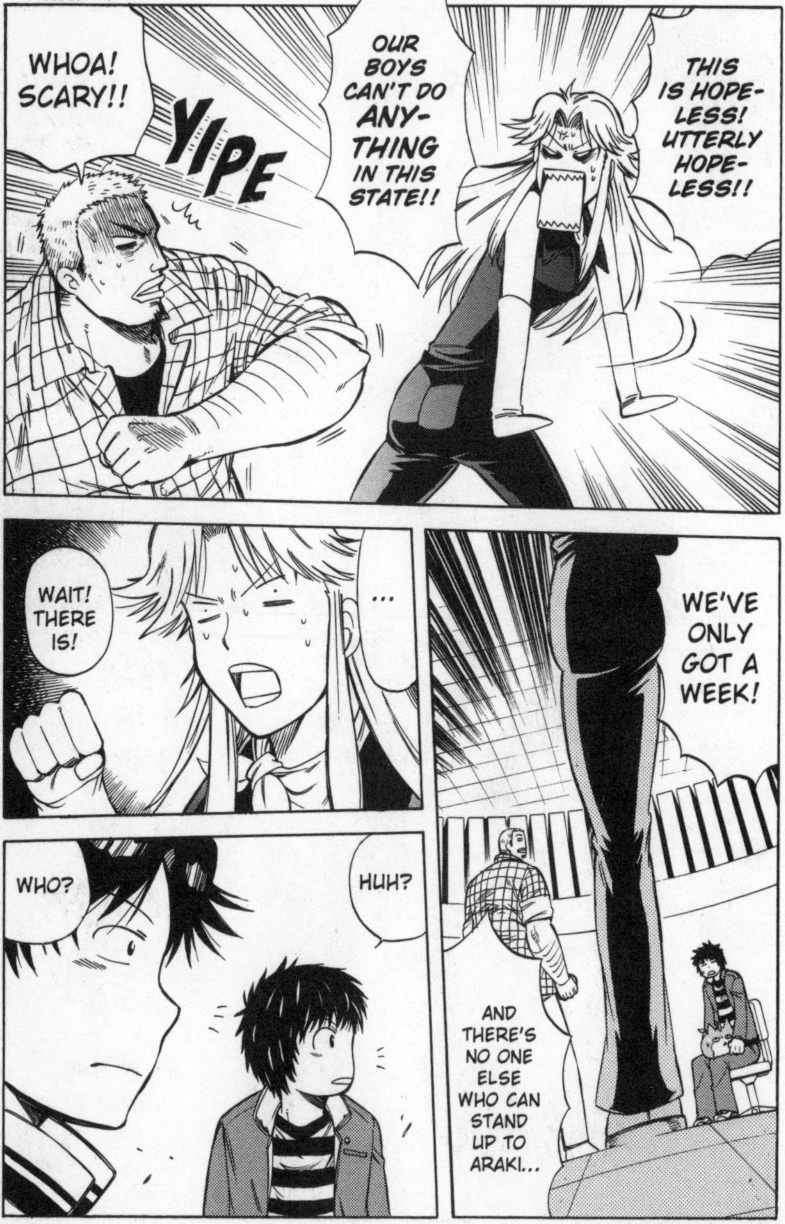
THIS IS HOPE-LESS! UTTERLY HOPE-LESS!!
OUR BOYS CAN'T DO ANY-THING IN THIS STATE!!
YIPE
WHOA! SCARY!!
WE'VE ONLY GOT A WEEK!
AND THERE'S NO ONE ELSE WHO CAN STAND UP TO ARAKI...
...
WAIT! THERE IS!
HUH?
WHO?

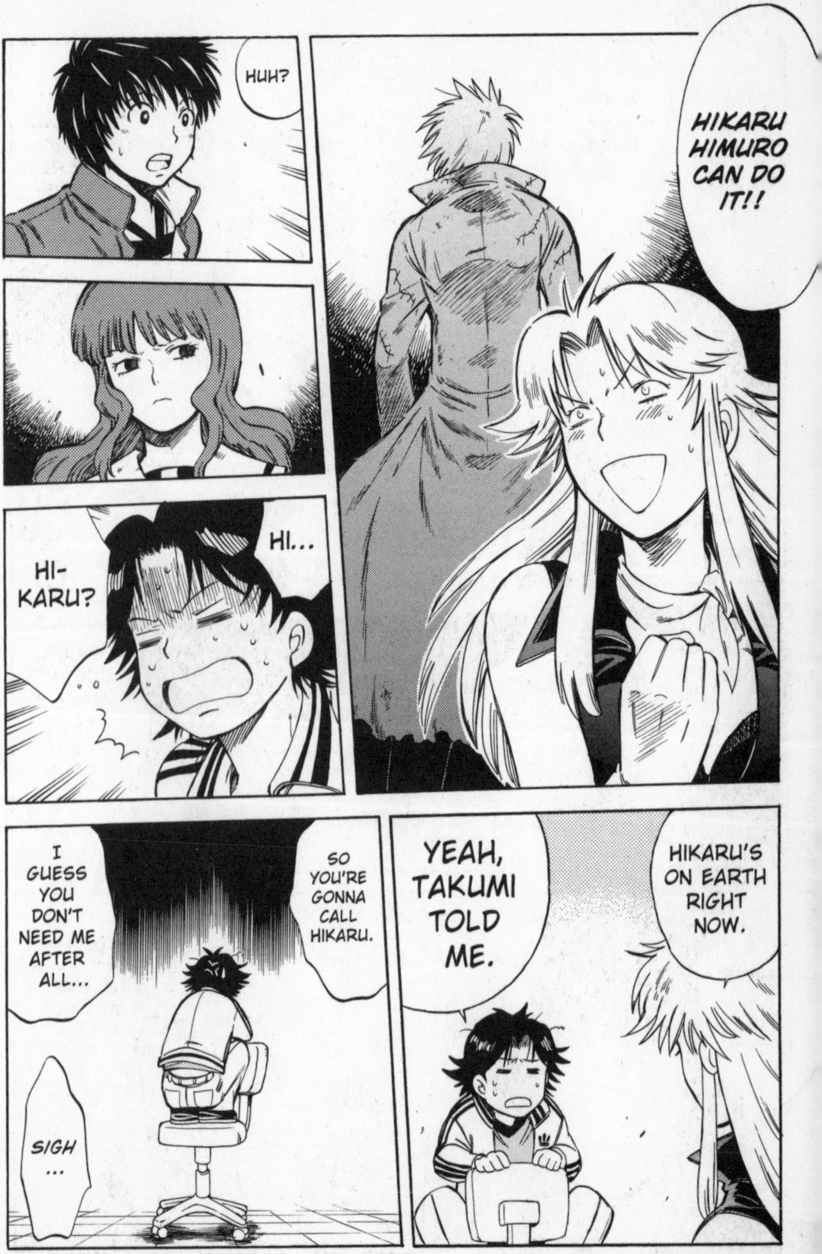
HIKARU HIMURO CAN DO IT!!
HUH?
HI...
HI-KARU?
HIKARU'S ON EARTH RIGHT NOW.
YEAH, TAKUMI TOLD ME.
SO YOU'RE GONNA CALL HIKARU.
I GUESS YOU DON'T NEED ME AFTER ALL...
SIGH...

READ THIS WAY

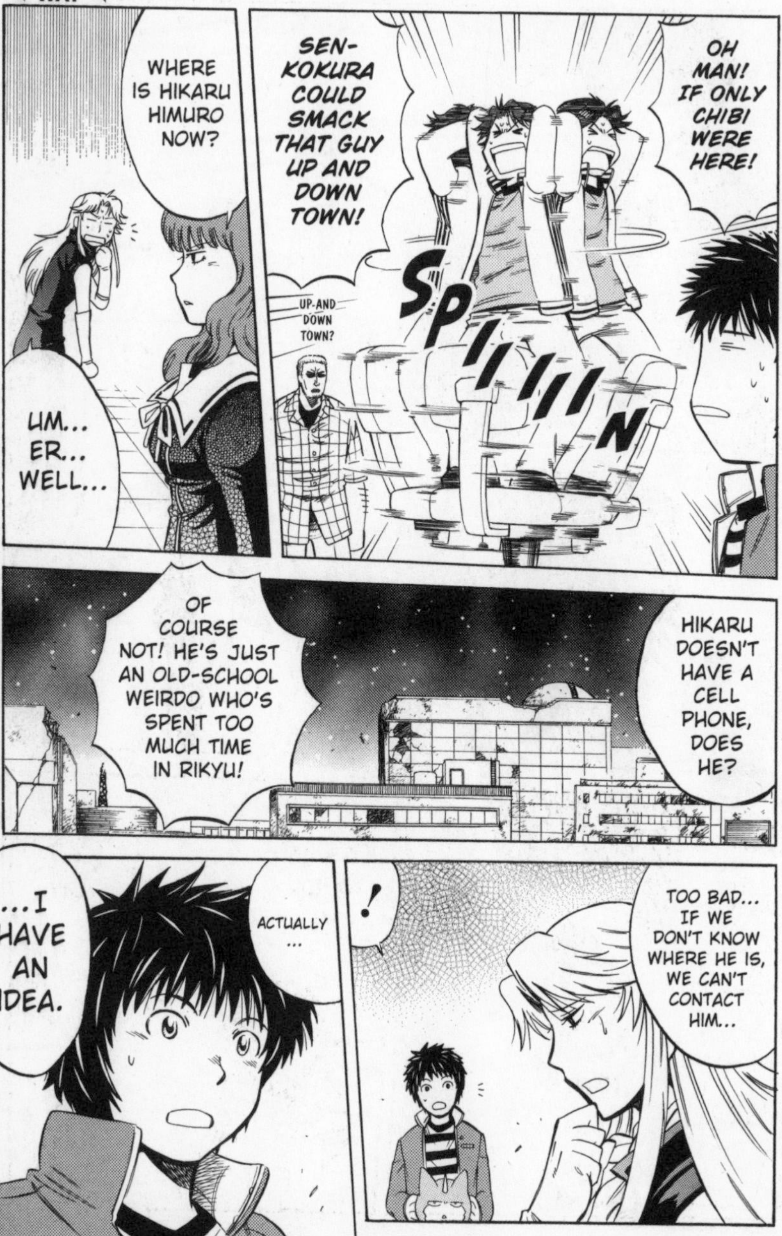
OH MAN! IF ONLY CHIBI WERE HERE!
SEN-KOKURA COULD SMACK THAT GUY UP AND DOWN TOWN!
SPIIIIIN
UP-AND-DOWN TOWN?
WHERE IS HIKARU HIMURO NOW?
UM... ER... WELL...
HIKARU DOESN'T HAVE A CELL PHONE, DOES HE?
OF COURSE NOT! HE'S JUST AN OLD-SCHOOL WEIRDO WHO'S SPENT TOO MUCH TIME IN RIKYU!
TOO BAD... IF WE DON'T KNOW WHERE HE IS, WE CAN'T CONTACT HIM...
!
ACTUALLY ...
...I HAVE AN IDEA.

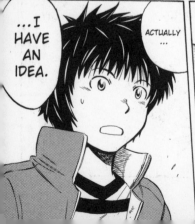

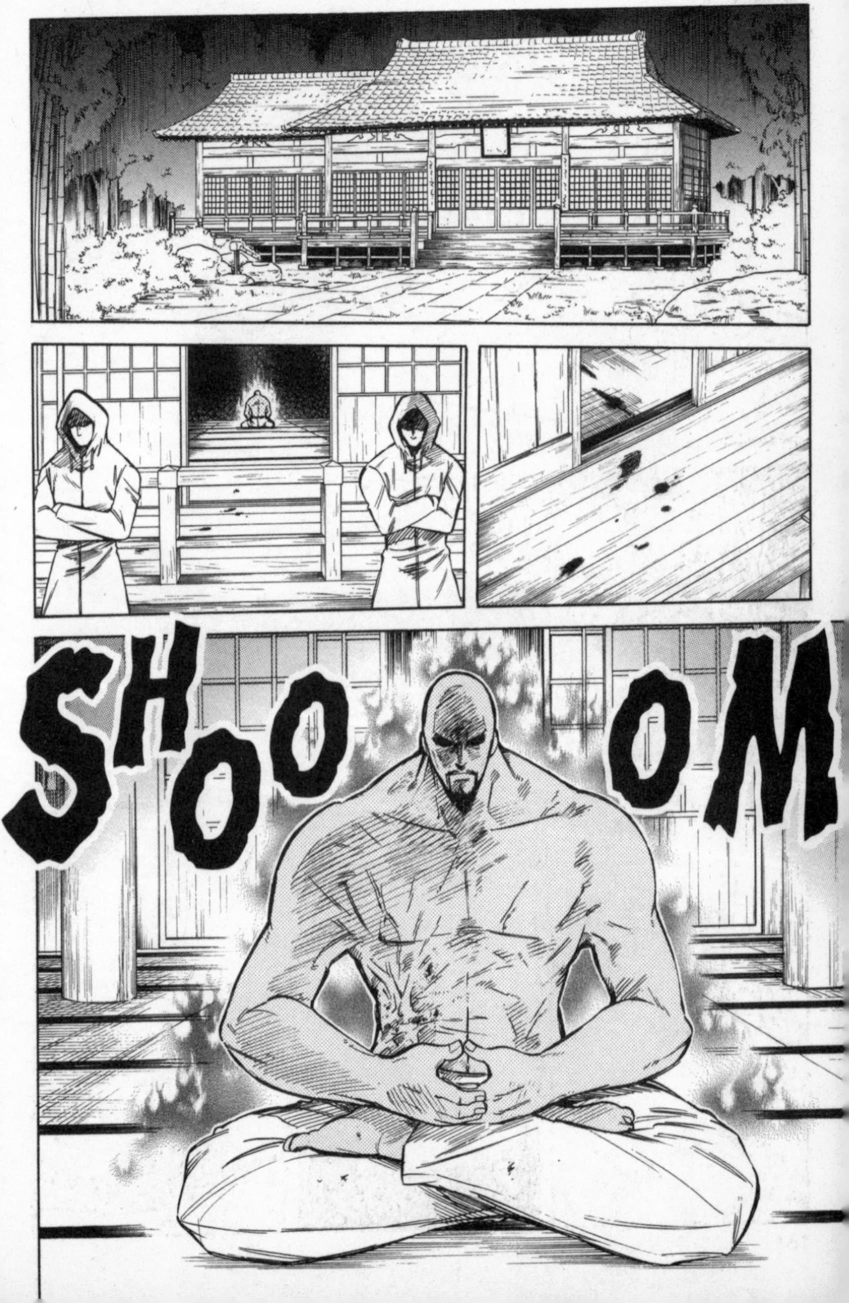
SHOOOM

READ THIS WAY

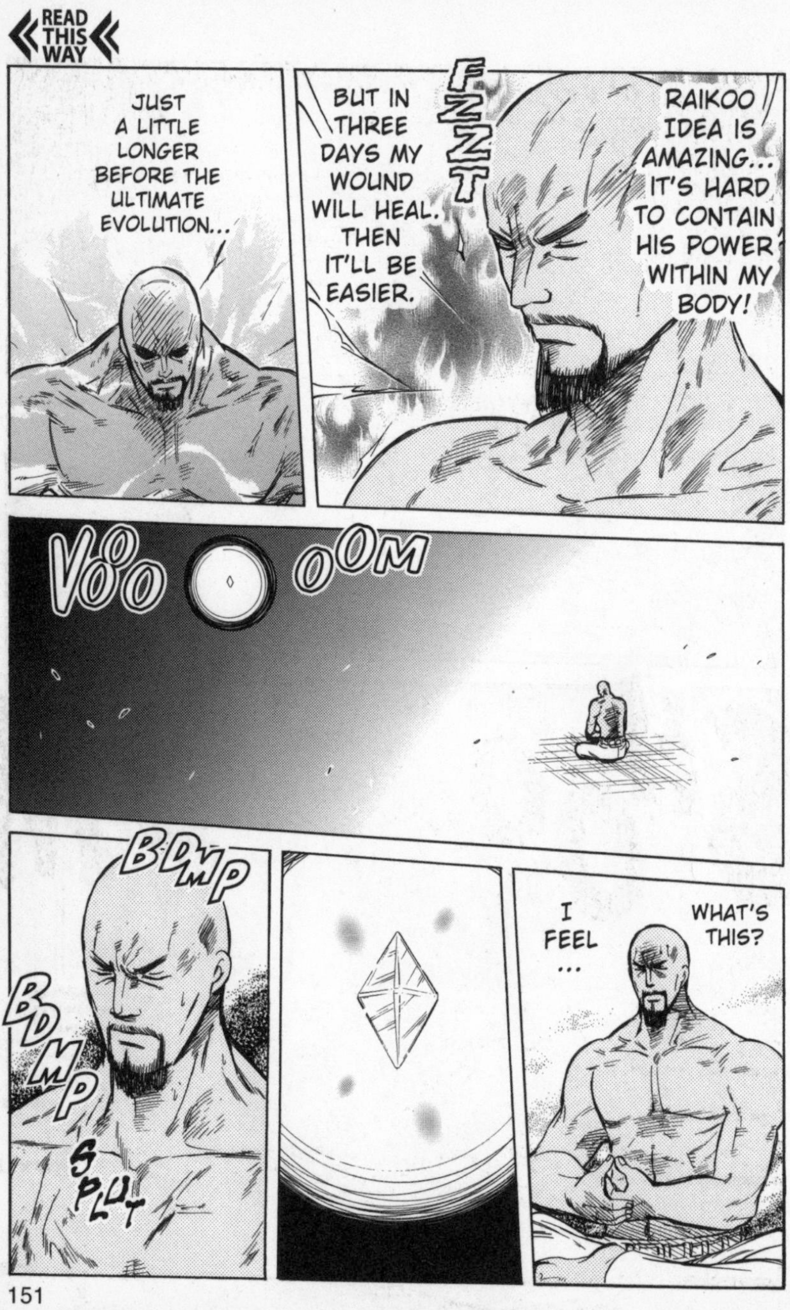

RAIKOO IDEA IS AMAZING... IT'S HARD TO CONTAIN HIS POWER WITHIN MY BODY!
FZZT
BUT IN THREE DAYS MY WOUND WILL HEAL. THEN IT'LL BE EASIER.
JUST A LITTLE LONGER BEFORE THE ULTIMATE EVOLUTION...
VOOOOOOM
WHAT'S THIS?
I FEEL ...
BDMP
BDMP
SPLUT

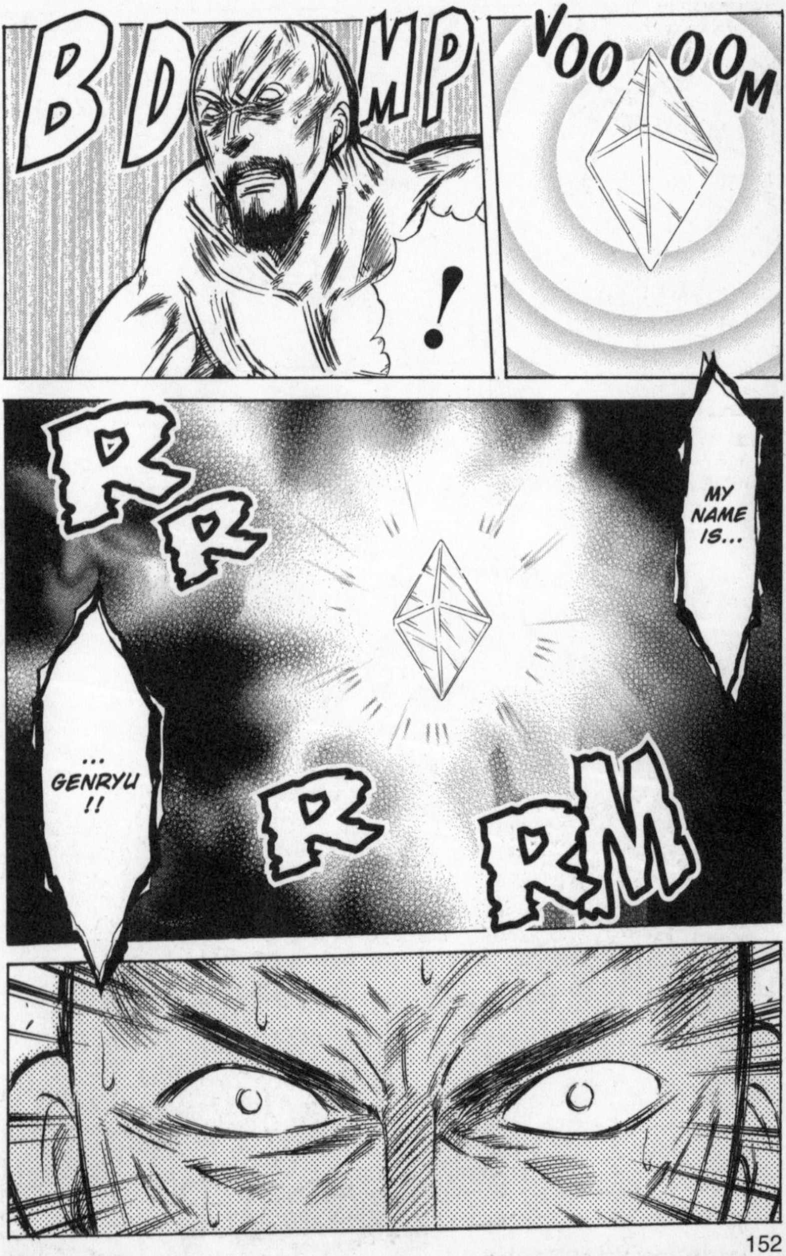
VOO OOM
BD MP
!
MY NAME IS...
RR
...GENRYU!!
R RM

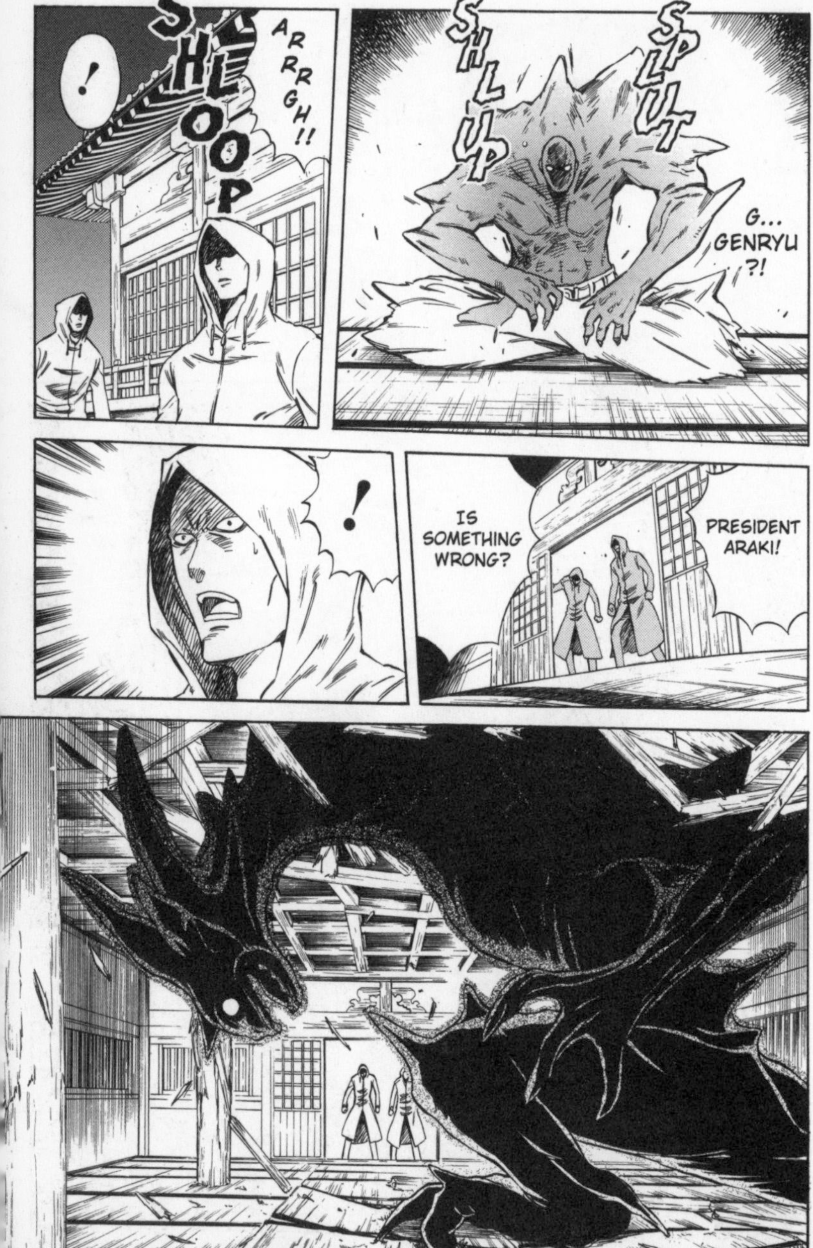
SPLUT
SHLUP
G... GENRYU ?!
ARRGH!!
SHLOOP
!
PRESIDENT ARAKI!
IS SOMETHING WRONG?
!

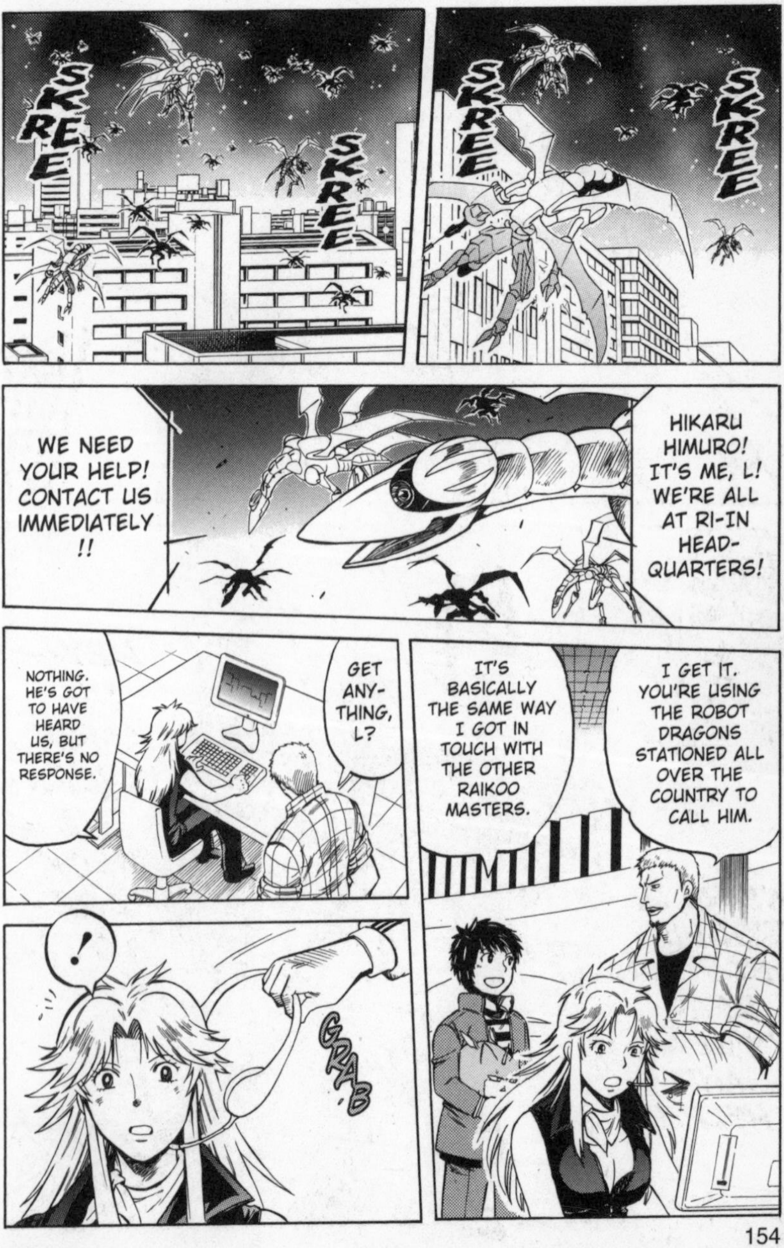
SKREE
SKREE
SKREE
SKREE
HIKARU HIMURO! IT'S ME, L! WE'RE ALL AT RI-IN HEAD-QUARTERS!
WE NEED YOUR HELP! CONTACT US IMMEDIATELY!!
I GET IT. YOU'RE USING THE ROBOT DRAGONS STATIONED ALL OVER THE COUNTRY TO CALL HIM.
IT'S BASICALLY THE SAME WAY I GOT IN TOUCH WITH THE OTHER RAIKOO MASTERS.
GET ANY-THING, L?
NOTHING. HE'S GOT TO HAVE HEARD US, BUT THERE'S NO RESPONSE.
GRAB
!

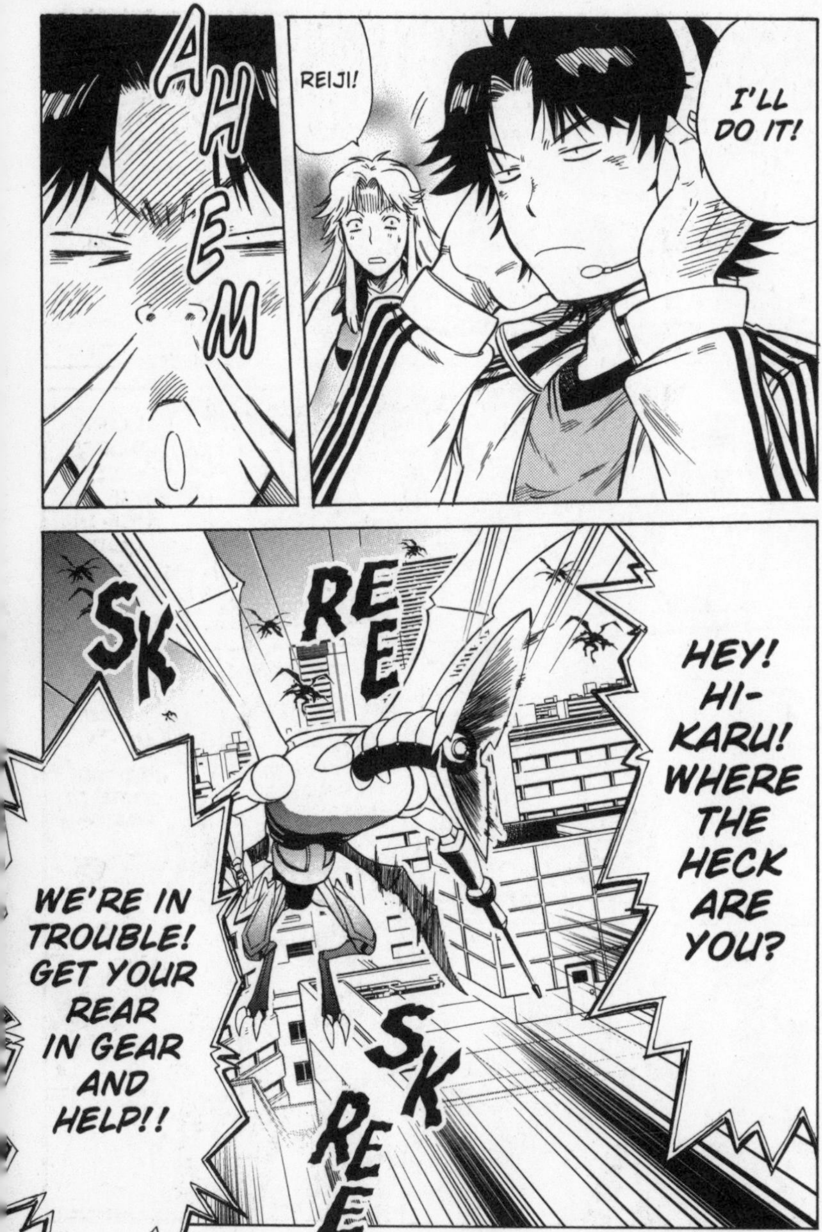
I'LL DO IT!
REIJI!
AHEM
SKREE
HEY! HI-KARU! WHERE THE HECK ARE YOU?
WE'RE IN TROUBLE! GET YOUR REAR IN GEAR AND HELP!!
SKREE

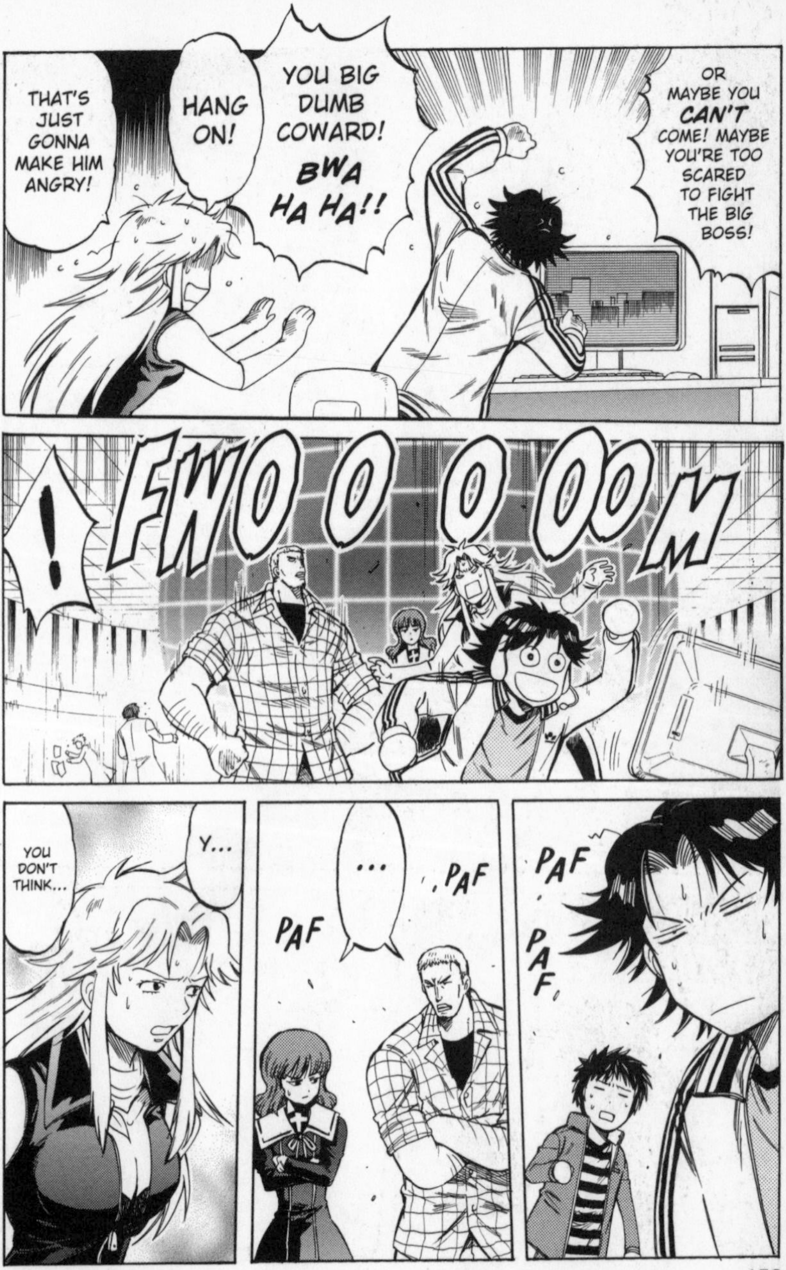
OR MAYBE YOU CAN'T COME! MAYBE YOU'RE TOO SCARED TO FIGHT THE BIG BOSS!
YOU BIG DUMB COWARD!
BWA HA HA!!
HANG ON!
THAT'S JUST GONNA MAKE HIM ANGRY!
FWO O O OOM
!
PAF
PAF
PAF
...
PAF
PAF
Y...
YOU DON'T THINK...

READ THIS WAY

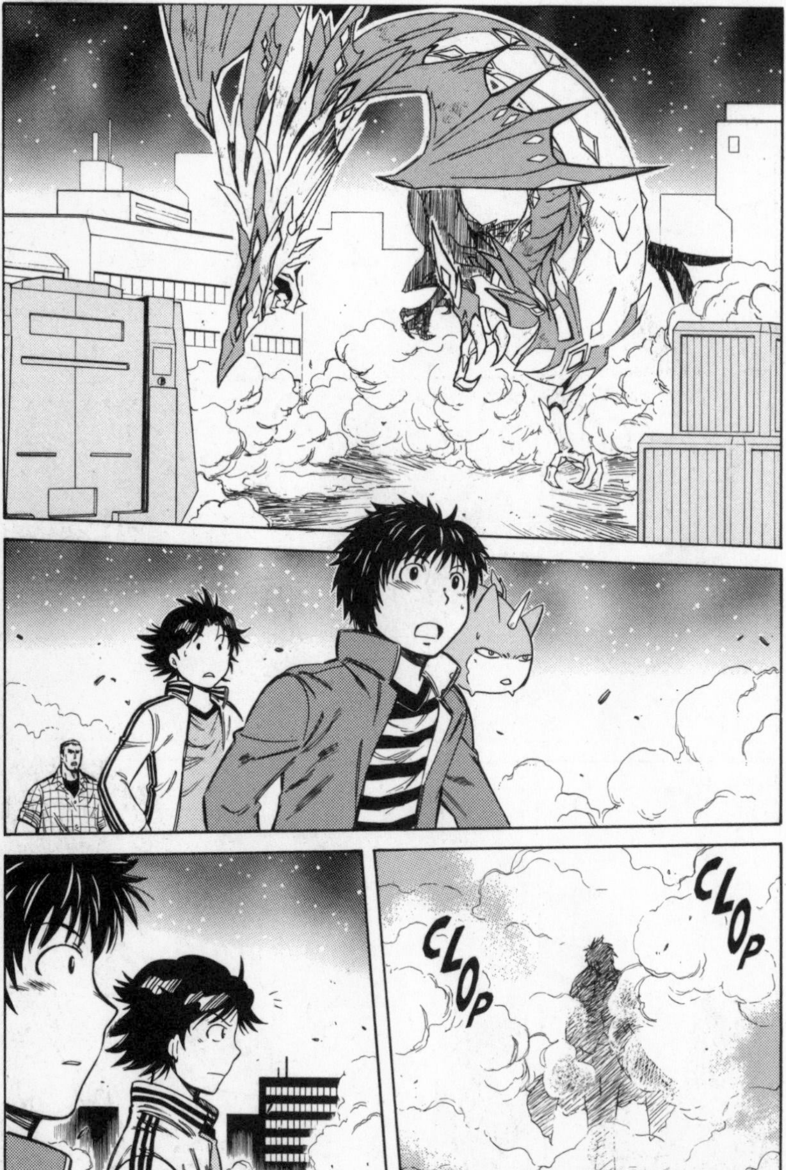
CLOP
CLOP

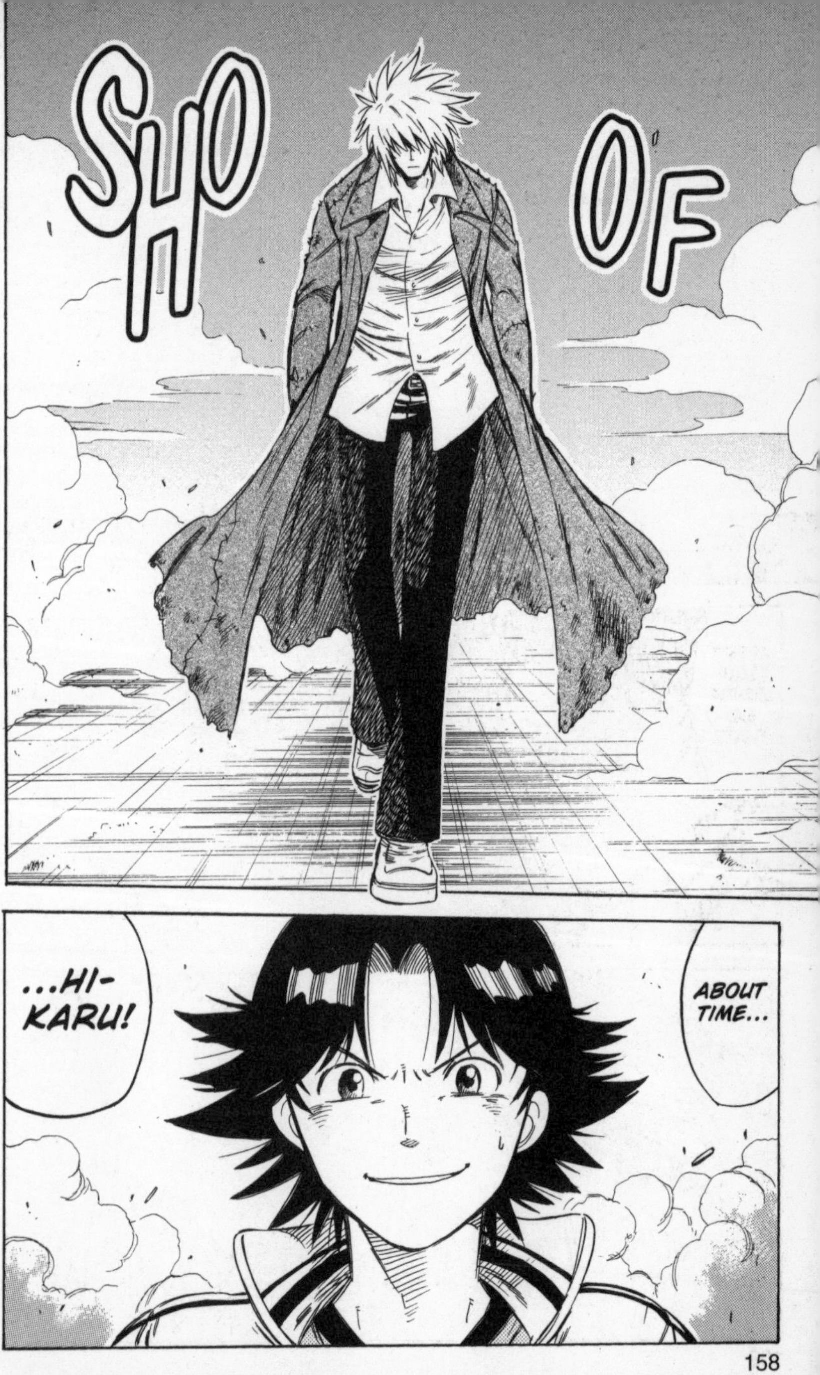
SHOOF
ABOUT TIME...
...HI-KARU!

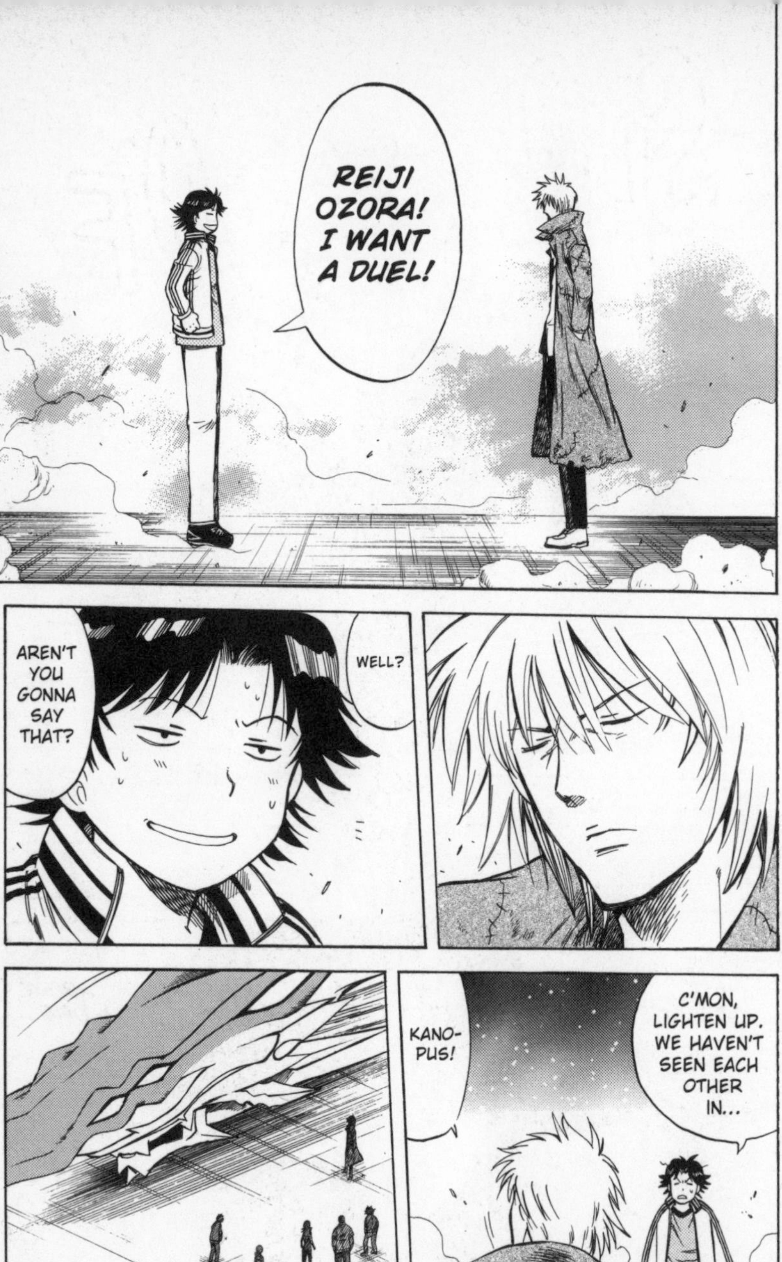
REIJI OZORA! I WANT A DUEL!
WELL?
AREN'T YOU GONNA SAY THAT?
C'MON, LIGHTEN UP. WE HAVEN'T SEEN EACH OTHER IN...
KANO-PUS!

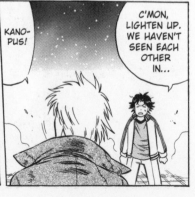

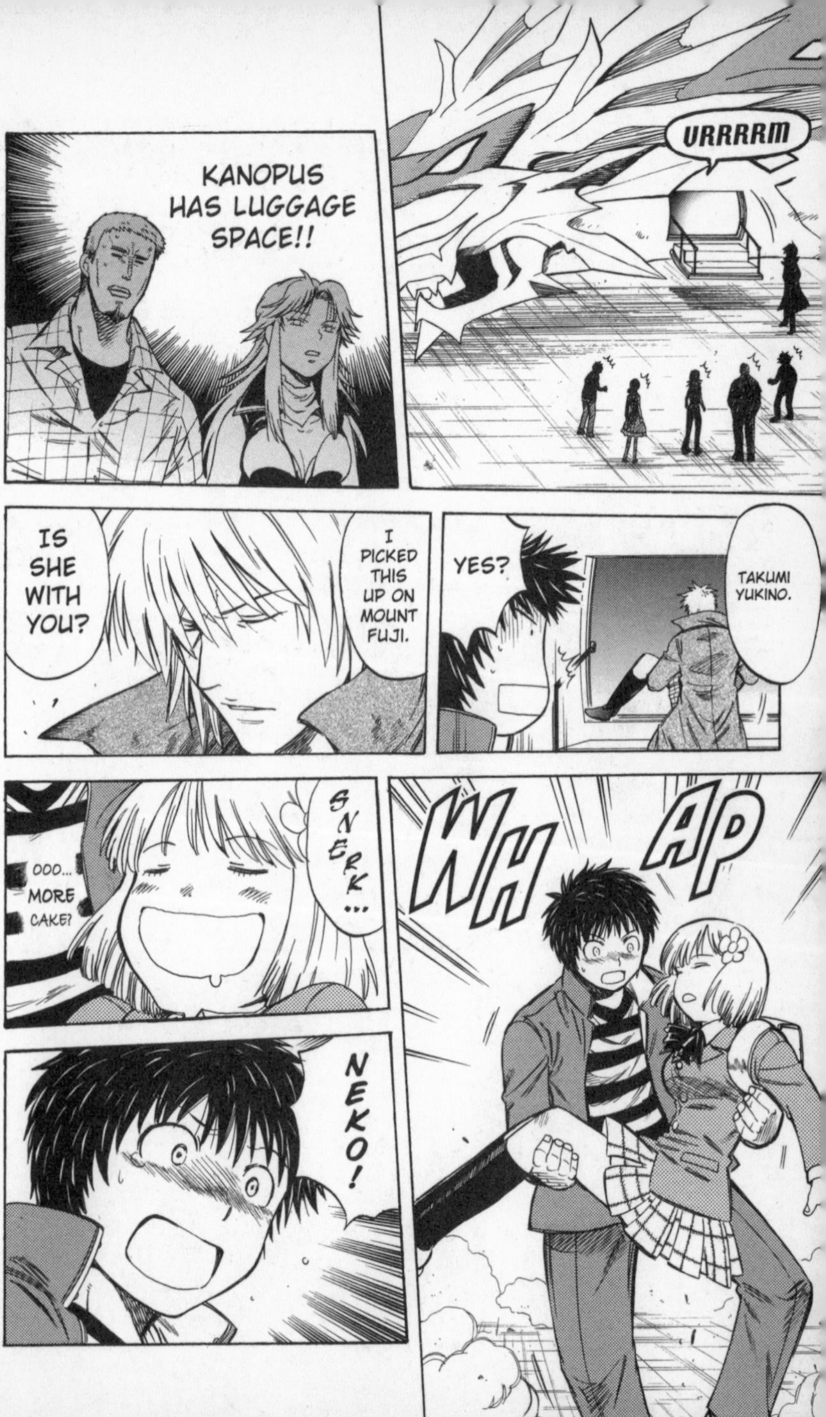
URRRRM
KANOPUS HAS LUGGAGE SPACE!!
TAKUMI YUKINO.
YES?
I PICKED THIS UP ON MOUNT FUJI.
IS SHE WITH YOU?
WH AP
SNERK...
OOO... MORE CAKE?
NEKO!

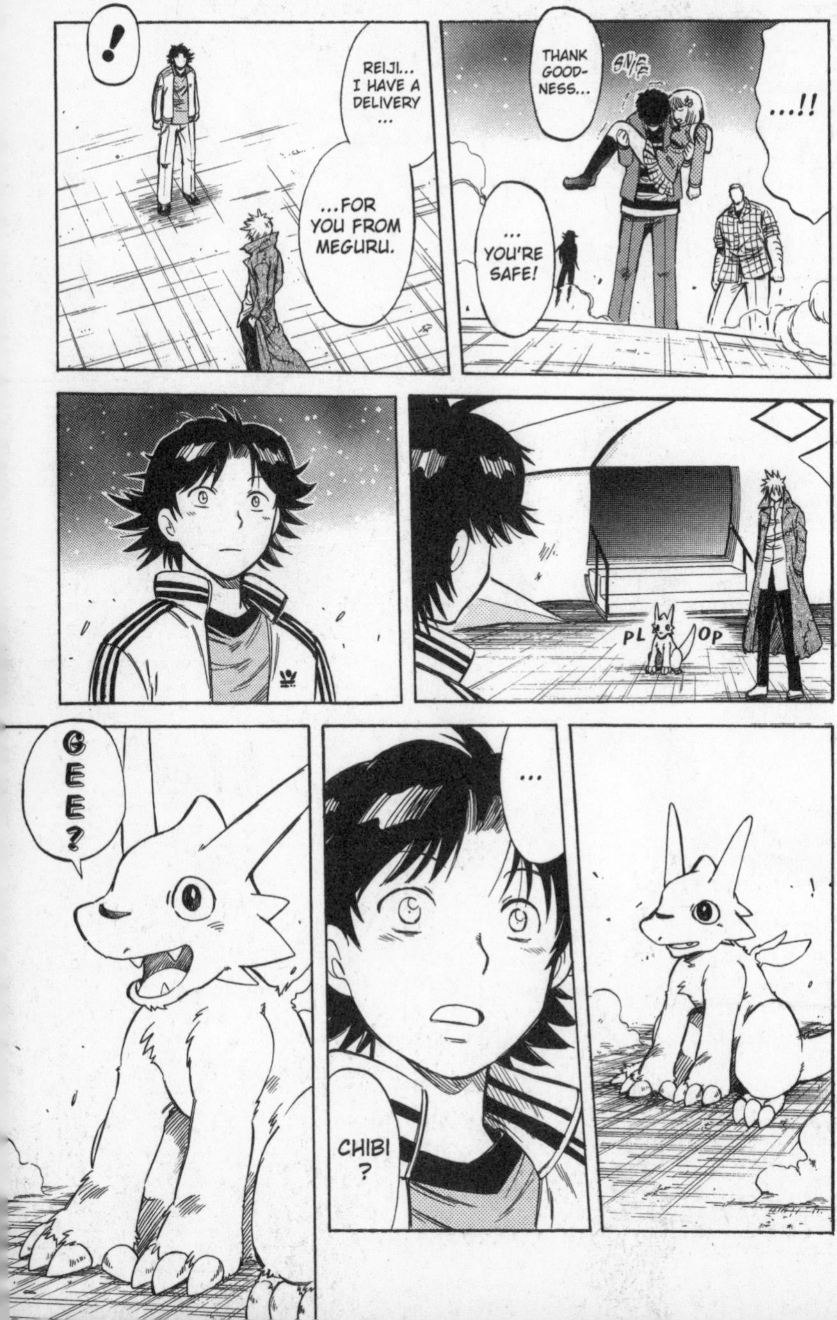
...!!
THANK GOODNESS...
SNIFF
...YOU'RE SAFE!
REIJI... I HAVE A DELIVERY ...
...FOR YOU FROM MEGURU.
!
PLOP
!
...
CHIBI?
GEE?

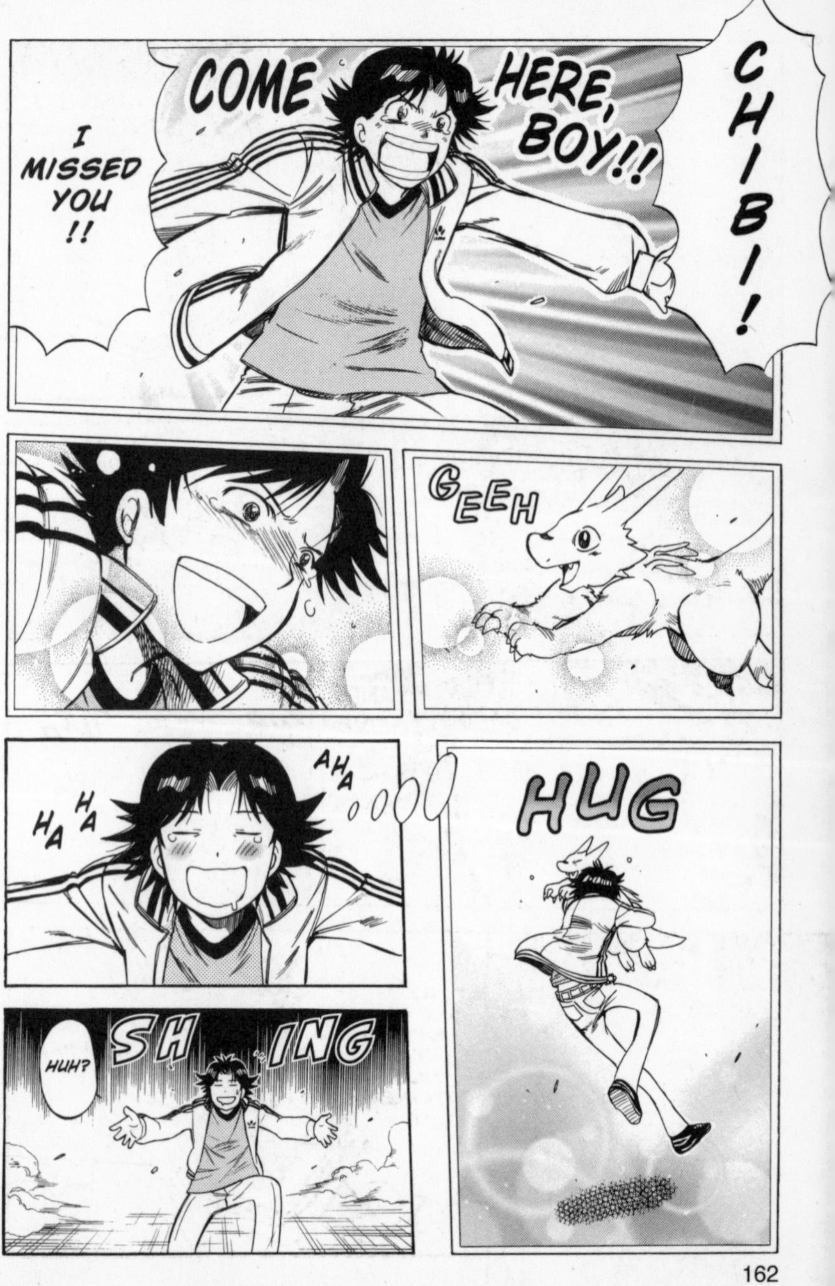

CHIBI!
COME HERE, BOY!!
I MISSED YOU !!
GEEH
HUG
HA HA
AHA
SH ING
HUH?

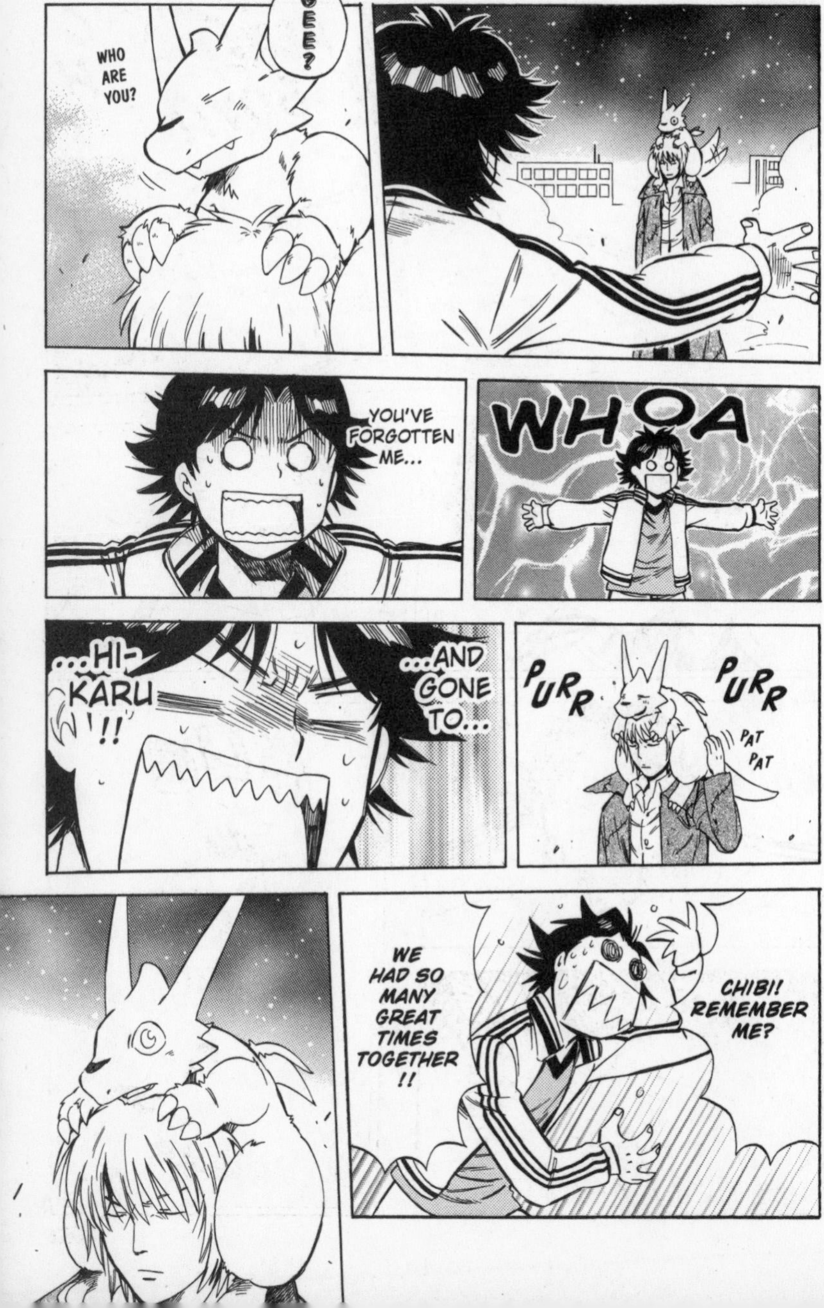
GEE?
WHO ARE YOU?
WHOA
YOU'VE FORGOTTEN ME...
PURR
PURR
PAT PAT
...AND GONE TO...
...HI-KARU!!
CHIBI! REMEMBER ME?
WE HAD SO MANY GREAT TIMES TOGETHER!!

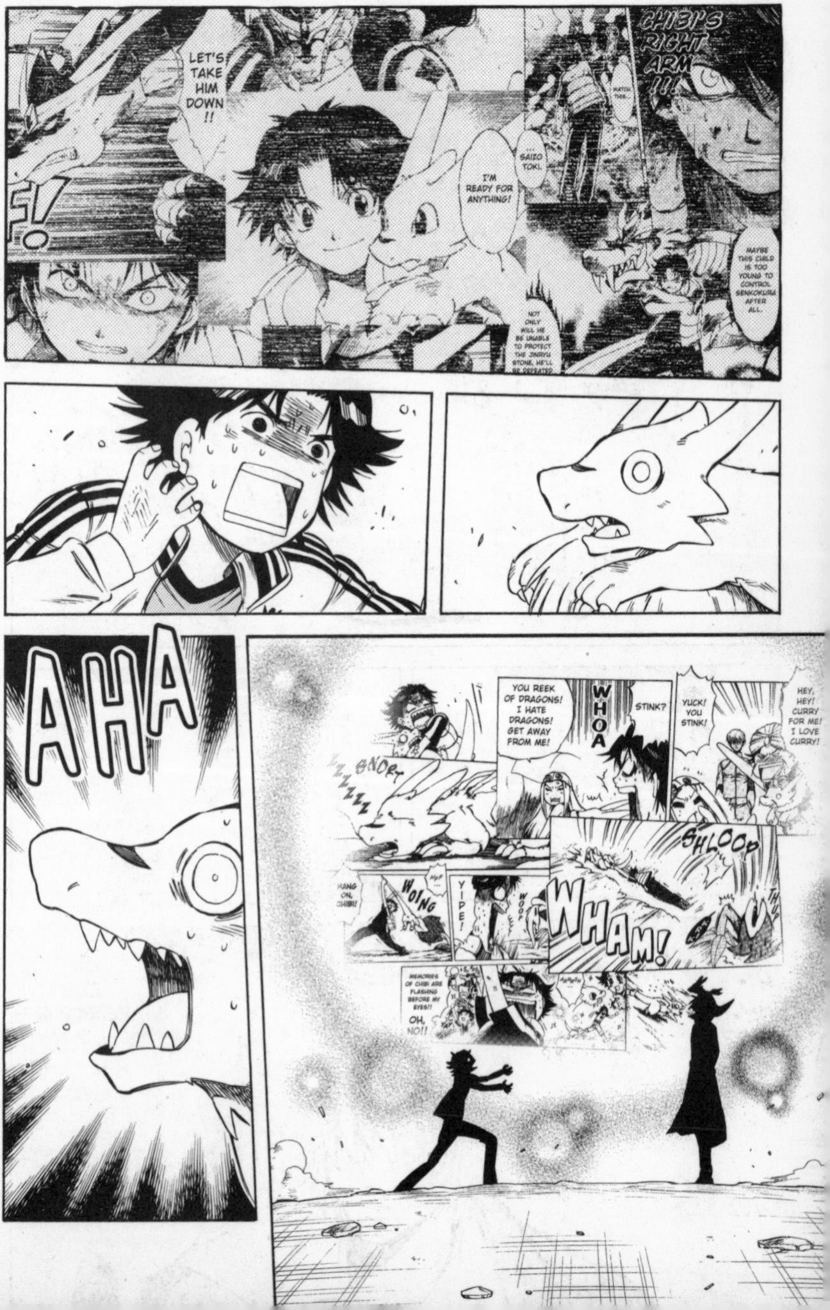
CHIBI'S RIGHT ARM!!!
WATCH THIS...
MAYBE THIS CHILD IS TOO YOUNG TO CONTROL SENKOKURA AFTER ALL.
...SAIZO TOKI.
I'M READY FOR ANYTHING!
NOT ONLY WILL HE BE UNABLE TO PROTECT THE JINRYU STONE, HE'LL BE DEFEATED
LET'S TAKE HIM DOWN!!
AHA
HEY, HEY! CURRY FOR ME! I LOVE CURRY!
YUCK! YOU STINK!
STINK?
WHOA
YOU REEK OF DRAGONS! I HATE DRAGONS! GET AWAY FROM ME!
SNORT
ZZZZZ
SHLOOP
WHAM!
WOOP
YIPE!
HMF...
WOING
HANG ON, CHIBI!
MEMORIES OF CHIBI ARE FLASHING BEFORE MY EYES!!
OH, NO!!

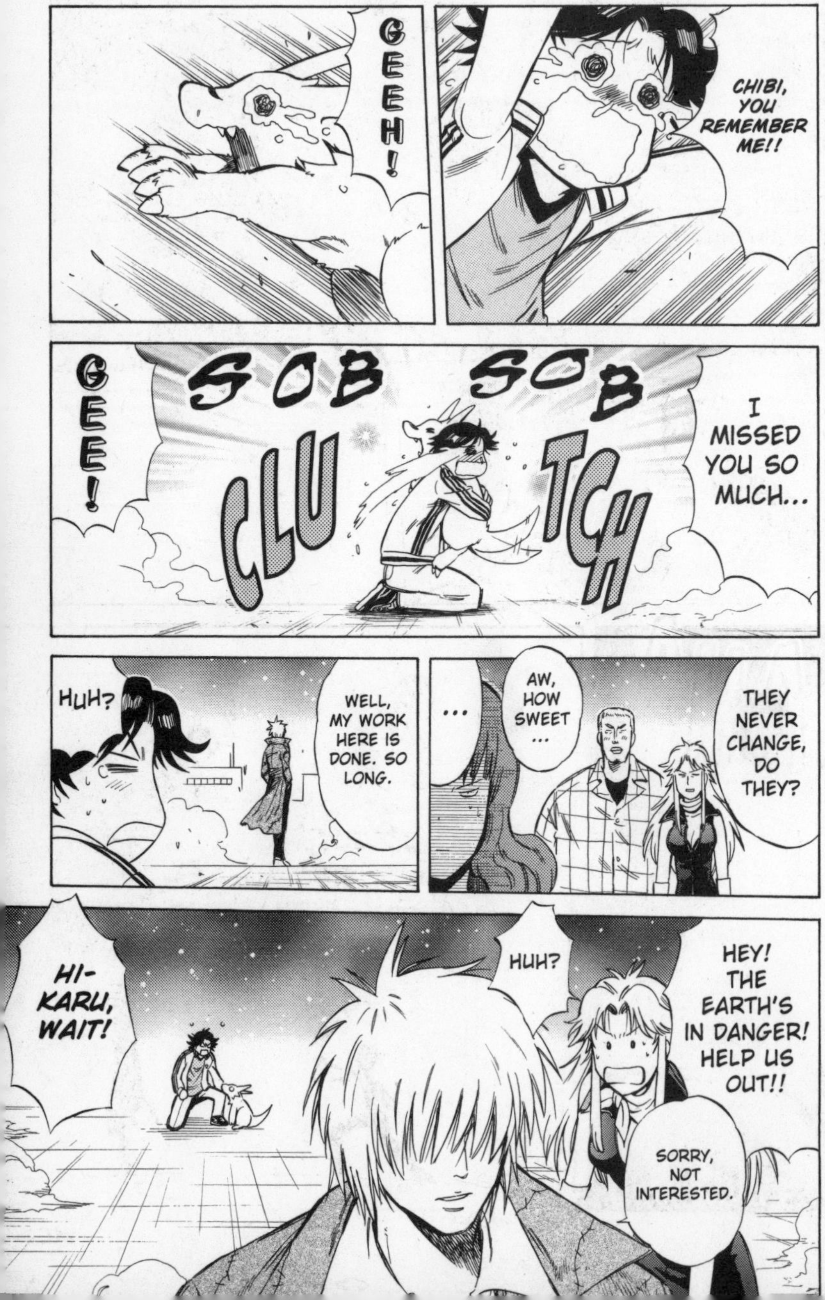
CHIBI, YOU REMEMBER ME!!
GEEH!
I MISSED YOU SO MUCH...
SOB SOB
CLUTCH
GEEE!
THEY NEVER CHANGE, DO THEY?
AW, HOW SWEET ...
...
WELL, MY WORK HERE IS DONE. SO LONG.
HUH?
HEY! THE EARTH'S IN DANGER! HELP US OUT!!
HUH?
HI-KARU, WAIT!
SORRY, NOT INTERESTED.

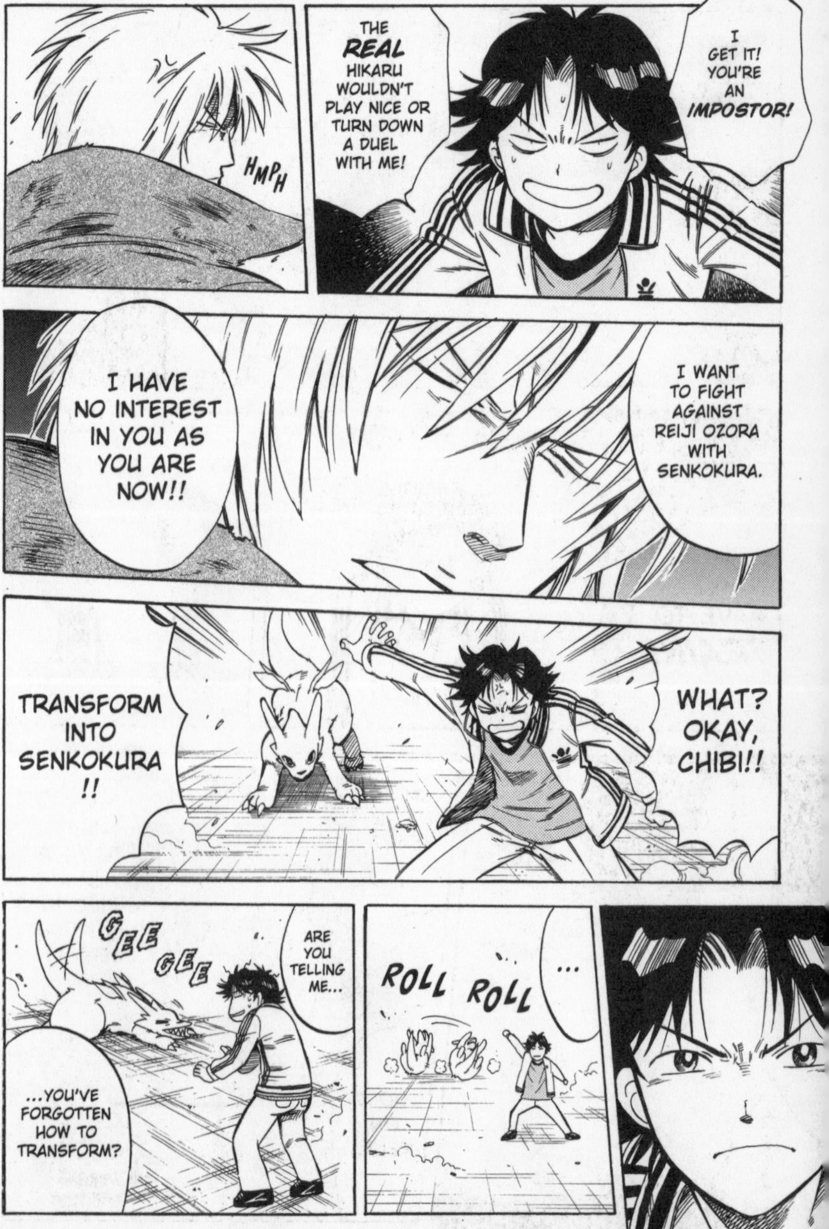
I GET IT! YOU'RE AN IMPOSTOR!
THE REAL HIKARU WOULDN'T PLAY NICE OR TURN DOWN A DUEL WITH ME!
HMPH
I WANT TO FIGHT AGAINST REIJI OZORA WITH SENKOKURA.
I HAVE NO INTEREST IN YOU AS YOU ARE NOW!!
WHAT? OKAY, CHIBI!!
TRANSFORM INTO SENKOKURA!!
...
ROLL ROLL
ARE YOU TELLING ME...
GEE GEE
...YOU'VE FORGOTTEN HOW TO TRANSFORM?

READ THIS WAY

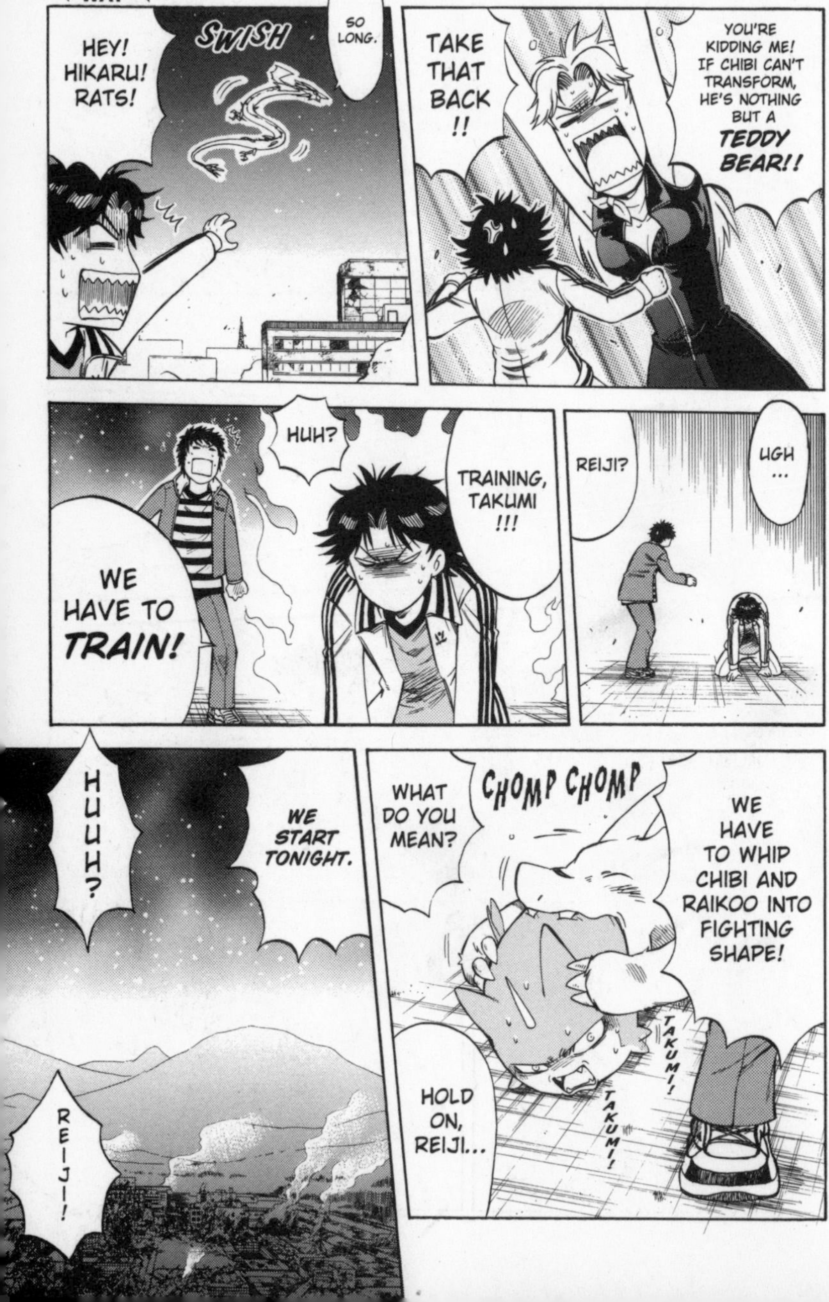
YOU'RE KIDDING ME! IF CHIBI CAN'T TRANSFORM, HE'S NOTHING BUT A TEDDY BEAR!!
TAKE THAT BACK !!
SO LONG.
SWISH
HEY! HIKARU! RATS!
UGH ...
REIJI?
TRAINING, TAKUMI !!!
HUH?
WE HAVE TO TRAIN!
WE HAVE TO WHIP CHIBI AND RAIKOO INTO FIGHTING SHAPE!
CHOMP CHOMP
WHAT DO YOU MEAN?
TAKUMI! TAKUMI!
HOLD ON, REIJI...
WE START TONIGHT.
HUUUH?
REIJI!

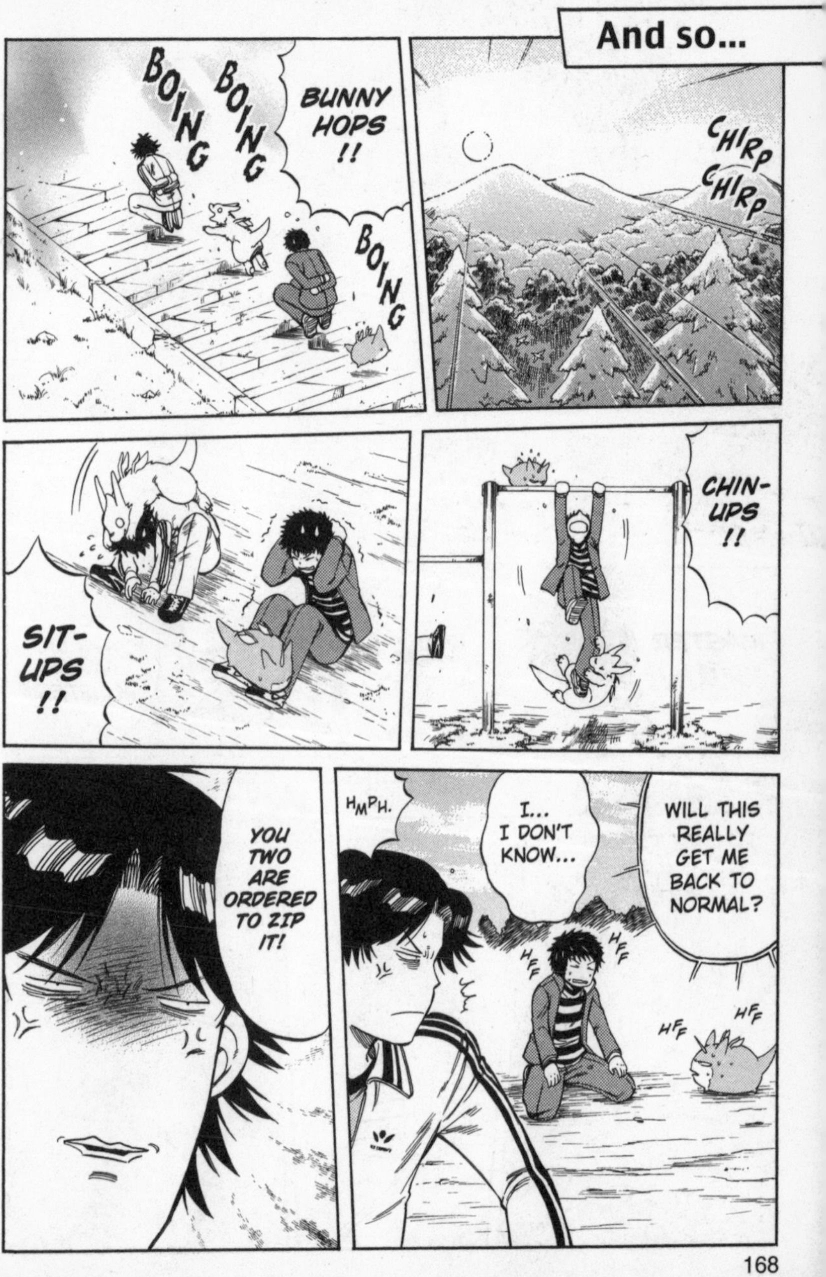

And so...
CHIRP CHIRP
BOING
BOING
BUNNY HOPS !!
BOING
CHIN-UPS !!
SIT-UPS !!
WILL THIS REALLY GET ME BACK TO NORMAL?
I... I DON'T KNOW...
HFF
HFF
HFF
HFF
HMPH.
YOU TWO ARE ORDERED TO ZIP IT!

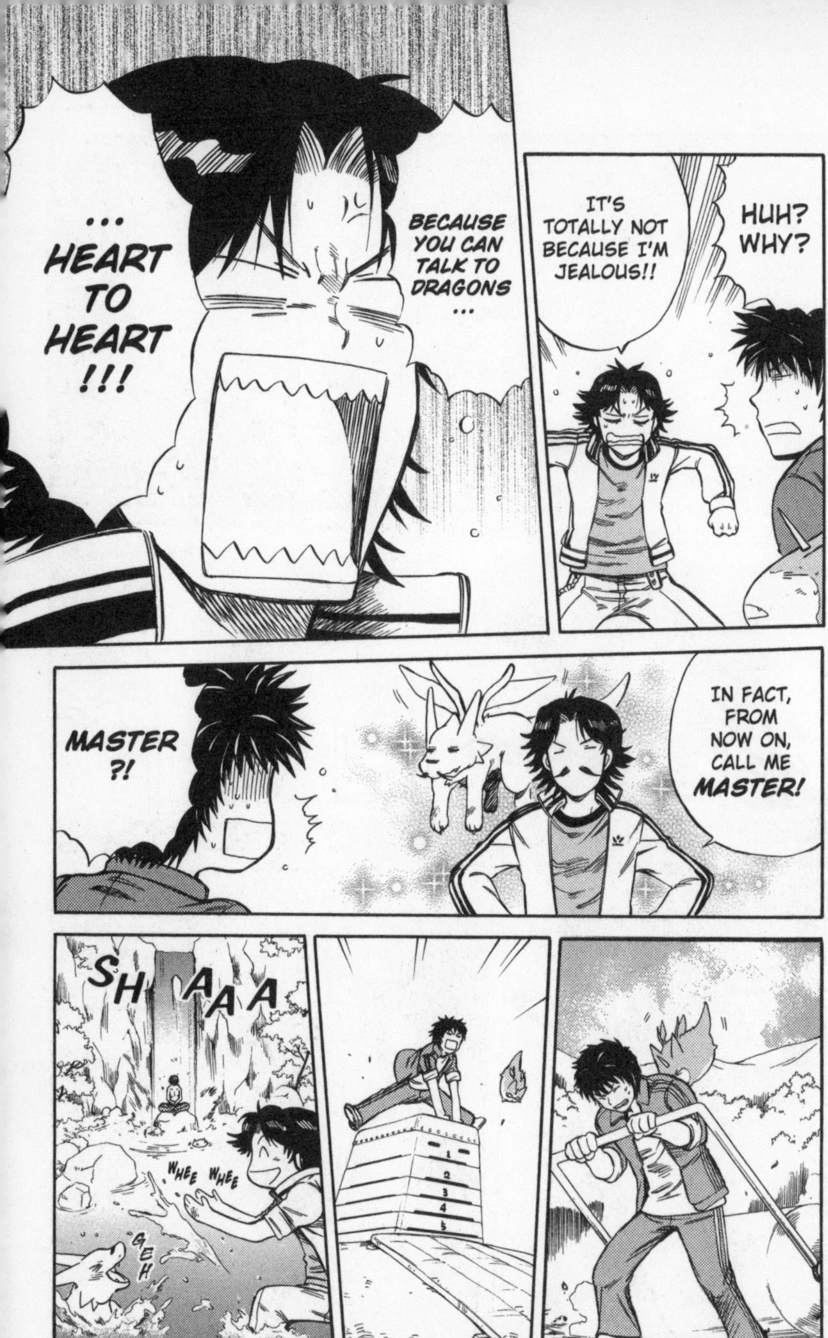
HUH? WHY?
IT'S TOTALLY NOT BECAUSE I'M JEALOUS!!
BECAUSE YOU CAN TALK TO DRAGONS...
... HEART TO HEART!!!
IN FACT, FROM NOW ON, CALL ME MASTER!
MASTER?!
SHAAA
WHEE WHEE
GEH

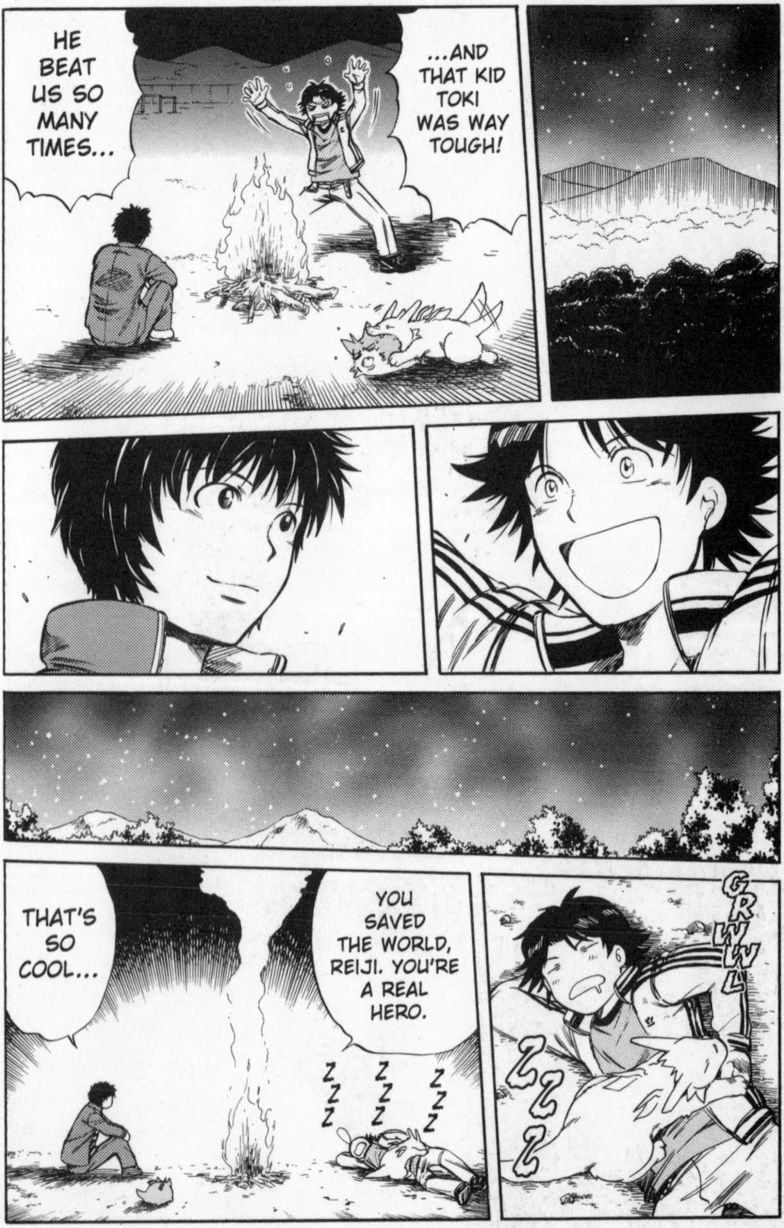
...AND THAT KID TOKI WAS WAY TOUGH!
HE BEAT US SO MANY TIMES...
GRWL
ZZZ
YOU SAVED THE WORLD, REIJI. YOU'RE A REAL HERO.
ZZZ ZZZ ZZZ
THAT'S SO COOL...

READ THIS WAY

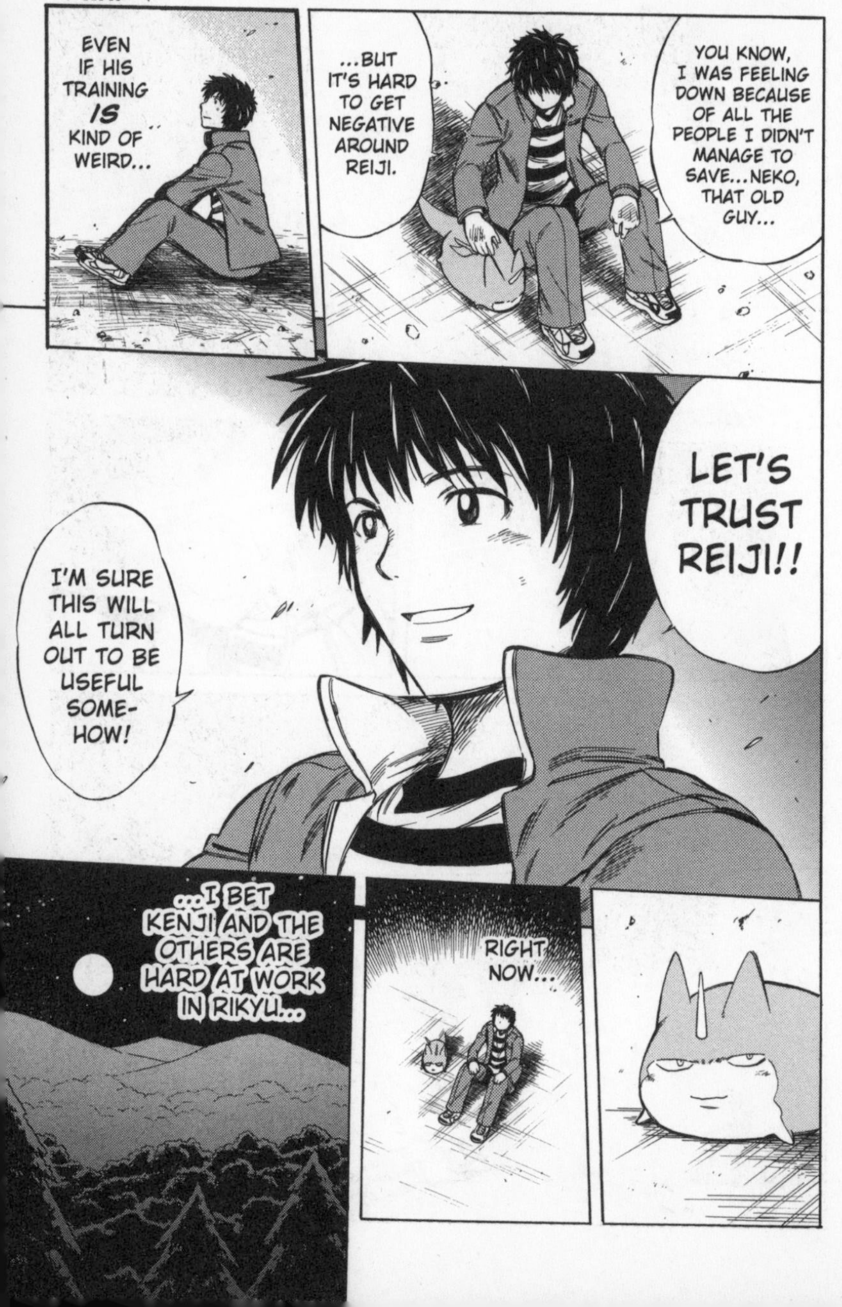
YOU KNOW, I WAS FEELING DOWN BECAUSE OF ALL THE PEOPLE I DIDN'T MANAGE TO SAVE...NEKO, THAT OLD GUY...
...BUT IT'S HARD TO GET NEGATIVE AROUND REIJI.
EVEN IF HIS TRAINING *IS* KIND OF WEIRD...
LET'S TRUST REIJI!!
I'M SURE THIS WILL ALL TURN OUT TO BE USEFUL SOME-HOW!
RIGHT NOW...
...I BET KENJI AND THE OTHERS ARE HARD AT WORK IN RIKYU...

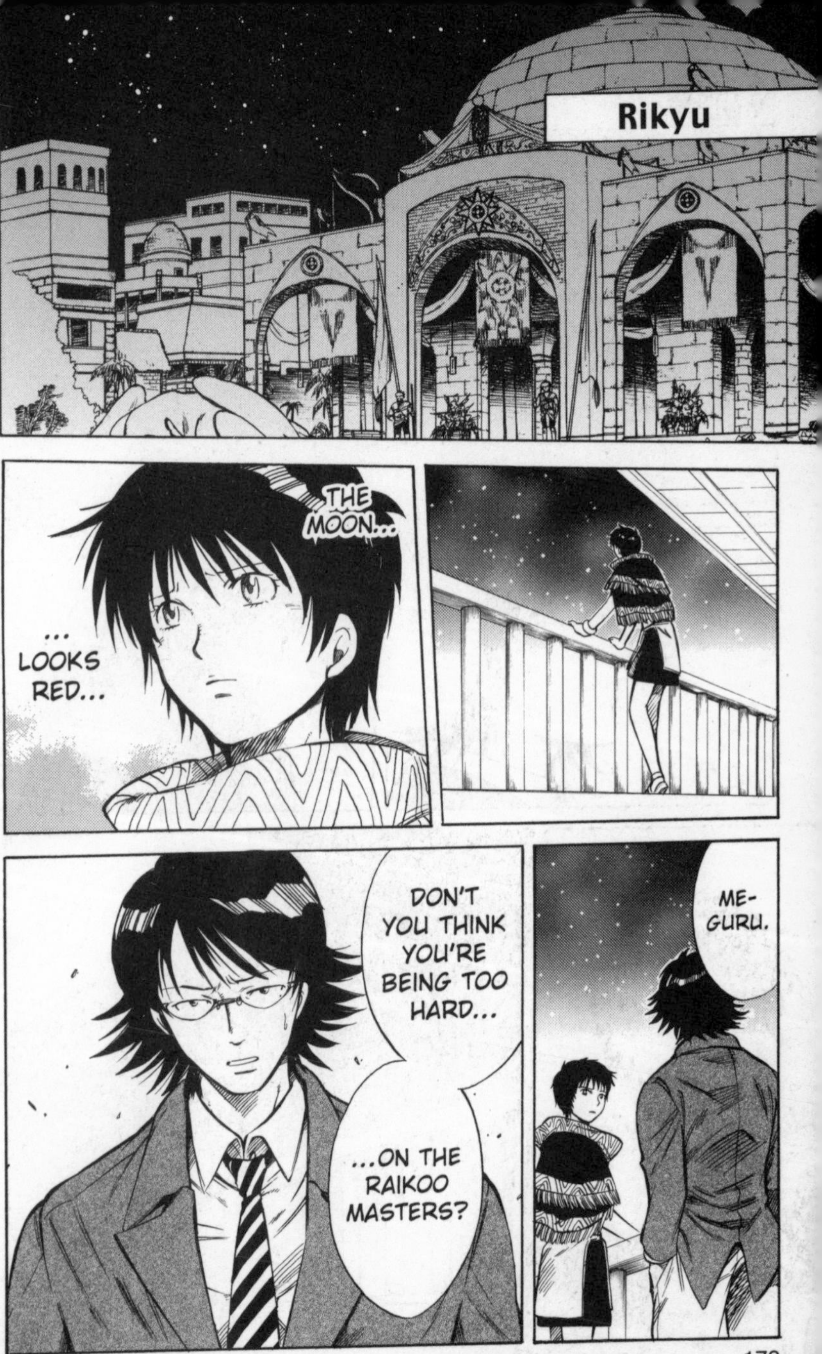
Rikyu
THE MOON...
...LOOKS RED...
ME-GURU.
DON'T YOU THINK YOU'RE BEING TOO HARD...
...ON THE RAIKOO MASTERS?

READ THIS WAY

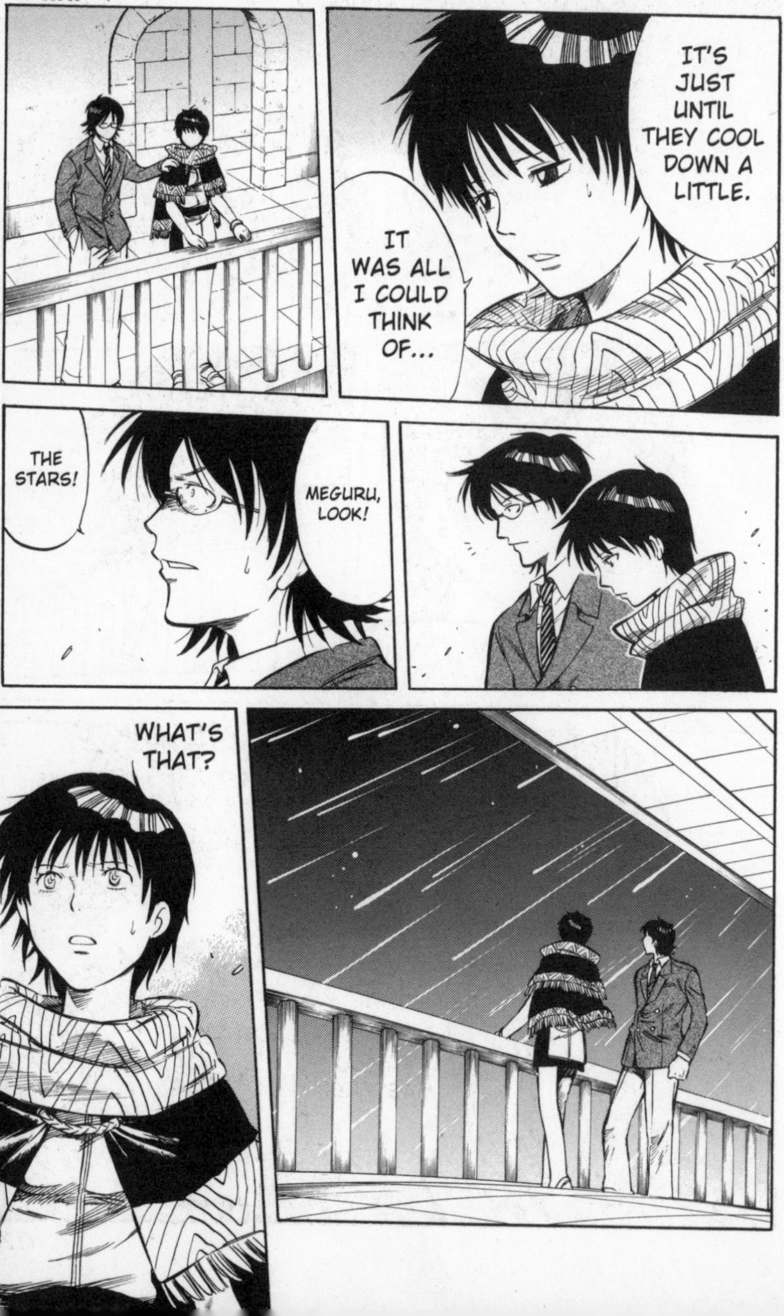
IT'S JUST UNTIL THEY COOL DOWN A LITTLE.
IT WAS ALL I COULD THINK OF...
MEGURU, LOOK!
THE STARS!
WHAT'S THAT?

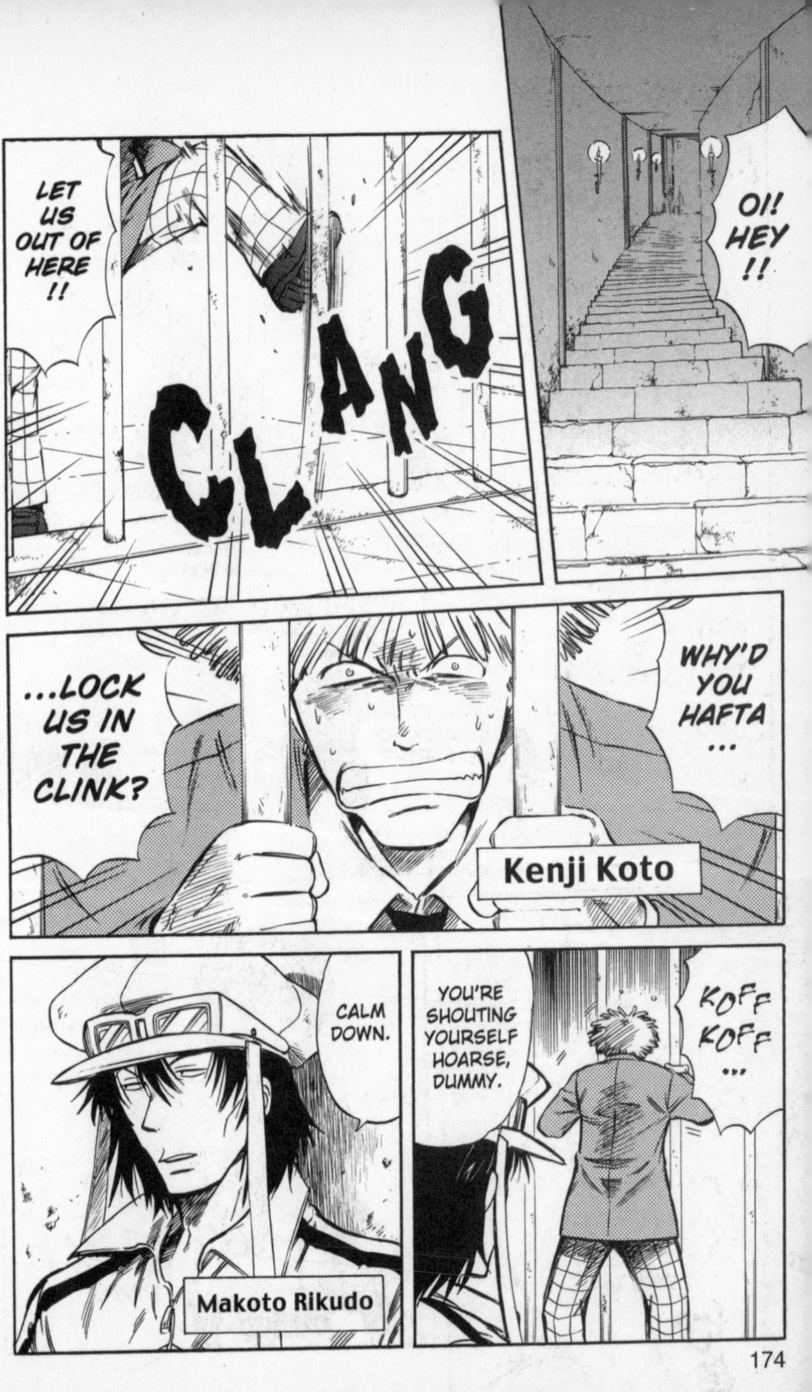
OI! HEY !!
LET US OUT OF HERE !!
CLANG
WHY'D YOU HAFTA ...
...LOCK US IN THE CLINK?
Kenji Koto
KOFF KOFF ...
YOU'RE SHOUTING YOURSELF HOARSE, DUMMY.
CALM DOWN.
Makoto Rikudo

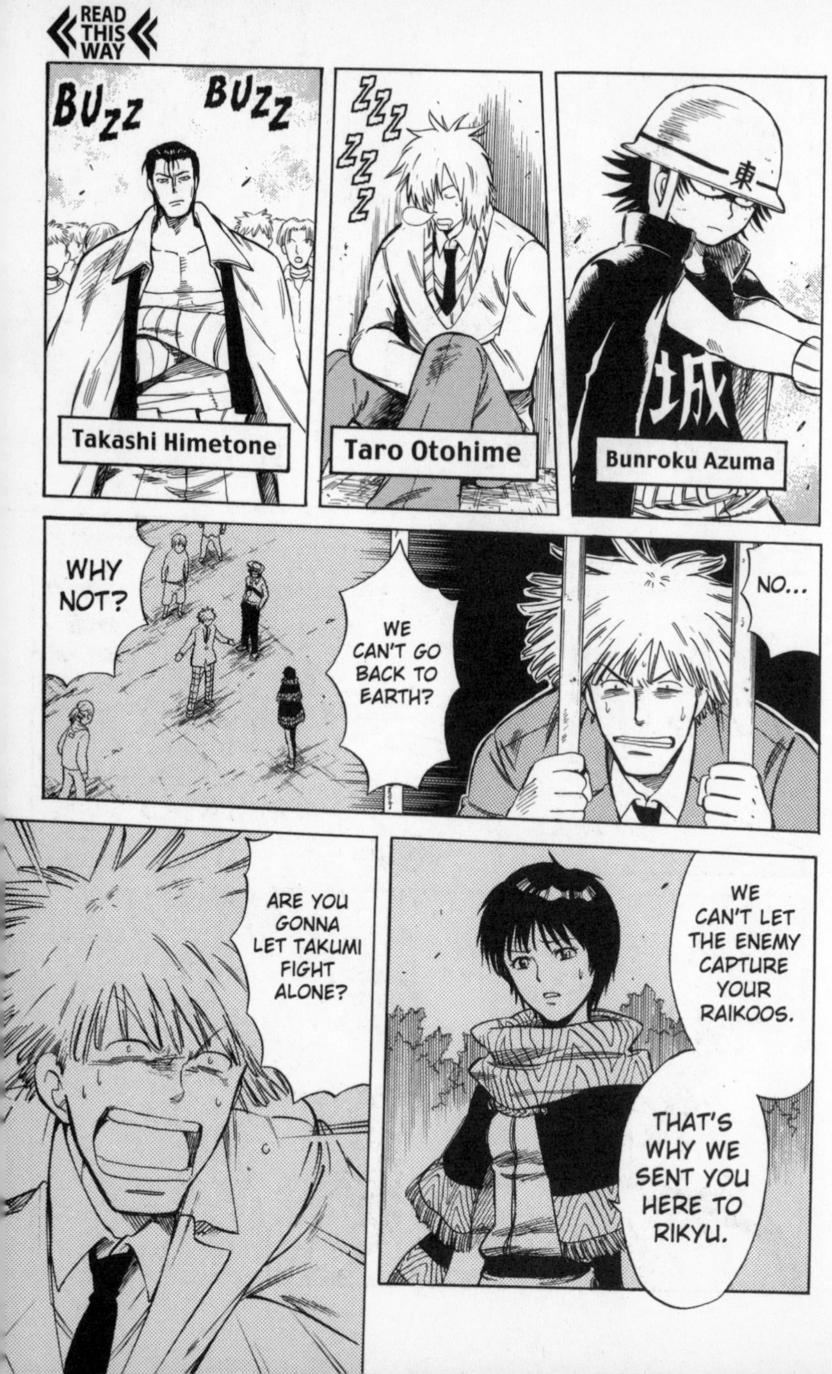
READ THIS WAY
Bunroku Azuma
ZZZ ZZZ
Taro Otohime
BUZZ BUZZ
Takashi Himetone
NO...
WE CAN'T GO BACK TO EARTH?
WHY NOT?
WE CAN'T LET THE ENEMY CAPTURE YOUR RAIKOOS.
THAT'S WHY WE SENT YOU HERE TO RIKYU.
ARE YOU GONNA LET TAKUMI FIGHT ALONE?

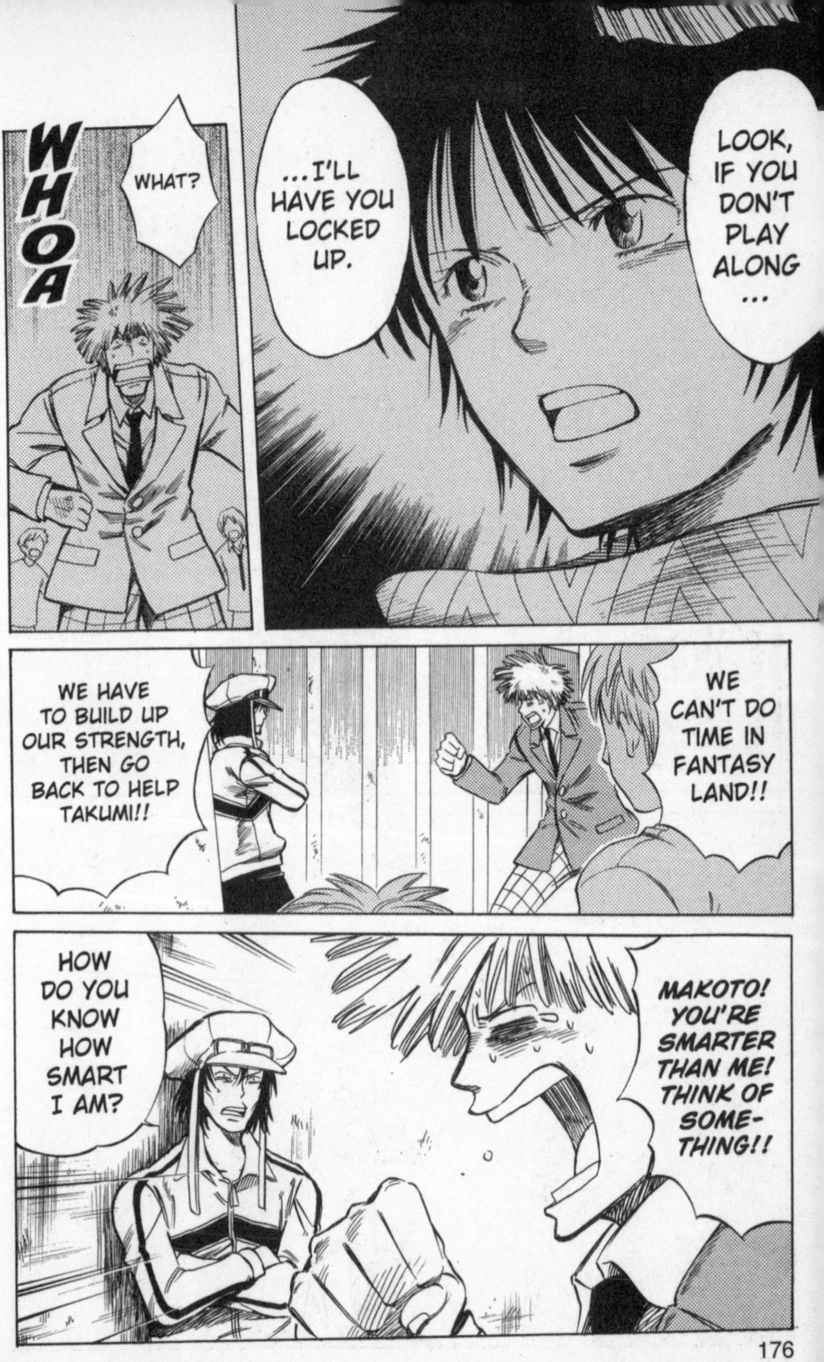
LOOK, IF YOU DON'T PLAY ALONG...
...I'LL HAVE YOU LOCKED UP.
WHAT?
WHOA
WE CAN'T DO TIME IN FANTASY LAND!!
WE HAVE TO BUILD UP OUR STRENGTH, THEN GO BACK TO HELP TAKUMI!!
MAKOTO! YOU'RE SMARTER THAN ME! THINK OF SOME-THING!!
HOW DO YOU KNOW HOW SMART I AM?

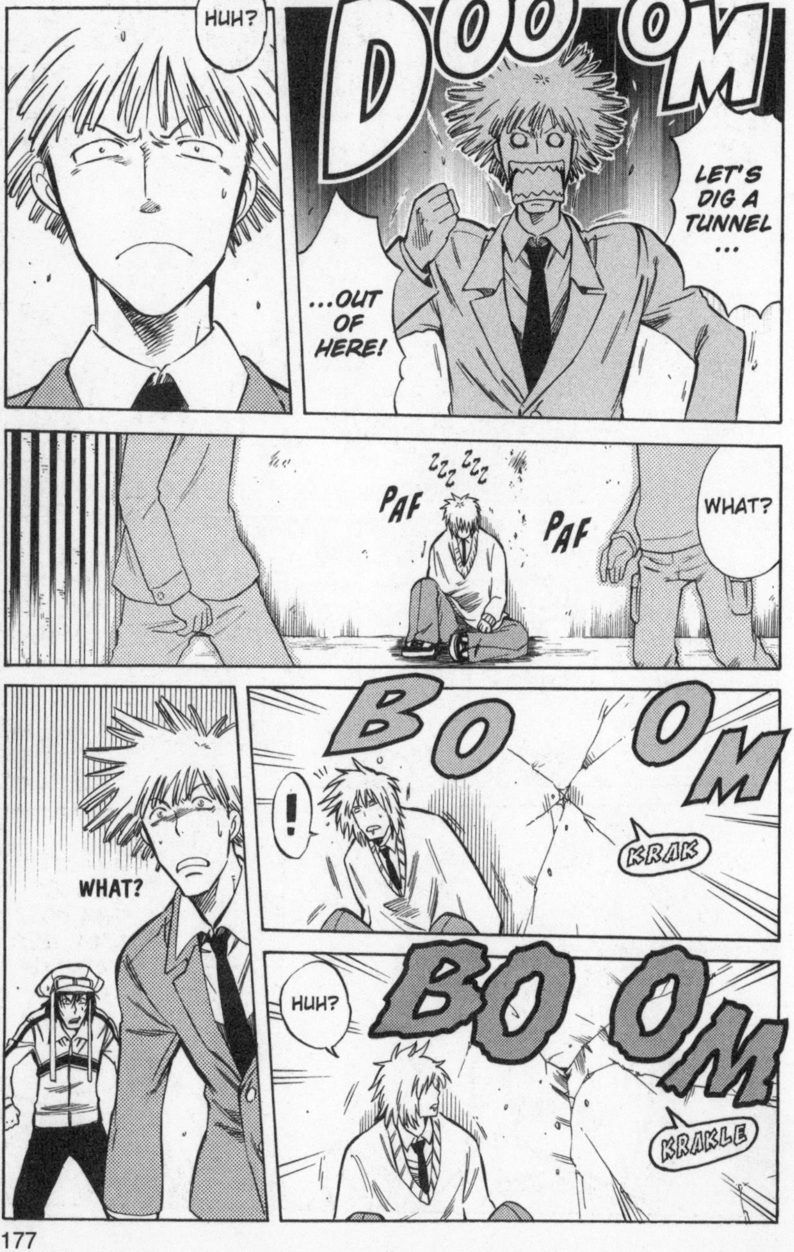
DOOOM
LET'S DIG A TUNNEL ...
...OUT OF HERE!
HUH?
WHAT?
PAF
ZZZ ZZZ
PAF
BOOM
!
KRAK
BOOM
HUH?
KRAKLE
WHAT?

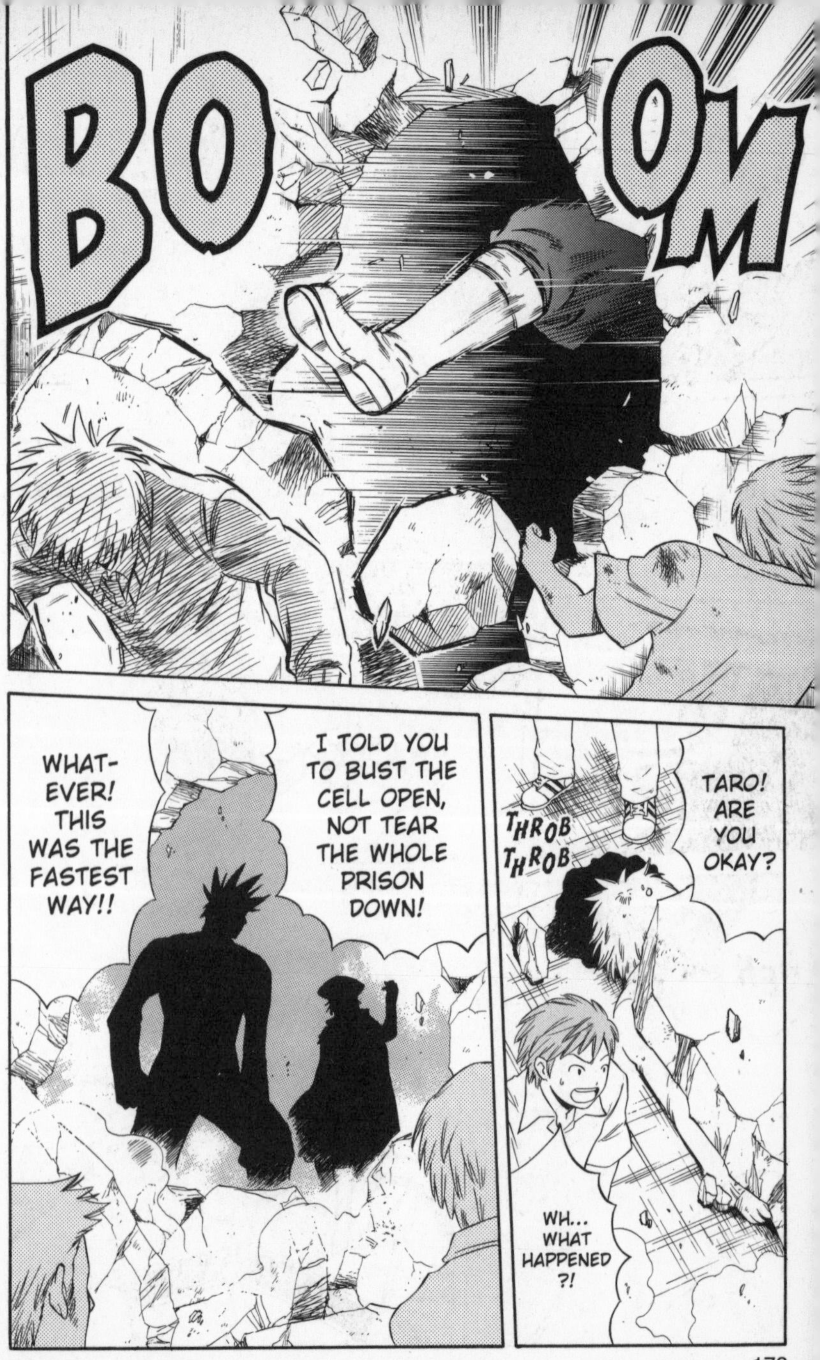
BOOM
TARO! ARE YOU OKAY?
THROB THROB
WH... WHAT HAPPENED ?!
I TOLD YOU TO BUST THE CELL OPEN, NOT TEAR THE WHOLE PRISON DOWN!
WHAT-EVER! THIS WAS THE FASTEST WAY!!

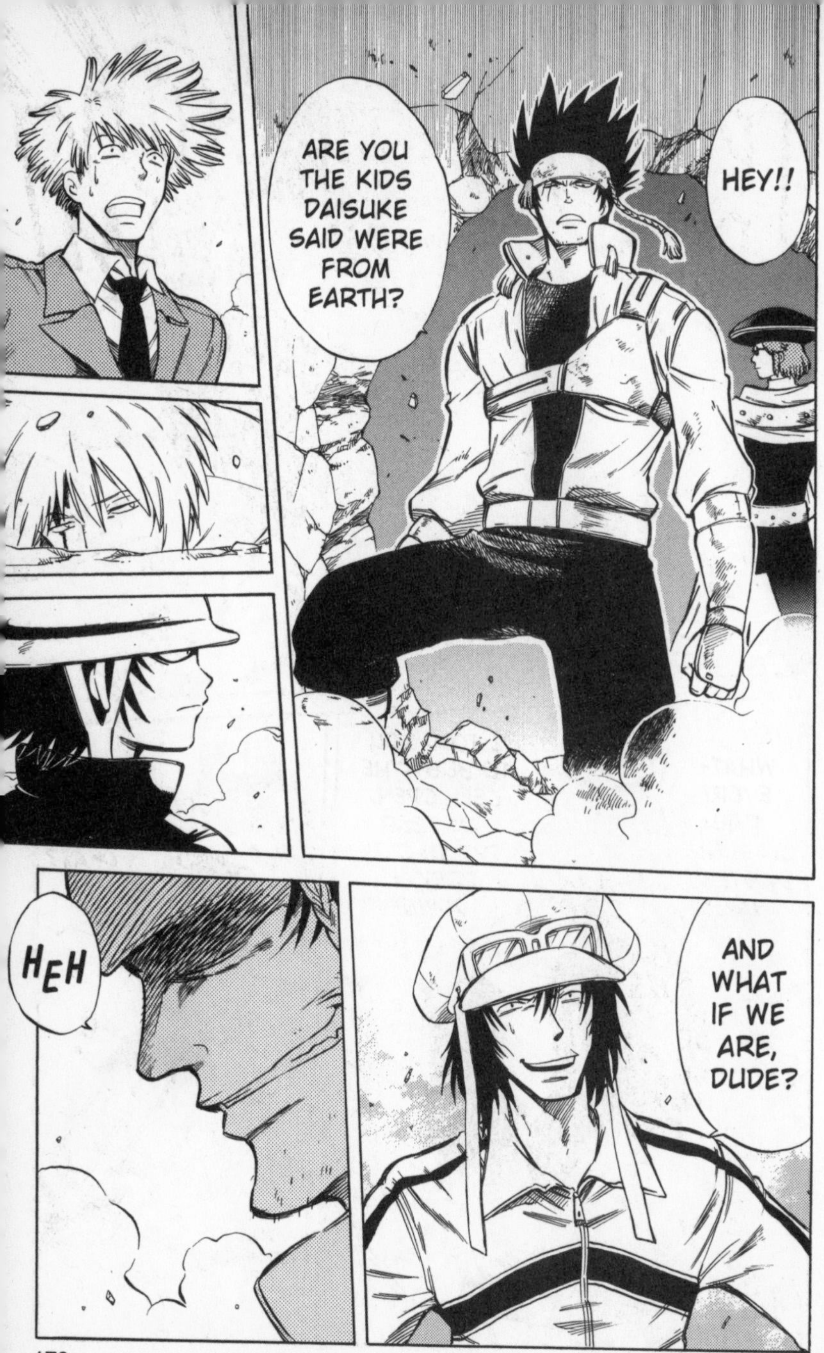
HEY!!
ARE YOU THE KIDS DAISUKE SAID WERE FROM EARTH?
AND WHAT IF WE ARE, DUDE?
HEH

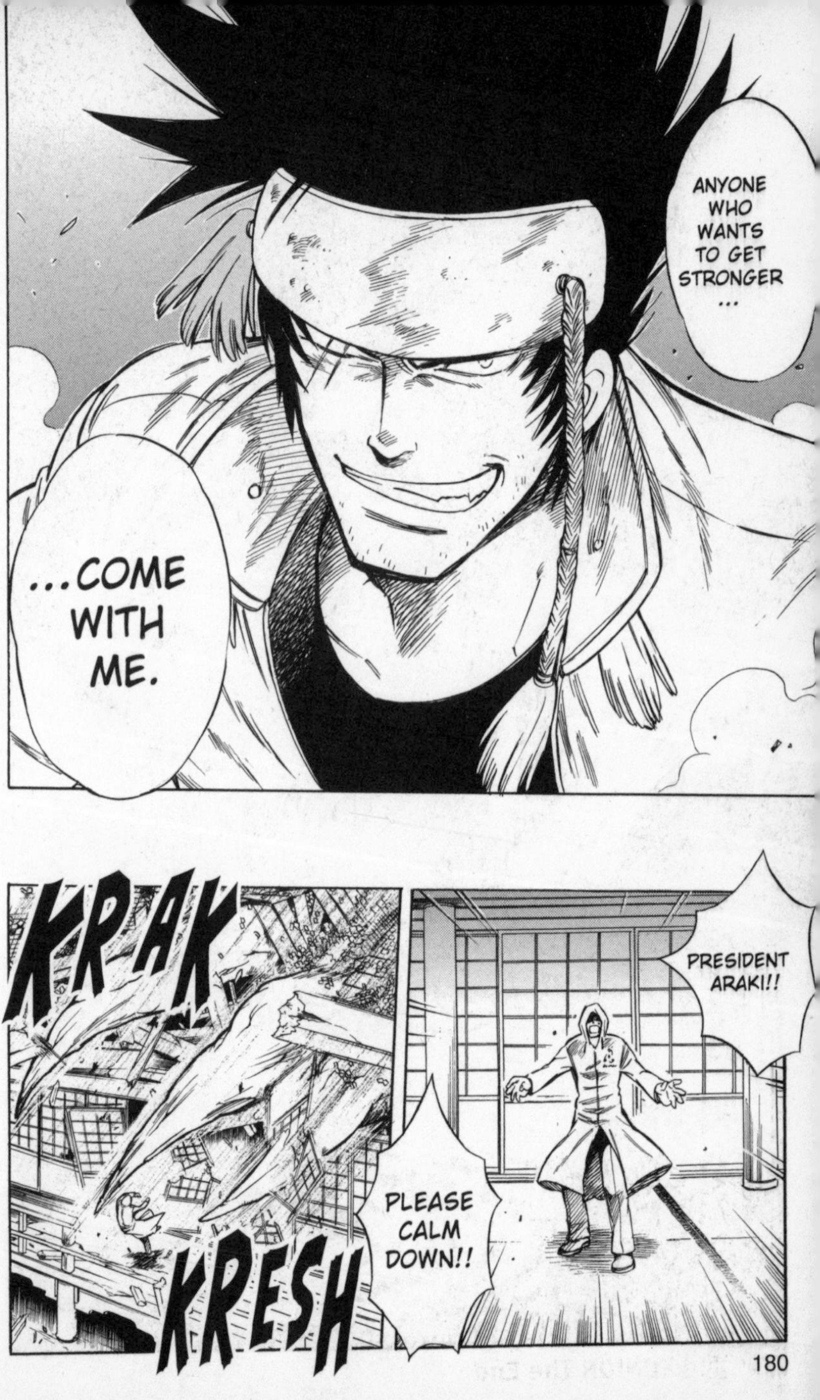
ANYONE WHO WANTS TO GET STRONGER ...
...COME WITH ME.
PRESIDENT ARAKI!!
PLEASE CALM DOWN!!
KRAK
KRESH

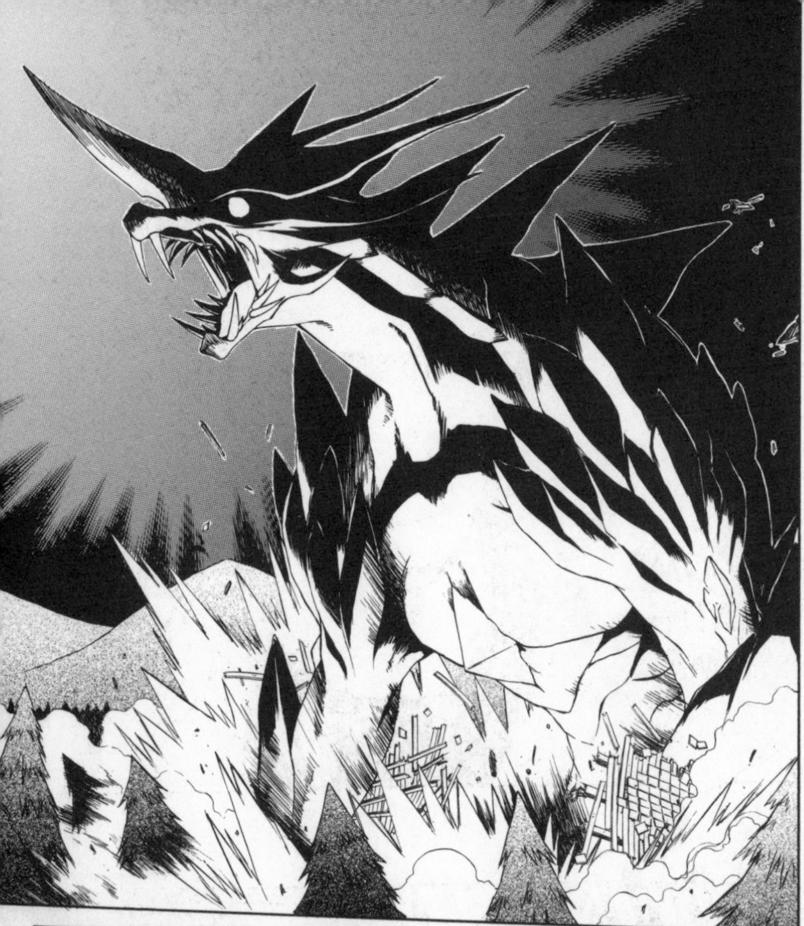

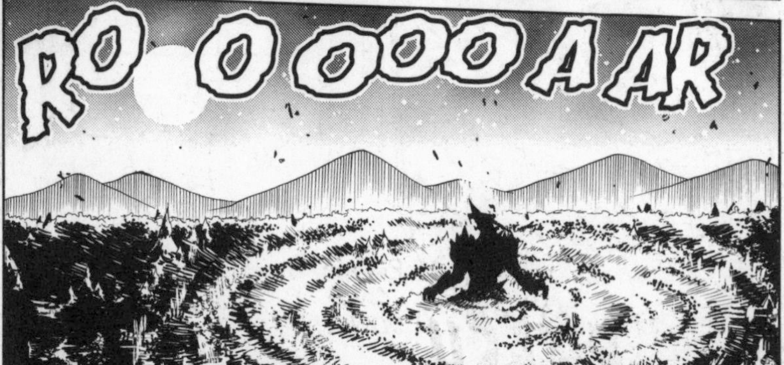
RO O OOO A AR

IT'S HERE!! THE D.D. CARD GAME TRAINING MANGA (REALLY!) THAT WAS A BIG HIT IN JAPAN'S *V-JUMP* MAGAZINE!

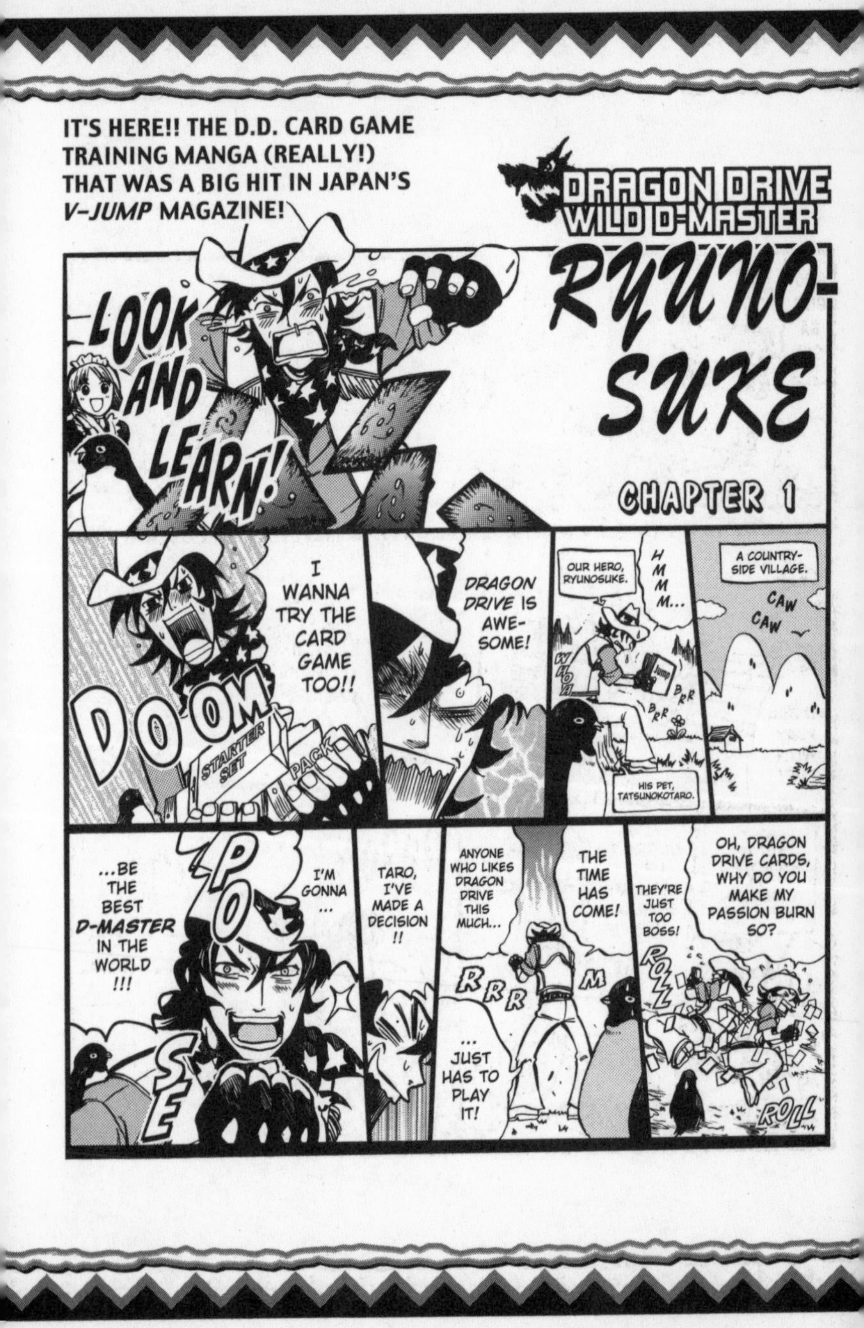
DRAGON DRIVE
WILD D-MASTER
RYUNO-SUKE
CHAPTER 1
LOOK AND LEARN!
A COUNTRY-SIDE VILLAGE.
CAW
CAW
HMMM...
OUR HERO, RYUNOSUKE.
WHOA
Jump
BRR
BRR
HIS PET, TATSUNOKOTARO.
DRAGON DRIVE IS AWE-SOME!
I WANNA TRY THE CARD GAME TOO!!
DOOM
STARTER SET
PACK
OH, DRAGON DRIVE CARDS, WHY DO YOU MAKE MY PASSION BURN SO?
THEY'RE JUST TOO BOSS!
ROLL
ROLL
THE TIME HAS COME!
ANYONE WHO LIKES DRAGON DRIVE THIS MUCH...
RRRM
...JUST HAS TO PLAY IT!
TARO, I'VE MADE A DECISION!!
I'M GONNA...
...BE THE BEST D-MASTER IN THE WORLD!!!
POSE

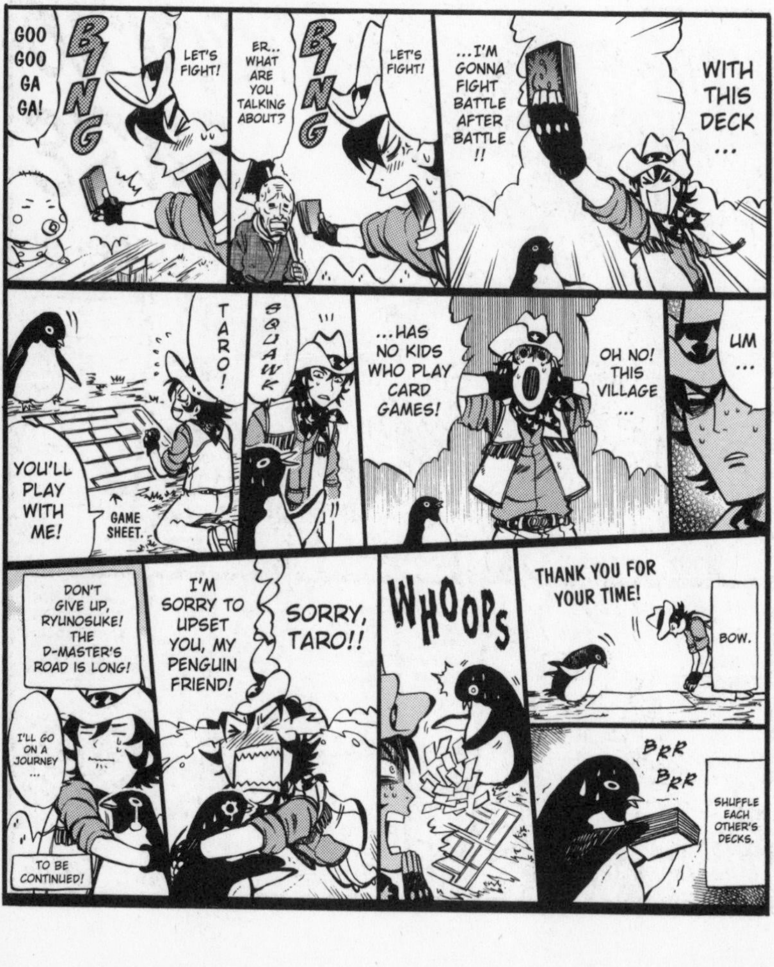
WITH THIS DECK ...
...I'M GONNA FIGHT BATTLE AFTER BATTLE !!
BING
LET'S FIGHT!
ER.. WHAT ARE YOU TALKING ABOUT?
BING
LET'S FIGHT!
GOO GOO GA GA!
UM ...
OH NO! THIS VILLAGE ...
...HAS NO KIDS WHO PLAY CARD GAMES!
SQUAWK
TARO!
YOU'LL PLAY WITH ME!
GAME SHEET.
THANK YOU FOR YOUR TIME!
BOW.
BRR BRR
SHUFFLE EACH OTHER'S DECKS.
WHOOPS
SORRY, TARO!!
I'M SORRY TO UPSET YOU, MY PENGUIN FRIEND!
DON'T GIVE UP, RYUNOSUKE! THE D-MASTER'S ROAD IS LONG!
I'LL GO ON A JOURNEY ...
TO BE CONTINUED!

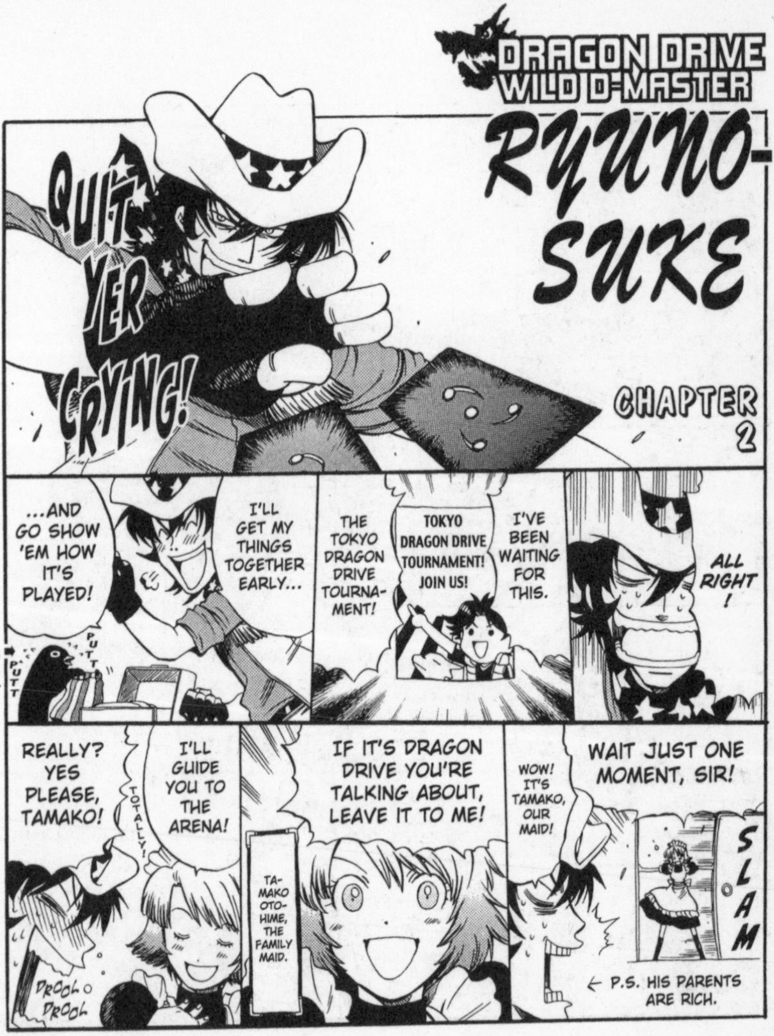
DRAGON DRIVE WILD D-MASTER
RYUNOSUKE
CHAPTER 2
QUIT YER CRYING!
ALL RIGHT!
I'VE BEEN WAITING FOR THIS.
TOKYO DRAGON DRIVE TOURNAMENT! JOIN US!
THE TOKYO DRAGON DRIVE TOURNAMENT!
I'LL GET MY THINGS TOGETHER EARLY...
...AND GO SHOW 'EM HOW IT'S PLAYED!
PUTT PUTT PUTT
HIS PET, TARO.
WAIT JUST ONE MOMENT, SIR!
WOW! IT'S TAMAKO, OUR MAID!
SLAM
P.S. HIS PARENTS ARE RICH.
IF IT'S DRAGON DRIVE YOU'RE TALKING ABOUT, LEAVE IT TO ME!
TAMAKO OTOHIME, THE FAMILY MAID.
I'LL GUIDE YOU TO THE ARENA!
TOTALLY!
REALLY? YES PLEASE, TAMAKO!
DROOL DROOL

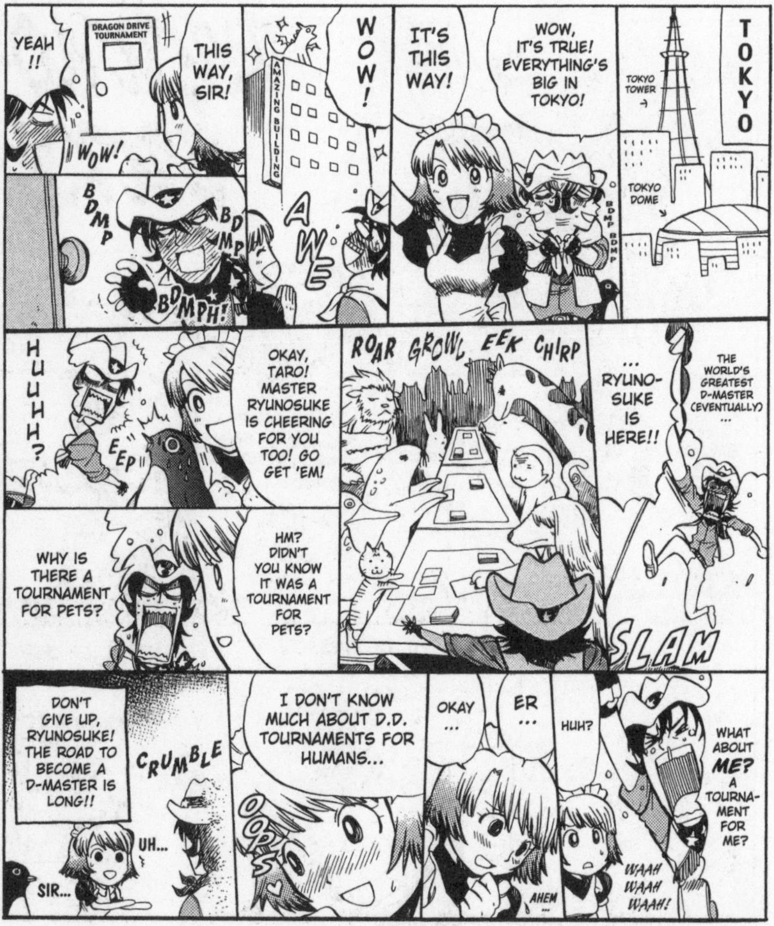
TOKYO
TOKYO TOWER
TOKYO DOME
WOW, IT'S TRUE! EVERYTHING'S BIG IN TOKYO!
IT'S THIS WAY!
BDMP BDMP
WOW!
AMAZING BUILDING
AWE
THIS WAY, SIR!
DRAGON DRIVE TOURNAMENT
YEAH!!
WOW!
BDMP
BDMP
BDMPH!
... RYUNOSUKE IS HERE!!
THE WORLD'S GREATEST D-MASTER (EVENTUALLY)...
SLAM
ROAR GROWL EEK CHIRP
OKAY, TARO! MASTER RYUNOSUKE IS CHEERING FOR YOU TOO! GO GET 'EM!
EEP
HUUHH?
HM? DIDN'T YOU KNOW IT WAS A TOURNAMENT FOR PETS?
WHY IS THERE A TOURNAMENT FOR PETS?
WHAT ABOUT ME? A TOURNAMENT FOR ME?
WAAH WAAH WAAH!
HUH?
ER...
OKAY...
AHEM...
I DON'T KNOW MUCH ABOUT D.D. TOURNAMENTS FOR HUMANS...
OOPS
CRUMBLE
UH...
DON'T GIVE UP, RYUNOSUKE! THE ROAD TO BECOME A D-MASTER IS LONG!!
SIR...

※THERE ISN'T.

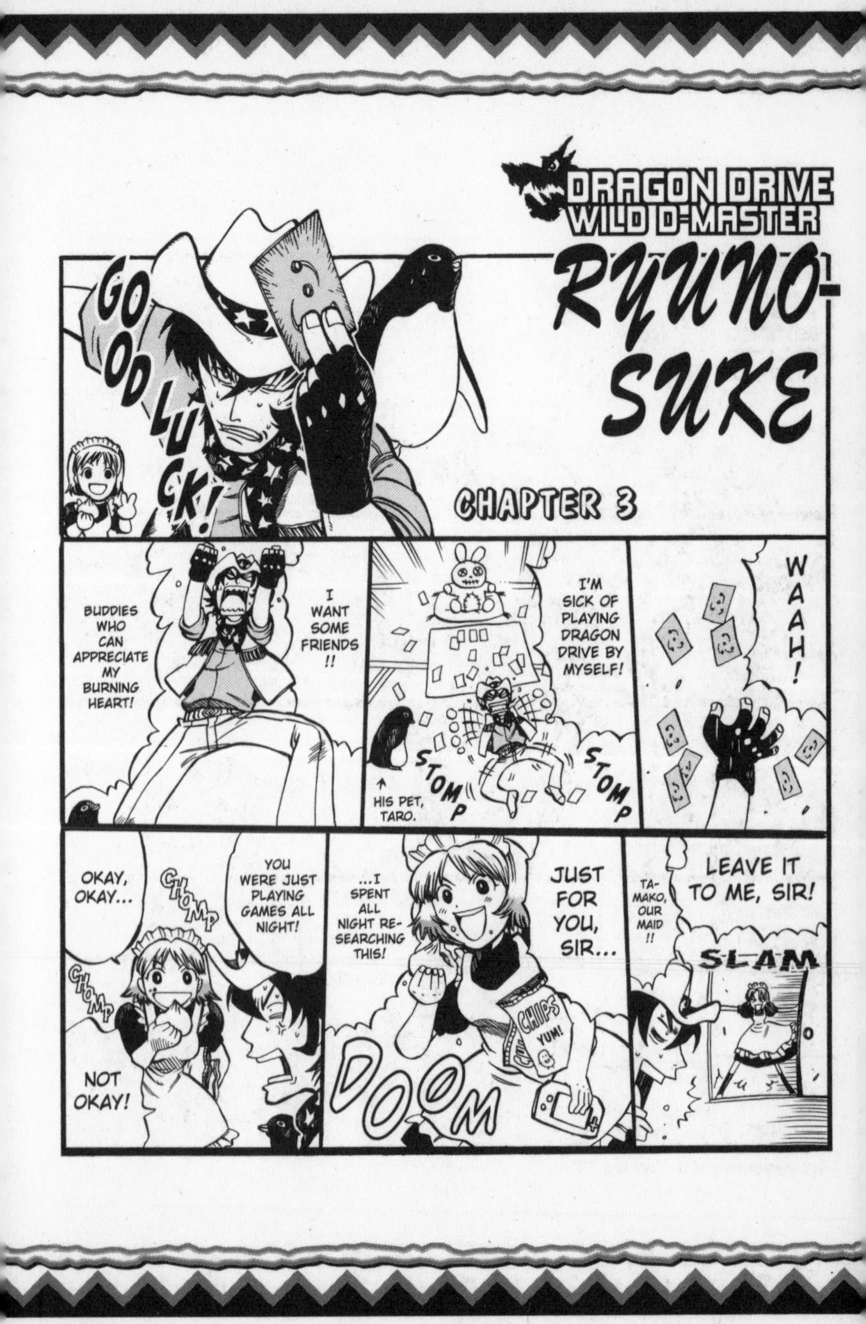
DRAGON DRIVE WILD D-MASTER
RYUNOSUKE
CHAPTER 3
GOOD LUCK!
WAAH!
I'M SICK OF PLAYING DRAGON DRIVE BY MYSELF!
STOMP
STOMP
HIS PET, TARO.
I WANT SOME FRIENDS!!
BUDDIES WHO CAN APPRECIATE MY BURNING HEART!
LEAVE IT TO ME, SIR!
TAMAKO, OUR MAID!!
SLAM
JUST FOR YOU, SIR...
...I SPENT ALL NIGHT RESEARCHING THIS!
CHIPS
YUM!
DOOM
YOU WERE JUST PLAYING GAMES ALL NIGHT!
OKAY, OKAY...
CHOMP
CHOMP
NOT OKAY!

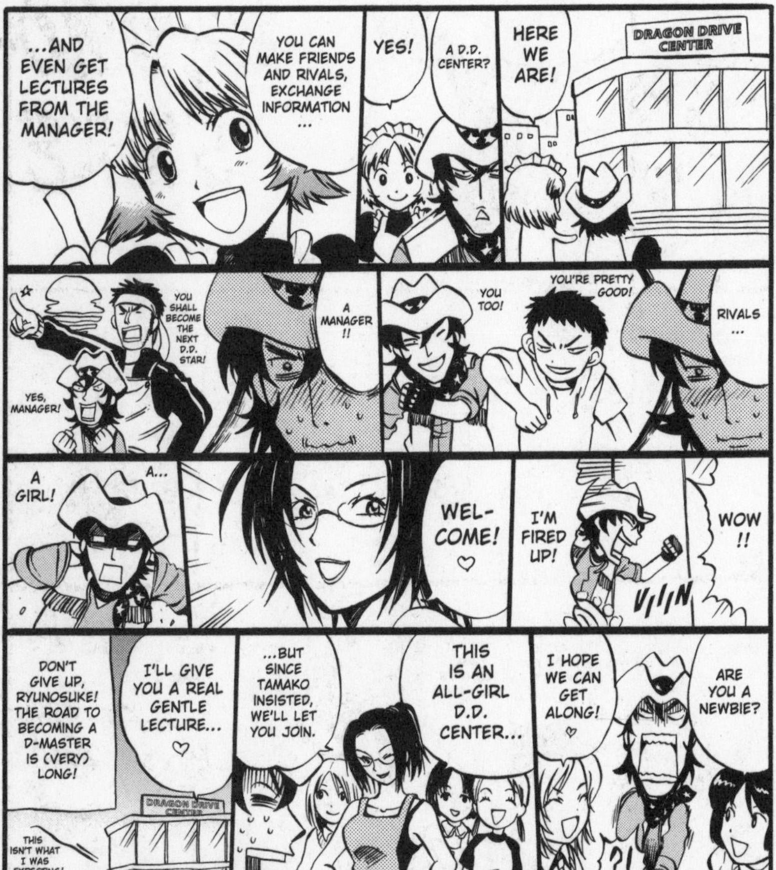
DRAGON DRIVE CENTER
HERE WE ARE!
A D.D. CENTER?
YES!
YOU CAN MAKE FRIENDS AND RIVALS, EXCHANGE INFORMATION ...
...AND EVEN GET LECTURES FROM THE MANAGER!
RIVALS ...
YOU'RE PRETTY GOOD!
YOU TOO!
A MANAGER !!
YOU SHALL BECOME THE NEXT D.D. STAR!
YES, MANAGER!
WOW !!
I'M FIRED UP!
WEL-COME! ♡
A...
A GIRL!
ARE YOU A NEWBIE?
?!
I HOPE WE CAN GET ALONG! ♡
THIS IS AN ALL-GIRL D.D. CENTER...
...BUT SINCE TAMAKO INSISTED, WE'LL LET YOU JOIN.
I'LL GIVE YOU A REAL GENTLE LECTURE... ♡
DON'T GIVE UP, RYUNOSUKE! THE ROAD TO BECOMING A D-MASTER IS (VERY) LONG!
DRAGON DRIVE CENTER
THIS ISN'T WHAT I WAS EXPECTING!

To be continued in Volume 14!

VOGUE
!!

BY MOTSU

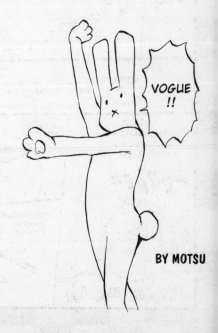